1

A HISTORY
OF COMPUTING
TECHNOLOGY

PRENTICE-HALL SERIES IN COMPUTATIONAL MATHEMATICS

Cleve Moler, Advisor

A HISTORY
OF COMPUTING
TECHNOLOGY

Michael R. Williams
University of Calgary

Prentice-Hall, Inc.
Englewood Cliffs, N.J. 07632

Library of Congress Cataloging in Publication Data

Williams, Michael R. (Michael Roy) (date)
  A history of computing technology.

  Bibliography: p.
  Includes index.
  1. Mathematical instruments—History.
2. Calculating-machines—History.
3. Computers—History. I. Title.
QA71.W66 1985   681'.75   85–6357
ISBN 0–13–389917–9

Editorial/production supervision and
  interior design: Tracey L. Orbine
Cover design: Diane Saxe
Manufacturing buyer: Gordon Osbourne

10 9 8 7 6 5 4 3 2 1

ISBN 0-13-389917-9 01

Prentice-Hall International (UK) Limited, *London*
Prentice-Hall of Australia Pty. Limited, *Sydney*
Prentice-Hall Canada Inc., *Toronto*
Prentice-Hall Hispanoamericana, S. A., *Mexico*
Prentice-Hall of India Private Limited, *New Delhi*
Prentice-Hall of Japan, Inc., *Tokyo*
Prentice-Hall of Southeast Asia Pte. Ltd., *Singapore*
Editora Prentice-Hall do Brasil, Ltda., *Rio de Janeiro*
Whitehall Books Limited, *Wellington, New Zealand*

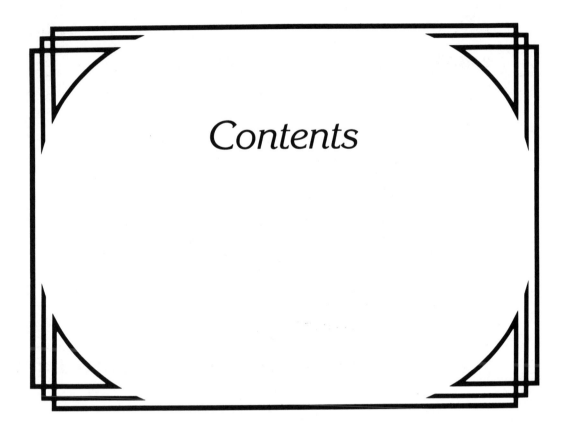

Contents

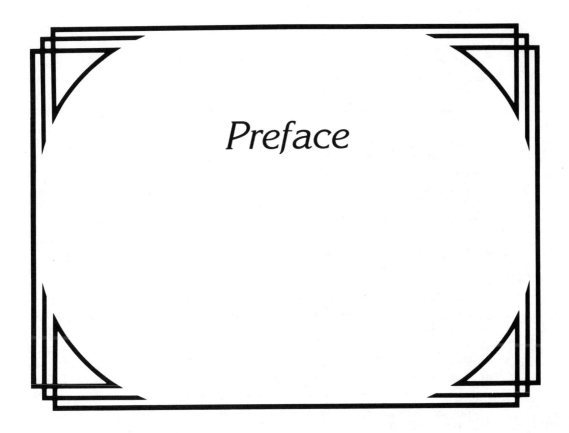

Preface

First look backward in order to look forward.
Thomas J. Watson, Sr.

In this day of ever greater and greater scientific advances it is very tempting
to pursue a course of study which concentrates on the advancing frontier of
scientific knowledge. People who take this path often find that, although they
are well equipped to deal with the latest ideas and machines, they lack an understanding of how these ideas germinated and why some of the latest tools
are in their current forms. They also occasionally find that they produce, after
a great deal of work, a process or instrument that is already well known to
more experienced workers in the field, but had never come to their attention
because of their own consuming interest in the "outer limits" of the subject.
This is particularly true of the very rapid development, and subsequent abandoning, of various tools and techniques of computer science.

Many works have been written about the early history of the more traditional scientific subjects such as mathematics, chemistry, or physics, but very

few have attempted to outline the historical development of some of the newer disciplines. This is unfortunate because most scientists are both more interesting to their friends and better prepared to meet new challenges if they have some understanding of how their subject has developed from is earliest beginnings.

Of all the different scientific topics that have been the subject of investigation, arithmetic is one that best combines an abstract character with universal use in all other branches of knowledge. This abstract character has led to the development of very elegant theories and the usefulness of the subject has resulted in the creation of many different machines, in almost every conceivable form of technology, to aid in the automation of the arithmetical processes.

It is the purpose of this book to explain and describe some of the historical aspects of "calculation" with an emphasis on the physical devices that have been used, in different times, to aid people in their attempts at automating the process of arithmetic. It is quite impossible to cover all the different ideas and inventions that have been produced to this end, and even more impossible to adequately describe the complete series of technological breakthroughs that led to the very rapid development of the electronic computer during the late 1950s and early 1960s. Not only are some of these developments the product of hundreds of different people working in very advanced laboratories, but some of them are considered as trade, or even state, secrets, and the owners of these rights are not about to let a simple historian in on their development sequence. I hope, however, that I have at least touched the highlights of the major advances in arithmetic from the beginnings of counting, through the three most important developments in the subject: the invention of the zero, logarithms, and the electronic computer. Along the way there are a lot of interesting stories about both the machines and the scientists who produced them.

In attempting to set this material down in some logical form and sequence, a difficulty arose relative to the arrangement of the subject matter, whether each subject should be considered in strictly chronological order or a full description be given to one aspect of the subject before going on to the next. After considerable debate, I have determined to use neither plan, but to use one or the other as best suited the subject matter.

As always in works of this kind, there will be errors. I have attempted to use only original source documents for many of my claims and statements but, when these were not available, I have resorted to secondary (and sometimes even remoter) sources. The errors remain, of course, mine. When I have neglected a certain line of development, it was usually for a good reason, but the fact remains that I may simply be unaware of its existence. I would welcome correspondence on any topic a reader feels has been misrepresented or simply skipped completely.

I would like to say a simple word of thanks to the National Engineering and Science Research Council of Canada and to the Social Science and Humanities Research Council of Canada, both of whom have provided several opportunities for me to gather the information contained in this volume. My colleagues and students at the University of Calgary, some of whom consider me mad because of my interest in the history of this subject, were the inspiration for this work. I would like to acknowledge their assistance in brewing tea for me at all hours of the night. Finally, I should thank my wife and family for being so understanding of my activities that they could condone my nocturnal habits and not complain when my nocturnal work (and tea drinking) interrupted our family life.

This work is dedicated to those computer pioneers I have met and admired, and to those whose life spans did not permit our actual meeting but whose work will stand as proof of their genius and hard work. It is also dedicated to my colleague, the man who writes strange programs, whose friendship I have enjoyed for over twenty years, may it last another forty!

Michael R. Williams

A HISTORY
OF COMPUTING
TECHNOLOGY

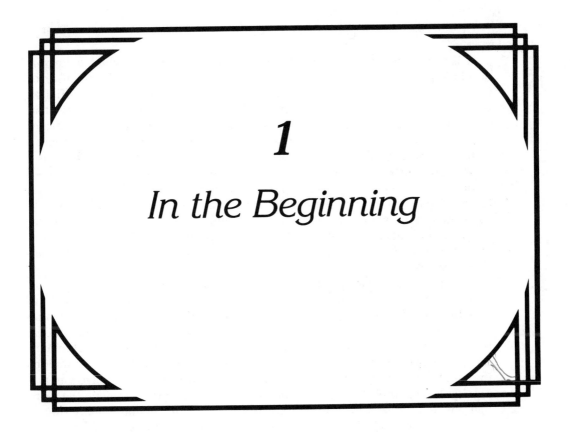

1

In the Beginning

1.1 NUMERATION

> Our system of numeration, if not a machine, is machinery; without it (or some-
> thing equivalent) every numerical problem involving more than a very limited
> number of units would be beyond the human mind.[1]

One of the first great intellectual feats of a young child is learning how
to talk; closely following on this is learning how to count. From earliest childhood we have been so bound up with our system of numeration that it is a feat
of imagination to consider the problems faced by early humans who had not
yet developed this facility. Careful consideration of our system of numeration
leads to the conviction that, rather than being one of the facilities that comes
naturally to a person, it is one of the great and remarkable achievements of
mankind.

[1]F. P. Barnard, *Report on the Machinery and Processes of the Industrial Arts* (New York: Van
Nostrand, 1869).

1

It is now impossible to determine the sequence of events which led to our developing a sense of number. Even the most backward tribe of humans ever found has had a system of numeration which, if not advanced, was sufficient for the tasks they had to perform. Our most primitive ancestors must have had little use for numbers; instead their considerations would have been more of the kind "Is this enough?" rather than "How many?" when they were engaged in food gathering, for example. When early humans first began to think and reflect about the nature of things around them, they discovered that they needed a concept of number simply to keep their thoughts in order. When they began to live a settled life, grow plants and herd animals, the need for a reasonably sophisticated number system became paramount. How and when this ability at numeration developed we will never know, yet it is certain that numeration was well developed by the time humans had formed even semi-permanent settlements.

It is very popular, in works dealing with the early history of arithmetic, to quote "facts" about the so-called "primitive" peoples and their levels of numeration. These "facts" generally note that the primitive peoples of Tasmania are only able to count *one, two, many*; or the natives of South Africa count *one, two, two and one, two two's, two two's and one*, and so on. Although often correct in themselves, these statements do not explain that in realistic situations the number words are often accompanied by gestures to help resolve any ambiguity. For example, when using the *one, two, many* type of system, the word *many* would be used to mean, "Look at my hands and see how many fingers I am showing you." This type of system is limited in the range of numbers which it can express, but this range will generally suffice when dealing with the simpler aspects of human existence.

The lack of ability of some cultures to deal with large numbers is not really surprising. Our own European languages, when traced back to their earlier versions, are very poor in number words and expressions. The translation of the Gospels made by Bishop Ulfilas in the fourth century for the Goths uses the ancient Gothic word for ten, *tachund*, to express the number 100 as *tachund tachund*, that is, ten times ten. By the seventh century the word *teon* had become interchangeable with the *tachund* or *hund* of the Anglo-Saxon language, and the Gospels of that period denote 100 as *hund teontig*, or ten times ten. The average person alive in seventh-century Europe was not as familiar with numbers as we are today. The seventh-century Statute of Shrewsbury laid down the condition that, in order to qualify as a witness in a court of law, a man had to be able to count up to nine. To apply such a condition today would seem ludicrous.

Perhaps the most fundamental step in developing a sense of number is not the ability to count, but rather the ability to see that a number is really an abstract idea instead of a simple attachment to a group of particular objects. It must have been within the grasp of primitive humans to conceive that four birds are distinct from two birds; however, it is not an elementary step to associate the number 4, as connected with four birds, to the number 4, as connected with four rocks. Associating a number as being one of the qualities of a specific object is a great hindrance to the development of a true number sense. As soon as the number 4 can be registered in the mind as a specific word, independent of the object being referenced, the individual is ready to take a first step toward the development of a notational system for numbers and, from there, to arithmetic. As was noted by Bertrand Russell:

> It must have required many ages to discover that a brace of pheasants and a couple of days were both instances of the number two.[2]

Traces of the very first stages in the development of numeration can be seen in several living languages today. Dantzig, in his book *Number,*[3] describes the numeration system of the Thimshian language of a group of British Columbia Indians. This language contains seven distinct sets of words for numbers: one for use when counting flat objects and animals, one for round objects and time, one for people, one for long objects and trees, one for canoes, one for measures, and one for counting when no particular object is being numerated. Dantzig conjectures that the last set of words is a later development while the first six groups show the relics of the old system. This diversity of number names is not confined to obscure tribal groups, however—it can be found in widely used languages such as Japanese, for example.

Intermixed with the development of a number sense is the development of an ability to count. Counting is not directly related to the formation of a number concept because it is possible to count by matching the items you wish to count against a group of pebbles, grains of corn, or the counter's fingers. These counting aids must have been indispensable to very primitive people who would have found the process impossible without some form of mechanical aid. Such aids to counting, although in different form, are still used by even the best educated professionals today, simply because they are convenient. All counting ultimately involves reference to something other than the things being counted. At first it may have been grains of corn but now it is a memorized sequence of words which happen to be the names of the integers. This matching process could have been responsible for the eventual development of the various number bases which came into existence because the act of counting usually takes the form of counting into small groups, then counting the number of groups, then groups of groups, and so on.

The maximum number of items that is easily recognizable by the human mind at one glance is small, say five or less. This may be why initial groups consisted of about five items, and would account for the large number of peo-

---

²As quoted in T. Dantzig, *Number, The Language of Science* (New York: The Free Press, 1967), p. 6.
³Ibid.

ples whose number systems were of base 5. The process of counting by matching with fingers undoubtedly led to the development of the different number systems based on ten.

By the time that a number system has developed to the point where a base such as 5, 10, 20, or even 60 has become obvious to an outside observer, the eventual development of its use in higher forms of arithmetic and mathematics has probably become fixed. If the base is too small, then large numbers of figures or words are required to represent a number and the unwieldy business of recording and manipulating large strings of symbols becomes a deterrent to attempting any big arithmetical problems. On the other hand, if the number base is too big, then a very large number of separate symbols are required to represent each number, and a great many rules must be learned in order to perform even the elementary arithmetical operations. The choice of either too small or too large a number base becomes a bar to the later development of arithmetic abilities.

A study of various forms of numeral systems yields the fact that a great variety of bases have been used by different peoples in various places over the globe. By far the most common is, of course, the number systems based on ten. The most obvious conclusion is that a very large percentage of the human race started counting by reference to their ten fingers. Although 5, 10, or 20 was the most popular choice for a number base, it is by no means uncommon to find systems based on 4, 13, or even 18. It is easy to advance a possible explanation of systems based on 5 and 20 because of the anatomical fact of there being five fingers on each hand and a total of 20 such attachments on both hands and feet. It is not quite so easy to see how the other scales may have developed in such a natural way.

If modern linguistic evidence can be trusted, the scale of 20 must have been very widespread in ancient times. It has been pointed out by several authors that some of the Eskimo people have a well-developed system which uses terms such as *one-man* for the number 20, *two-men* for 40, and so forth. This obviously implies that a base 20 number system was in use at one time, but it is difficult to see how an early Eskimo could have had access to his toes for counting—unless he was inside a relatively warm igloo. This could imply that the Eskimos brought their number system with them when they moved into North America. In fact, it is possible to trace remnants of various number systems based on 20 all the way back to the very early people living in the tropical regions of southern Asia.

The European languages also show a marked preference for the grouping together of 20 objects. It is entirely possible that the general prevalence of base 10 numbers among the Indo-European peoples developed later from an original base 20 system. The most modern example of this is the French use of *quatre-vingt* (four-twenty) instead of *huitante* for 80, and *quatre-vingt-dix* (four-twenty-ten) instead of *nonante* for 90. If we are willing to look at forms of the language which died out in the thirteenth century, then the terms *six-vingt* (120), *sept-vingt* (140), *huit-vingt* (160), and even *quinze-vingt* (15–20 for 300) show that the base 20 system was no stranger. The English word *score*, as in the Biblical "three score and ten years" or Lincoln's famous "Four score and seven years ago . . ." is another modern example of Europeans dealing in groups of 20. The term *score* will be discussed further in the section dealing with tally sticks.

Once the sense of number as an entity separate from the thing being counted has developed, there arises a need to assign names to the integers. This sequence of names, once decided upon, often becomes one of the most stable parts of a people's language. Thus, although languages may evolve so that almost all the words acquire vastly different forms, the sequence of integer names remains almost intact. The original meanings of the names of the integers are likely, therefore, to be quite obscure. The similarity of number names across related languages is easily seen by examining a table of these names in the family of Indo-European languages. Although the actual names differ from one language to another, the basic form remains constant.

Number	Ancient Greek	Latin	Sanskrit	French	German	English
1	en	unus	eka	un	eins	one
2	duo	duo	dva	deux	zwei	two
3	tri	tres	tri	trois	drei	three
4	tetra	quantour	catur	quatre	vier	four
5	pente	quinque	panca	cinq	fünf	five
6	ex	sex	sas	six	sechs	six
7	epta	septem	septa	sept	sieben	seven
8	octa	octo	astra	huit	acht	eight
9	ennea	novem	nava	neuf	neun	nine
10	deca	decem	daca	dix	zehn	ten

This stability of number names has been a good tool of the philologists. They have made extensive collections of the number names in many languages in an attempt to see which languages have common roots. Care must be taken in any exercise of this sort because a common set of names could have resulted from simple mixtures of languages, trade between two peoples, or simple coincidence.

George Peacock, in his *Arithmetic*,[4] points out the situations that can arise by simple coincidence. He compares the number words of the Nanticocks (a tribe of Indians who used to reside on the south bank of the Chesapeake) with those of the Mandingoes (of Africa):

---

[4]George Peacock, "Arithmetic," *Metropolitan Encyclopedia* (London: J. Mawman, 1826), pp. 369–524.

Number	Nanticocks	Mandingoes
1	killi	killim
2	filli	foola
3	sabo	sabba
4	nano	nani
5	turo	loolo
6	woro	soro
7	wollango	oronglo
8	secki	sec
9	collango	conanto
10	ta	tang

The similarity is striking yet can only be attributed to coincidence because any mixing of the languages due to geographic proximity or cultural contacts via trade is ruled out.

The opposite side of the coin can be shown by comparing the number words from languages which are known to be related. In Europe, the languages spoken by the Finnish and Hungarian people can be traced back to a common root, yet the number words in these languages have very little common.

Number	Finnish	Hungarian
1	yksi	egi
2	kaksi	ketto
3	kolme	harum
4	nelja	negy
5	viisi	et
6	kussi	hat
7	sietseman	het
8	kahdeksan	nyoltz
9	yhdeksan	kilentz
10	kymmenen	tiz

The ability to count must soon have led to the need to record the results of counting. This probably first took the form of setting aside the pebbles used in the matching process, but would soon lead to the use of tally sticks, knotted cords, and the actual invention of numerals.

1.2 THE INVENTION AND DEVELOPMENT OF A WRITTEN NUMBER SYSTEM

There appear to be two distinct stages in the development of written record-keeping systems, the pictorial stage and the symbolic stage. The inscriptions done by people in the pictorial stage will correspond with the earliest stage in the development of a number sense. The inscriptions will have a picture of ten cattle to represent ten cows or ten tents may indicate ten family groups. This stage is most easily seen in some of the records made by North American Indians just about the time they came into contact with Europeans.

The symbolic stage, on the other hand, will show a picture of a cow followed by five strokes to represent five cattle. At this stage the strokes no longer represent objects but have become a determinative (a sign used to qualify the meaning of the object sign). In other words, the strokes have become adjectives rather than nouns. In many societies this step must have come at the same time as the development of numbers as abstract ideas. This stage is best illustrated by some of the early stone carvings left by the Egyptians.

Once a particular society has reached the symbolic stage of recording numbers, the notation system which it develops will be almost entirely dependent on cultural influences. The use of fingers or pebbles for counting, the number of items counted into a group before a new group is started (the number base), and the materials available for making a lasting record of the result are all culturally determined. Once these variables have been determined, the result will lead to one of two different types of notational systems: the additive system or the positional system.

1.2.1 The Additive Number System

In this system there is a distinct symbol for each kind of group made during the counting process, and this symbol is repeated as often as necessary to indicate how many of each group are needed. The Egyptian number system is the classical example of an additive system, however, most people are more familiar with the additive system used by the Romans. In the Old Roman system, before the subtractive forms of IV for 4 and IX for 9 were in use, it was possible to express any number less than 5000 by a sequence of symbols in which no individual symbol need be repeated more than four times. For example, the number 2976 would be represented as MMDCCCCLXXVI. Although it was the custom to write down the symbols in decreasing order of value (M = 1000, D = 500, C = 100, L = 50, X = 10, V = 5, I = 1), this is by no means necessary. The value of a number in an additive system has nothing to do with the position of any symbol within the string representing the number. It is quite unambiguous to write the number 2976 as ILVCMCXDMXCC but, of course, ease of reading always precluded its being written otherwise than in order of descending value.

The pure additive system is quite easy to use for simple calculations, even though it does not appear so at first glance. Addition involves the two-step process of simply writing down the group symbols from each number, then collecting together the sequences of smaller valued symbols to make larger valued ones so that the number regains its canonical form. For example:

$$
\begin{array}{rl}
2319 = & \text{MM CCC X V IIII} \\
+\ 821 = & \quad\ \text{DCCC XX\ \ I} \\
\hline
3140 = & \text{MMDCCCCCXXXVIIIII}
\end{array}
$$

The second step now takes over and, because IIIII = V, VV = X, CCCCC = D, DD = M, the final result is written as MMMCXXXX.

Multiplication, although slow, is not really difficult and only involves remembering multiples of 5 and 10. For example:

$$
\begin{array}{r}
28 = \text{XXVIII} \\
\times\ 12 = \quad\ \text{XII} \\
\hline
336
\end{array}
$$

XXVIII times I =   XXVIII
XXVIII times I =   XXVIII
XXVIII times X =   CCLXXX
                                     ——————————
                        CCLXXXXXXXXVVIIIIII

which would be written as CCCXXXVI.

The operations of division and subtraction are a little more cumbersome; however, division was aided by operations (as was multiplication) which are no longer in use today. These operations, called "duplation" and "mediation," are described in more detail in Section 1.3 on Egyptian arithmetic.

Although more cumbersome than systems of positional notation, the additive systems are not without their merits, and computation is not difficult once the rules are mastered. The modification of such a number system to include subtractive elements, such as the IV = 4 or IX = 9 of the Modern Roman system, tend to make matters very much more difficult as far as arithmetic is concerned. However, this development is a late modification of the Old Roman number system and is not to be found at all in most examples of additive notation. Examples of the use of IV for 4 or IX for 9 can be found as early as 130 A.D., but these symbols did not become popular until about 1600 A.D. when Roman numerals were no longer so important in everyday use.

1.2.2 The Positional Systems

In positional number systems, the counting groups are denoted entirely by the position of the symbol in the string of characters denoting the number. This means that it is usually necessary to have a zero symbol to indicate an empty group. It is possible to do away with the need for a zero symbol if the system has some regular way of positioning the other symbols to indicate that one position is empty. This latter method was used by the Chinese and will be discussed in detail in the section dealing with their numerals. The positional system used by some early cultures, for example, the Babylonians prior to 400 B.C., did not have a zero symbol and thus their written numbers were ambiguous.

The rules of calculation in a positional system are more complex than those used with additive systems, and they usually require that the user memorize some form of multiplication table. Because everyone is familiar with the working of our own positional number system, no attempt will be made to describe it in detail. It will be more instructive to examine a small selection of some of the other number systems that have been used by various cultures during the course of history.

The following description of various number systems and their written representations is not meant to be exhaustive. Indeed some of the world's most important and widespread numerical systems will not be mentioned at all. The intent is simply to heighten awareness of the different number systems and the numerals used among the world's peoples. The exception to this is the discussion of the European number system, which is included to provide some historical background on this very important development.

1.3 THE EGYPTIANS

Our knowledge of the Egyptian forms of numerical notation and arithmetical procedures stem from the translation of the many documents which have survived in the very dry air of the Nile valley. The earliest written records to have survived, which date from just before 3000 B.C., reveal a system of number representation that remained essentially the same from the third millennium B.C. right up to the last days of the ancient Egyptian culture. With such a vast time span to consider it is only natural that both the spoken and written languages, together with the arithmetic abilities and needs of the people using them, changed quite considerably. Yet because of the very conservative nature of the educated Egyptian, who generally belonged to the priestly class, the changes are not as vast as they might have been in other, less conservative societies.

The lack of money or coinage in the early centuries led to the development of very detailed accounting systems for the amounts of grain and beer stored in various places and paid out to the workers as salary. These accounts are one of the main sources of information concerning the forms of notation and the arithmetical operations in use during the first part of the Egyptian era. There also exist two major mathematical works, the Rhind papyrus and the Moscow papyrus, which give a very good indication of the level of mathematical knowledge of the scribes. They do not show all the processes the scribes might have used when doing the calculations, but they provide some answers to the basic questions of how the operations were sometimes carried out.

The earliest form of Egyptian writing is the hieroglyphic script so familiar to anyone who has ever read about Egypt. This type of picture writing is quite suitable for inscribing public monuments or temple walls, and was used in this capacity right up into the Christian era, but it is not very useful when attempting to take quick notes with paper and ink. When hieroglyphics are written quickly they tend to become just quick sketches of the original figures with the lines drawn in a more cursive and connected style. With time, these shorthand forms became standardized into what is now known as Hieratic script. The Hieratic was further shortened and modified until, about the fourth century B.C., it had developed into what is known as the Demotic script. Most of the arithmetical and mathematical works that have survived are written in Hieratic script on papyrus, a form of paper made from reeds.

The Egyptian number system was strictly based on 10, but was additive rather than positional in nature. In later times some small changes were made to represent very large numbers by a multiplicative method, but these were a very late development. The following seven basic signs were all that were necessary to represent a number:

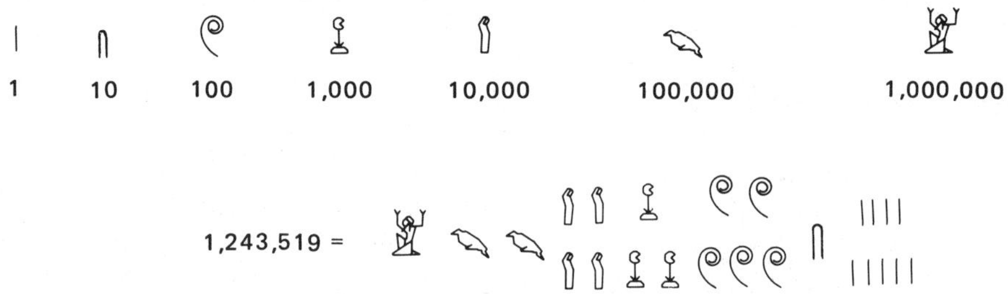

| 1 | 10 | 100 | 1,000 | 10,000 | 100,000 | 1,000,000 |

1,243,519 =

Figure 1–1. The classic Egyptian hieroglyphic additive number system.

The symbol for 1 is a simple vertical stroke, likely representing a stick or reed used in the primitive counting process. The symbol for 10 is of unknown origin, but the figure also occurs in the written word for a horse's heel and the two words are very much alike in their pronunciation (yes, we do know how to speak ancient Egyptian!) so it is possible that the symbol was adopted simply because of a similarity of sound. Since modifications of the sign for 10 are also found in words representing sacks or baskets, however, the symbol might be connected with a container holding ten objects. The symbol for 100 represents a coiled rope, perhaps of 100 units length; it is by association with this symbol, and the Egyptian practice of land measurement with ropes, that the Greeks referred to the Egyptian mathematicians as "rope stretchers." The symbol for 1,000 represents a lotus plant, of which a great many grow along the banks of the Nile. A finger pointing at the sky (to the stars?) is thought to be the derivation of the 10,000 figure. The Nile was full of tadpoles, so what could be more natural than to use such a symbol to represent a larger number like 100,000. The final sign, that of the god Heh who held up the sky, for the number 1,000,000 was used in the early days but seems to have gone out of style during the later era of Egyptian civilization.

The construction of the numbers was very regular. The highest valued symbol always preceded the lower valued ones but, because Egyptian was written either right to left or left to right (and sometimes even top to bottom), it is not possible to predict which way the numbers would be written without consulting the text in which they are contained. It is unfortunate that we have very few examples of texts in which the names of the numbers are actually spelled out (that is, eight thousand twenty-seven instead of 8027), so we have little real idea of how the Egyptians thought of their numbers.

The hieroglyphic text in Figure 1–2 shows a typical set of accounts relating to the Royal Court from about 1800 B.C. (transcribed from the Hieratic into Hieroglyphics). The first line reads "the harem, 45" (units of beer), the second line "the nursemaids, 61," the third "members of the household, 38," the fourth "the total, 143." If you are quick at mental addition, you will see that this example contains the earliest arithmetic error known to the author. That poor scribe must turn in his grave when he sees us still remembering his error 3700 years after he made it.

In the later part of the Egyptian era the multiplicative device, mentioned above, was occasionally employed. As Figure 1–3 illustrates, this consisted of writing the number of times a symbol should appear beneath the symbol itself. This device has obvious advantages in cutting down the number of complex symbols used to represent a number, a large saving in effort if your writing medium is a sandstone block and a copper chisel.

As with Roman numerals, the operations of addition and subtraction are quite straightforward and easily implemented. The implementation of multiplication was another matter. A scribe wishing to find the answer to the question, "How much is 23 taken 13 times?" would proceed as follows:

He would write down the first number (23) in the first column and the number 1 in the second as shown in Figure 1–5. Beneath these, he would write down two times each number (an easy operation when you only have to write down each symbol twice as often as it occurred in the number above), and keep up this doubling process until he had gone far enough for his needs—generally until the number of the second column was about to become larger than the

Figure 1–2. A redrawing of part of an Egyptian royal household account, circa 1800 B.C., containing one of the earliest known errors in arithmetic.

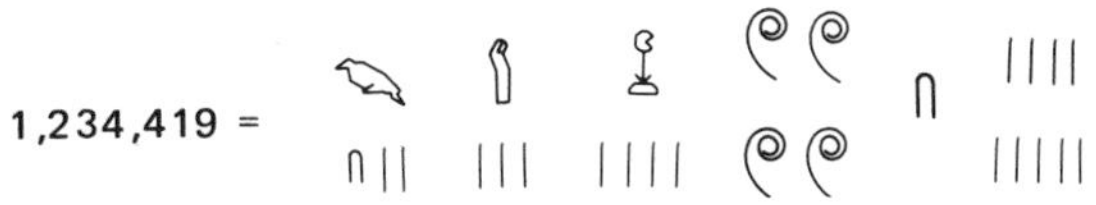

$1,234,419 =$

Figure 1–3. The later Egyptian multiplicative method of number representation.

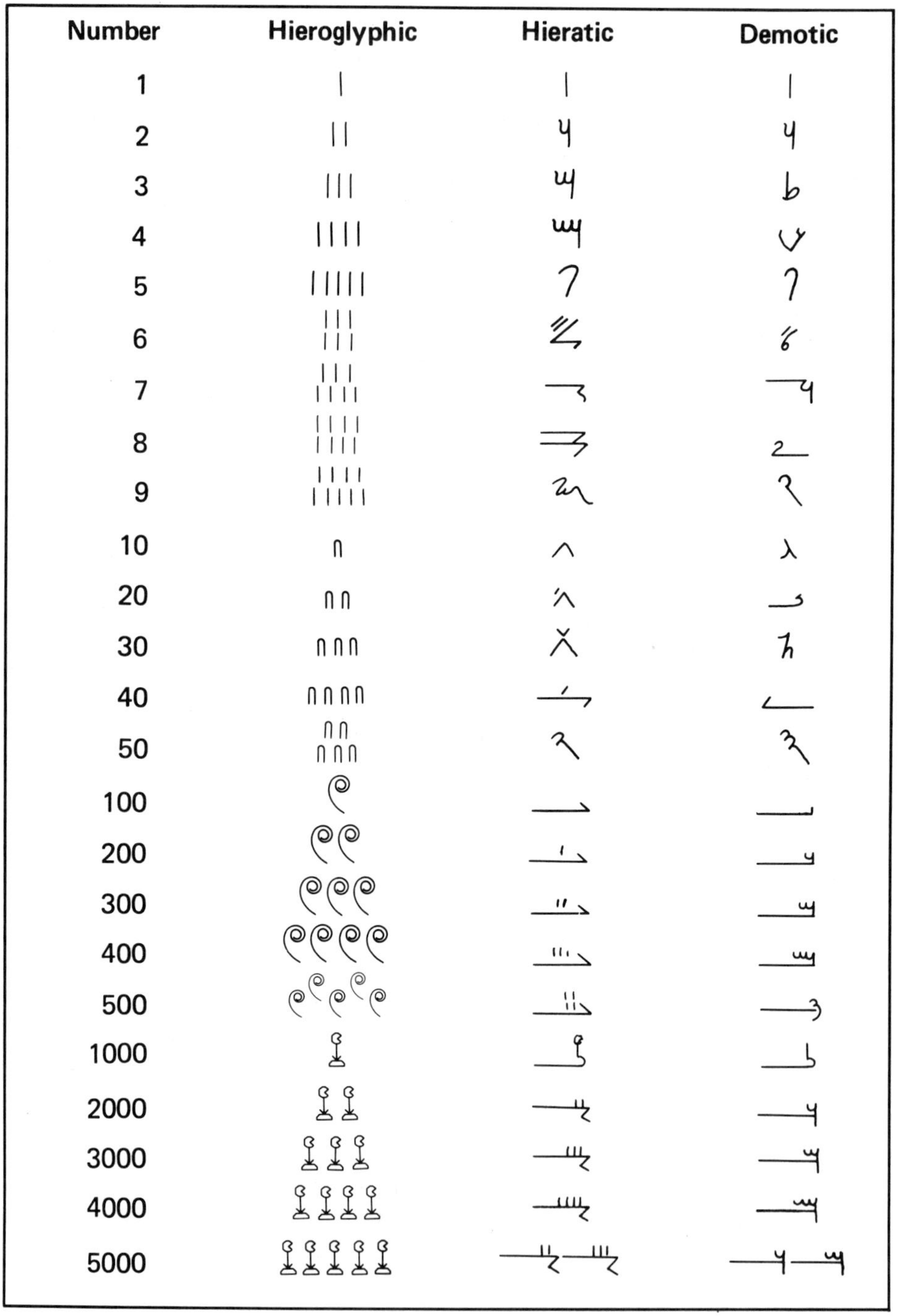

Number	Hieroglyphic	Hieratic	Demotic
1						
2						
3						
4						
5								
6				/				
7				/				
8				/				
9				/					
10				
20				
30				
40				
50				
100				
200				
300				
400				
500				
1000				
2000				
3000				
4000				
5000				

Figure 1–4. A table of hieroglyphic, hieratic, and demotic numbers.

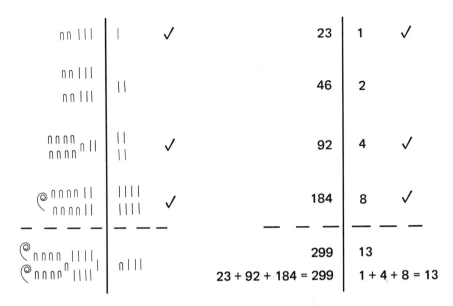

Figure 1–5. A sample of Egyptian multiplication.

multiplier in use, 13 in this case. He would then inspect the second column and put a mark beside those numbers which would add up to the value of the multiplier (the first, third, and fourth in this case because 13 = 1 + 4 + 8). The scribe would then add up the corresponding numbers in the first column to obtain the desired result.

A number of points are worth noting about this operation. First, the tick marks made by the scribe along the numbers in the second column are really just a mechanism of determining the binary representation of the value of the multiplier (13 in binary is 1101). The multiples of 23 which corresponded to binary '1' positions in the multiplier would then be added together to form the final product. This is exactly the same technique that is used in the "shift and add" binary multiplication scheme implemented on modern electronic computers. Although the Egyptians did not seem to follow through with any other results using binary notation for numbers, their methods of operation relied on it heavily. In addition, an intelligent scribe would occasionally throw in a multiple of 10 if he could see that it might be useful, as in Figure 1–6.

Doubling was the basic operation involved in this method of doing multiplication and, because the Greeks adopted the technique for use in their schools, this mechanism spread into Europe. Until the introduction of the Hindu-Arabic numerals, Europeans used the Egyptian doubling methods for multiplication and a similar halving technique for division. These methods were so much a part of the system that most of the early European textbooks on arithmetic instructed the readers that there were six fundamental arithmetic

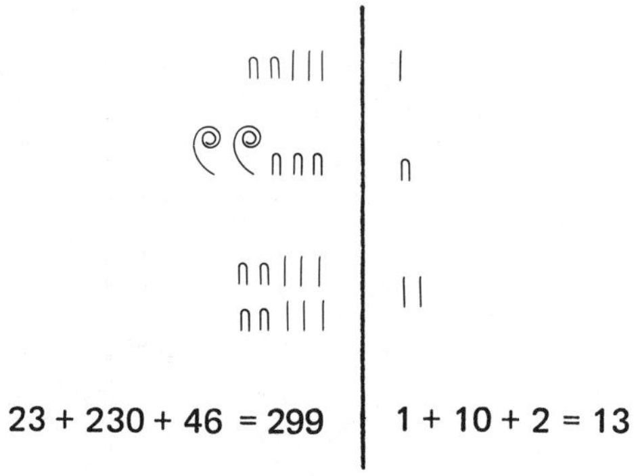

$$\begin{array}{c|c}
\text{nn|||} & | \\
\text{℘℘nnn} & \text{n} \\
\text{nn|||} & \\
\text{nn|||} & || \\
\hline
23 + 230 + 46 = 299 & 1 + 10 + 2 = 13
\end{array}$$

Figure 1-6. Modified Egyptian multiplication.

operations they had to learn: addition, subtraction, multiplication, division, duplation (doubling), and mediation (halving).

Division was the simple inverse operation to multiplication and its implementation was along similar lines. It did lead to the complication of fractions being needed to represent some of the results, and this led to the development of a rather strange and complex system of fractional notation. A complete discussion of Egyptian fractions is beyond the scope of this work, and the interested reader is referred to some of the more modern reference works on the subject, the work by Gillings being an ideal place to start.

1.4 THE GREEKS

The Greek civilization has always been of interest to Europeans and its history has been quite well documented. The Greeks were some of the greatest mathematicians of the ancient world, at least in the fields of geometry and number theory. When it came to the consideration of arithmetic processes, they had a firm dividing line between the common methods of doing arithmetic, which they termed "logistic," and the more advanced topics of number theory, which was called "arithmetic." The theoretical side of the Greek studies, their "arithmetic," was used both as a mental exercise and for telling of fortunes and other cabalistic processes. Because this area of study interested the early European mathematicians and historians, much is known about their theorems, while the simple knowledge of how they actually did their arithmetic operations, "logistic," has been largely ignored.

Many Greek inscriptions contain numbers which are spelled out, and obviously the reason pertains to official documents where it is important that there be no confusion as to the exact meaning intended. But this system is impractical for everyday use. The Greeks eventually developed two separate forms of numerical notation which were both in use at the same time, one form or another being dominant depending on the relative political influence of Athens and the other major city states.

The "Attic" system, sometimes called "Herodianic" because of its being found on a document attributed to Herodian, was in use from at least as early as 454 B.C. to about 95 B.C. It appears to have been adopted in Athens and, because of that city's influence, spread to other parts of the Greek world. The numerals appear to have been derived from the first letter of the names of the numbers, except the symbol for 1, which was represented in the Egyptian fashion by a simple line. The symbol for 5, Π, was derived from the first letter of the Greek word *pente*, the symbol for 10, Δ, from *deca*, and so on. It is interesting to note that the system is strictly decimal with the exception of having a separate symbol for 5. This may well be a holdover from an early Greek number system based on 5 rather than on 10, and this view is supported by the fact that Homer uses the term *to five* meaning "to count" (Odyssey, iv, 412).

| | 1

Γ 5

Δ 10

H 100

X 1,000

M 10,000   **Figure 1–7.**   The Attic numerals.

The Attic symbols were combined in an additive system to form any number up to 50,000. The number of repetitions of each symbol was limited to four by combining the Π with the others to produce a compound symbol for the numbers 50, 500, and 5,000. The symbols for the higher values always came before the lower valued ones.

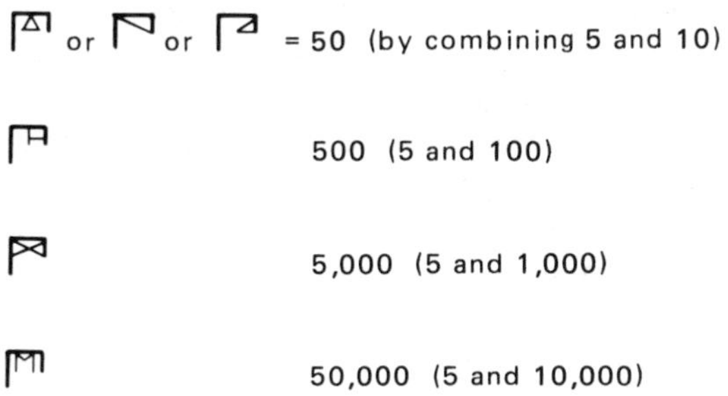

Γ△ or Γ or Γ△ = 50 (by combining 5 and 10)

ΓΗ   500 (5 and 100)

ΓΧ   5,000 (5 and 1,000)

ΓΜ   50,000 (5 and 10,000)

Figure 1–8.   The combined Attic numerals.

The second set of numerals, usually called the alphabetic numerals, likely developed in the Greek part of Asia Minor some time between 800 B.C. and 500 B.C. The earliest surviving inscription which uses this system dates from about

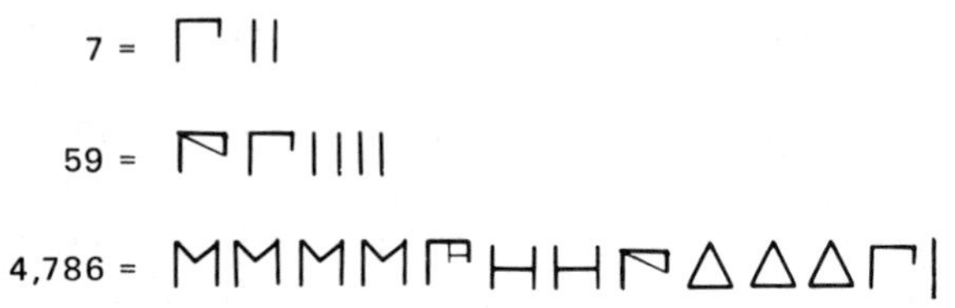

7 = ⌐ ||

59 = ⊓⌐||||

4,786 = MMMM⌐HH⊓ΔΔΔ⌐|

Figure 1–9. Examples of Attic numerals.

450 B.C., but evidence about the order in which the Greeks considered their letters puts the invention several centuries earlier. It is usually thought that the Greeks obtained their alphabet from the Phoenicians and that they changed some of the consonants to represent vowels, which were not written in Phoenician. They then assigned values to the various letters as follows:

THE GREEK ALPHABETIC NUMERALS

A	= 1	I	= 10	P	= 100
B	= 2	K	= 20	Σ	= 200
Γ	= 3	Λ	= 30	T	= 300
Δ	= 4	M	= 40	Υ	= 400
E	= 5	N	= 50	Φ	= 500
Ϛ	= 6	Ξ	= 60	X	= 600
Z	= 7	O	= 70	Ψ	= 700
H	= 8	Π	= 80	Ω	= 800
Θ	= 9	Ϙ	= 90	Τ	= 900

The system uses three letters that were not in the classical Greek alphabet of 24 letters, but appear to be older forms of letters or characters that have been borrowed from other alphabets for the purpose of the numeral system. This use of the alphabet to represent numerical quantities was not unique to the Greeks. In fact they may well have obtained the idea through trade contacts with other groups who used the same scheme. The same technique is known to have been used by the Hebrews, early Arabs, Hindus, and many others.

The symbols were used in a strictly additive system, the resulting notation being very concise but not exactly easy to use. These alphabetic numerals eventually replaced the Attic system, partially because the concise nature of the notation allowed them to be used on coins and other places where the space is limited. Their first official use was on a coin, from 266 B.C., found at Alexandria and bearing the head of Ptolemy II. They eventually started showing up in official documents from mainland Greece about 200 B.C. and appear to have displaced the Attic notation entirely some time after 100 B.C. They lasted for a remarkably long period of time, being in use in different parts of the world long after the Greeks had given them up. In the early part of the fourteenth century, a monk named Barlaam wrote several books on geometry and arithmetic in Greek using these alphabetic numerals. Some of these works were published as late as 1564 in Strassburg.

15      $I\,E$

758      $Y\,N\,H$

2,000 $\dfrac{\beta}{M}$

40,000 $\overset{\triangle}{M}$

85,485 $\overset{H'}{M}\,E\,Y\,\pi\,E$ **Figure 1–10.** Examples of Greek alphabetic numerals.

In general, it was usual to write down a number with the higher valued symbol first, but examples are known, particularly from Asia Minor, where the reverse was true. A few examples are known where the scribe wrote the letters down in apparently random order. Any number from 1 to 999 can easily be represented by no more than three characters, and this range would have sufficed for most of the problems encountered in everyday life. When larger numbers were needed, the system was simply repeated with an identifying mark added before or after the letter to indicate that it was now to be considered as 1,000 times larger than it had been before. For 10,000 and up, the alphabetic numerals were augmented by the character used in the Attic system, M (for myriad), which was placed either before, after, or underneath the letter to signify that it stood for 10,000 times as much as it normally would.

The two different numeral systems each had some slight advantages and disadvantages, but both were awkward to use when doing arithmetic, particularly the alphabetic numerals. Cantor, when describing the alphabetic numerals, sums up the situation by saying:

Instead of an advance we have here to do with a decidedly retrograde step, especially so far as its suitability for the further development of the numeral system is concerned. If we compare the older "Herodianic" numerals with the later signs which we have called alphabetic numerals, we observe in the latter two drawbacks which do not attach to the former. There now had to be more signs, with values to be learnt by heart; and to reckon with them required a much greater effort of memory. The addition

$$\triangle\triangle\triangle \;+\; \triangle\triangle\triangle\triangle \;=\; \Gamma\triangle\triangle \;(30 \,+\, 40 \,=\, 70)$$

could be coordinated in one act of memory with that of

$$HHH \;+\; HHHH \;=\; \Gamma HH \;(300 \,+\, 400 \,=\, 700)$$

in so far as the sum of 3 and 4 units of the same kind added up to 5 and 2 units of the same kind. On the other hand Λ + M = O did not at all immediately indicate that T + Υ = Ψ. The new notation had only one advantage over the other, namely that it took less space. Consider, for instance, 849, which in the "Herodianic" form is ⲦHHHΔΔΔΔΓ | | | |, but which in the alphabetic system is Ω M Θ. The former is more self explanatory and, for reckoning with, has most important advantages.[5]

To present the other side of the coin, it does appear that people who have taken the trouble to learn the Greek alphabetic numerals, for example, those engaged in modern translations of older Greek works, report no real difficulty in performing simple arithmetic operations. Problems do arise, however, when users attempt to do slightly more advanced work which requires familiarity with multiplication tables.

Perhaps the most damning indication that the alphabetic system was awkward to use comes from Ptolemy who, when producing the tables for his great work, *The Almagest*, opted to use the Babylonian number system rather than the Greek because it was easier to manipulate. It was his adoption of the Babylonian number system with its base 60 that ultimately resulted in our having 60 seconds to the minute, 60 minutes to the hour, and angular measurement based on multiples of 60.

Of course, when you use alphabetic characters to represent the digits of your number system, it is entirely possible that an expression may be understood both as a number and a verbal concept. This ambiguity was generally avoided by marking the letters which should be considered a number, either by a line at the start and end of the letter group or, more commonly, by a line drawn over the top of the numbers. It was likely the use of these alphabetic numbers, in Greek and other cultures, that encouraged the development of the various cabalistic cults and fortune-telling schemes. The Hebrews used a similar alphabetic number scheme, and their religious beliefs show through quite clearly in the way some of their numbers were represented. The Hebrew letters for 10 and 5, for example, just happened to be the first two letters for Jehovah and, because it was not considered proper for God's name ever to be written down, even in abbreviated form, they had to represent the number 15 by (9 + 6) instead of (10 + 5). Of course, this led to some rather awkward rules which had to be remembered when doing arithmetic.

The actual process of doing arithmetic with either the Attic or the alphabetic numerals has never been adequately examined. This may well be because it was not considered to be all that interesting and, as a consequence, very few early Greek documents survive which describe the methods they used. It is known that they used the Egyptian methods of doubling and halving for performing multiplication and division but, if the average person had any other methods in addition to these, they have been lost. Certain mathematicians are

[5]M. B. Cantor as quoted by T. L. Heath in *A History of Greek Mathematics* (New York: Oxford University Press, 1921), p. 37.

known to have used other methods. Hero of Alexandria, for example, was known to do multiplications by factoring out powers of 10 whenever possible. For example, if he needed to multiply 13 by 18, he would note down the problem as (10 + 3) (10 + 8) which can be rewritten as 10 (10 + 8) + 3(10 + 8) which gives 100 + 80 + 30 + 24 = 234. By this method he could avoid the problems of having to know a huge multiplication table, and often could represent part of the problem by just doing a multiplication by 10, which was done by simply moving over to the next set of nine letters—almost as simple as our own method of just adding a zero (see table on page 16). When he had to do an actual multiplication, it was likely done by simply looking up the answer in a table. The final additions would be done with the aid of an abacus.

We know that the Greeks made use of a form of the table abacus to do a lot of their actual computation because there are a number of references to the need for an abacus and counters in Greek literature. This subject will be explored to greater depth in the section dealing with the use of the table abacus.

There was one further addition to the Greek system. Archimedes wrote an essay for Gelon, the king of Syracuse, in which he described how to extend the alphabetic number system. In its classical form, the system could be used to represent a myriad of myriads, or 10^8. By taking this as the new base unit and combining it with all the other previous symbols, a notation was developed for any number less than 10^{16}. He called the numbers between 10^8 and 10^{16} the "numbers of the second order." Taking 10^{16} as the base for his "third order numbers" he was able to develop a representation for integers less than 10^{24}. He continued in this way until reaching numbers of the ninth order, or 10^{64}. The system does not seem to have been used in any way other than being an academic exercise for Archimedes and his readers.

1.5 THE EUROPEAN NUMBER SYSTEM

Our own number system is so familiar to us that it is not worth describing. However, it is worth devoting some effort to a brief investigation of its origins. The Roman Empire spread through essentially all of Europe and left its mark in European cultures by leaving behind various versions of the Latin language and the system of numeration used by the Roman soldiers and tradesmen. These Roman numerals were in such widespread use that they have lasted right up to the present day, at least for certain special functions such as marking the hours on clocks and numbering chapters in books, especially formal works such as the Bible.

The advent of what we call the Hindu-Arabic number system, together with its strict positional or place value scheme and the zero that must be used to show an empty place, was one of the great inventions of mankind. It enabled the development of mathematics and arithmetical methods which were far in advance of anything that had been known before. From our vantage point of

being able to look back in history, it seems that the invention of a strictly positional number system, and a character to represent a zero, should have been
an obvious extension of some of the early positional number systems. This idea
can be easily put aside by noting that some of the greatest of all the ancient
authors, even when they were aware of the shortcomings of their own number
systems, did not conceive of the simple system we use today. The French mathematician Pierre-Simon Laplace (1749–1827) noted:

> How difficult it was to invent such a method one can infer from the fact that it
> escaped the genius of Archimedes and of Apollonius of Perga, two of the greatest
> men of antiquity.[6]

The use of a zero was not uncommon in certain early positional number
systems. The Babylonians used a zero-like character to represent an empty column in the middle of a number as early as 200 B.C., but it was not a consistent
part of their system. If a number, such as 1024 required a zero to separate the
digit 1 from the digit 2, they would use their zero symbol in the same way we
do. If, however, they had to represent a number such as 1000, they appeared
to be unable to conceive of the fact that the zero symbol could be used to simply
"pad out" the last several places, and they would represent the number as 1
and leave the reader to figure out that it meant 1000 and not 10, 100, or
even 1.

Exactly where and when humans first used our current positional number
system, and the ten digits on which it relies, remains unclear. It certainly came
into Europe from the Arabs, and it is quite clear that they in turn obtained it
from the people on the Indian subcontinent. Where or when the Indians obtained the system is not known. It may have been an indigenous invention, it
may have come from further east in Indo-China, or it may have been a development out of the Babylonian use of an "empty" column symbol. In early India,
as in a lot of societies, the art of arithmetic was developed to a degree beyond
that needed for commerce because of its importance to the local religion. All
three of the early Indian religions (Jainism, Buddhism, and Hinduism) considered arithmetic important, as is shown by its being listed as one of the fundamental studies required for the priesthood.

The earliest use of Indian "mathematics" occurs in early works written
in verse form, in which complex literary devices were employed to represent
numbers in order to preserve the rhyme and meter of the poems. Even the
documents which use numerals to denote numbers are not always reliable
guides to when this practice first appeared. It seems that, some time in the
eleventh century, an attempt was made to rationalize the system of land own-
ership in part of India and this led to many people producing forged documents

---

[6]Pierre-Simon Laplace quoted in F. Cajori, *A History of Mathematical Notions* (La Salle, Ill.:
Open Court Publishing, 1974), p. 70.

to aid their claims to various endowments. Of the 17 known inscriptions using numerals from before the tenth century, all but two have been shown to be forgeries. The earliest undoubted occurrence of a zero in a written inscription in India was in 876 A.D. with the numbers 50 and 270 being represented in the local version of the Indian digits.

The history of our number system becomes much clearer about the ninth century A.D. In the seventh century, when the dynasty of the Caliphs was founded in Baghdad, the learning of the adjacent countries was being absorbed into the newly expanded Arabic culture. As the Arabs conquered a country, they would often take over the mode of writing—particularly the notation of numerals—of the conquered people and search out the sources of knowledge in the literature which may have survived the ravages of war.

The great leader of the Eastern part of the Arab empire, the Caliph Al-Mamun, established an academic center known as the House of Wisdom in Baghdad some time about the year 800. This House of Wisdom was a combination of library, university, and institute for translating foreign works into Arabic. It was likely the most important such school since the destruction of the one in Alexandria. This school acquired and translated works from their original Greek, Persian, Sanskrit, and Coptic sources into Arabic. In fact our only knowledge of several of the early scientific works in these languages comes from their Arabic translations—or the later Latin versions—because the originals have long since been lost. These translations were first undertaken under the Caliph Al-Rashid, but the majority were done during the reign of Al-Mamun. Unfortunately, history repeated itself when the House of Wisdom, like its predecessor in Alexandria, was completely destroyed in 1258 by the grandson of Genghis Khan, Hulagu Khan, who destroyed Baghdad together with all its libraries and museums.

One of the scholars attached to Al-Mamun's House of Wisdom sometime early in the ninth century was Mohammed ibn Musa Al-Khowarizmi (Mohammed, the son of Moses, from Khowarizm—the modern city of Kiva in the U.S.S.R.). Al-Khowarizmi, as he is usually known, had contact with Indian astronomers who had been brought to the court of Al-Mamun to provide the Arabs with the resources of Indian astronomy and mathematics. Al-Khowarizmi wrote textbooks on both arithmetic and algebra and calculated astronomical tables for use in Baghdad. In his *Arithmetic*, he distinctly indicates that the system came to him from the Indians. Although none of the original Arabic versions is extant, we do have copies of translations that were made into other languages. The *Arithmetic* begins with the subject of numeration, then discusses the digits and the use of the zero at great length, and follows this with a systematic discussion of the fundamental operations upon integers.

Al-Khowarizmi's work was very influential, since it was evidently copied many times and later Arabic writers often based their own mathematical works on Al-Khowarizmi's model. The use of the Hindu numerals quickly spread through out the entire Arab empire.

The eventual spread of these Hindu numerals into Europe is most easily explained by the contacts generated between Arabs and Europeans by trade and war. It is likely that the Italian traders would know of the accounting systems of their trade partners, and the soldiers and priests returning from the Crusades would also have had ample opportunity to have made contact with the Arabic system of notation and arithmetic. The oldest known European manuscript to contain the Hindu-Arabic numerals was written in the Albelda Cloister in Spain in 976 A.D. The new numerals are also found in another Spanish manuscript of 992 A.D., a tenth-century manuscript found in St. Gall, and a Vatican document of 1077 A.D. Their use was very rare during this early period, however, and it is likely that very few people would have understood the system before the middle of the thirteenth century.

The first great attempt to introduce this new form of notation was made by Leonardo of Pisa (1175–1250?), better known by the name of Fibonacci (which came from *filius Bonaccio*, the son of Bonaccio), who ranks as one of the best European mathematicians of the Middle Ages. During Fibonacci's time, Pisa was one of the great trading cities of Italy, and it had connections all through the Mediterranean area. His father was the head of one of Pisa's overseas custom houses, in Bugia on the coast of North Africa. Bugia was an important center for merchants and scholars so when, at the age of 12, Fibonacci was sent to join his father, he had a first-class opportunity to observe the methods of the Arabs. He certainly obtained part of his schooling while in Bugia, and legend has it that he was taught Arabic and arithmetic by a local grocer. He later visited Egypt, Syria, Greece, and France where he took pains to enquire into the local systems of arithmetic. He found all these numerical systems so inferior to those of the Arabs that, when he returned to Pisa, he wrote a book to explain the Arabic system of numerals and computation. This book, entitled *Liber Abaci*, The Book of the Abacus, was first published in 1202, and revised and extended in 1228. It was a massive tome for its day, consisting of 459 pages divided into 15 chapters. Chapters 1 through 7 introduced the Arabic notation and the fundamental operations on integers, chapters 8 to 11 dealt with various applications while the remainder were devoted to methods of calculation involving series, proportion, square and cube roots, and a short discussion of geometry and algebra. It was in one of these later chapters that he introduced the famous rabbit problem and the series of numbers which now bears his name.

The *Liber Abaci* was not as influential as it might have been because it was rather large, and thus difficult to copy in the days before printing. It also contained advanced material suitable only for scholars so that it was known only to a few people, none of whom seemed to have had much influence on the methods of calculation used in everyday transactions.

Although the efforts of Fibonacci were of little success, the idea of the Hindu-Arabic numerals gradually spread into Europe. The main source of information was the various translations, or partial translations, of Al-Khowarizmi's *Arithmetic*. The fact that Arabic was completely different from any

Figure 1–11. A hypothetical portrait of Leonardo of Pisa (Fibonacci).

European language was a great bar to the dissemination of Arabic scientific ideas. In order to learn Arabic it was usually necessary to travel to an Arabic-speaking country, and this was a dangerous task as some Arabs did not take kindly to Christian visitors (and vice versa). This problem was partially solved when, in 1085, Alphonso VI of Leon recaptured Toledo from the Moors and a large Arabic-speaking population came into the sphere of European influence. The majority of the early translators, or at least the people who aided the translators, came from this population.

The two main works which spread the knowledge of Hindu-Arabic arithmetic through Europe were the *Carmen de Algorismo* (The Poem of Algorism) by Alexander De Villa Dei from about 1220 and the *Algorismus Vulgaris* (Common Algorism) by John of Halifax, better known as Sacrobosco, from about 1250 A.D. Both of these works were based, at least in part, on the works of Al-Khowarizmi or one of his successors. They were both designed for use in the European universities then starting up in places such as Paris and Oxford, and were not meant to be complete explanations of the system; rather they simply gave the basics so that a lecturer could explain them, line by line, to his students. The *Carmen de Algorismo* was particularly difficult to follow, especially in the discussion on the calculation of roots, because it was written in hexameter verse. Despite this it became very popular, being copied many times in its Latin original and even being translated into English, French, and Icelandic. Part of its popularity was due to the fact that Alexander de Villa Dei (?–1240), who was a native of Normandy and wrote and taught in Paris, was already very well known for a Latin Grammar, also in verse, which was widely used in schools of the period. Also, being only 284 lines long, it was easily copied by scribes, and a hundred copies could be made and distributed in the time it would take to make one copy of *Liber Abaci*. The same was true of the *Algorismus Vulgaris* which was only about 4,000 words long.

Sacrobosco, who also taught in Paris during the first half of the thirteenth century, was well known for a work on astronomy, and this undoubtedly contributed to the success of his *Algorismus Vulgaris,* which continued to be used as a university text on arithmetic even after the invention of printing. Printed editions are known from as late as the fifteenth and sixteenth centuries.

One of the first translators of Al-Khowarizmi's work was Adelard of Bath who, about the year 1120, produced a Latin text whose first words "Dixit Algorismi . . ." (Thus said Algorismi) resulted in this new science being known as *algorism*. This term, and the various corruptions of it generated by different authors, eventually spread through every European language to the point where the process of doing arithmetic with the Hindu-Arabic numerals was termed algorism, and this in turn has given us the term *algorithm* which is so familiar to students of computer science. Before very long the connection of "Algorismi" with Al-Khowarizmi was lost and various authors invented different people, such as King Algor, to whom the origin of these methods could be attributed.

The copiers of these translations were very faithful in rendering exact copies down through the centuries. One example of this comes from an English translation of Sacrobosco's work in which the ten digits are described as:

$$0 \quad 9 \quad 8 \quad \wedge \quad 6 \quad 7 \quad \& \quad 3 \quad 7 \quad /$$

which is just opposite to the order in which any European would have written them down. They had obviously been copied faithfully, through version after version, from the order in which they appeared in the original Arabic (which would have been read right to left) several centuries earlier.

The switch from the additive Roman numerals to the positional system of the Hindu-Arabic numerals came slowly over a period of centuries. It was not easy for the Europeans to comprehend the use of the zero which, while representing nothing itself, could magically make other digits dramatically increase in value. The Hindu word for the zero sign was *sunya* which, appropriately enough, meant "empty" or "blank." When the system was

Figure 1–12.   The first page of the 1501 edition of Sacrobosco's *Algorismus*. Note the later corrections to the form of the numerals on the eighth last line.

adopted by the Arabs, they used their own word for "empty," which is generally written as *sifr* in our alphabet. This Arabic word was simply transliterated into Latin either as *zephirum*, from which we get our word "zero," or as "cipher," from which we derive the older English form "to cipher," meaning to do arithmetic. Some of the mystery with which the new system was considered can be observed by the fact that this same root word has given rise to terms that have been involved in magic and secret writing, such as to "cipher" or "decipher" a coded text. This air of mystery was heightened by the attitude of some people who, after they knew algorism, thought that it was knowledge to be kept for a select few and not explained to the common people. This attitude is illustrated in several pictures from the late Middle Ages, one of which is reproduced here. The picture, which dates from the late 1400s and was used in a book designed to teach arithmetic to the Queen of Spain, shows two individuals doing arithmetic, one using the old methods of the table abacus while the other, hiding the work from the first, was using the new algorism.

By 1375 the Hindu-Arabic numerals had a firm hold on Europe. They began to appear in many different documents and were well enough known for Chaucer, who called them "the figures newe" to write a poem explaining their power:

The Wedde

Shortly it was so full of bestes
That though Argus the noble counter
Y sate to reckin in his contour
For by the figures newe all ken.

If they be crofty, reckin and nombre
and tell of every thing the nombre
Yet shull he fail to reckin even
The wonders we met in my sweven.

Even though they were becoming well known, there was still a great deal of resistance to adopting the new numbers. In 1299 the city of Florence issued an ordinance which prohibited the use of Hindu-Arabic numerals on the grounds that they were very easy to alter or forge, for example, changing a 0 to a 6 or a 9 would have been quite easy. The merchants had developed various tricks to prevent this sort of thing with Roman numerals; for example, XII would be written as Xij so that an extra i could not be added to the end without arousing suspicion and, by making the first character a capital, they prevented anyone from adding characters to the left-hand side of a number. It would only be a short time before the same sorts of devices were developed for the new figures but, even as late as 1594 the merchants of Antwerp were warned not to use them in contracts or bank drafts.

The Italians, quick to see the usefulness of the system for mercantile purposes, led Europe in the general adoption of the place value system. Algorism was known throughout Europe by about 1400, but the more conservative merchants kept their records in Roman numerals until about 1550, and many monasteries and colleges used them until the middle of the seventeenth century. A number of interesting documents show the change actually taking place. A set of family records in the British Museum shows the first child being born in Mijc.Lviii (1258, the "ijc" being a form of writing 200), the second was born in Mijc.Lxi, the third in Mijc.63, while the fourth and fifth children were born

M. Mandekens invent. I. Neeffs sculpsit.

Figure 1–13. Both the abacus and algorism being used to do arithmetic. (Source: *Amussis Ferdinandea*, circa 1430.)

in 1264 and 1266.[7] Obviously this family accommodated to the new system in only three or four years. Even as late as 1681 we find evidence that the new system was not entirely understood. A book published in that year had its chapters numbered as: 1, 2, 3, 4, 5, 6, 7, 8, 9, X, X1, X2, X3, X4, . . . , XXX, XXX1, 302, 303, . . . , XXXX, 401, 402, ...[8]

This hanging onto the old methods of notation was caused, not by a lack of knowledge of the new, but by the fear that, without a complete understanding of the system, something might go wrong. This type of fear is seldom seen today, but two examples from the seventeenth century might help to illustrate this phenomenon. William Oughtred, whom we will meet again in the discussion about the slide rule, would often calculate $ab + ac$ rather than $a(b + c)$ because of a fear that some sort of error might enter into an abbreviated system.

[7]This is cited by Robert Steele, *The Earliest Arithmetics in English* (London: Oxford University Press, 1922).

[8]This is noted in G. F. Hill, "On the Early Use of Arabic Numbers in Europe," *Archaeologia*, 62 (part 1), p. 37.

In 1673 John Wallis from Oxford wrote to John Collins and admitted that he had doubts about writing $\sqrt{12}$ as $2\sqrt{3}$ simply because no one had ever done it that way before and, although he knew it to be the same value, he "durst not without precedent, . . . introduce a new way of notation."[9]

Many different forms of the numerals have been used in Europe, some of which would not even be recognized for what they are today. The manuscript versions of the old works are particularly difficult to read because the author and copyist used the forms of numerals with which they were most familiar. Books produced a few years, or even a few miles, apart would use different characters for at least some of the ten numerals. It was the invention of the printing press which standardized them into the forms we now know, although even the forms of 5 and 7 vary slightly between some Europeans and Americans. It is interesting to note that, despite the fact that the Europeans obtained the system from the Arabs, the two cultures use remarkably different forms of the numerals today. The European tourist is constantly having problems with the fact that the symbol "0" is used in Arabic countries as the symbol for the digit five and a large dot is used as the symbol for zero.

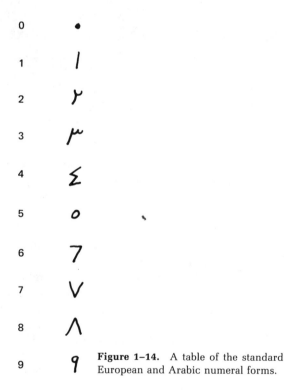

Figure 1–14. A table of the standard European and Arabic numeral forms.

[9]Cited in A. De Morgan, *Arithmetical Books from the Invention of Printing up to the Present Time* (London: Taylor and Walton, 1847).

1.6 THE FAR EAST

Although there is a lot known about the old forms of numerals and their computational use in China, there is great difficulty in establishing exact dates for the introduction of various concepts and practices. This difficulty stems from the fact that the ancient Chinese had a high veneration for the works of very old authors and, much like the European Medieval tradition of considering Aristotle to be the ultimate authority, they would confine their research to elaborating the knowledge set down by the ancients. If anyone did propose a new method of computation, it was almost always attributed to one of the ancient authors whose writings were, of course, no longer available. Several authors have been taken in by this practice of attributing results to the ancients and have credited the Chinese with a very sophisticated arithmetic system by as early as 3500 B.C. Although some evidence exists to show that abilities in arithmetic existed that early, the major developments in this area did not take place until about 600 B.C.

Most of our knowledge of early Chinese numbers comes from monuments and coins because the written works on arithmetic have not survived the ravages of either human or natural disaster. One of the worst of these ravages was perpetrated by Chi Hwang-ti, the first emperor of the Tsin dynasty, in 213 B.C. when he ordered all the books in China to be burned and the scholars buried alive. He was, unfortunately, reasonably successful in this undertaking. There are some texts which survived the purge, dating from about 540 B.C., which indicate that the Chinese had a well-developed decimal place value notation that had been in use for several hundred years. The best estimate is that they used a positional decimal number system from about 1300 B.C., possibly even earlier.

It has been conjectured that the development of a place value notational system depends on the style of writing adopted by a people. Those civilizations which had an alphabetic writing system tended to use the alphabetic symbols to represent integers and, like the Greeks, saw no real reason to stop equating symbols with integers when the digits from 1 to 9 had been assigned their signs. The Chinese ideographic writing system did not tempt one to assign individual symbols to numbers greater than nine because there would have been no built-in compulsion to use up all of the symbols in an alphabet. It is likely that the Chinese were the first people to use a completely formed decimal representation for numbers.

The characters used by the Chinese undoubtedly were simple pictures of the sticks they used for the primitive counting process. Like the Egyptian system, the integers from 1 to 5 were just represented by simple vertical strokes but, for representing numbers from 6 to 9, they employed the shorthand device of a horizontal stroke representing five together with enough vertical strokes to make up the required digit. The system is illustrated in Figure 1–15.

During computation, the numbers were represented by a special set of

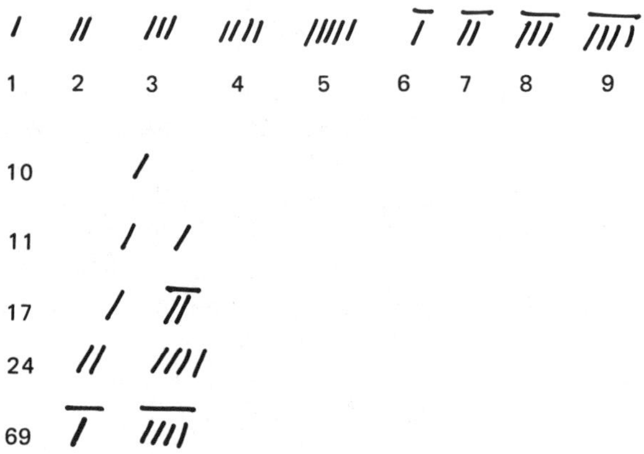

/	//	///	////	/////	̄/	̄//	̄///	̄////
1	2	3	4	5	6	7	8	9

10 /

11 / /

17 / ̄//

24 // ////

69 ̄/ ̄////

Figure 1–15. Examples of early Chinese numerals.

calculating rods which would be laid down in such a way as to form the ideographs of the required numerals. When attempting to represent a number such as 24 (see Figure 1–15), it is very easy to confuse the rods belonging to one digit with those belonging to its neighbor. In order to overcome this problem the technique of rotating every second digit through 90 degrees was evolved. This meant that the digit 1 would be represented as | if it was used in the units, hundreds, ten thousands, or millions position, and by — if it was used in the tens, thousands, or hundred thousands position. For example:

$$198{,}617 = \ ^{-} \ \overline{////} \ \_\underline{!}\_ \ \overline{7} \ - \ \overline{//}$$

Figure 1–16. An example of 90-degree rotation of early Chinese digits.

In later years it became the practice to perform arithmetic on a large squared board, much like a checker board, with each digit of a number occupying a separate square. This eliminated the need to rotate adjacent digits by 90 degrees but, because of the lack of any device to indicate an empty column (zero) when writing down the result, the orientation of the numerals was still vital to their understanding. An arithmetic text from the third century A.D. starts off with:

> In making a calculation we must first know the positions. The units are vertical and tens horizontal, the hundreds stand while the thousands lie down; thousands and tens therefore look the same, as also the ten thousands and the hundreds.[10]

A representation for zero was added to the system, probably from contact with India, about the year 800 A.D.

[10]J. Needham, *Science and Civilisation in China*, Vol. III (Cambridge: Cambridge University Press, 1959), p. 8.

The rods and squared board provided a substitute for the modern use of a pencil and paper. Two numbers to be added together were first laid out on the board, one above the other, then the result of adding together the various columns of digits would be represented by another line of rod numerals below the first two. Subtraction was done by placing the rod numeral answer above the two lines which represented the given problem, in effect creating the complementary addition problem. Multiplication and division, while not exactly equivalent to our pencil and paper methods, would be readily understood by a modern individual. The conjecture has been made that, because the Chinese always wrote from top to bottom, their horizontal use of the calculating board indicates that it may have been introduced from another culture. There is no real evidence to support this conjecture, but it is not beyond the realm of possibility that the system was adopted from either the Indian or Tai people. It is interesting to note that the Tai number words are very similar to the Chinese number words but that the two languages have almost no other words in common.

One indication of the sophistication of this system is that the early Chinese had some notion of negative numbers. The computing rods came in two colors, red for use when representing positive quantities and black for negative ones. There is also some indication that, at least in later years, the calculating rod system was modified by having numbers engraved upon the individual rods. Almost nothing is known of the use of this system but it is possible that it was a primitive attempt at the use of decimal representation, much like Gerbert's "apices" described in Section 2.3.

A complete set of traditional calculating rods contained 271 pieces, each of which was about 0.1 in. in diameter and 6 in. long. Initially they were constructed from bamboo, but after 400 B.C. they were often constructed from ivory, bone, or horn, and some time between 600 A.D. and 900 A.D. they were fashioned from cast iron. One very old way of indicating the wealth or status of a man was to imply that he was so rich he could afford to "calculate with ivory rods."

Calculating rods continued to be used in China up to about the year 1600 when, due to the increasing popularity of the wire and bead abacus, no further references are found in the literature. The wire and bead abacus is, undoubtedly, easier and quicker to use than the calculating rods on a squared board, but the rods were a useful tool in the hands of a trained manipulator. In the eleventh century A.D. an astronomer was described as being able to "move his counting rods as though they were flying, so quickly that the eye could not follow their movements before the results were obtained."[11] The date of the introduction of the wire and bead abacus is not known for certain, but it is known that a calendar reform done in the year 1281 A.D. was accomplished by the calculations being done with calculating rods while another calendar re-

[11]Needham, *Science and Civilisation*, p. 72.

Figure 1–17.   A Chinese illustration of a counting board in use.

form in 1384 was aided by the astronomers using a wire and bead abacus. Thus the calculating rods must have been displaced by the more modern abacus starting some time about the year 1300 A.D.

In later years the Chinese used three distinct numeral systems. The first were those that occur in normal written material, the second were a special set of numerals for use in legal documents because of the ease with which the first set could be forged or altered, while the third set (the counting rod numerals) were those which, because of their simple construction, were normally used for written arithmetic or accounting work.

The second, or legal, set of numerals were the ideographs for certain words which, because of historical and poetic connotations, came to be associated with certain numbers:

The numeral for	Means
1	perfection
2	to assist
3	an accusation
4	to expose publicly
5	to associate
6	a mound of earth
7	a tree
8	to divide
9	a stove
10	to collect

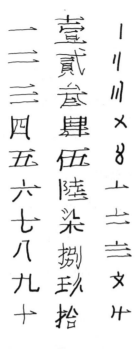

Figure 1–18. A table of the three different Chinese numerical character sets.

From China the use of the calculating rods, and the numeral representation based on them, spread to Korea. Here they took a much firmer hold than they did in China, not even being completely displaced when the wire and bead abacus was introduced. Even as late as the nineteenth century the use of the calculating rods was still so widespread that they were obvious to foreigners. In 1881 the French missionaries at Yokohama published a book about Korea, *Grammaire Coreene*, in which they stated:

> The Coreans, to make their calculations, use small rods in nonfixed number, which are placed from right to left, isolated or in groups, in order to represent the units, tens, hundreds, etc. Disposed vertically they indicate each unit of the order of the units or of the tens etc.; disposed horizontally, they are worth five units of the same order.[12]

Shortly after the introduction of Buddhism into Japan, in 552 A.D., two Korean scholars came to Japan in order to teach more about this new faith. They not only brought the teachings of Buddha but were also responsible for the introduction of the Chinese calendar and the Chinese system of astrology. With these came the knowledge of the calculating rods and the rod numerals. By 600 A.D., when the Japanese adopted the Chinese system of measures, the use of the calculating rods was well established.

---

[12]T. de la Couperie, "The Old Numerals, the Counting Rods, and the Swan Pan in China," *Numismatic Chronicle, 3, 297.*

One of the annoying problems of doing arithmetic with the calculating rods is their tendency to roll around, particularly if the calculating board is not perfectly flat. The Japanese solved this problem by making their rods with a square cross section. This rather obvious improvement does not seem to have been passed back to the Koreans or Chinese, perhaps because the circular rods were already too firmly embedded in these other two cultures, or it may simply be that because the mainland peoples considered the Japanese to be barbarians they were reluctant to accept any of their ideas.

1.7 OTHER FORMS OF NOTATION

Earlier sections of this chapter have illustrated several of the different ways that people used writing materials to record the results of their computations. It should be kept in mind, however, that the majority of the early societies in this world were not fortunate enough to have access to reasonable sources of writing materials. Clay or wax tablets, as used by the Babylonians and Greeks, were not always available due to different climate or geological conditions. Even when the raw materials for these media could be readily obtained, they were often not used because of the need to bake the clay or keep the wax cool in order to preserve the records which had been so carefully inscribed upon them. What to us would seem like more reasonable modes of recording information, by the use of pen and ink on paper or parchment, was again not suitable because these materials represent relatively late technological developments. Papyrus was not known outside of Egypt until about 600 B.C., and parchment was not available until about 400 B.C. Even those societies that had items like paper or parchment would not often use them—except for recording important data—because they were difficult to produce and consequently quite expensive. Because of these factors, large sections of the world's population had to develop alternate physical representations for information. A variety of different materials was used, but knotted cords or notches cut into "tally sticks" were the most common forms.

1.7.1. Knotted Cords for Record Keeping

All cultures used threads or ropes for everyday tasks. It would only be natural for them to think of using knots in these ropes to represent elementary forms of data. The knotted rope was superior to the other obvious alternative, that of keeping a bag of pebbles as a number record, because it was not subject to the same type of information corruption that could take place if the recording device were accidentally dropped. A knotted cord would also have been an obvious choice as a simple memory tool for many societies because they were already familiar with it from its use in the contexts of magic and religion—although which association would come first is a debatable point. The knot has had a long history as a tool of the witch doctor. The association has survived right up to modern times in such cross-cultural expressions as to "bind" or "untie" a spell.

Although there are many historical records to indicate that knotted strings were used for remembering information, this technique seems to have been almost lost by modern societies except for the occasional ceremonial use, mainly by religious groups. For example, the ancient Hebrews were known to have used knotted strings as a memory device, and Deuteronomy 6:6–8 exhorts them to tie cords around the hands and head (seen today in the Jewish phylacteries or frontlets) to remind them of the laws. According to tradition, God showed Moses the exact form of tying these knots to make them the most suggestive. A similar device is the fringe of white and blue cords, worn on Orthodox Jewish clothing, tied with knots at different distances to remind them of the Commandments.

Other Biblical references to knots can be seen in some of the Old Testament descriptions. For example, Ezekiel 40:3 records the prophet's vision of a man "with a line of flax and a measuring reed in his hand" who took down the exact dimensions of the future temple. It has long been supposed that the "line of flax" (the word *cord* would be a more accurate translation from the Hebrew) was being used to record these measurements by means of a series of knots. The fact that the cord was being used as a recording device would have been obvious to people in Ezekiel's time, but the connection is lost on the modern reader.

Even as late as the third century A.D. the tax gatherers in Roman Palestine were using knotted strings both for their own records and for receipts. Even when this mechanism was replaced by writing, the receipts were still referred to as "publican's knots."

The literary references to the use of knots is not just confined to Biblical sources. There are countless references in old Arabic sources which refer to digits as knots. Although it is highly likely that the Arabic references stem from an early use of knotted strings as recording devices, some care must be taken with this statement because many of the early references reserve the term *knot* only for multiples of 10—that is 10, 20, 30, and so on. This may be some indication that the term *knot*, meaning number, arose from sources other than the use of knotted strings, or that knots were only used to represent multiples of 10 while the units digits were represented by some other mechanism, for example, the number of strands in the cord, or some form of marking on the lower sections of the cords.

China, too, has historical records indicating knotted cords were once in use as recording devices. In an appendix to a historical work, Confucius writes:

> In great antiquity knotted cords served them for the administration of affairs. During the following generation, the saintly man Fou-Hi replaced these by writing.[13]

---

[13]S. Gandz, "The Knot in Hebrew Literature," *Isis*, 14, 214.

Tradition places Fou-Hi about 2800 B.C. Although this passage would indicate that the use of knots died out very early in Chinese history, it is likely that this is just one more example of the corruption of the historical record by crediting discoveries to the ancients. Other Chinese references refer to the use of knotted cords until the start of the Han dynasty (about 300 B.C.).

Even after writing materials were in common use in China, some very old customs concerning the representation of numbers by knots managed to survive. As in other societies these were generally involved with magic or religion. The magical or divinatory work known as the *I Ching* contains two diagrams of undoubted antiquity. Their source, according to legend, was that they were presented to an ancient emperor (Yu the Great) by two magic animals which came out of the Yellow River. These diagrams represent a 3 by 3 magic square (in which the sum across any row, column, or diagonal adds up to 15) and a square in which are represented all the integers from 1 to 10. The numbers, in each case, are represented by cords with knots tied in them; the cords representing even (yin) numbers are black while those representing odd (yang) numbers are white.

Not all examples of the use of knots to record information come from the distant past. In Germany, up to the end of the nineteenth century, millers would use knots to record the amount and kind of flour they delivered to the bakers. The strings used to close the flour sacks would be knotted in specific ways to record the sack's contents. One measure of flour was indicated by a simple overhand knot, two measures by an overhand knot with an extra string passed through it, and more complex knots were used to record five and ten measures of flour. The type of flour was recorded by a special series of loops tied in the ends of the cords.

A further modern example comes from India. During the census of 1872 the illiterate among the census takers would use four different colors of cord to record the population of rural villages. They would tie one knot for each individual, using a black cord for a man, a red cord for a woman, white for a boy, and yellow for a girl.

The practice of using knotted records was also common among various groups of American Indians from the interior of British Columbia to the middle of South America. The Incas, from the northwest coast of South America, were the only ones to really develop the system beyond the simple recording of elementary items such as the number of days that had elapsed from a given event. The Incas were an anomaly; they were a highly civilized people with a sophisticated government and yet had little in the way of a written language. Their use of knotted strings reached its highest development in the fifteenth- and sixteenth-century Inca empire device known as a quipu (*quipu* was the Inca word for knot). The quipu had two basic functions: It would record purely numerical information, and it also would act as an aide-memoire for the record keepers in recalling historical traditions, poems, lists of kings, and so on.

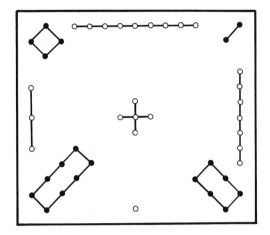

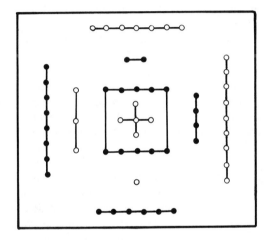

Figure 1–19. The Chinese magic squares represented by knot numerals.

1   2   5   10

Figure 1–20. German miller's knots.

The quipu's method of operation was based upon the decimal system of notation, and different kinds of records were indicated by the thickness or color of the strings. Most of the quipus in existence today were discovered in graves along the Pacific coast of Peru and, through improper handling (both before and after their owners' demise) tend to resemble nothing more than a well worn and tangled string mop.

One of the best early descriptions of the quipu comes from a Spaniard (Pedro de Ciera de Leon, born in Seville in 1519) who went to the new world when he was 14. Unlike most of the other early Europeans in the Americas, he was quite careful to record the life style of the Incas and, when talking about their records, he states:

> The Peruvian quipus are of twisted wool, and consist of a large cord with finer threads attached to it by knots. These fringes contained the contents of the quipu, which were denoted either by single knots or by artificial intertwinings. The different colours of the threads had different meanings, and not only was the colour and mode of intertwinings of the knots to be considered in reading a quipu, but even the mode of twisting the thread, the distance of the knots from each other and from the main cord. The registers of tribute, the enrollment of the tribes, lists of arms and troops, inventories of the contents of storehouses; all of these were the primary uses of the quipus. They were also available for recording the most striking events and thus supplied the place of the chronicles![14]

Another Spaniard (Garcilasso de la Vega) implied that the quipus were used for actually doing arithmetic:

> They knew a great deal of arithmetic and had an admirable method by knots made on strings of different colours . . . they added up, and multiplied by these knots, and to know what portions referred to each village, they divided the strings by grains of maize or small stones, so that their calculation might be without confusion.[15]

It is likely that de la Vega was confused in this regard for, from other sources, it appears as though the Incas actually used a form of abacus to do their calculations. This abacus used grains of corn or small stones in its operation, and it is possible that de la Vega became confused as to the actual role of each device when he witnessed an Inca using an abacus to do calculations involving data stored on a quipu.

The most common form of quipu consisted of a main cord with the various pendant strings looped around it. These pendant cords were generally tied together by top cords which acted as grand totals of the information on the pendant strings. The information would be recorded either by single or multiple knots, and the distance from the main cord indicated its decimal position, with the units digit being the furthest from the main cord. Figure 1–21 shows a quipu which might have been used to record the number of pages in the first edition of Knuth's *The Art of Computer Programming*. Reading from left to right, the pendant strings indicate that there are 225 pages in Chapter 1 and 229 pages in Chapter 2, giving a combined total of 454 pages in the first volume, as seen

[14]Ibid., p. 200.
[15]Ibid., p. 201.

Figure 1–21. A drawing of an Inca quipu keeper, as illustrated in one of the early Spanish documents.

in the top string. Volume II (438 pages) is made up of 155 pages in Chapter 3 and 283 pages in Chapter 4. Volume III is made up of 379 pages in Chapter 5 and 162 pages in Chapter 6, giving a total of 541 pages. The last pendant string, which would be a different color from the others, indicates that there is a grand total of 1433 pages in the first three volumes.

1.7.2 Tally Sticks

Another obvious device which could be used to record information is the notched stick. Again, this form of data recording has been used in almost every civilization, although most modern cultures show little or no sign of its once having been of importance. The earliest example that has come to light is the so-called Ishango bone found on the shore of Lake Edward in Zaire (Congo). This small bone, about 8,000 years old, has a little piece of quartz stuck in a

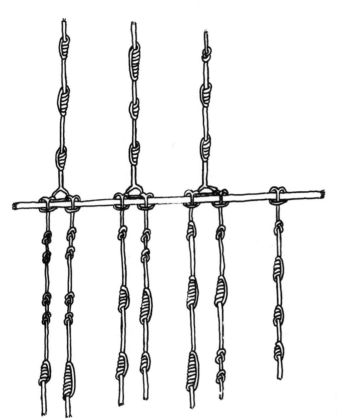

Figure 1–22. Knuth's table of
contents in the form of a quipu.

groove at one end and has three columns of notches cut into the sides of the
bone itself. Microscopic examination of the bone indicates that the notches
were made by some 39 different tools, thus it likely represents a record of events
rather than a random decoration scratched into the bone. There is some limited
evidence that suggests the markings may represent a record of some activity
based upon a lunar calendar. If that is the case, then the notations record a
series of events over a time span of almost six months. If the Ishango bone is
really a numerical record rather than just a decoration, then traces of this type
of recording system can be found from as early as the Upper Paleolithic cultures of 30,000 B.C.

　　There are so many examples of the use of knotched sticks in different
parts of the world that it is impossible to describe them all. The stick is almost
universal in its availability and the cutting tools would be at hand in every
culture that was sufficiently advanced to need its record-keeping functions.
Most ethnographic museums contain several examples of its use in one form

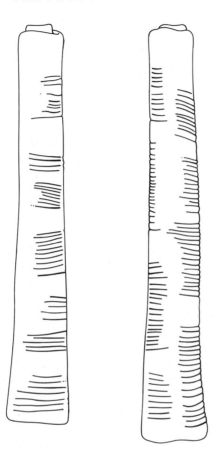

Figure 1–23. A diagram of the Ishango bone—an 8,000 year old tally stick.

or another. As typical examples of the device, we need only examine them in the forms found in China and in England.

The Chinese used tally sticks about the same time that they were using knotted strings. The inhabitants of the Liu-Chhiu islands have some cultural traditions which likely date back to the time when the use of knotted strings and tally sticks were common all over China. The people of Liu-Chhiu were basically isolated from their neighbors and, being very conservative, were slow to adopt new cultural ideas even when contact was established. These people used a very simple set of tally sticks to keep records of rice, money, and so on. The sticks were from 1 to 2.5 ft long and 1 to 1.5 in. thick. On the sticks were scratched a primitive set of numerals, much like the old rod numerals of mainland China, but they showed a marked preference for the base 5 system, much like the traditional numerals of Korea.

Figure 1-24. The old Chinese character meaning "contract."

One obvious remnant remains of tally stick usage in mainland China. The old written character for an agreement or contract is made up of three radicals, two on the top and one on the bottom. The first top radical is a stick with cuts shown across it, the second is a pictorial representation of a knife, and the lower radical is the character meaning "large" or "big"; thus a contract is literally "a large tally stick."

The high point of the use of tally sticks occurred in the British Exchequer during the thirteenth to nineteenth centuries. Any debts or payments were recorded on lengths of elm wood by means of special notches cut into the sides of the stick. The stick was then split lengthwise into two pieces, a thin piece called the foil (from the French word for leaf), and a thick piece called the stock. The Exchequer kept the foil and the other party kept the stock as an invoice or receipt. When further payments were to be made, the two parts of the original tally were compared to ensure that no forging of receipts had taken place by either party. This practice was so widespread in British commerce that it has resulted in many words which reflect this heritage. For example, if a person deposited money in a bank a tally would be cut of the amount, the bank would keep the foil and the depositor would keep the stock, thus becoming literally a "stock holder" in the bank. Today we no longer trade stocks in our stock markets—we have evolved to the point where we only trade stock certificates! Phrases such as "to tally up the bill" or the "counter foil" one fills out to record the issue of a cheque come from this same source.

The Exchequer tallies were customarily cut as follows: The notch for 1000 pounds was to be as large as the hand is wide; for 100 pounds the notch was to be as wide as the thumb with a rounded bottom, for 20 pounds it was to be as wide as the little finger, for 1 pound it was to be the size of a grain of barley, for 1 shilling it was to be just large enough to be seen as a notch, and for 1 pence it was to be a simple cut with no wood removed. If it was necessary to represent half of any of these quantities, as, for example, when recording 10 pounds, then the notch was to be made with one straight and one slanted side. The notch for 20 shillings (one pound) was the first time that any substantial amount of wood had to be removed (or scored) from the tally, and this led to the adoption of the English term *score* for 20.

Charles Dickens was very interested in administrative reform and his description of the eventual fate of the Exchequer tallies is rather interesting:

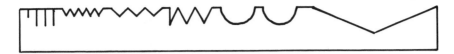

Figure 1–25. A diagram of an English tally stick recording the sum 1253 pounds, 5 shillings, 3 and one-half pence.

Ages ago a savage mode of keeping accounts on notched sticks was introduced into the Court of the Exchequer and the accounts were kept much as Robinson Crusoe kept his calendar on the desert island. In the reign of George III an inquiry was made by some revolutionary spirit whether, pens and paper, slates and pencils being in existence, this obstinate adherence to an obsolete custom ought to be continued, and whether a change ought not to be effected. All the red tape in the country grew redder at the bare mention of this bold and original conception, and it took until 1826 to get these sticks abolished. In 1834 it was found that there was a considerable accumulation of them; and the question then arose, what was to be done with such worn-out, worm-eaten, rotten old bits of wood? The sticks were housed in Westminster, and it would naturally occur to any intelligent person that nothing could be easier than to allow them to be carried away for firewood by the miserable people who lived in that neighbourhood. However, they never had been useful, and official routine required that they should never be, and so the order went out that they were to be privately and confidentially burned. It came to pass that they were burned in the stove in the House of Lords. The stove, over-gorged with these preposterous sticks, set fire to the panelling; the panelling set fire to the House of Commons; the two houses were reduced to ashes; the architects were called in to build others; and we are now in the second million of the cost thereof.[16]

Thus the House of Commons and the House of Lords, so easily recognized in tourist photographs of central London, owe their existence to the British practice of keeping tax records on tally sticks.

1.7.3 Other Methods of Numerical Notation

There were, of course, lots of other methods used to record and manipulate numerical information during the long span of human history. Special situations would require some unique system to be constructed, for example, the invention of the Braille system of numbers and letters to enable the blind to both read and record information. In many cases the invention of a new system

---

[16]Quoted by T. Dantzig in *Number: The Language of Science*, 4th ed. (New York: Macmillan, 1954), pp. 23–24.

was intended to enable a single individual or a small group of individuals with
some form of handicap to function in society. A typical example of this type
of system was the one developed by Dr. Nicholas Saunderson (1682–1739), who
contracted smallpox when he was only one year old, which left him totally
blind. When he was a young boy, he invented a notational system for helping
him in doing the usual school arithmetic exercises. His system consisted of a
smooth thin board about one foot square, upon which was drawn a grid of
horizontal and vertical lines about 0.1 in. apart, a small hole being drilled at
the intersection of each horizontal and vertical line. It is possible to consider
this board as being covered by a multitude of tiny three by three grid patterns.
For example:

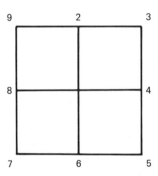

Figure 1–26.   Saunderson's numerical grid.

Saunderson considered that each of the small grids represented a single decimal digit, and would indicate which digit was being represented by sticking a
pin in one of the holes. The center hole indicated a 1, the hole immediately
above it a 2, and so on, as indicated in Figure 1–26. In order to indicate a zero,
a special pin with an extra large head was placed in the center hole. The units,
tens, and hundreds digits were arranged beside one another just as we would
do with pencil and paper. Saunderson kept a large stock of pins, with their
points cut off to avoid pricking his fingers, in two separate boxes, one for the
normal small-headed pins and one for the large-headed pins used to represent
a zero. In order to locate any particular digit of any number recorded on the
instrument, he placed a series of notches along two sides of the square, the

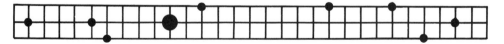

Figure 1–27.   The numbers 14709 and 2368 as they would be represented on Dr. Saunderson's board.

notches marking the center of each three by three grid. He was said to have acquired great facility and quickness in the use of this board for performing the standard arithmetic operations.

Although he remained totally blind, Saunderson became such a good mathematician that he was eventually made Lucasian Professor of Mathematics at Cambridge in 1711, created a Doctor of Laws in 1728, and became a Fellow of the Royal Society in 1736. It is interesting to note that, while at Cambridge, he became very famous for his advanced course on optics. It is rather remarkable that a man, totally blind since he was an infant, could become famous for his lectures on such optical phenomena as the use of a prism for creating rainbows.

FURTHER READING

AL-DAFFA, A. A. (1977). *The Muslin Contribution to Mathematics.* Atlantic Highlands, NJ: Humanities Press.

BAGGE, L. M. (1906). "The Early Numerals," *Classical Review,* 20, 259–67.

BALL, W. W. R. (1888). *A Short Account of the History of Mathematics.* London: Macmillan and Co.

BENEDICT, S. R. (1914). *A Comparative Study of the Early Treatises Introducing the Hindu Art of Reckoning Into Europe,* Ph.D. Thesis, Ann Arbor, University of Michigan.

BONNYCASTLE, J. (1810). *Introduction to Arithmetic.* London.

CAJORI, F. (1894). *A History of Mathematics.* London: Macmillan and Co.

———, F. (1928). *A History of Mathematical Notations.* La Salle, IL: Open Court Publishing Co. (reprinted by Open Court in 1974).

CHAMBERLAIN, B. H. (1898). "A Quinary System of Notation Employed in Luchu," *Journal of the Anthropological Institute,* 27, 338–95.

CHENG, D. C. (1925). "The Use of Computing Rods in China," *American Mathematical Monthly,* 32, 492–99.

CONANT, L. L. (1956). "Counting," in *The World of Mathematics,* ed. J. R. Newman. New York: Simon and Schuster.

DANTZIG, T. (1930). *Number, the Language of Science.* New York: The Macmillan Co., (various printings by different publishers).

DATTA, B., and A. N. SINGH (1962). *History of Hindu Mathematics.* Bombay: Asia Publishing House.

FILON, L. N. G. (1925). "The Beginnings of Arithmetic," *Mathematical Gazette,* 12 (177).

DE LA COUPERIE, T. (1883). "The Old Numerals, the Counting Rods, and the Swan Pan in China," *Numismatic Chronicle,* 3, 297.

DeMORGAN, A. (1847). *Arithmetical Books from the Invention of Printing up to the Present Time.* London: Taylor and Walton.

GANDEZ, S. (1931). "The Origin of the Ghubar Numerals," *Isis, 16,* 393–424.

GANDZ, S. (1930). "The Knot in Hebrew Literature," *Isis, 14,* 189–214.

GILLINGS, R. J. (1972). *Mathematics in the Time of the Pharaohs.* Cambridge: MIT Press.

GUNN, B., and E. T. PEET (1965). "Four Geometrical Problems from the Moscow Mathematical Papyrus," in *The Treasury of Mathematics* ed. H. Midonick. New York: Penguin Books.

HEATH, T. (1921). *A History of Greek Mathematics,* 2 vols. Oxford: Clarendon Press.

HILL, G. F. (?). "On the Early Use of Arabic Numbers in Europe," *Archaeologia, 62* (Part 1), 37.

KARPINSKI, L. (?). "Augrim Stones," *Modern Language Notes, 27* (7), 206–9.

——. and G. WINTER (1930). *Robert Chester's Latin Translation of the Algebra of Al-Khowarizmi,* Vol. II in *Contributions to the History of Science.* Ann Arbor: University of Michigan.

——. (1923). "Michigan Mathematical Papyrus," *Isis, 5,* 20–25.

LENARD, P. (1933). *Great Men of Science,* trans. from the German by S. Hatfield. London: Bell and Sons.

LESLIE, J. (1817). *The Philosophy of Arithmetic,* Edinburgh: Archibald Constable and Co.

LOCKE, L. (1965). "The Ancient Quipu," reprinted in Midonick, *The Treasury of Mathematics.* New York: Penguin Books.

MENNINGER, K. (1969). *Number Words and Number Symbols.* Cambridge: MIT Press.

MIDONICK, H. (1965). *The Treasury of Mathematics.* New York: Penquin Books.

NEEDHAM, J. (1959). *Science and Civilisation in China, Vol. III.* Cambridge: Cambridge University Press.

NEUGEBAUER, O. (1952). *The Exact Sciences in Antiquity.* Princeton: Princeton University Press.

NEWMAN, J. R. (1956). *The World of Mathematics.* New York: Simon & Schuster.

PEACOCK, G. (1829). "Arithmetic," in *Metropolitan Encyclopedia.* London: J. Mawman.

PEET, T. E. (1965). "The Rhind Mathematical Papyrus," in *The Treasury of Mathematics,* ed. H. Midonick.

SCOTT, J. F. (1960). *A History of Mathematics.* London: Taylor and Francis Ltd.

SINGER, C. (1959). *A Short History of Scientific Ideas to 1900.* Oxford: The Clarendon Press.

SMELTZER, D. (1958). *Man and Number.* London: Adam and Charles Black.

SMITH, D. E. (1923). *Our Debt to Greece and Rome: Mathematics.* London: George Harrap & Co.

——. (1923). *History of Mathematics.* Boston: Ginn and Co., (reprinted by Dover Publications, 1958).

——. and Y. MIKAMI (1914). *A History of Japanese Mathematics.* Chicago: Open Court Publishing Co.

STEELE, R. (1922). *The Earliest Arithmetics in English.* Early English Text Society, Oxford University Press.

TATON, R. (1963). *History of Science,* trans. from the French by A. J. Pomerans. New York: Basic Books, Inc.

VAN DER WAERDEN, B. L. (1963). *Science Awakening*. New York: John Wiley.

WALLIS, J. (1683). "The Antiquity of the Numeral Figures," in *The Philosophical Transactions and Collections to the End of the Year 1700*, London (actual printing done in 1722).

YELDHAM, F. A. (1926). *The Story of Reckoning in the Middle Ages*. London: George G. Harrap & Co.

ZASLAVSKY C. (1973). *Africa Counts*. Boston: Prindle, Webster & Schmidt.

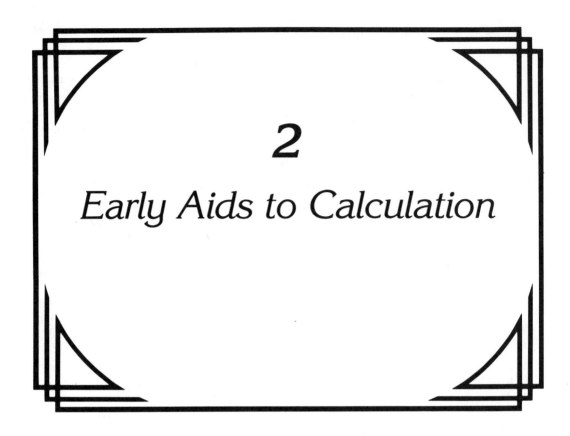

2

Early Aids to Calculation

2.1 INTRODUCTION

The establishment of a number system and the development of the necessary rules for doing arithmetic within that system are only the first step toward gaining a real flexibility with arithmetic processes. In the very early days, the average person probably had no need for an ability to calculate beyond simple addition and subtraction, with an occasional requirement to multiply small integers. The problems which required more in the way of sophisticated arithmetic abilities likely first arose in problems of trade, taxes, calendar making, and military organization. These were probably dealt with by highly trained individuals, but it would not be long before most people would also need access to greater arithmetical power.

    Of all the early number systems, only the Chinese came close to allowing computations to be easily performed by "nonprofessionals." The simple operations of addition and subtraction are easily performed in most systems, particularly the additive systems like those developed in Egypt, Greece, or Rome, but the other operations, such as division and obtaining square roots, were very difficult in most systems, and almost impossible in some. Part of this difficulty arose from the fact that no suitable materials existed upon which to write down either the problem or the intermediate workings to help someone arrive at a final answer. Clay or wax tablets were not always available because of differing geological or climatic conditions and paper was not known, except in a few small areas of the world, until sometime after 600 B.C. Even after the development of the process to produce parchment in about 400 B.C., it remained very expensive and was used only for recording important information, not for the actual calculations.

A large variety of different calculational aids were developed to overcome the problem of the lack of suitable writing materials. Even after writing materials were in common use, new technology continued to produce devices to aid in the arithmetic process. These ranged from elementary methods of using one's fingers to the very sophisticated analogue slide rule, which was so common until it was replaced by the hand-held electronic calculator. In between these two extremes, we have the development and use of different forms of the abacus, a great variety of analogue astronomical and navigational instruments, the sector, Napier's bones, and what was to be the ultimate calculational aid until the invention of the electronic computer—the simple table of logarithms. Each of these subjects will be dealt with in turn, with very little regard to the many centuries that passed between the developments at either end of the spectrum. It is also worth noting that people were (and sometimes still are) using one of the more sophisticated calculational aids, such as the slide rule or log tables, while at the same instant they were keeping various totals on some of the more primitive devices such as an abacus or even on their fingers.

2.2 FINGER RECKONING

The human fingers have been used in at least three distinct ways to aid people in their calculations. The first of these, simple counting on the fingers, is so widespread among schoolchildren that it needs no comment. The second involved a complex series of finger positions used to represent numbers when people were both illiterate and innumerate and yet needed some way to communicate numbers across language barriers. This same mechanism was also used to let the fingers act as a sort of accumulating register while doing mental calculations. The third use of the fingers involved a more direct arithmetical function and was an extension of the simple finger counting schemes, used when doing addition, to a system which would be useful for multiplication.

The use of the fingers to indicate a number is surely one of the oldest forms of numeration. It is, however, rather limited in its scope because of the fact that humans can use only ten fingers at any one time. As mentioned in Chapter 1, the Eskimo practice of using the terms *one-man* for the number 20, *two-men* for the number 40, and so on implies that several groups were able to use all 20 appendages for display purposes, but that still leaves the vast majority of integers without any reasonable way of having their value displayed.

At some time in the distant past, it became obvious that a good system for displaying numbers on the fingers would have certain advantages. If you did not speak the language being used in a marketplace, you had a hard time concluding a bargain without some way of indicating that you were willing to trade 47 of your objects for 13 of someone else's. Although this might sound like a flippant example, it must have been a very real problem in conducting international commerce and even in bartering between tribes and villages in many parts of the world. We do not know exactly when a unified system of number representation on the fingers was reached, but we do know that it eventually spread throughout all of North Africa, the Middle East, Europe, and may well have stretched into India and parts of the Far East. The system was mainly used to indicate a number to another person, often when involved in trade negotiations, but could also be used for simple forms of arithmetic as will be explained later.

We know, from the works of Herodotus, that the system was in widespread use among the Greeks of the fifth century B.C., but since he neglects to give us any details, all we can do is assume that it is the same as the finger notation used in later periods. It is entirely possible that the system dates from very much earlier than that, but nobody was kind enough to leave us any physical evidence which would indicate exactly when and where it may have started. About the only evidence we have is literary references to some form of finger computation being in use. Generally it is assumed that the reader would be so familiar with the system being mentioned, that no descriptions were necessary. A typical comment of this type comes from the Roman politician Cicero (106–43 B.C.) who, when writing to his friend Atticus to discuss the difference between simple and compound interest, states: "What difference this makes, if I know your fingers, you have certainly computed."[1] To "know your fingers" (*si tuos digitos novi*) is usually translated as "know your skill at reckoning." Similarly, the Roman orator Quintilian (d. 96 A.D.) says:

> If a speaker, by any uncertain or awkward movement of the fingers differs from the accepted mode of calculation, he is thought poorly trained.[2]

It is clear from the sermons of St. Augustine (354–430 A.D.) that he expected his listeners to understand some system of finger reckoning, for he often makes reference to numbers being held on the hand and occasionally asks his audience to follow some particularly complex calculation by moving their fin-

---

[1] Quoted in J. L. Richardson, "Digital Reckoning among the Ancients," *American Mathematical Monthly, 23.*

[2] Quoted in Richardson, "Digital Reckoning."

gers with his as he expounds upon some obscure cabalistic subject. In his great work, *The City of God,* he notes:

> He puts aside the fingers of the computers and orders silence, who says "It is not for you to know the times, which the Father has put in his own power."[3]

The earliest complete descriptions of the system come to us from the eighth century A.D. Nicolaus Rhabda of Smyrna and the monk known as the Venerable Bede both set down a description of the system then common among the people. Bede (672?–735), who is the best known of these gentlemen, was a monk who resided near the mouth of the river Tyne on the northeast coast of England. For his day, he was a prolific writer and produced several different works on various subjects, one of them being a treatise, written in 725 A.D., on the calendar together with information for calculating the date of such important Christian feast days as Easter. This subject required his readers to be familiar with methods of calculation, so he devoted the first chapter of his *De Temporum Ratione* to the usual methods of finger reckoning. In the process he described the finger signs to be used when representing numbers up to one million, although it is unlikely that anything more complex than 999 was in general use by the population.

As Bede described them, the signs for all the numbers from 1 to 99 could be made with only the left hand, the right hand being reserved for representing numbers from 100 to 9900. This fits in very well with some of the earlier literary references; for example, Juvenal (60–130 A.D.) writes, "Happy is he who had delayed the hour of his death so long and finally numbered his years on his right hand."[4] If that was Juvenal's only criterion for happiness, he must have died with a sorrowful heart, for he could easily have numbered his years on his left hand.

The numbers were expressed by the hand being held upward, the palm flat, the fingers together and the thumb, unless otherwise noted, being held out to one side. By comparing the following description with the diagram by Pacioli, it should be obvious how the different numbers were represented. The system is quite cunning in that it only uses the third, fourth, and fifth fingers, either bent at the middle joint or fully closed upon the palm, to represent all digits from 1 to 9. This leaves the thumb and index finger free to represent the multiples of 10 (10, 20, 30, . . . 90), so that two sets of finger positions can be used in any combination to represent the numbers from 1 to 99. In some descriptions, for example, the one by Bede, there were signs for numbers between 10,000 and 1,000,000 which were made by the hands touching various parts of

[3]Ibid.

[4]Quoted in D. E. Smith, *History of Mathematics* (New York: Dover Publications, 1958), *Vol. II*, p. 197.

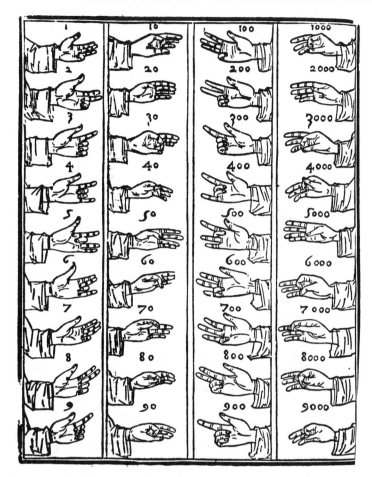

Figure 2–1. An illustration of the Finger Numerals. (Source: *Suma de Arithmetica Geometria* of Pacioli of Venice, 1494.)

the body, but these were evidently known only to a few people and not part of the regularly used system.

It seems obvious from sources such as St. Augustine's sermons, which often describe every step of a particular cabalistic calculation, that the finger numerals were used not only for simply communicating between people who could not speak each other's language (and would be unlikely to recognize a written number if they ever saw one), but were also used as a simple notational device when doing elementary arithmetic. If several numbers had to be added together, the first of them was noted on the fingers, the second added to it mentally and the result noted on the fingers, the third added mentally to the total noted on the fingers, and so on. This provided a simple notational device for relieving the mind of the chore of remembering intermediate results in a

	Left Hand
1	5th finger bent at the middle joint
2	4th and 5th fingers bent at the middle joint
3	3rd, 4th, and 5th fingers bent at the middle joint
4	3rd and 4th fingers bent at the middle joint
5	3rd finger bent at the middle joint
6	4th finger bent at the middle joint
7	5th finger closed on the palm
8	4th and 5th fingers closed on the palm
9	3rd, 4th, and 5th fingers closed on the palm
10	tip of the index finger touching the middle joint of the thumb
11–19	represented by the sign for 10 and the signs for 1 to 9 being made at the same time
20	thumb touching the base of the third finger
30	thumb and index finger form a circle
40	thumb and index finger held vertical and close together
50	thumb bent at both joints and held flat against the palm
60	thumb set as for 50 with the index finger bent over it
70	first joint of the index finger held on the first joint of the thumb, which is held vertical
80	tip of index finger held on the first joint of the thumb
90	thumb bent over the first joint of the index finger

	Right Hand
100 to 900	were represented by the right hand making the same signs as for 10 to 90 on the left hand
1000 to 9000	were represented by the right hand making the same signs as for 1 to 9 on the left hand

longer computation and would enable the operator to devote full concentration to the mental arithmetic. If one was interrupted, it was only necessary to hold the hands in their current position and the calculation could be taken up again later without the bothersome detail of attempting to remember the last result.

This very simple method of representing numbers, for both communication and as an accumulating register, died out with the advent of easily obtainable writing materials, the introduction of the Hindu-Arabic numeral system, and an increase in the general level of education.

The other major use of the fingers, for doing multiplication, was completely different from the scheme described above. It is hard for us to imagine that multiplication of small integers was a difficult process for an educated person, but even as late as the 1600s the subject of multiplication was often left until university level studies. Samuel Pepys (1633–1703), who was well educated by the standards of his day and eventually rose to become the Secretary to the Admiralty, was forced to hire a private tutor to teach him the multiplication and division skills for the jobs he had been assigned. Until the 1800s, the majority of well-educated people, only knew the multiplication table up to 5 × 5, so it is not really surprising to find a system in use which would enable them to perform multiplication beyond this limited range.

If a person knew the multiplication tables up to five times five, then it was possible to perform finger operations which would automatically yield the product of any pair of integers in the range from 6 to 10. One variation of this scheme required that the hands be held with the palm up and the fingers clenched. To multiply 7 times 8, you extend two fingers on the left hand, generally the thumb and the first finger, and three fingers on the right hand. The number of fingers extended represents the excess of the number over five—two for the left hand because 5 + 2 = 7, and three on the right because 5 + 3 = 8. The final product is obtained by adding together the number of fingers extended to give the tens digit of the result (2 + 3 = 5) and multiplying together the number of fingers still clenched in the left hand by the number still clenched in the right (3 × 2 = 6) to give the units digit—thus 56! Because there are only five fingers on each hand, the multiplication will never exceed five times five, and thus it is only necessary to know the multiplication tables up to that point. If a result greater than 10 is obtained when doing the multiplication, the tens digits of this result must be added to the tens digits of the final answer (obtained when adding together the extended fingers).

Perhaps the easiest way of stating these rules is by the following formula (e represents the number of fingers extended on the left hand, e' the number

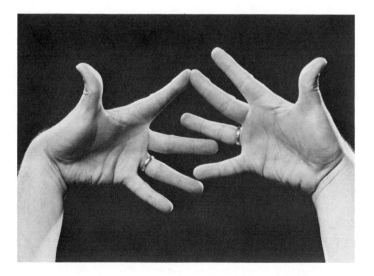

Figure 2–2. An example of finger multiplication (7 times 8). The tens digit is represented by the touching fingers and those above (i.e. 2 + 3 = 5) while the units digit is found from the fingers remaining below (2 × 3 = 6).

extended on the right hand, c the number clenched on the left, and c' the number clenched on the right):

$$\text{product} = 10(e + e') + cc'$$

In general, it is possible to extend the system to other ranges of integers as follows:

Range of numbers being multiplied	Formula for the result
6–10	$10(e+e') + cc'$
11–15	$10(e+e') + cc' + 100$
16–20	$20(e+e') + cc' + 200$
21–25	$20(e+e') + cc' + 400$
26–30	$30(e+e') + cc' + 600$

If it was necessary to multiply two numbers which were not in the same range, for example, 8×14, then the larger number could be split to bring it within the same range as the smaller number, for example, $(8 \times 8) + (8 \times 6)$. It is unlikely that the average person knew or used anything beyond the first or second range of numbers. The finger multiplication scheme is probably still in use in some parts of the world, for it is known to have been taught to at least some students, as part of their usual primary education, in the Ukraine as late as the 1940s. A search of school subject matter could quite easily reveal that it is still being taught in other areas.

Two other systems of finger notation and reckoning are known to have existed, and it is almost certainly the case that many others have been developed from time to time which have not been noticed by the modern investigator. It is worth describing these other two methods just to see the different range of ideas that have been used.

The first scheme was developed by a Mexican priest, Buenaventura Francisco de Ossorio, who used his fingers as a computational device to help him calculate the dates of all the movable Christian feasts. Ossorio described his system in a small booklet published in 1757. The system is quite complex and requires that many different positions on the hand be memorized as to their significance, but it would do all the computations—a job which would normally require Ossorio to have access to 35 different almanac tables! A complete description of Ossorio's scheme can be found in Florian Cajori's work listed in the reference section.

The second system was used in China and the southern parts of India. It involved using the joints of each finger of the left hand to represent the numbers from 1 to 10,000. This provided a scheme for displaying numbers during trade talks or for use as an accumulating register in much the same way as the previously described system was used. Each finger has three joints, and each joint has a right, middle, and left side so that it is possible to consider the finger

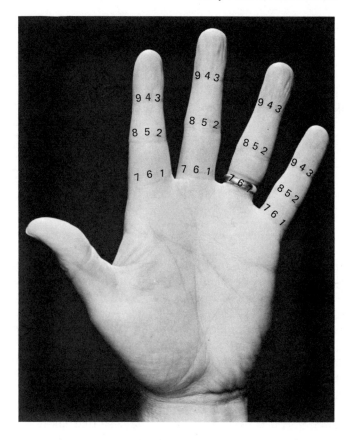

Figure 2–3. Finger notation positions used in China.

to have nine separate areas, each of which can represent one of the digits from 1 to 9 as shown in Figure 2–3. The fingernails of the right hand can be used to touch the different positions on the left hand in order to represent any digit in each of the four possible positions. Not touching a particular finger would represent a zero in that particular position. Thus, any number from 1 to 9,999 can be easily represented by the simple touch of one hand on the other.

2.3 THE ABACUS

The abacus is usually considered as being an object in the same class as a child's toy. This is quite the wrong impression for, in the hands of a trained operator, it is a powerful and sophisticated aid to computation. Some appreciation of the

power of the abacus can be gained by noting the fact that, in 1947, Kiyoshi
Matsuzake of the Japanese Ministry of Communications used a soroban (the
Japanese version of the abacus) to beat Private Tom Wood of the U.S. Army of
Occupation, who used the most modern electrically driven mechanical calculating machine, in a contest of speed and accuracy in calculation. The contest
consisted of simple addition and subtraction problems, adding up long columns
of multiple digit numbers, and multiplication of integers. Matsuzake clearly
won in four out of the five contests held, being only just beaten out by the
electrically driven calculator when doing the multiplication problems. Although both men were highly skilled at their jobs, it should be pointed out that
it took Matsuzake several years of special training in order to develop such a
high order of skill at using the soroban. It is unlikely that the average abacus
user would ever develop such speed and accuracy of operation. However, it
does illustrate that, at least in the hands of even a moderately skilled operator,
the abacus is far from being only an interesting toy.

The origin of the abacus is, literally, lost in the dusts of time. It likely
started out as pebbles being moved over lines drawn in the dirt. Most cultures
have used an abacus or counting board at some stage in their development but,
as in most European cultures, once paper and pencil methods were available
the use of an abacus died out so completely that it is hard to find any cultural
memory of its once having been an important part of the arithmetic process.
Today we tend to think of the abacus as a Far Eastern device, only because
that is one of the few places where its use is still noticeable. In fact the abacus,
in its present form, was only introduced into China in historical times (about
1200 A.D.) and was taken from there to Korea about 1400 A.D. and to Japan about
1600 A.D.

Although we know that the abacus was in general use in Europe until
only about 250 years ago, we have remarkably little physical evidence of its
presence, particularly from the earliest Greek and Roman times. What evidence
we have is usually of the form of quotations from the ancient writers. For example, Demosthenes (ca.384 B.C.–ca.322 B.C.) wrote of the need to use pebbles
for calculations that were too difficult to do in your head.

The Greeks were some of the greatest mathematicians of the ancient world
but they tended to divide mathematics into two separate studies: logistic was
the art of calculation, and arithmetic was what we would now call number
theory. The number theory studies were considered to be important and, as
such, have been passed down to us almost intact, while logistic was considered
a "vulgar and childish art" (Plato). Thus, if any treatises were written describing the Greek methods of computation, they were not considered worthy of
preservation. About the only thing we do know is that they did use a form of
the table abacus because one is illustrated on the side of a large vase and another has been found in archeological excavations, but as to the actual method
of use, we have only the statement, made by Herodotus when writing about
the Egyptians, that

. . . they write their characters and reckon with pebbles, bringing their hand from right to left while the Greeks go from the left to the right.[5]

Some of the earliest physical evidence about the form of the abacus comes to us from archeological excavations of Greek sites. In 1851 a very large vase, about 4 feet tall, was discovered which was covered with pictures of people engaged in various tasks. This so-called "Darius" vase, now housed in a Naples museum, has one figure which appears to be a king's treasurer keeping track of tribute being brought to him by various other figures. The treasurer is holding a wax tablet, possibly for recording the tribute, in one hand while he seems to be manipulating some counters on a table with the other. There is not enough detail shown to be certain that the artist intended to represent a table abacus, but it seems likely that a treasurer would have to do some elementary calculations when recording tribute and that the intent was to illustrate an abacus.

The second bit of evidence is a lot clearer than the Darius vase. It is an actual abacus table, found on the island of Salamis just a few miles off the Greek coast near Piraeus. The Salamis abacus is now broken into two pieces, but was once a large marble slab about 5 ft long and 2 ft 6 in. wide. There is no indication of when it might have been made. From its size, it must have been used in some large public institution, perhaps as a bank or money changer's table. We know very little about how it may have been used except that it seems to be designed for counters to be placed on or between the various lines, and the inscriptions appear to refer to numerical values and to certain types of coins

Figure 2–4. A drawing of the Greek abacus in use. (Source: From an illustration on the "Darius" vase.)

[5]Quoted in T. Heath, *A History of Greek Mathematics* (Oxford: Clarendon Press, 1921), p. 48.

such as drachmae, talents, and obols. It has been speculated by many different people that the spaces between the five separate lines at one end of the abacus are intended for calculations involving fractions of the drachma.

The word *abacus* itself can be of some help in determining the origins of the European version. The manipulation of pebbles in the dust, or the use of the finger or a stylus in fine dust or sand spread upon a table, is known to have been used as an aid to calculation from the earliest times. The Semitic word *abaq* (dust) is thought by many to be the root of our modern word *abacus*. From the Semitic, the word seems to have been adopted by the Greeks who used *abax* to denote a flat surface or table upon which to draw their calculating lines. The term then appears to have spread to the Romans who called their table an abacus.

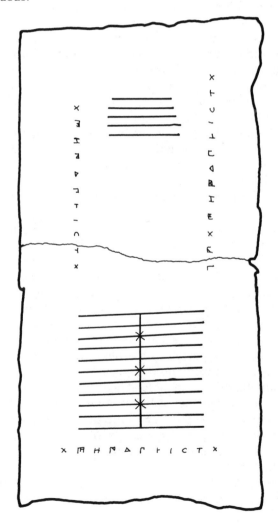

Figure 2–5. A drawing of the Salamas abacus. Note that the original stone has been broken in two pieces.

The term *abacus* has meant many different things during its history. It has been applied to the simple dust table, or wax tablet, which was generally used only as a substitute for pen and ink, as well as to the various forms of table abacus and different wire-and-bead arrangements used in the Far East. Because most early arithmetic was done on the abacus, the term became synonymous with "arithmetic," and we find such oddities as Leonardo of Pisa (Fibonacci) publishing a book in 1202 called *Liber Abaci* (The Book of the Abacus) which did not deal with the abacus at all but was designed to show how the new Hindu-Arabic numerals could be used for calculation. In northern Europe, the phrase *Rechnung auff der linien* (calculating on the lines) was in common use as a term meaning "to do arithmetic" even long after the use of the abacus had been abandoned.

Many of our modern mathematical and commercial terms can be traced to the early use of the table abacus. For example, the Romans used small limestone pebbles, called *calculi,* for their abacus counters; from this we take our modern words *calculate* and *calculus.* A more modern example comes from the fact that, in England, the table abacus was generally referred to as a "counting board" or simply a "counter"; of course, every merchant would have a "counter" in his shop upon which to place the goods being purchased and upon which the "account" could be calculated.

The spread of the Hindu-Arabic numerals into Europe, together with the development of cheap rag paper upon which to scribble, sounded the death knell for the table abacus. Its use died out in Italy in the 1500s but, due to generally lower standards of living and more conservative practices in northern Europe, it remained the dominant mode of performing arithmetic there until well into the eighteenth century.

By the thirteenth century the European table abacus had been standardized into some variant of the form shown in Figure 2–6. It consisted of a simple table, sometimes covered by a cloth, upon which a number of lines were drawn in chalk or ink. The lines indicated the place value of the counters. Thus the bottom line represented units, and each line above increased by ten times the value of the line below; also each space between the lines counted for five times that of the line below it. No more than four counters could be placed on a line and no more than one in any space. As soon as five counters appeared on a line, they were removed and one placed in the next higher space; if two appeared in a space, they were removed and one placed on the next higher line. When performing a computation on the table abacus, any counters in a space were considered to be grouped together with those on the line below, so that the space was simply a device to keep the eye from being confused by having a large number of counters on one line. A cross or star was usually placed next to the fourth (thousands) line to guide the eye, much as we use a comma today to mark off groups of three digits.

Very few reckoning tables still exist. We know that they once existed in great numbers for they are often mentioned in wills and in household inven-

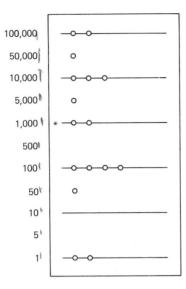

100,000	—o—o—————————
50,000	o
10,000	—o—o—o———— —
5,000	o
1,000	* —o—o—————————
500	
100	—o—o—o—o—————
50	o
10	—————————————
5	
1	—o—o—————————

Figure 2–6. A table abacus set out to represent 287,452.

tories but, being a common object, nobody thought to preserve them, and only three or four are known to still exist in various museums.

By the thirteenth century the counters had changed from the simple pebbles used in earlier days into specially minted coin-like objects. They first appeared about 1200 in Italy but, because it was there that the use of Hindu-Arabic numerals first replaced the abacus, the majority of the counters now known come from north of the Alps. These coin-like counters were cast, thrown, or pushed on the abacus table; thus they were generally known by some name associated with this action. In France they were called *jetons* from the French verb *jeter* (to throw), while in the Netherlands they were known as *werpgeld* (thrown money). The older English usage of "to cast up an account" or "to cast a horoscope" also illustrates the mode of operation of a good abacist.

The counters, now commonly called jetons, are still to be found in quite large numbers. This is not surprising when you realize that the average numerically literate person would possess at least one set of copper jetons while a merchant would likely have several. Wealthier individuals or those with some authority in the community would often have their jetons struck in silver with their coat of arms or portraits as the decoration. The business of producing jetons was, at one time, a major industry in parts of Europe, Nuremberg being a noted center of production.

A new "nest" of between 20 and 100 jetons was considered a very suitable gift to celebrate New Year's Day. The old set would be disposed of in order that the errors of last year's accounts could be discarded with the jetons themselves. The usual method of disposing of an old set of jetons appears, for some unknown reason, to have been the simple expedient of throwing them into the local river. They now tend to come to light during dredging operations on German rivers. Examples can often be found in stores selling coins and tokens to collectors. F. P. Barnard managed to examine over 100,000 individual jetons before he wrote his classic description *The Casting Counter and the Counting Board*.[6]

The custom of using jetons for a New Year's Day gift soon led to the French minting special jetons to be used in this way. These were usually decorated with kings' heads on one side and some allegorical scene depicting the major events of the previous year on the other. The French kings and their ministers made formal presentations of such specially struck jetons to each of their officials every year. The king's set was sometimes minted in gold (which was often later melted down to provide the raw material for a table service), the more senior officials would have their gifts cast in silver, and the lesser individuals would have to make do with copper or brass. The dies of these jetons would then be used to strike sets to be sold to the general public.

The growing importance of the French colonies demanded that some form of jeton be made available for calculation in the New World. Starting in 1738, the French began to ship quantities of jetons to their North American colonies both for commercial calculation and for use by the growing number of taxation officials. In 1750 a separate Department of the Colonies was organized to deal with colonial finances, and these officials had a new series of commemorative jetons struck for their 1751 New Year's Day gifts. Further jetons were issued each year until 1759, when French fortunes in North America suffered such reverses that there was no longer anything positive to commemorate. The reverse side of four such colonial jetons are shown in Figure 2–7. The obverse side generally shows a bust of Louis XV, although examples are known with other designs. This selection does no more than illustrate the general type, and the interested reader is encouraged to look for further examples in the works noted in the references.

As the Hindu-Arabic numerals gained a foothold in Europe, the table abacus was quickly abandoned. Its use was forgotten to the extent that, when Napoleon invaded Russia in 1812, his soldiers brought back examples of the Russian abacus as being a curiosity of the area; this was at a time when their own great grandfathers had been daily users of the device in France.

As with the tally sticks described earlier, the table abacus continued to be used for the longest period in Britain. Figure 2–8 shows one page from the first widely used printed book on arithmetic in the English language. This book, by Robert Recorde, was in print from 1542 right up to the start of the 1700s. It clearly shows (besides two errors in the illustration which are left as a puzzle for the reader) that abacus arithmetic was being taught to schoolchildren throughout this period. The illustration from Recorde's book shows the usual method of working a table abacus. For addition the two numbers were simply

---

[6]F. P. Barnard, *The Casting Counter and the Counting Board* (Oxford: Clarendon Press, 1916).

Figure 2-7.   Some examples of the French colonial jetons of 1751–1758. (Photographs courtesy of the Glenbow Museum, Calgary, Canada.)

set down side by side, and the two groups of jetons were then moved together to accomplish the operation. Subtraction was slightly more difficult but was aided by the fact that one could literally "borrow" a jeton from a higher valued row. The methods for multiplication and division were slightly different in various parts of Europe, but they largely retained the doubling and halving processes that were started by the Egyptians.

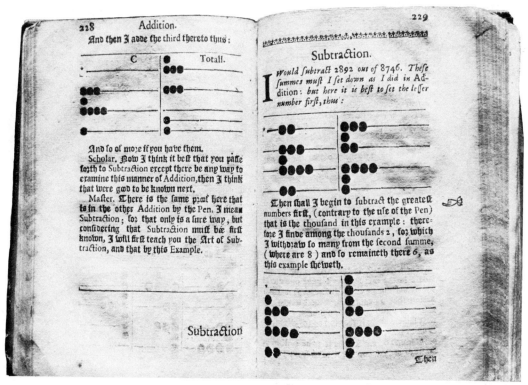

Figure 2–8. A page from Robert Recorde's book on arithmetic.

The most famous table abacus was that used by the English national accounting office, the Court of the Exchequer. This tax calculator was a table 10 ft long by 5 ft wide, bordered by a ledge 4 in. high and covered with a dark russet cloth. It was divided into squares by intersecting chalk lines, within which a sum was denoted by jetons according to their position—the column farthest to the right for pence, the next for shillings, and so on. The calculator sat about half way down the table, and the king and nobles who had come to pay their taxes sat around the room. Although this exchequer table has given its name to the modern government department dealing with finance, it is only when we come to fill out our income tax forms that we might wish life to be simple enough for our accountant to still use an exchequer table as the main computing instrument.

In early times the English paid their taxes not in money but in goods, and the counters were of different sizes and colors to represent the different goods being considered. Almost any token could be, and was, used for a counter, but besants, coins from eastern Europe, were favorites until after the fourteenth century because of their size and weight. Whenever the exchequer obtained foreign coins, for example, from taxes imposed on merchants trading with the Continent, they were put aside for use by the exchequer calculator.

The scheme used by the exchequer to represent various digits was quite different from that used by the ordinary abacist using a table abacus. The first few integers were simply represented by rectangular arrays of jetons while a single jeton, placed above and to the right of the rectangular array, would count for 5 or, if above and to the left, it would count for 10. The scheme can be best appreciated by studying Figure 2–9. In later times, the officials of the Exchequer would revert to using this type of notation even when pens and ink were available. There are several examples of ink dots appearing on state papers, the latest on a document from 1676 in which the pattern in Figure 2–10 is evident. This pattern represents the sum of 4,438 pounds 10 shillings 4 pence. Note that

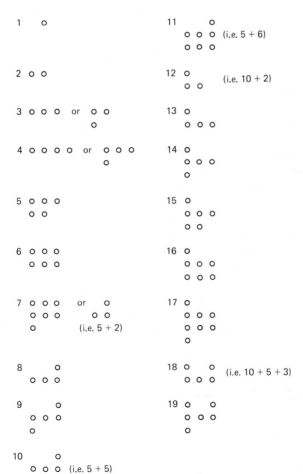

Figure 2–9. The merchant's accounts numerals.

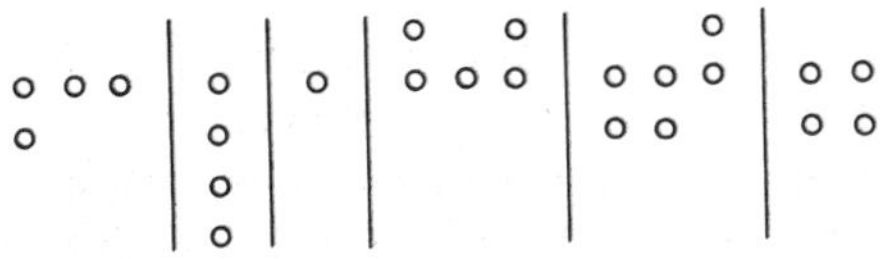

Figure 2-10. Pattern of ink dots appearing in a document of 1676.

the single counter in the third digit from the left stands for 20 (a score of) pounds.

There were at least two attempts to replace the standard European table abacus with one which used fewer counters. The first of these was by the Roman philosopher Boethius, who was beheaded in 524 A.D. when he fell out of favor with the Goth king. Boethius wrote a book on geometry which contained a section on the abacus. In this work he described how, instead of using many counters to represent a number on one line of the abacus, it was possible to use only one counter, or "apice," upon which was inscribed the required digit in Roman numerals. This would have required the abacist to possess several sets of jetons with the digits from 1 to 9 engraved on the top surface. There is no record that this type of abacus was ever used in any extensive way, but the British Museum has several small counters engraved with various Roman numerals and drawings of hands showing finger numerals, which they classify as "gaming pieces."

The second attempt was made by a monk, Gerbert of Aurillac in Auvergne, who was later to become Pope Sylvester II. Gerbert is known to have studied under Bishop Hatto of Vich in Barcelona during the period 967–970 A.D. He may have had some contact with the Hindu-Arabic numerals from this time, but he is also known to have possessed a copy of Boethius' *Geometry* and thus may have obtained his ideas from the "apices" it described. Whatever the source, Gerbert described the use of a new form of abacus in a work he wrote about the year 1000 A.D. This abacus consisted of a smooth board divided into 30 columns, three of which were for use with fractions and the other 27 were grouped together in nine groups of three columns each. Each column, in the groups of three, was headed C for *centum* (hundred), D for *decem* (ten), or S for *singularis* (unit), and the apices could then be placed under the appropriate column to represent any three-digit number. At least one twelfth-century description of Gerbert's abacus, from a manuscript found in St. John's College in

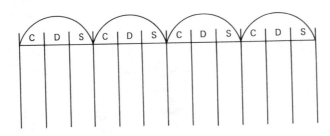

Figure 2-11. Gerbert's abacus of about 1000 A.D.

Cambridge, still groups the columns in threes, but correctly labels each of them with the figures for thousands, ten-thousands, and so on.

Gerbert's use of the abacus with digits engraved on the "apices" shows a lack of understanding of the true nature of the zero, but it was a natural step between the use of an abacus and written arithmetic using the Hindu-Arabic notation. There is also the possibility that Gerbert did fully understand the new numerical notation and decided to describe this intermediate step because he realized that most of the European scholars of the day would not be able to comprehend, and thus dismiss, a fuller explanation.

Gerbert's abacus never became popular, but it was used from time to time, and several different descriptions of it can be found in later years. It is known that Bercelinus (ca. 1000 A.D.), Radulph of Laon (ca. 1100), and Gerland (ca. 1200) all used Gerbert's abacus in their work.

Gerbert is known to have been a very good scientist for his day. It is fortunate that he was Pope during the period around 1000 A.D., for many people firmly believed that the world would come to an end at the start of the second millennium and Gerbert, by calculating the times of eclipses due in the year 1000 and publishing them in advance, managed to keep Christian Europe from dissolving into complete panic. Like all men of his age, he was a firm believer in some aspects of astrology and fortune telling. A soothsayer had once told him that he would die in the Holy Land, so he carefuly avoided ever going there. It is a little ironic that he was taken with a seizure and died while celebrating mass in the Jerusalem Church in Rome!

The Oriental wire-and-bead abacus appears to have its origin in the Middle East sometime during the early Middle Ages. A type of abacus was developed which had several wires, each of which was strung with ten beads. The Turks called this a *coulba*, the Armenians a *choreb*, and the Russians, where it can still be seen in use today, referred to it as a *stchoty*. This device almost certainly entered the Far East via the standard trade routes of the day, so that it was probably first adopted by the merchant class and then slowly spread to the upper levels of society. Its introduction may well have been helped by international traders, such as Marco Polo, who had to travel through several different countries on their way to China and thus had ample opportunity to pick up different techniques along the way.

By the time it was firmly entrenched in Chinese society, about the year 1300 A.D., it consisted of an oblong frame of wood with a bar running down its length, dividing the frame into two compartments. Through this bar, at right angles to it, are usually placed 17 (but sometimes more) small dowels with seven beads strung on each one, two on the upper side (heaven) of the bar and five on the lower (earth) side. Each bead in the lower section is worth one unit, while those in the upper section are worth five. Thus it is possible to represent any number from 1 to 15 on the individual dowels, although anything greater than 9 would only naturally occur as an intermediate result in the process of a calculation. The Chinese called this device a "swan pan" (counting board),

Figure 2–12. The Chinese swan pan storing the number 279.

and the term *swan* was derived from and older term meaning to "reckon with the rods."

From China the concept of a wire-and-bead abacus spread to Japan. Again, it was probably the merchant class who actually spread the idea, for there was a great deal of trade going on between the two countries during the period from 1400 to 1600 A.D. It is entirely possible that the soroban was being used in Japan for at least 100 years before it was officially noticed by the ruling classes some time about 1600. At that time, the rulers of Japan were known to despise the lower classes, and any knowledge of business affairs—even the value of the different coins—on the part of the nobility was considered a sign of inferior breeding. The soroban generally resembles the swan pan except that there is only one bead in heaven, and four in earth, and the beads themselves have been modified to provide a sharper edge so that the operator's fingers can make

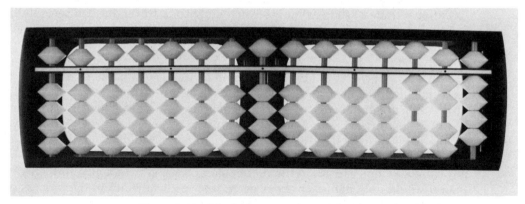

Figure 2–13. The Japanese soroban storing the number 279.

better contact for flipping them up and down the dowels. These changes mean that the Japanese operator has to be a little more aware of how to work quickly with additions or substractions which may require a carry, or borrow, to or from the next column. It is perhaps with the soroban that the abacus reached its ultimate development. As was pointed out earlier, a well-trained soroban operator can compete with an electrically driven, four-function mechanical calculator as far as speed and accuracy are concerned.

The use of the abacus was not confined to the Old World. We know very little about the various forms of abacus used by the Indians of North and South America, but we do know that some of these groups used the device. In 1590 a Jesuit, Joseph de Acosta, recorded some facts about the Inca culture that would indicate the common use of an abacus.

> In order to effect a very difficult computation for which an able calculator would require pen and ink . . . these Indians make use of their kernels of grain. They place one here, three somewhere else and eight I know not where. They move one kernel here and three there and the fact is that they are able to complete their computation without making the smallest mistake. As a matter of fact, they are better at calculating what each one is due to pay or give than we should be with pen and ink.[7]

It would seem obvious that there were a number of American Indian cultures that were advanced enough to require some form of calculating device be in common use, but almost no records remain of anything even as primitive as de Acosta's description. It is likely that the abacus was in common use but that very few Europeans were concerned with recording anything except their own conquest of these Indian cultures.

2.4 THE QUADRANT

Most of the devices discussed so far have had their beginnings so far back in history that it is impossible to determine exactly when or where they were first used. The quadrant was an astronomical and calculational tool which had been in existence for hundreds of years before it became the subject of several attempts to improve on its usefulness. Some of the ancient astronomers, such as the later Babylonians and Greeks like Ptolemy, undoubtedly used various sighting devices to measure the angles between stars and, from these humble beginnings, the quadrant was slowly improved as a sighting and measurement device. During the sixteenth century there arose a new educated class of Europeans who demanded that the tools of calculation, navigation, and sun dialing be made available to them without the years of tedious study that were

---

[7]H. Wassen as quoted by James R. Newman in *The World of Mathematics* (New York: Simon and Schuster, 1956), pp. 463–64.

required in order to learn the complete theory behind all the different movements of the heavenly bodies. This resulted in many different modifications of basic instruments, some of which quickly died out while others, like the improved quadrant, were to remain as a standard instrument which would be possessed by every man of learning who had the means of obtaining one.

The quadrant is known in many different forms with differing tables engraved upon it. One of the best known, because it has survived in the greatest numbers, is the so-called "Gunter's quadrant," which was devised by Dr. Edmund Gunter, a Professor of Astronomy at Gresham College in London. The scales engraved on Gunter's quadrant are the same ones found on an equally ancient instrument, the "astrolabe," which Gunter folded into four parts and compressed so that they would fit on a quarter circle. Gunter was a very important figure in the popularization of all kinds of mathematical devices, including the "sector" and tables of logarithms, and his life and contributions will be described in greater detail in later sections of this book.

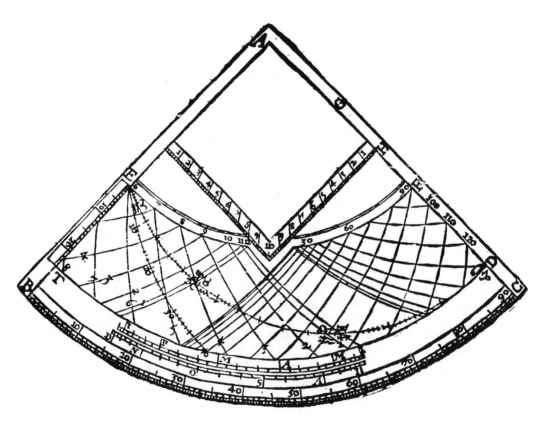

Figure 2–14. A Gunter's quadrant, as illustrated in *The Works of Edmund Gunter*, 1680 edition.

Because the scales of Gunter's quadrant require some knowledge of astronomy before they can be fully appreciated, a slightly simpler, but no less powerful, instrument developed by William Leybourn (1626?–1700) will be described in detail. Leybourn was a teacher of mathematics in London who became very well known for his textbooks on such topics as mathematics, astronomy, surveying, arithmetic, Napier's "bones," and slide rules. It should be kept in mind that Leybourn actually lived during the seventeenth century, and did most of his work after 1650, but that other types of quadrants were available to the general public long before this time. The description of his quadrant is being included here simply as a representative of the general type of instrument that was available.

There are at least three examples of the Leybourn quadrant that have survived the ravages of time. The one pictured in Figure 2–15 is to be found on display in the Physics Department of the University of St. Andrews, Scotland. Exactly how it came to be there is not known for certain, but it appears to have been one of a set of instruments which were purchased for use in the University some time in the last part of the seventeenth century. It is made of brass and is slightly less than six inches along the edge. It has two large holes along one edge which, at one time, contained sights which would have been used to take elevations of stars, buildings, and so on. There is another hole at the center of the quarter circle which once had a string threaded through it. This string would have been used as a plumb bob when taking elevations of the stars, to extend readings from one scale to another, and for marking off distances between the scales. The owner of the quadrant would also need to have had a pair of dividers to lay off measurements on some of the scales, although a sliding bead on the plumb bob string would have done at least part of this job if the dividers were not right at hand.

Before it is possible to comprehend the variety of tasks the Leybourn quadrant is capable of performing, it is necessary to review the old forms of trigonometric functions. The modern system of defining trigonometric functions is by the ratios of the lengths of the sides of a right-angled triangle. Long before this system was adopted, the trigonometric functions were considered as the lengths of various lines drawn in and around a circle of some convenient radius. Figure 2–17 shows a circle and an angle (theta) marked off along the circumference. With respect to the given radius, the various trigonometric functions were defined as the lengths of specific lines, for example:

- chord of theta was the lenth of the line BD
- sine of theta was the length of the line BE
- versed sine of theta was the length of the line DE
- tangent of theta was the length of the line DC
- half tangent of theta was the length of the line AF (the half tangent is really the tangent of half the angle)
- secant of theta was the length of the line AC

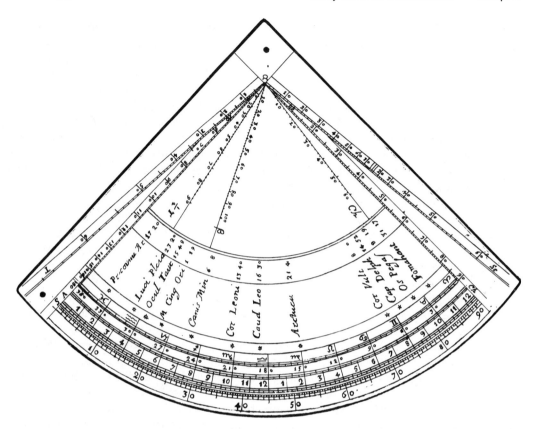

Figure 2–15. A drawing of the Leybourn quadrant, both front and back views. The holes along one limb once held a pair of sights.

Of course, the lengths of these lines would change each time a circle of different radius were used, so the mathematician consulting any trigonometrical table had to be aware of exactly how long the defining radius was for the tables then in use. This system was rather cumbersome, and we can be thankful that it was eventually replaced by our more modern system of ratios.

Returning now to the actual scales on the quadrant, those on the front face are primarily concerned with computations involving trigonometric functions, navigation, and astronomical observations. The short line in the center, divided into 100 equal units, is the defining radius for most of the trigonometric scales. This radius is short enough to allow for the representation of the lengths of all tangents from 0 to 65 degrees (on the scale marked T), the length of the versed sines from 0 to 180 degrees (on the scale marked VS), the length of all half tangents from 0 to 90 degrees (1/2 T), the length of the chords of angles from 0 to 60 degrees (small scale marked Ch), and the lengths of the sines of

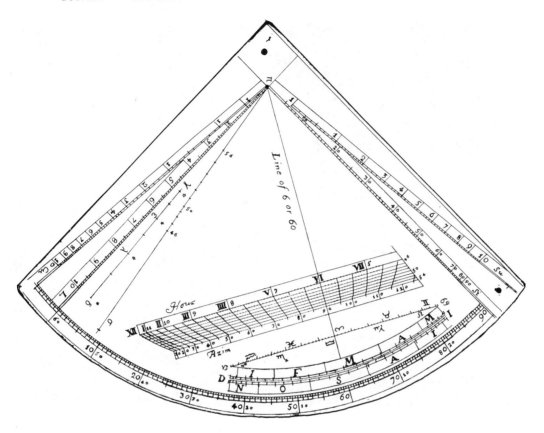

Figure 2–15. (cont.)

angles from 0 to 90 degrees, and the secants from 0 to 60 degrees. Both sines and secants are measured along the scale marked Se, with the sines occupying the first part of the scale and the secants the latter part. The one other large linear scale, marked Ch is not related to the standard base radius and is intended for use with some of the scales on the rear side of the quadrant.

The circular scales were to aid in astronomical observations such as finding various stars, telling time both day and night, and casting horoscopes. Working from the inmost circle to the edge of the quadrant they are:

- a list of 12 prominent stars with their declinations from the equator; adjacent to each name is a star point so that the string may be stretched across this point and the outer scales read from the position of the string

- the signs of the zodiac, together with a division of the quadrant into 360 equal parts

Figure 2–16. The use of a quadrant for taking sights. (Source: "Amussis Ferdinandea," ca. 1430.)

- a division of the quadrant into 24 parts which indicate the position of the star in terms of the number of hours it would take the first point of Aries to reach the star's position at midnight
- the usual division of a quadrant into 90 degrees

The scales on the rear of the quadrant are divided into two different sets, a set for computing squares, square roots, cubes, and cube roots, and another set for determining the position of the sun at any time during the year and for constructing sundials.

The scale marked L is called a "scale of equal parts" because it is divided into ten equal-sized units, each of which is subdivided into ten smaller units. This scale is the main one to be used when doing simple arithmetic. For example, a measurement taken from this scale (either with dividers or the movable bead on the plumb bob string), of x units, will yield the value of x^2 or x^3 when measured against the "Su" (for "Surds") or "Cu" (for "Cubes") scales,

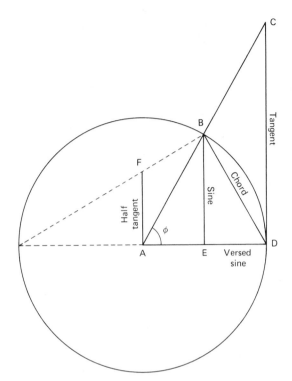

Figure 2–17. The old method of defining trigonometric functions according to the length of lines in relation to a given circle.

respectively. Square and cube roots could be obtained by the reverse process. Multiplication and division could also be performed using the scale of equal parts when aided by the use of the plumb bob string and a pair of dividers. The method was essentially that used on the device known as a "sector" (to be described in the next section), but Leybourn's own words, although slightly ambiguous, are sufficient to describe the process:

> Take the lesser of the two Numbers to be multiplied out of the line, and with that distance of the Compasses, set one foot in the Term of the greater Number; and bring the thred to the nearest distance: Then from 10 at the end of the line, take the nearest distance to the thred; this distance shal reach from the beginning of the line to the Product of those two Numbers being multiplied together.[8]

This description is not as difficult as it first appears to be, particularly when you have a quadrant and dividers at hand to follow each stage with a particular example. It was possible to include any of the trigonometric scales in each calculation. Thus, except for its lack of digital accuracy, it is very much equivalent to the modern pocket calculator.

[8] W. Leybourn, *Panorganon: or a Universal Instrument* (London, 1672), p. 25.

The calendar scale is found close to the outer edge of the quadrant. The months on the scale are noted as "I,F,M,A,M,I,I,A,S,O,N,D" and are used in conjunction with the zodiac scales and hour scales just above and the degree scales just below. If the plumb bob string is held so that it passes just over a given date, then the sun's position in the zodiac can be determined from the intersection of the string and the dotted zodiac scale. For example, the date of March 20 will yield the fact that the sun is in the tenth day of Aries, and by stretching the string further out to the degree scale, it is seen that the sun is just over 4 degrees north of the equator (by using the degree markings in small figures in the outer most scale). It must be kept in mind that all this calendar information is based on the use of the old Julian calendar rather than our modern Gregorian system.

The complex scale in the center of the quadrant is a table of the sun's position for every day of the year, for all latitudes between 46 and 54 degrees north of the equator. For example, if it were required to find the sun's azimuth (the angle along the horizon as measured from a point due south) at 3:20 p.m. for an observer at 50 degrees north latitude, the string is stretched over the intersection of the 50-degree line and the line denoting 3:20 p.m. (Roman numerals are p.m., Arabic numerals are a.m.). This string will cut the azimuth scale at 45 degrees, which is the required azimuth. The other half of this problem is to determine how high the sun is above the horizon at 3:20 p.m. on March 20 for an observer at 50 degrees north latitude? This is easily solved by stretching the plumb bob string across the calendar scale point representing March 20 and measuring (with a pair of dividers) the distance between the string and the line denoting 3:20 p.m. (Again, the measurement is taken along the line marked for 50 degrees north latitude.) This distance, when laid out on the linear scale of sines marked Si will yield 27 degrees 30 minutes which is, of course, the height of the sun above the horizon. The place at which the string cuts the 50 degree north latitude line will yield the time of sunrise and sunset for March 20 (5:40 a.m. and 6:20 p.m.). Thus, in the days before the pocket watch, this quadrant provided a handy pocket-sized timepiece as well as containing all the information and tables that would be required for simple horoscope calculation.

A glance at the mathematical textbooks of the fifteenth and sixteenth centuries will reveal that the science of constructing sundials was not only well developed, but also practiced on a large scale. It was a common practice for a professor of mathematics or astronomy to publish simplified directions for the construction of sundials upon both horizontal and vertical surfaces. Leybourn himself wrote a book about how to create sundials, in which he even described how to make a sundial on the ceiling of a room, the sun being reflected to it by a mirror on the windowsill. Two of the most common dials are a horizontal dial and a vertical dial on a south facing wall. The sundial shown in Figure 2–18 is a horizontal dial designed for a latitude of 51 degrees north. It was drawn with the aid of the linear scales on the rear of the quadrant marked with

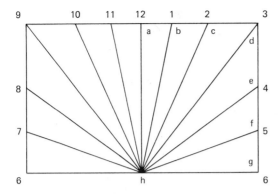

Figure 2–18. A sundial constructed using Leybourn's quadrant.

the letters gamma and delta. The basic measurement (a–h) of the dial is the secant of 39 degrees (that is, 90 − 51 = 39; for a vertical dial it would have been the secant of 51 degrees) obtained from the scale of secants on the front of the quadrant. The positions for the lines denoting 1, 2, 3, 4, and 5 o'clock are obtained from the short scale marked by the letter γ, and the required lengths are indicated by the stars on the scale. The height of the shadow-casting gnomon is easily obtained from the scale marked σ. The end from which the measurement is taken depends on whether it was a horizontal or a vertical dial under contruction.

The large scale of sines marked Si on the back of the quadrant is constructed to the radius of the "Line of 6 or 60" and may be used to create sundials which are to be mounted on inclined planes or on walls facing southwest, for example. The techniques of constructing such dials were well known to scientifically educated gentlemen of the time.

The modern mathematician, computing scientist, or astronomer would be hard pressed to design an instrument capable of so many functions with such limited equipment, yet the functions we have described are only a fraction of the ones for which the instrument was designed. Leybourn wrote a book of 260 pages in which he hoped to describe the observations and calculations which could be done with this quadrant, but even that did not suffice to explain it all completely. One can only admire the genius of men such as Leybourn, Gunter, and others, who laid out the design for instruments such as this and thus considerably eased the burden of computation for all of us.

2.5 TWO LEGGED INSTRUMENTS

The slide rule was the main "quick calculating" instrument for at least a century before its position was usurped by the inexpensive electronic pocket calculator during the 1970s. Although the slide rule has a long and honorable history, it did not always occupy the position of leadership among analog calculating devices. There was another series of analog instruments which were used before the invention of the slide rule and, to a large extent, competed with it until the middle of the nineteenth century. These instruments, generally known as sectors, were developed in the late 1500s from an instrument dating back to at least Roman times, called a proportional compass.

2.5.1 The Proportional Compass

A proportional compass is very similar to a set of dividers except that the legs are hinged in the middle with a set of points at both ends of each leg. Their main use was by draftsmen for reducing and enlarging drawings in any given proportion, dividing a circle into an equal number of parts, and determining square and cube roots. The trick which allowed such a simple instrument to perform all these tasks was the fact that the point at which the two legs were hinged was adjustable and it was possible to move the pivot up and down the legs to create different lengths of leg between the top and bottom points.

Engraved on both sides of the legs were various scales which were used in adjusting the pivot point. There were generally four scales: lines, circles, planes, and solids. The scale of lines was used when enlarging or reducing drawings in various proportions. When the pivot was set on 2 (on the scale of lines), any measurement taken with the large points would be twice that indicated by the small points. The scale of lines was usually graduated from 1 to 10.

The scale of circles was used to divide the circumference of a circle into any number of parts from 2 to 20. The scale was such that, when the large points were opened up to the diameter of the circle, the small points gave the length of the chord which would divide the circle into the correct number of equal parts.

The scale of planes was essentially a mechanism for obtaining square roots. It was usually used to expand or reduce the areas of a diagram. For example, if the compass is adjusted to 3 on the scale of planes and the small points are used to measure the side of a square, then the square constructed on the length of side indicated by the large points will have three times the area of the original square. This scale could also be used to expand or reduce the area of any regular figure.

The scale of solids was used to enlarge or reduce a figure in proportion to its volume in the same way as that of the scale of planes, except that the relationship between the points reflected the cube root of the scale rather than the square root.

2.5.2 The Sector

As the level of technology (mainly military technology) expanded in the second half of the sixteenth century, there arose a need for a calculating instrument

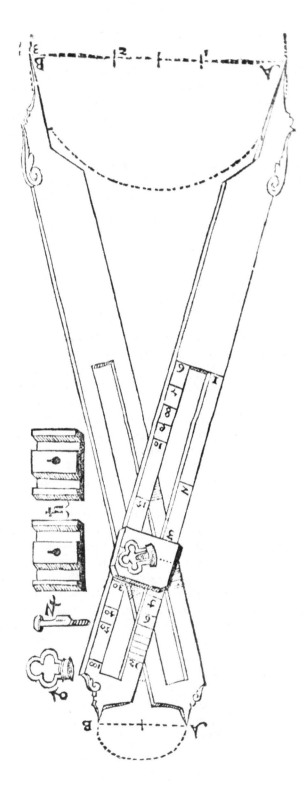

Figure 2-19. An early drawing of a proportional compass.

as easy to use as the proportional compass, yet much more powerful. Several different people seemed to have hit on the mechanism of the sector at about the same time. Between 1584 and 1606 independent inventions were published in Antwerp, London, and Padua. Although all of these inventions were similar, the one created in Padua by Galileo was the most useful and the most widely copied of the early sectors. He first published a description of his sector in 1606, but manuscript copies of his work indicate that he was working on the device as early as 1597 and may well have actually produced several examples even earlier than that. He called his invention the "geometric and military compass" because it found its initial uses in the problems faced by artillery men. We shall see, in a later section, how it was the demands of the descendants of these artillery men who caused another great leap forward in computing technology during the Second World War. Galileo set up a small factory and hired an instrument maker to help satisfy the demand for copies of his instrument. He is known to have manufactured over 300 before he shut down the shop in 1610 when he moved from Padua to Florence.

Before continuing to describe the sector, it is worth a short digression to see the types of problems that concerned the people of the artillery corps in Galileo's day. The discovery, about 1500, of the techniques of casting cannons had a major influence on the conduct of war in Europe. By the end of that century there were many thousands of cannons being used by the different nations, and with these came the need to perform calculations when aiming and firing these new devices. Several very elementary instruments were in common use by sixteenth-century gunners to determine the elevation of the gun barrel, the size of the cannon ball, and the amount of powder to be used, all of which would help to determine the range of fire.

The "gunner's compass" was a device which looked very much like a carpenter's square with one leg longer than the other. A plumb line hung from the corner, and a cross piece between the legs was marked off into 12 divisions or "points." The long leg would be put down the mouth of the gun and the plumb line would then indicate the "points" of elevation of the piece; 6 points would be 45 degrees, for example, and 2 points would be 15 degrees. In the days when the figure zero was still looked upon with some suspicion in Europe, the marking for the zero point on the gunner's compass was just left blank. Thus a level gun was said to be at "point blank" range. This old system of ranging can still be clearly seen marked on the sides of older cannon kept for display purposes.

On the back of the gunner's compass were usually engraved a primitive set of tables designed to solve the problem of caliber. This problem can be best stated as: Given a correct amount of powder for a certain type of ball in a cannon of known diameter, find the amount of powder needed to give the same range in a cannon of different diameter or with a ball of different material. The tables seldom contained the data needed for the problem at hand and, even if they did, they were often inaccurate. The usual result of experimenting to solve

Figure 2–20. The gunner's compass in use to find the elevation of a gun.
(Source: *La Nova Scientia* by N. Tartaglia, 1537.)

the caliber problem was wasted ranging shots or, worse still, a burst cannon and a dead artillery crew.

The sector, in its final form, consisted of two arms joined together by a hinge, much like the folding carpenter's ruler in use today. The arms were usually 6 to 12 in. long and were engraved with a number of different scales, most of which radiated out from the hinge pivot point. The accuracy of the sector depended on the manufacturer establishing the exact center of this hinge, and the care with which the hinge was constructed was a measure of the quality of a sector. Each arm would be engraved with an identical set of scales. They were usually made of brass, but some wealthier individuals had theirs made from silver. Just after 1850 it became the fashion to have one made out of an inexpensive nickel and copper alloy (electrum) which resembled silver in its white shine. (It is not only our own age that likes to have its cheaper "plastic" imitations of the real thing!) Although it started out as a cheap imitation of silver, electrum was eventually used for a lot of instruments because it turned out to be better than either brass or silver. It was stiffer and lighter than silver and did not discolor or corrode the way brass does.

The usual operating mechanism for the sector was to take a measurement with a pair of dividers and open the sector until the dividers spanned the distance from a point on the scale of one arm to the identical point on the same scale of the other arm. Leaving the sector open at this angle, one can find the

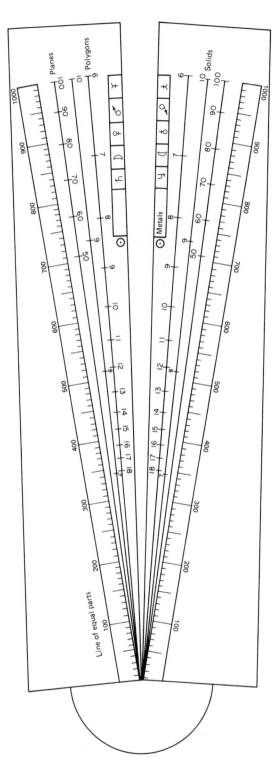

Figure 2–21. A sector designed by the author.

answer by noting the distance between other points on scales spanning the two arms. For example, to find the answer to a simple arithmetic problem such as 100/7, use the two scales marked "line of equal parts." This line runs from the hinge to the end of each arm and is usually divided into 1000 equal divisions on the larger sectors and 200 divisions on the smaller ones. Using a pair of dividers, measure off 100 units on the line of equal parts. Now find two numbers, one of which is seven times the other, on the line of equal parts (say 20 and 140). Open the sector until your dividers (measuring 100) just span the distance between the points marked 140 on each arm. The distance between the points marked 20 on each arm will now give the answer to 100/7, which is approximately 14.25. The process is most easily illustrated by examining the drawing of a man shown using a sector. A very similar procedure would be used to divide a line into seven parts. The length of the line would again be measured by the dividers and the sector opened so that the dividers spanned the distance between the points on the two arms marked 140. The distance between the two arms at the points marked 20 would be 1/7 of the original line.

There were usually several different scales engraved on a sector, the exact complement being determined by the use to be made of the device. Questions

Figure 2–22. Drawing of a man using a sector. (Source: The frontpiece of *The Works of Edmund Gunter,* 1680 edition.)

such as the problem of caliber were answered by making use of a scale marked off according to the volumes of equal weights of various metals and stones, together with a scale similar to the "scale of solids" found on the proportional compass. With these and other standard scales, a simple gunner could solve any caliber problem in a matter of a few seconds. It should be remembered that this was in the days when there were no analytical methods of dealing with this type of problem. Even the great Galileo, who first put these scales on the sector, would not have known how to produce a workable formula to solve all caliber questions. It is strange, therefore, that some of the more "pure" mathematicians of the time derided the use of these devices. One of the most vocal critics was William Oughtred, the man who invented the slide rule, who stated:

> . . . the true way of Art is not by Instruments . . . it is a preposterous course of vulgar Teachers, to begin with Instruments, and not with the Sciences, and so instead of Artists, to make their Scholars only doers of tricks, and as it were Iuglers . . .[9]

Even the great Descartes is said to have responded to visitors who wanted to see his instruments by opening a box to show them a pair of compasses with one broken leg and a folded piece of paper which would act as his ruler.

Despite the fact that a number of famous men ridiculed the use of instruments for solving mathematical problems, the sector proved so useful that it was quickly modified by the addition of several scales to make it more useful for both the land-oriented surveyor and the navigator at sea.

One of the driving forces behind the adoption of the sector was a Mr. Edmund Gunter. Born about 1581, Gunter went at age 18 to Christ Church College in Oxford where he took degrees in mathematics and general arts. About 1606 he heard of the sector and, being very impressed with its use, wrote a description of it in Latin. This work was never published but was extensively copied by hand and enjoyed a wide circulation. He was eventually selected as Professor of Astronomy at Gresham College, London, in 1619 (at the same time that Henry Briggs was Professor of Geometry), and one of his first tasks was to translate his work on the sector into English. This work, which included several other chapters on various topics, was finally published in 1623.

Gunter's book, which not only described his modifications of the sector but was also the first English-language logical treatment of the nature of sines, chords, tangents and their uses, was so successful that a great many English-speaking people referred to the device as "a Gunter." His later description of a logarithmic scale—"Gunter's Line of Numbers"—led to an early form of the slide rule being known as a "sliding Gunter." Gunter's book went through many, many editions long after the author's death. It was reprinted so many times,

[9]As quoted in F. Cajori, *William Oughtred—A Great 17th Century Teacher of Mathematics* (Chicago: Open Court Publishing Co., 1916), p. 88.

usually with the title *The Works of that Famous Mathematician Mr. Edmund Gunter*, that is is not at all unusual to find it in the collections of larger libraries.

By the beginning of the nineteenth century the sector had been combined with a number of older instruments to create a single device that would serve several functions. As one example of this, it is useful to examine the development of the gunner's compass. From a simple pair of sticks, it had developed into a sophisticated instrument which combined the calculating abilities of a sector with the devices necessary to take the diameter of a cannon ball, determine the bore or caliber of a cannon, and calculate the weight of a shot and the amount of powder to be used in both land-based and naval artillery. It had the usual form of a sector, that of two thin brass rulers joined by a hinge at one end, but the inner surfaces of these rulers were curved to accommodate the curvature of a cannon ball. A number of scales and tables were engraved on both sides, including:

- a scale for measuring the inside diameter of a cannon
- a scale showing the weight of shot to be used in guns of various diameters
- a semicircular scale on the hinge to measure the elevation of a cannon
- a shot diameter scale to indicate the diameter of any shot placed between the jaws of the instrument
- a table giving the proof and service charges for brass guns
- a line of lines (a linear scale for using the device as a sector)
- a scale giving the weight of any iron shot being measured in the jaws
- tables giving the weight of powder needed to charge iron guns from 0.5 to 42 pounders
- scales of weights and specific gravities of different metals, stones, wood, water, and so on
- tables showing the amount of powder needed to charge the chambers of brass mortars and howitzers

Sectors were not all simple compass-like instruments. Several examples exist to show that the more inventive individuals attempted to mechanize, at least to some extent, the idea of the sector. Perhaps the most famous example of this type of device was produced by Sir Samuel Morland, of whom more will be said in the section dealing with the development of mechanical adding machines. Morland's device combined the basic sector with some simple gearing to produce a robust "trigonometrical calculating machine."

Figure 2–24 shows one of the two extant examples of Morland's machine. It was once owned by Charles Babbage, as part of his collection of books and equipment dealing with calculation, but now resides in the Science Museum in London. The device, which is a little over 11 in. on each side, is made of brass with a coating of silver on its front surface. The two handles on the lower

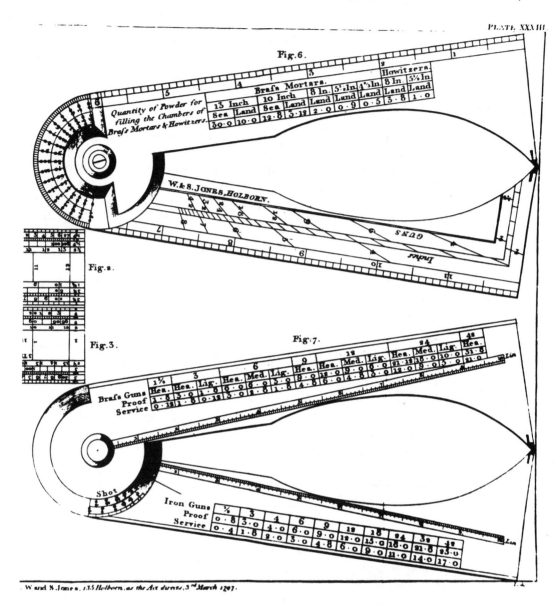

Figure 2–23.   The gunner's sector-compass.

portion are geared in two different ways. The left-hand one is used to turn the large central circle while the other is used, via a simple gear rack, to move the central horizontal bar up and down across the face of the instrument. The two arms of the sector were arranged so that one of them, the one pointing up in the photograph, was fixed to the central disk while the other could either be

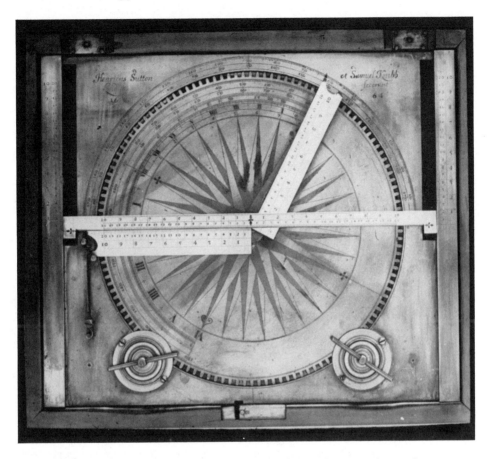

Figure 2–24. Samuel Morland's trigonometrical calculating machine. (Photograph courtesy of the Science Museum, London.)

fixed in a horizontal position via the spring clip shown on the left-hand side of the instrument, or could be carried around by the rotation of the central wheel. The scales engraved on the disk, and on the semicircular markings on the face of the instrument, were used to set and measure angles in either degrees, hours and minutes, or according to the points of the compass. The sliding horizontal scale essentially took the place of the dividers normally required when using a simple sector.

This device, because of its mechanical settings, had obvious advantages over the elementary sector when being used for navigational calculations at sea. In addition, the mechanical settings would often allow much finer readings from the scales than were possible when using a simple pair of dividers to transfer readings from one scale to the next.

2.6 NAPIER'S "BONES"

2.6.1 Napier and His Bones[10]

John Napier, Baron of Merchiston, was born in 1550 just as the Scottish reformation was starting. Details of Napier's life and his involvement in the Protestant reformation are given in the section dealing with the development of logarithms. He is, of course, best known for his invention of logarithms, but he spent a large part of his life devising various other schemes for easing the labor involved in doing arithmetic. As Napier himself said:

> The difficulty and prolixity of calculation, the weariness of which is so apt to deter from the study of mathematics, I have always, with what little powers and little genius I possess, laboured to eradicate. And with that end in view, I have published of late years the Cannon of Logarithms. . . . [F]or the sake of those who prefer to work with the natural numbers as they stand, I have excogitated three other compendious modes of calculation, of which the first is by means of numbering rods and these I have called Rabdologia. Another, by far the most expeditious of all for multiplication, and which on that account I have not inaptly called the Promptuary of Multiplication, is by means of little plates of metal disposed in a box. And lastly, a third method, namely Local Arithmetic performed upon a chess board. . . .[11]

He undoubtedly used these mechanical devices in the calculation of his first table of logarithms. The best known of these devices is his *Rabdologia,* or as they are more commonly known "Napier's bones." The name *bones* arose from the fact that the better quality sets were contructed from horn, bone, or ivory. Various authors have preferred to call them "numbering rods," "multiplying rulers," or even "speaking rods," but the name *bones* just refused to die out. Today they are considered a mere curiosity, while his other two devices have been almost entirely forgotten. The "Promptuary of Multiplication" was simply a modified version of his bones which, at the expense of being more difficult to construct, eliminated some of the problems of multiplying one multidigit number by another. It was an interesting idea but never became popular. The best description, other than the short one included later in this section, is contained in the article by W. F. Hawkins in the reference section. The "local arithmetic" device was simply a standard chess or checkerboard used as a modification of the table abacus. Each row and column represented a power of two higher than the one below or to the right. Again, it was never really used by the public because of the seemingly unnatural use of binary numbers. Its use

[10]Some of the material in the following section has appeared in an article by the author, "From Napier to Lucas," in *Annals of the History of Computing,* 5, No. 3 (July 1983), 279–96.

[11]A translation by Mark Napier, a descendant of John, of a Latin letter of dedication to Alexander Seton appearing in the introduction to Napier's *Rabdologia* (Edinburgh, 1617), p. 414.

is explored in the article by Martin Gardner in *Scientific American* which is also noted in the reference section.

Napier did not at first consider these inventions worthy of publication; however, several friends, particularly Alexander Seton the Earl of Dumferm-line and High Chancellor of Scotland, pressed him to write them up, if only to avoid others claiming them as their own. His descriptions appeared in 1617, the year of his death and three years after the publication of his description of logarithms, in a small book entitled *Rabdologia*.

The idea for the bones undoubtedly came from the gelosia method of doing multiplication. This ancient method probably originated in India and spread to Arab, Persian, and Chinese societies by the late Middle Ages. The method was introduced into Italy sometime in the fourteenth century where it obtained its name from its similarity to a common form of Italian window grating. The method consists of writing down a matrix-like grid, placing one digit of the multiplicand at the head of each column and one digit of the multiplier beside each row, the product of each row and column digit was then entered in the appropriate box of the matrix—the tens digit above the diagonal and the units digit below. The final product was obtained by starting in the lower right-hand corner and adding up the digits in each diagonal, with any carry digits being considered as part of the next diagonal. The adjacent illustration of the gelosia method shows 456 multiplied by 128, with the product (058368) being read off starting from the upper left-hand corner.

Napier's "bones" are simply a collection of strips of all possible columns of this gelosia table as is shown in Figure 2–26. To perform the multiplication of 456 by 128 one would simply select the strips headed 4, 5, and 6, place them side by side and read off the partial products of 456 times 1, 456 times 2 and 456 times 8 (by adding up the digits in each parallelogram to obtain each digit of the partial product), then add together the partial products. Division was aided by the bones in that multiples of the divisor could be easily determined, and thus save the time that would normally be spent in trial multiplication.

The two larger "bones" in the diagram were used to extract square and cube roots. The clearest way of describing their use is by following through the

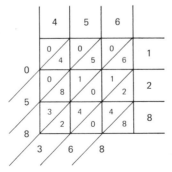

Figure 2–25. The gelosia method of multiplication.

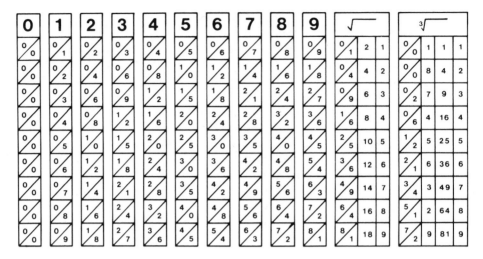

Figure 2–26. A set of Napier's bones.

sample calculation illustrated in the diagrams of Figures 2–27 through 2–29. These illustrate the use of the square root "bone" in determining the square root of 910116 using the notation which would have been common in the seventeenth century. The first process is to divide the number into two-digit groups, the normal practice being to put a dot under the rightmost digit and then under every second digit to the left. Taking the square root "bone," one looks in the diagonally divided column to find the largest number that is less than or equal to the first pair of digits (91); in this case the number is 81, which is then entered below the horizontal lines, and the digit from the rightmost column of the "bone" is entered between the lines. The difference between the square found on the "bone" (81) and the square required (91) is entered above the original number. This upside-down form of subtraction was one of the common methods in use in Napier's day.

The number from the middle column of the "bone" (18 in this case) is then used to perform the second step. The individual "bones" for 18 are placed to the left of the square root "bone," and the process just described is repeated for a number consisting of the digits on the topmost line and the digits from the original number up to the next dot (1001 in this instance). The closest root to 1001 is the number 925, which is found on row five of the combined "bones," and this is subtracted from 1001 in the same way as was described earlier. The form of the computation at this step is shown in Figure 2–28.

The individual "bones" are now shifted left one place, and the "bone" indicated by the number in the middle column of the square root "bone" is inserted between them and the larger root "bone." In this example, the number found in the middle column of row five was a 10, which means that the individual "bones" are now those for the digits 1, 9, and 0. This final step is illus-

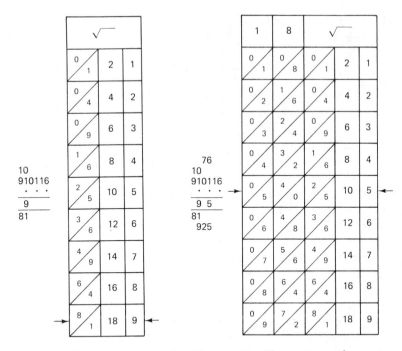

Figure 2–27. The square root bone—step A.

Figure 2–28. The square root bone—step B.

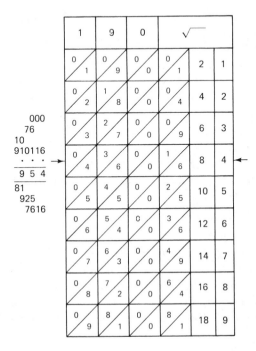

Figure 2–29. The square root bone—step C.

trated in Figure 2–29, which also shows that the number 7616 can be found exactly on row four of the combined "bones." This means that 954 is the exact square root of 910116, and the process is complete.

If the result had not been exact, we could have repeated these steps as often as necessary to obtain the required number of significant figures. The process is nothing more than a way of aiding in our standard pencil and paper methods for determining square roots. The cube root bone is used in a similar way, and anyone with enough interest can quickly determine the method by trying a simple example.

The use of Napier's "bones" spread rapidly and, within a few years, examples could be found in use from Europe to China. It is likely the two Jesuits Schott and Kircher, whose story will be told a little later in this section, were partially responsible for this dissemination, particularly to China where two Jesuits held office in the Peking Astronomical Board.

The obvious disadvantage of the "bones" was that the user had to write down and add up all the partial products of the multiplicand. In an appendix to *Rabdologia*, Napier described his "Multiplicationis Promptuarium," a larger set of strips operating on the same principle as the "bones," which would eliminate the need for recording and later adding up the partial products. This "Promptuary of Multiplication" consisted of a large box with slots in two of its sides. These slots held strips of wood or brass, one set being engraved with a sequence of digits, and the other having triangular holes cut into specific areas. There were at least ten copies of each species of strip for each digit from 0 to 9.

To obtain the product for 234 times 648, the user would select the "digit" strips for 2, 3, and 4 and place them on top of the box; then select the "hole" strips for 6, 4, and 8, and place them at right angles on top of the "digit" strips. The product (151632) could then be read off by adding up the figures showing through the holes in each of the main diagonals. The entire process is illustrated in Figure 2–31.

This device never became popular, probably because of the difficulty and expense of constructing the many different strips required for a full set. There is only one known example of the device which predates 1900, a lovely ivory set currently housed in a Spanish Museum. The one or two sets that were made in this century appear to have been constructed only for demonstration purposes.

2.6.2 *Gaspard Schott and Athanasius Kircher*

As was mentioned earlier, one of the chief agents in spreading Napier's "bones" around the world was the correspondence carried out by Gaspard Schott (1608–1666) and Athanasius Kircher (1602–1680) with various groups of Jesuits around

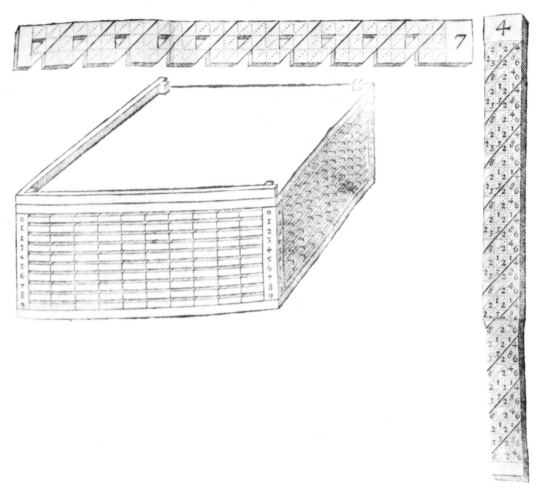

Figure 2–30. Napier's *Multiplicationis Promptuarium.* (Source: 1623 edition of *Rabdologia.*)

the world. Both Schott and Kircher were German Jesuit mathematicians during the time when the Jesuit order was sending its technically trained members around the world as missionaries for both the Christian faith and the wonders of European technology. Both men started their careers in the University of Würzburg, with Schott being a pupil of Kircher, but had to flee when that area was invaded by the Swedes in 1631. Schott went to Sicily and Kircher was called to Rome, where they each stayed for the next 20 years. The Jesuit order established Kircher as its unofficial information exchange center to whom all foreign Jesuits communicated their latest theory, observation, or invention.

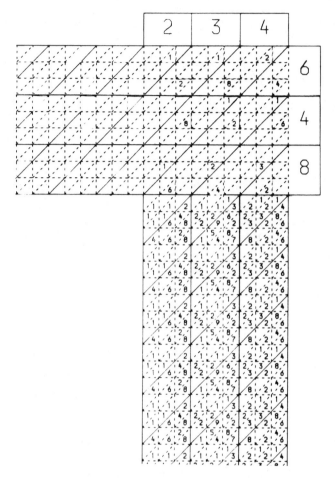

Figure 2–31. Using the *Multiplicationis Promptuarium* to find 234 times 648.

Kircher could not keep up with both his own work and the organization of the information sent to him so, in 1651, Gaspard Schott came to Rome with the intention of publishing all of Kircher's accumulated material. In 1657 Schott moved to take up the position of professor of mathematics and physics at Augsburg, but he continued to act as part of the Jesuit clearinghouse for technical information. The amount of information grew so large that, before Schott died in 1666, he had produced 11 massive texts detailing the wonders that had been communicated to him and Kircher by all the scientists of their day.

One of these large volumes was a description of the mathematical methods developed by Kircher to perform the calculations required by a technically oriented seventeenth-century gentleman. In producing this work, Schott included not only the algorithms to be used but also any mechanical aids which had been devised to aid in the computation. One such aid was a remarkable

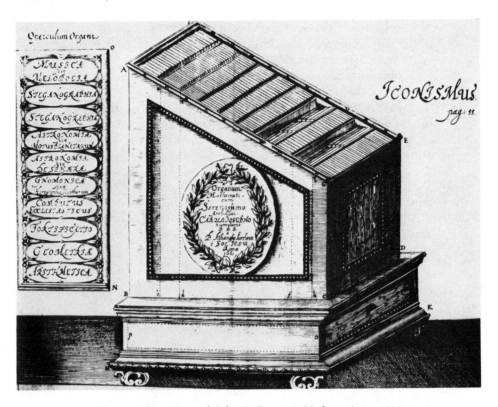

Figure 2–32. Gaspard Schott's *Organum Mathematicum*, 1666.

extension to Napier's "bones" which Schott called an *organum mathematicum*. It is a large box in which are stored ten different sets of bone-like tablets for performing a variety of different tasks. There were sets used for:

arithmetic: a standard set of Napier's bones together with addition and subtraction tables

geometry: tablets whose primary purpose was to solve problems encountered in survey work

fortification: tablets which would aid the gentleman soldier to get the details correct when contructing the more standard types of military fortifications

calendar: tablets which were used in determining the date of Easter and the dates of the other major Christian festivals

gnomics: tablets which would help in the calculation of the required parameters to construct sun dials on all surfaces independent of their direction or inclination

spherics: tablets which would help in the calculation to the movement of the sun, determine the times of sunrise and sunset for any given day of the year, and other similar problems

planetary movements: tablets to perform calculations to determine the motions of the planets and to cast horoscopes

earthworks: two sets of tablets dealing with the calculations involved in cut and fill problems for the construction of canals, for example

music: tablets which would aid the novice in composing music and creating melodies

Figure 2–33 shows a few of the music "bones" just to give an impression of how the tablets looked.

Schott was aware of the physical problems involved in using a standard set of arithmetic "bones"—such things as locating the correct "bones" and hav-

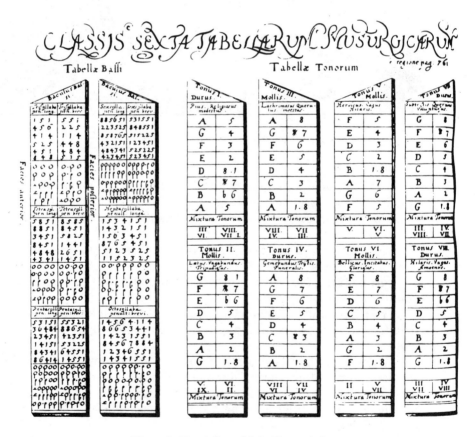

Figure 2–33.   A few of Schott's music bones.

ing some convenient device to ensure correct positioning. Although Samuel Morland (whose achievements will be described in a later section) had constructed his mechanical version of Napier's "bones" several years earlier, he had not yet produced his printed description of them; thus Schott was left on his own to invent a similar device. The result was a series of cylinders with a complete set of Napier's "bones" inscribed on each, the individual bones running the length of the cylinder. Several of these cylinders were then housed in a box that would permit turning the cylinders and examining individual "bones" through slits cut in the top of the box. Figure 2–34 shows Schott's device, which includes an addition table on the inside cover to aid the operator.

Although it was an interesting attempt at making the bones easier to use, the system proved to be a failure. The parallelograms containing the digits to be added together span two adjacent "bones," and the space required to mount the cylinders meant that these digits were widely separated. This led to a greater tendency to make mistakes and the device was soon abandoned. Schemes similar to Schott's were tried by different people in different countries (most notably by Pierre Petit, the Fench mathematician and friend of Pascal), but they all failed for the same reason.

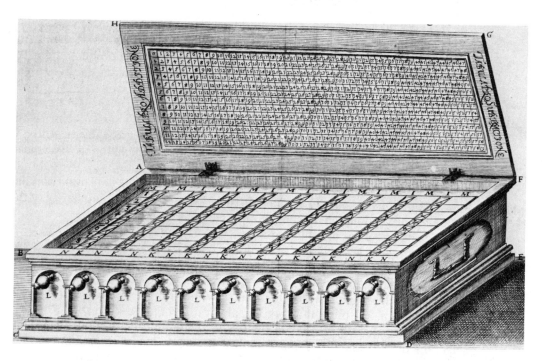

Figure 2–34.   Schott's version of Napier's Bones. (Source: 1668 edition of Schott's *Organum Mathematicum*.)

2.6.3 Early Versions of Napier's Bones

A different approach was tried by Sir Charles Cotterell when, in 1667, he constructed a set of "bones" housed in a small box, the lid of which consisted of a tiny wire-and-bead abacus to be used when adding together the partial products. The set came with a small brass wand to move the abacus beads and a brass "ladder" to act as a cursor for the "bones." Unfortunately very few of these sets have survived and those that have are all incomplete.

Sir Samuel Morland, an Enlish inventor and diplomat, constructed two different machines, one of which incorporated a version of Napier's "bones." These machines were intended to act as a pair, the first being a simple adding machine which could be used to add together the partial products that were generated by his "Napier's bones" machine. Although not a very sophisticated pair of machines, they required a good deal more mechanical knowledge in their construction and use than any of the machines mentioned in this section. These machines, together with the very first really workable mechanical calculating machine designed by William Schickard, which also used some of Napier's ideas, will be described in Chapter 3.

2.6.4 Genaille–Lucas Rulers

The final chapter in the development of Napier's "bones" as a computational instrument takes place in 1885 when, at the French Association for the Advancement of Science meetings, Edouard Lucas presented a problem on arithmetic which caught the attention of Henri Genaille, a French civil engineer working for the railway. Genaille, who was already quite well known for his invention of several different arithmetic aids, solved Lucas' problem and, in the process, devised a different form of Napier's "bones." These "rulers" eliminated the need to carry digits from one column to the next when reading off partial products. He demonstrated these rulers to the Association at their meetings in 1891. Lucas, who was known for a series of publications on recreational mathematics, gave these rulers enough publicity that they became quite popular for a number of years. Unfortunately he never lived to see the popularity of the device for he died at age 49 shortly after Genaille's demonstration.

The rulers, a set of which are shown in Figure 2–35, are similar in their use to a standard set of Napier's "bones." There is one ruler for each digit from 0 to 9. Each ruler is divided into nine sections with several digits inscribed in each section, and one or two arrows point to the left toward a particular digit in the next ruler. Figure 2–36 illustrates how to find the product of 3271 × 4, the rulers for 03271 (note the need for always having a leading zero ruler) are placed side by side. Starting with the fourth section of the rightmost ruler, you select the digit at the top of this section (4 in this case) and then simply follow the arrows toward the left, reading off the digits as you come to them—in this case, 13084.

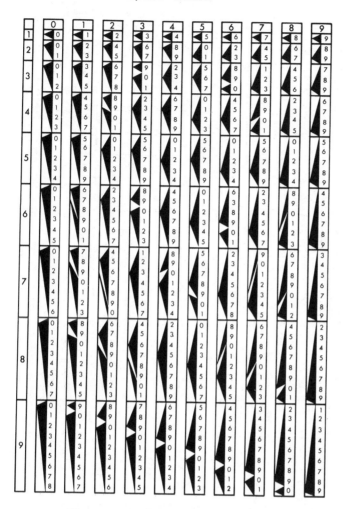

Figure 2–35. The Genaille-Lucas rulers.

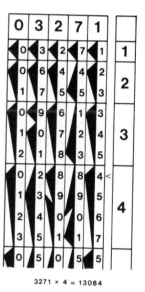

3271 × 4 = 13084

Figure 2–36. The Genaille-Lucas rulers in operation.

Once the problem of eliminating the carry digits had been solved by Genaille, the creation of a specific set of rulers for division was quickly accomplished. The division rulers are similar to the multiplication ones except that the large arrows are replaced by a multitude of smaller ones. Figures 2–37 and 2–38 show a complete set of division rulers together with an example of how they could be used to divide the number 6957 by 6. Note that a special ruler marked R must be placed on the right-hand side of the set in order to determine the remainder, if any, of the division operation. The division rulers are used in the opposite direction from the multiplication ones. In order to divide the

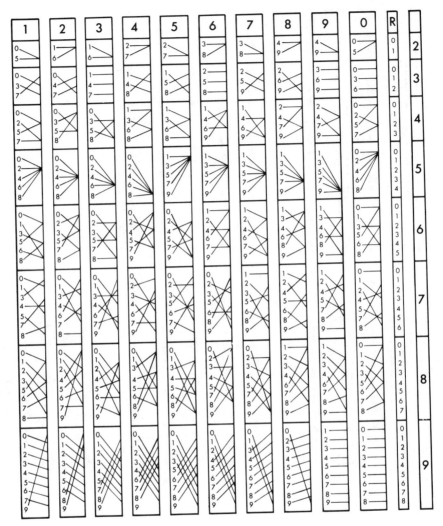

Figure 2–37. The Genaille-Lucas division rulers.

number by 6, you start at the left-hand side of the sixth section with the topmost digit (1 in the case shown here) and proceed to the right, following the arrows and reading off the digits as they are encountered (1159 with a remainder of 3).

Although the oldest surviving set of Napier's "bones" date from 1620, just three years after Napier's death, no one seems to know where Napier's actual bones lie. There are conflicting reports of his being buried in at least two different parishes in Edinburgh. The only thing that is certain is that his bones (and his "bones") served mankind well during their period of use.

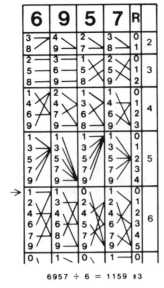

$$6957 \div 6 = 1159 \; \text{R}3$$

Figure 2–38. The Genaille-Lucas division rulers used to divide 6957 by 6.

2.7 LOGARITHMS

John Napier has already been mentioned in Section 2.6.1, but this section is the appropriate one in which to describe his life and times. The Napier family, who spelled their names as Napier, Napeir, Napair, Nepeir, Naper, Napare, Neper, or even Naipper, had long been one of the noble houses of Scotland. It is incorrect to assume that the life of a Scots baron of the time was one of culture and learning. The Scottish reformation was just starting as Napier was born in 1550, and the upheavals that it caused only added to the misery of the nobles and the common folk alike. In the middle of the sixteenth century, Scotland was torn apart by both political and religious strife, with war between the different groups being a constant occurrence. It was a country where the only recognized activity for a nobleman was either protecting his estates, hunting, military adventures, or engaging in religious controversy. The cultural level of the time is said to have seldom risen above that of barbarous hospitality. Before Napier's time Scotland had produced several men of note in the field of literature but only one in science, the thirteenth-century mathematician Michael Scott. With the study of academic subjects being held in low regard, it is very surprising that one of the most fundamental advances in mathematics and computation should have come out of this environment.

Napier was born near Edinburgh, but that is almost all we know of his early life. His father was one of the first people to take up the cause of the Protestant movement in Scotland, and it was presumably he who influenced

Figure 2-39.   John Napier. (Illustration taken from the works of Mark
Napier.)

John from his earliest days to believe that the Pope was the sole bar to the
salvation of all mankind. Certainly John held this belief right up to the time he
died in 1617. In 1563 John's mother died, and he was sent off to St. Salvator's
College at the University of St. Andrews. He was only 13 at the time, but it was
not an uncommon age for people of that time to enter St. Andrews. He was
boarded with a Dr. John Rutherford, then head of St. Salvator's, who was one
of the leading Protestant figures in Scotland and was known for his negative
views about the Roman Catholic Church, probably because he had suffered at
the hands of the Inquisition a few years earlier when he had been living in
Lisbon. Rutherford was an able academic and, besides adding to Napier's anti-

Rome views, gave him a good grounding in Latin and the other subjects then taught at St. Andrews. There is no record of Napier's ever having graduated—in fact there is no record of exactly what he did for the next several years. It has been speculated that he may have been sent off to travel on the Continent, but it is unknown how he managed to obtain the rest of his training in the sciences.

In 1593 a small book entitled *A Plane Discovery of the Whole Revelation of St. John* was published by Napier in Edinburgh. This book is noteworthy in at least two respects: It was the first work of Biblical interpretation ever published in Scotland, and it gave Napier the reputation of a fine theologian. This reputation likely saved him from prosecution when he dabbled in magic and witchcraft later in his life. Although the book was the product of many years of thoughtful Bible reading, it is really little other than an all-out attack on the Roman Catholic Church in general and the Pope in particular. It became so popular that it went through five editions in English, three in Dutch, nine in French, and four in German. Napier is known to have considered this book his major life's work and to have looked upon his mathematics as simply a secondary interest. In fact his mathematical research was likely third or fourth on his list of priorities because he had to spend most of his time running the vast Napier estates.

Many writers have suggested that the invention of logarithms came like a bolt from the blue, with nothing leading up to them. This is not exactly the case because, like almost every other invention, examples can be found of parallel development by other people. Napier is always given the credit for logarithms because these other developments were either left unpublished or, in some cases, not recognized for what they were at the time.

In the time before Napier the fear of computation was so strong that most mathematicians sought to create instruments to get around the problem. Developments such as the sector and various types of quadrant are the prime examples of this sort of thinking. The major computational problems of the day tended to involve astronomy, navigation, and the casting of horoscopes, all of which are, of course, interrelated. These problems had led to a number of sixteenth-century mathematicians' devoting their time to the development of trigonometry. About 25 years before Napier published his description of logarithms, the problem of easing the workload when multiplying two sines together had been solved by "the method of prosthaphaeresis" which corresponds to the formula:

$$\sin (a) \bullet \sin (b) = [\cos (a - b) - \cos (a + b)]/2$$

Once it had been shown that a rather nasty multiplication could be replaced by a few simple additions, subtractions, and an elementary division by 2, it is entirely likely that this formula spurred mathematicians, including Napier, to search for other methods to simplify the harder arithmetical operations. In fact several other such formulae were developed during Napier's time, but only the method of prosthaphaeresis was of any real use except in special circumstances. We know that Napier knew of, and used, the method of prosthaphaeresis, and it may well have influenced his thinking because the first logarithms were not of numbers but of sines.

Another factor in the development of logarithms at this time was that the properties of arithmetic and geometric series had been studied extensively in the previous century. We now know that any numbers in an arithmetic series are the logarithms of other numbers in a geometric series, to some suitable base. For example, the first of the following two series of numbers is geometric, with each number being 2 times the previous one, while directly underneath is an arithmetic series whose values are the corresponding base 2 logarithms.

natural numbers	1	2	4	8	16	32	64	128	256	512	1024
logarithms		0	1	2	3	4	5	6	7	8	9	10

It had long been known that, if you take any two numbers in the arithmetic progression, say 3 and 4, that their sum, 7, would indicate the term in the geometric series that was the product of the two corresponding terms in the geometric series; thus, $3 + 4 = 7$ and $8 \times 16 = 128$ (the third times the fourth = the seventh). This is starting to look very much like our own conception of logarithms as being the powers to which some base number is raised, a concept that was not understood in Napier's time. Often the use of a good form of notation will suggest some basic mathematical principle. Our use of indices to indicate the power to which a number is being raised seems to have an obvious connection with logarithms but, without this form of notation, the connection is vague at best.

Another notational problem at the end of the sixteenth century was with the mode of expressing decimal fractions. The decimal point had only been suggested a few years earlier in 1585 and was not yet in general use. Before the decimal point became common, it was the custom to indicate decimal fractions by one of three different methods. If you wished to write 3.14159, it would either be done as 3 1/10 4/100 1/1000 5/10000 9/100000 or, more commonly, 3,1′4″1‴5⁗9‴‴ or even 3(0) 1(1) 4(2) 1(3) 5(4) 9(5). Napier himself used this latter form of notation when writing his book *Rabdologia*. The Swiss mathematician Jobst Burgi (1552–1632), who is often credited with an independent invention of logarithms about the same time as Napier, was able to see some glimmer of the idea of an index in this system of recording decimal fractions. Burgi, whose real profession was watchmaker to Landgraf Wilhelm IV of Hesse, managed to combine this idea of an exponent with the studies he had been making on arithmetic and geometric series, and came up with an idea for logarithms. He did not publish anything on the subject until several years after Napier's description had appeared, and even then it was only an anonymous printing of a short table of what we would call antilogarithms. As Johann Kepler states in the introduction to his *Rudolphine Tables* (1627):

> . . . the accents in calculation led Justus Byrgius on the way to these very logarithms many years before Napier's system appeared; but being an indolent man, and very uncommunicative, instead of rearing up his child for the public benefit, he deserted it in the birth.[12]

Kepler's description of Burgi may have some truth in it because Kepler is known to have had several dealings with Burgi during his lifetime.

John Napier came upon the idea of logarithms not by algebra and indices, but by way of geometry. When first thinking about this subject, he used the term *artificial number* but later created the term *logarithm* from a Greek phrase meaning "ratio number." He decided on this term because his logarithms were based on the concept of points moving down lines where the velocity of one point was based on the ratio of the lengths of the line on either side of it. Consider two lines, AX and BY, and two points, P and Q, moving down these lines as shown in Figure 2–40. Point P is assumed to move along the line AX with constant speed while point Q, which starts at the same speed as P, is constantly having its speed changed so that it is at all times proportional to the distance QY. If you take the distance AP as being the magnitude of a number, then the logarithm of that number is given by the magnitude of the distance BQ. This explanation seems a little strange to modern mathematicians, but it fits in very well with Napier's desire to determine logarithms of sines for, as was mentioned in the section on quadrants, it used to be the case that a sine was considered as the length of a line, not as a ratio of sides in a triangle.

We know almost nothing about how long Napier worked before he felt that the idea of logarithms was sufficiently refined to be worthy of publication, but in July of 1614 he published a small volume of 56 pages of text and 90 pages of tables entitled *Mirifici Logarithmorum Canonis Descriptio* which is best translated as *Description of the Admirable Cannon (Table) of Logarithms*. It was common in those days to dedicate a book to a nobleman, often in the hope that some patronage would result from it. Unfortunately Napier had the bad luck to dedicate the *Descriptio* to the then Prince of Wales, who, when he later became King Charles I, was beheaded by Cromwell.

Figure 2–40. Napier's method of developing logarithms.

---

[12]Quoted in M. Napier, *Memoirs of John Napier of Merchiston* (Edinburgh: William Blackwood, 1834), p. 392.

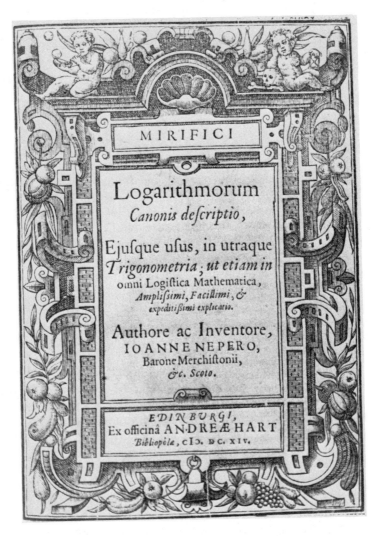

Figure 2–41. The title page of the *Descriptio*, 1614.

The *Descriptio* was just that, a description of the cannon or table of logarithms of sines, with the rules to be followed when using them to perform multiplication, division, or the computation of roots and powers. It contained a statement that, if these tables were accorded the reception which Napier hoped they would get from fellow mathematicians, he would describe in some future publication exactly how they were discovered and the methods used to calculate them. Ever mindful of his background in theology, and following the example of many other writers of his day, he ended off the *Descriptio* with:

Let those who reap the harvest of this small work pay a tribute of glory and thank-fullness to God, sovereign author and dispenser of all good.[13]

Our story now shifts to London, where one of the most famous English mathematicians of the day, Henry Briggs, was professor of geometry at Gresham College. Briggs (1561–1631) had obtained his education at St. John's College in Cambridge and had become famous enough that he was selected as the very first professor of geometry at Gresham College in 1596. By the early years of the 1600s his reputation had spread far enough that people like Johann Kepler were consulting him on the properties of the ellipse. In the later months of 1614 he obtained a copy of Napier's *Descriptio* and in March of the following year was exclaiming that

Napier, lord of Markinston, hath set my head and hands at work with his new and admirable logarithms. I hope to see him this summer, if it please God; for I never saw a book which pleased me better, and made me more wonder.[14]

Briggs immediately began to popularize the concept of logarithms in his lectures and even began to work on a modified version of the tables. Several years later, in 1624, Briggs' newly calculated logarithms were published and he stated in the Latin preface:

That these logarithms differ from those which that illustrious man, the Baron of Merchiston published in his Cannon Mirificus must not surprise you. For I myself, when expouding their doctrine publicly in London to my auditors in Gresham College, remarked that it would be much more convenient that 0 should be kept for the logarithm of the whole sine. . . . And concerning that matter I wrote immediately to the author himself; and as soon as the season of the year and the vacation of my public duties of instruction permitted I journeyed to Edinburgh, where, being most hospitably received by him, I lingered for a whole month.[15]

What Briggs was suggesting was that the base of the logarithms should be changed in order to make them easier to use. Napier had seemingly already seen the same thing, for as Briggs states:

But as we held discourse concerning this change in the system of Logarithms, he said, that for a long time he had been sensible of the same thing, and had been

---

[13]Quoted in P. M. d'Ocagne, "Some Remarks on Logarithms Aprops to their Tercentenary," *Annual Report of the Smithsonian Institution* Washington, D.C.: The Smithsonian Institution), p. 176.

[14]As quoted in D. E. Smith, *History of Mathematics, Vol II* (New York: Dover Publications, 1958), p. 516.

[15]C. G. Knott, ed., *Napier Tercentenary Memorial Volume* (London: Longmans, Green for the Royal Society of Edinburgh, 1915), p. 126.

anxious to accomplish it, but that he had published those he had already prepared, until he could construct tables more convenient, if other weighty matters and his frail health would suffer him so to do. But he conceived that the change ought to be effected in this manner, that 0 should become the logarithm of unity, and 10,000,000,000 that of the whole sine; which I could but admit was by far the most convenient of all. So, rejecting those which I had already prepared, I commenced, under his encouraging counsel, to ponder seriously about the calculation of these tables; and in the following summer I again took journey to Edinburgh, where I submitted to him the principal part of those tables which are here published, and I was about to do the same even the third summer, had it pleased God to spare him so long.[16]

The result of these changes was to create the common, base 10 logarithms that we know today.

There is an interesting tale told about the first meeting between Briggs and Napier. It seems that a certain John Marr, an advisor to both Charles I and James I, was staying at Merchiston Castle at about the time that Briggs was due to arrive for his first visit. Napier, who suffered badly from gout, was left in his bedroom while Marr went to greet Briggs. Marr later told the story to the astrologer Lilly who relates that ". . . he brought Mr. Briggs into my Lords chamber, where almost one quarter hour was spent, each beholding the other with admiration, before one word was spoken.[17]

It was not only Briggs who was impressed by Napier's *Descriptio.* In 1617, the year of Napier's death, Johann Kepler first saw the *Descriptio* in Prague. He was too busy to pay it much attention but did acknowledge its existence in a letter to his friend William Schickard, where he indicated:

> A Scottish baron has started up, his name I cannot remember, but he has put forth some worderful mode by which all necessity of multiplications and divisions are commuted to mere additions and subtractions. . . .[18]

Further on in the same letter, Kepler made a few statements which indicate that he did not fully appreciate the power of the new system, but he can be forgiven this misunderstanding because it was during this period that he was hard at work on his third law of planetary motion. About a year later he had time to reread the *Descriptio,* and he became as firm a convert to the new system as Briggs had been when first seeing publication in 1614. Kepler wrote to Napier expressing his admiration and letting him know that he must publish the promised *Constructio* as soon as possible. Unfortunately, Napier had been dead for two years before the letter arrived. The letter may, however, have

---

[16]M. Napier, *Memoirs of John Napier,* p. 410.

[17]Ibid., p. 409.

[18]Ibid., p. 391.

spurred John's son, Robert Napier, into putting the finishing touches on his father's notes and overseeing the publication of the *Constructio* in 1620.

Henry Briggs never did finish his complete recalculation of Napier's logarithms. His tables, first published in 1624, contained the logs of the numbers from 1 to 20,000 and from 90,000 to 100,000, all calculated to 14 decimal places. There are 1161 errors in these original tables, or just under 0.04% of the entries. Almost all of them are simple errors of plus or minus 1 in the last decimal place;

ARITHMETICA

LOGARITHMICA

SIVE

LOGARITHMORVM

CHILIADES TRIGINTA, PRO

numeris naturali ferie crefcentibus ab vnitate ad 20,000 : et a 90,000 ad 100,000. Quorum ope multa perficiuntur Arithmetica problemata et Geometrica.

HOS NVMEROS PRIMVS

INVENIT CLARISSIMVS VIR Iohannes Neperus Baro Merchiftonij : eos autem ex eiufdem fententia mutavit, eorumque ortum et vfum illuftravit Henricvs Briggivs, in celeberrima Academia Oxonienfi Geometriæ profeffor Savilianvs.

DEVS NOBIS VSVRAM VITÆ DEDIT ET INGENII, TANQVAM PECVNIÆ, NVLLA PRÆSTITVTA DIE.

LONDINI,
Excudebat GVLIELMVS
IONES. 1624.

Figure 2–42. The title page of the *Arithmetica Logarithmica*, 1624.

however, several more are printing or copying errors such as the printing of 3730 instead of 4730, but these are easily seen by users of the tables because they stand out as being quite different from the surrounding entries. Briggs introduced the term *mantissa* from the Latin word meaning "the addition" which was often used to mean an appendix to a book. The term *characteristic* was also suggested by Briggs, but first used in print by the Dutchman Adrian Vlacq.

The concept of logarithms spread rapidly. In the same year as Briggs' tables appeared, Kepler published his first set of logarithms and, a year later, Edmund Wingate published a set in Paris called *Arithmetique Logarithmique*, which not only contained logarithms for the numbers from 1 to 1000, but also contained Edmund Gunter's newly calculated log sines and log tangents. The first complete set of logarithms for the numbers from 1 to 101,000 was published by a Dutch printer, Adrian Vlacq (1600?–1667?), who was noted for his ability at printing scientific works. He filled in the sections missing from Briggs' work and published the whole table in 1628. Vlacq's tables were copied by many others in later years. Although the publishers seldom acknowledged the source of the logarithms, it was obvious where they came from because Vlacq's original errors were copied along with the correct logarithms. It was not until the first quarter of the nineteenth century, when Charles Babbage published his famous log tables, that correct sets of tables were readily available at a price the average tradesman could afford.

One of the most famous attempts to construct error-free tables occurred during the period 1794–1799 when, due to the introduction of the metric system in France, the quadrant was redivided into 100 degrees, and this required that all trigonometric tables be recomputed. G. Riche de Prony was assigned to organize the effort, and he started by asking several famous mathematicians (including Legendre) to produce the methods and formulae which should be used. He then hired professional calculators to determine some important primary results and then, using a method of differences, had large squads of workmen do the actual additions. The majority of these workmen came from among the hairdressers of Paris because the abandonment of powdered wigs had put them all out of work. Being a good student of human nature, Prony knew that some workmen would likely copy the results of others just to get out of doing their own work and, as he hoped to check the calculations by having them done over several different times, this had to be avoided at all costs. He, therefore, set up his calculating centers in different parts of France and took some pains that people in different centers should not communicate with each other. The resulting tables were never published, due largely to lack of government support, but extracts from them have appeared from time to time to solve specific problems.

Within 20 years of the time that Briggs' tables first appeared, the use of logarithms had spread all the way around the world. From being a limited tool of great scientists like Kepler, they had become commonplace in the school-rooms of the civilized nations. The 1646 edition of the major English language textbook on arithmetic, Robert Recorde's *Ground of Arts*, contains the statement: "For the extraction of all sorts of roots, the table of logarithms set forth by M. Briggs are most excellent and ready." Logarithms were used extensively in all trades and professions that required calculations to be done. It is hard to imagine an invention which has helped the process of computation more dramatically than has logarithms, the one exception being the modern digital computer. During a conference held in 1914 to celebrate the 300th anniversary of the publication of the *Descriptio* it was estimated that, of all the calculation done in the previous 300 years, the vast majority had been done with the aid of logarithms.

2.8 THE SLIDE RULE

The story of how John Napier invented logarithms has already been told in the previous section. Although they were usable as they stood, it was the work of Henry Briggs, a professor at Gresham College in London, that actually made them easier to use. Brigg's work naturally came to the notice of Edmund Gunter, another professor at Gresham College, who, as had already been described in the section on quadrants, was a very practically minded teacher of astronomy and mathematics. Gunter was primarily interested in the problems of astronomy, navigation, and the construction of sundials (the only reasonable method of telling time in his day), all of which required large amounts of calculation involving trigonometric elements. Because of the trigonometric content of these problems, the logarithm tables being produced by Briggs were only of marginal help, so Gunter sat down and completed the calculations for tables of the logarithms of sines and the logarithms of tangents for each minute of the quadrant. These eight-figure tables were published in 1620 and did much to relieve the burden of calculation for finding your position at sea.

Gunter has already been mentioned as one of the people who contributed to the sector's becoming the most useful calculating instrument of the day, so he was quite familiar with the process of using a pair of dividers to measure off various distances on the sector scales. This experience soon led him to realize that the process of adding together a pair of logarithms could be partially automated by engraving a scale of logarithms on a piece of wood and then using a pair of dividers to add together the two values. Not only did this method eliminate the mental work of addition, but it also eliminated the time-consuming process of looking up the logarithms in a table. Gunter's piece of wood soon became known as "Gunter's Line of Numbers." Its use spread rapidly through England and was quickly popularized on the Continent by Edmund Wingate, who described his contribution as follows:

In Anno 1624, I making a journey into France, had the happiness to be the first transporter of the use of these inventions into those parts; where as soon as I arrived divers Mathematicians of the chiefest note in Paris, resorting to my chamber, and I communicating unto them first, the manifold used of the Logarithmes described upon Master Gunters Crosse-staff, they earnestly importuned me to expresse them by some short Tractite in the French tongue.[19]

Gunter's line of numbers consisted of a simple piece of wood, about two feet long (often the shaft of a cross-staff, a simple navigational sighting instrument of the time), marked off with a logarithmic scale, much the same way as one axis of a piece of logarithmic graph paper is marked today. If he wished to multiply A times B, he would open up a pair of dividers to the distance from 1 to A on his line of numbers, and putting one point of the compass on the point B, he would read off the number at which the other point sat. The accuracy was a little limited, but he had produced the first logarithmic analogue device to be able to multiply two numbers together. Gunter would likely have added further refinements to his line of numbers, for he was a master at the design and use of instruments, but he died in 1626 at age 45 before he was able to get enough time from his other duties to return to the subject of logarithmic calculating instruments. The next developments were to be left to a highly individualistic clergyman named William Oughtred.

William Oughtred (1574?–1660) was one of the leading mathematicians of his day. In 1604, after having taken a degree at Cambridge, he was appointed rector of a small parish in Surrey and, a few years later, was moved to the parish of Albury where he lived for the rest of his life. He was the bane of his bishop, being the subject of several complaints that he was a pitiful preacher because he never studied anything other than mathematics (which tends to make for dull sermons). In the days before regular scientific journals, information was published by sending it to individuals who were known to be in regular contact with other scientifically minded people. Athanasius Kircher, mentioned in connection with Napier's bones, and Fr. Martin Mersenne of Paris, for example, were the noted "post boxes" on the Continent while William Oughtred was one of the main distribution points for England.

Oughtred offered free instruction in mathematics to anyone who was sufficiently interested to journey to his home in Albury. It must have been very good instruction, because a great many of the next generation of English mathematicians received their training at Oughtred's table. It must also have been very frustrating because Oughtred kept unconventional hours, often staying up for two or three nights in a row and ignoring meals when he had a good idea to pursue. There are stories of his wife hiding the candles in an effort to force him to get some rest. He made up for these late night sessions by refusing to get out of bed until at least 11:00 a.m. on most days, and often staying there all day working with a pen and ink pot that hung from the end of the bed.

[19]E. Wingate, *The Construction and Use of Logarithmetical Tables* (London, 1648), preface.

Figure 2-43. William Oughtred (1574?-1660), the inventor of the slide rule. (Photograph courtesy of the Science Museum, London.)

Oughtred was what we would now classify a pure mathematician. Although he had a contempt for the computational side of mathematics and considered the people who used calculational instruments simply "the doers of tricks," this did not deter him from becoming familiar with the mathematical instruments then available. Records indicate that he paid a visit to Henry Briggs in 1610 and, while there, met Edmund Gunter who discussed mathematical instruments with him at great length.

Oughtred had noted that Gunter's line of numbers required a pair of dividers in order to measure off the lengths of logarithmic values along the scale and quickly came up with the idea that, if he had two such scales marked along the edges of the pieces of wood, he could slide them relative to each other and thus do away with the need for a pair of dividers. He also saw that if you had two disks, one slightly smaller than the other, with a line of numbers engraved around the edge of each, they could be pinioned together at their centers and rotated relative to one another to give the same effect as having Gunter's scale engraved on two bits of wood.

Because of his general disdain for mathematical instruments he did not consider it worth his trouble, time, or effort to publish a description of how he had improved Gunter's line of numbers into a practical slide rule. He did, however, describe the system to one of his pupils, Richard Delamain, who was a teacher of mathematics living and working in London. Delamain used Oughtred's ideas quite openly and would base his teaching on various methods of instrumental calculation.

Exactly when these ideas were communicated to Delamain is uncertain; indeed it is possible (though unlikely) that Delamain was an independent inventor of the circular slide rule. Whatever the case, Delamain published a description of the circular slide rule, in 1630, in a book he called *Grammelogia*, the name he applied to his instrument. In the dedication of the book to Charles I (a practice that today's writers emulate by getting someone famous to write a preface to their work—present author excepted!), Delamain states that he had made attempts to improve Gunter's scale ". . . by some motion so that the whole body of logarithms might move proportionally the one to the other, as occasion required."[20] It is also amusing to note that he stressed the ease with which his device could be used for calculation by stating that ". . . it is as fit for use as well on horseback as on foot."[21] I have never had, neither have I ever met anyone who has had, a pressing need for doing multiplication while astride a horse, but I assume that it might come in handy in certain military situations.

In the same year that Delamain published his *Grammelogia*, another of Oughtred's pupils, William Forster, happened to mention that, in order to gain more accuracy when using Gunter's line of numbers, he had resorted to using a scale six feet long and a beam compass to measure off the lengths. Oughtred then showed him how he could dispense with the beam compass by simply having two of Gunter's scales sliding over one another and also showed him a circular disk with Gunter's line of numbers marked off along the edge with two indices, like a pair of dividers, extending from the center. The latter device, which Oughtred called his "circles of proportion," he claimed to have invented sometime in 1622. Forster was so impressed that he demanded Oughtred publish a description of these inventions. Oughtred, still under the impression that these "playthings" were not suitable objects for the true mathematician, initially decided against it but, when Delamain's book appeared claiming them as his own invention, Oughtred agreed to publish and even let Forster translate his Latin into English so that the subject matter would be more widely distributed than if it had remained in academic Latin.

Forster's book, entitled *Circles of Proportion*, came out in 1632 and contained a very thinly disguised suggestion that Delamain had stolen the idea for the circular slide rule from Oughtred. This started a lifelong dispute between the two men, neither of whom ever admitted that he obtained the idea from the other. In 1633, probably to forestall Delamain from doing the same,

---

[20]Quoted in D. E. Smith, *A Source Book in Mathematics* (New York: McGraw-Hill, 1929), p. 157.

[21]Ibid.

Oughtred and Forster published *An Addition unto the Use of the Instrument called the Circles of Proportion*, which contained both the original *Circles of Proportion* and *The Declaration of the two Rulers for Calculation*, which described Oughtred's scheme for having two scales of Gunter's line of numbers engraved on sticks which could slide past one another. The complete story of the dispute between Oughtred and Delamain is still not entirely clear, and it awaits an intensive study by some historian with access to all the surviving documents and examples of the work of both men.

A few examples of Oughtred's circles of proportion still exist. They generally have eight different scales engraved around the circumference of the disk with two index scales fixed to the center. These were to be used to transfer distances from one part of the scales to another, although they are mostly missing in the surviving examples. The eight scales usually have one dealing with logarithms, the others being scales indicating the values of sines and tangents for various angles.

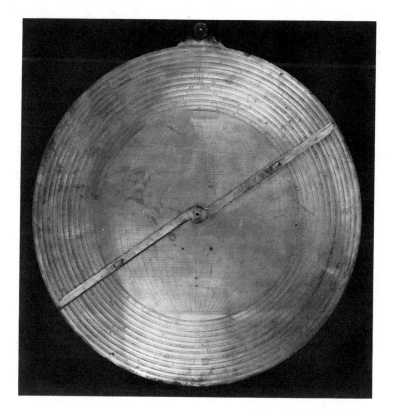

Figure 2–44. Oughtred's circles of proportion; this example was made by Elias Allen ca. 1634 and now belongs to St. John's College, Oxford. (Photograph courtesy of the Museum of the History of Science, Oxford.)

The slide rule may have been developed and publicized in the 1630s and obtained its current form as a movable slide between two other fixed blocks of wood about the middle 1650s, but very little use was actually made of the device for almost 200 years. Several special slide rules were developed and became quite popular, for example, a version for the use of timber merchants, but on the whole the sector remained the main analogue calculating instrument. This is surprising because the sector was difficult to make. Its hinge had to be manufactured with great care, and it had to exert enough force so that the arms would be held open at any given position yet be smooth enough to adjust the aperture by small amounts. Like the slide rule, the sector's accuracy increased with greater length, but longer arms put more strain on the hinge and created greater manufacturing difficulties. The slide rule may have been easier to manufacture, but the use of a pair of dividers was so ingrained into scientific thinking that the full power of the device was not exploited until the middle of the nineteenth century. Indeed the early examples of the slide rule which still survive usually show unmistakable signs of having been used, not in the intended way, but by having had a pair of dividers pick off lengths along the logarithmic scales. Undoubtedly another of the reasons for the lack of popularity was the fact that the scales put on slide rules were often crudely made and, as a consequence, the results were often inaccurate.

James Watt, better known for his work on the steam engine, was responsible, at least in part, for one of the first really well-made slide rules in the very late 1700s. He had spent the early part of his life as an instrument maker at Glasgow University and was thus familiar with the techniques of engraving accurate scales upon instruments. After he had set up a workshop for his steam engine busines in Soho, Birmingham, he discovered that he needed a device to let him perform quick calculations on the volumes and power levels of various engines. He devised a simple slide rule consisting of one sliding piece between two fixed stocks (a design which had been in use for a considerable period of time previously), carefully engraved the face with four basic scales, and put tables of various constants on the back. His rule was accurate enough that others soon requested copies for themselves and Watt manufactured this so-called "Soho Slide Rule" for several years. Even with the example of the Soho Slide Rule, the general public seemed to ignore the power of the instrument. The great English mathematician Augustus De Morgan, when writing an article about the slide rule for the popular press in 1850, had to explain that "for a few shillings most persons might put into their pockets some hundred times as much power of calculation as they have in their heads."[22]

The big breakthrough for the slide rule came in 1850 when a 19-year-old French artillery officer, Amedee Mannheim (1831–1906), designed a very simple slide rule much like that manufactured by Watt, but added the movable

[22]Quoted in R. T. Gunther, *Historic Instruments for the Advancement of Science* (London: Oxford University Press, 1925).

cursor which we think of as such an integral part of the slide rule today. This was not the first time that a movable cursor had been combined with the simple sliding logarithmic scales, indeed the first time had been almost 200 years earlier on a slide rule designed for British naval use, but it had been ignored and forgotten until Mannheim reinvented it. The cursor enabled fairly complex operations to be easily carried out on a simple, yet well-made, slide rule. Mannheim's design was adopted as the standard for the French artillery and, after a few years, examples of it began to crop up in other countries. Mannheim survived his army service and was eventually appointed to the post of Professor of Mathematics at the Ècole Polytechnique in Paris, a post which did nothing to harm the ever-growing reputation of his slide rule.

Despite the fact that the Europeans had begun to adopt the "slip stick" for most forms of quick calculation, it remained unpopular in North America until 1888 when several examples of the Mannheim design were imported. The North American market grew until, in 1895, there was enough of a demand that the Mannheim rules were manufactured in the United States. Even with a local source of manufacture, the slide rule remained suspect in North America until well into the twentieth century. A survey reported in the journal *Engineering News* that, as late as 1901, only one half of the engineering schools in the United States gave any attention at all to the use of the slide rule.

Once established, the progress of the slide rule was extremely rapid. Many different forms were produced by several different major manufacturers. The number of scales to be found on each instrument increased to the point where 18 or 20 different scales were regularly engraved on the better quality instruments. Both sides of the rule were used and the center, sliding portion could often be turned over or completely replaced to provide even more combinations of scales. Special slide rules incorporating such things as a scale of atomic and molecular weights were created for chemists, and almost every engineering specialty could boast that at least one manufacturer produced a slide rule de-

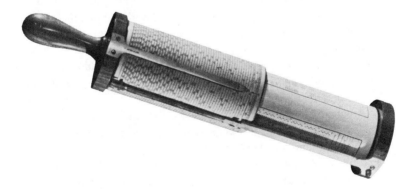

Figure 2–45. Fuller's slide rule.

signed for its particular use. The accuracy of the slide rule was improved by several individuals who modified the basic form so that the logarithmic scales were wrapped around cylinders or into spirals. One device, known as Fuller's slide rule, was equivalent to a standard slide rule over 84 feet long, yet could be easily held in the hand. It was possible to work correctly to four figures, and sometimes even five, with this particular unit.

The slide rule became a symbol of advancing technology of the twentieth century. It was, however, to be a transient symbol, quickly surpassed by the hand-held electronic calculator, which offered many times its accuracy and convenience. The demise of the slide rule was so rapid that it is possible to find many examples of people who differ in age by only four or five years, one of whom relied entirely on the slide rule for all the calculations required at the university, while the other, who took the same course of studies, would not know how to use it to multiply two numbers together.

FURTHER READING

ADAMS, G. (1803). *Geometrical and Graphical Essays.* London: W. and S. Jones.

BAGGE, L. M. (1906). "The Early Numerals," *Classical Review, 20,* 259–67.

BALL, W. W. ROUSE (1888). *A Short Account of the History of Mathematics.* London: Macmillan and Co.

BECHTEL, E. A. (1909). "Finger Counting Among the Romans in the Fourth Century," *Classical Philology, 4,* (January), 25–31.

BERNARD, F. P. (1916). *The Casting Counter and the Counting Board.* Oxford: Clarendon Press.

BRETON, P. N. (1894). *Illustrated History of Coins and Tokens Relating to Canada.* Montreal: P. N. Breton & Co.

BRYDEN, D. J. (1973). "A Didactic Introduction to Arithmetic, Sir Charles Cotterell's Instrument for Arithmeticke of 1667," *History of Education, 2,* (No. 1).

CAJORI, F. (1894). *A History of Mathematics.* London: Macmillan and Co.

——. (1908). "Notes on the History of the Slide Rule," *American Mathematical Monthly, 25,* 1–5.

——. (1909). *A History of the Logarithmic Slide Rule.* London: Constable.

——. (1916). *William Oughtred—A Great 17th Century Teacher of Mathematics.* Chicago: Open Court Publishing Co.

——. (1926). "A Notable Case of Finger Counting in America," *Isis, 8,* 325–27.

DANTZIG, T. (1930). *Number, the Language of Science.* New York: Free Press. (Reprinted by Collier-Macmillan, 1967.)

D'OCAGNE, P. M. (1905). *Le Calcul Simplifie.* Paris: Gauthier-Villars.

——. (1914). "Some Remarks on Logarithms Apropos to their Tercentenary," in *Annual Report of the Smithsonian Institution.* Washington, D. C.: The Smithsonian Institution, pp. 175–81.

DRAKE, S. (1976). "Galileo and the First Mechanical Computing Device," *Scientific American, 234* (No. 4), 104–13.

——. (1978). *Galileo Galilei: Operations of the Geometric and Military Compass.* Washington, D.C.: Smithsonian Institution Press.

DUMAS, M. (1972). *Scientific Instruments of the 17th and 18th Centuries and their Makers.* London: B. T. Batsford & Co.

ELWORTHY, F. T. (1895). *The Evil Eye.* London: John Murry and Co.

FAREY, J. (1827). *A Treatise on the Steam Engine.* London.

FULLER, G. (1879). *A New Calculating Slide Rule Equivalent to a Straight Slide Rule 83 Feet 4 Inches Long.* London.

GARDNER, M. (1973). "Mathematical Games," *Scientific American, 228* (No. 4), (This is an article on Napier's binary Local Arithmetic counting board.) 106–11.

GARVAN, A. N. B. (1962). "The Slide Rule and the Sector," *Proceedings of the 10th International Congress of the History of Science,* pp. 397–99.

GIBSON, G. A. (1915). "Napier's Logarithms and the Change to Briggs' Logarithms," in *Napier Tercentenary Memorial Volume,* ed. C. G. Knott. London: Longmans, Green for the Royal Society of Edinburgh, pp. 111–37.

GLAISHER, J. W. L. (1915). "Logarithms and Computation," in *Napier Tercentenary Memorial Volume,* ed. C. G. Knott. London: Longmans, Green for the Royal Society of Edinburgh, pp. 63–80.

GUNTER, E. (1673). *The Works of that Famous Mathematician Mr. Edmund Gunter.* London (6th edition revised by W. Leybourn).

GUNTER, R. T. (1937). *Early Science in Cambridge.* London: Oxford University Press.

——. (1927). "The Astrolabe: Its Uses and Derivatives," *Scottish Geographical Magazine,* 43 No. 1, 135–47.

——. (1932). *The Astrolabes of the World,* 2 vols. Oxford: Oxford University Press.

——. (1925). *Historic Instruments for the Advancement of Science.* Oxford University Press.

HALL, H. (1889). *The Antiquities of the Exchequer.* London: Elliot Stock.

HASKINS, C. H. (1911). "The Reception of Arabic Science in England," *English Historical Review, 30* (1911), 56–69.

HATTON, E. (1731). *An Intire System of Arithmetic.* London.

HAWKINS, W. F. (1979). "The First Calculating Machine (John Napier, 1617)," *New Zealand Mathematical Society Newsletter,* (Dec.).

HEATH, T. (1921). *A History of Greek Mathematics.* Oxford: Clarendon Press.

HOLDEN, C. A. (1901). Untitled article, *Engineering News, 45,* 405.

HORSBURGH, E. M. (1914). *Handbook of the Exhibition of Napier Relics and of Books, Instruments, and Devices for Facilitating Calculation.* Edinburgh: Royal Society of Edinburgh. (Reprinted in 1982 by Tomash Publishers, Los Angeles)

HUME-BROWN, P. (1915). "John Napier of Merchiston," in *Napier Tercentenary Memorial Volume,* ed. C. G. Knott. London: Longmans, Green for the Royal Society of Edinburgh, pp. 33–51.

IYER, R. V. (1954). "The Hindu Abacus," *Scripta Mathematica, 20,* 58–63.

JACOB, L. (1911). *Le Calcul Mecanique.* Paris: Gauthier-Villars.

KARPINSKI, L. C. (?). "Augrim Stones." *Modern Language Notes*, 27, No. 7, 206–9.

KNOTT, C. G, ed. (1915). *Napier Tercentenary Memorial Volume.* London: Longmans, Green for the Royal Society of Edinburgh.

LESLIE, J. (1817). *The Philosophy of Arithmetic.* Edinburgh: Archibald Constable and Co.

LEYBOURN, W. (1667). *The Art of Numbring by Speaking Rods: Vulgorly Termed Nepeir's Bones.* London.

———. (1672). *Panorganon: or a Universal Instrument.* London.

———. (1721). *Dialling Improvd.* (Leybourn's *Dialling* improved by Henry Wilson) London.

MACKAY, A. (1802). *The Description of the Sliding Gunter.* Aberdeen, Scotland.

NAPIER, J. (1593). *A Plaine Discovery of the whole Revelation of Saint John.* Edinburgh.

———. (1614). *Mirifici Logarithmorum Canonis Descriptio.* Edinburgh.

———. (1617). *Rabdologia.* Edinburgh.

———. (1620). *Mirifici Logarithmorum Canonis Constructio.* Edinburgh(?)

NAPIER, M. (1834). *Memoirs of John Napier of Merchiston, his Lineage, Life and Times, with a History of the Invention of Logarithms.* Edinburgh: William Blackwood; London: Thomas Cadell.

NEEDHAM, J. (1959). *Science and Civilization in China,* Vol. III. Cambridge: Cambridge University Press.

NORTH, J. D. (1974). "The Astrolabe," *Scientific American,* No 1 (January), 96–106.

OSSORIO, B. F. (1757). *Astronimica, y Harmoniosa Mano.* Mexico. (This work is discussed by Cajori.)

OZANAM, M. (1803). *Ozanam's Recreations,* Vol. I. London.

PEACOCK, G. (1826). "Arithmetic," *Metropolitan Encyclopedia.* London: J. Mawman & Co.

PICKWORTH, C. N. *The Slide Rule.* (There are many different editions by several different publishers, for example, Van Nostrand, Pitman, Emmott and Co.)

RECORDE, R. (1542). *The Grounde of Arts,* 27 different editions from 1542 to 1699.

RICHARDSON, J. L. (1916). "Digital Reckoning among the Ancients," *American Mathematical Monthly,* 23, 7–13.

SARTON, G. (1935). "The First Explanation of Decimal Fractions and Measures," *Isis,* 23, 153–245.

SCHOTT, G. (1668). *Organum Mathematicum.* Nüremberg.

SIMONS, L. G. (1932). "Two Reckoning Tables," *Scripta Mathematica,* 1, 305–8.

SMITH, D. E. (1921). "Computing Jetons," *Numismatic Notes and Monographs,* No. 9. New York: American Numismatic Society.

———. (1923). *History of Mathematics.* Boston: Ginn & Co. (Reprinted by Dover Publications 1958).

———. (1929). *A Source Book in Mathematics.* New York: McGraw Hill.

SMITH, D. E., and Y. MIKAMI (1914). *A History of Japanese Mathematics.* Chicago: Open Court Publishing Co.

STANLEY, W. F. (1888). *Mathematical Drawing and Measuring Instruments.* London: W. F. Stanley Co.

STEWART, D. and W. MINTO (1787). *An Account of the Life, Writings, and Inventions of John Napier of Merchiston.* Perth, Scotland.

THOMPSON, A. J. (1952). *Logarithmetica Britannica.* Cambridge: Cambridge University Press.

THOMPSON, J. E. (1952). *The Standard Manual of the Slide Rule.* New York: Van Nostrand Co.

TURNER, A. J. (1973). "Mathematical Instruments in the Education of a Gentleman," *Annals of Science, 30,* 51–88.

VAN DER WAERDEN, B. L. (1961). *Science Awakening.* New York: Oxford University Press.

VANHEE, L. (1926). "Napier's Rods in China," *American Mathematical Monthly, 23,* 326–28.

WARD, J. (1740). *The Lives of the Professors of Gresham College.* London.

WATERS, D. W. (1958). *The Art of Navigation in England in Elizabethan and Early Stuart Times.* London: Hollis and Carter.

WILF, A. (1952). *A History of Science in the 18th Century.* London: Allen and Unwin.

WINGATE, E. (1628). *The Construction and Use of the Line of Proportion.* London.

——. (1648). *The Construction and Use of Logarithmetical Tables.* London.

YELDHAM, F. (1926). *The Story of Reckoning in the Middle Ages.* London: George G. Harrap & Co.

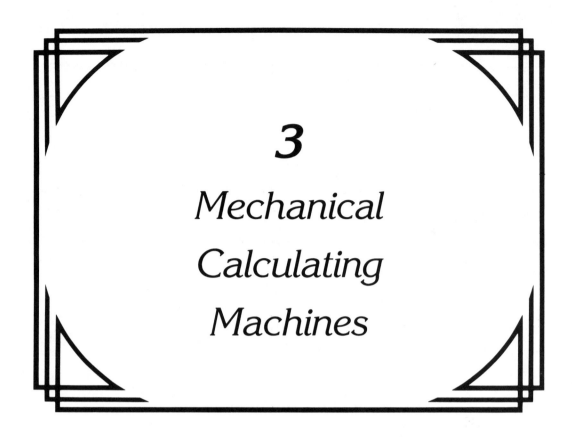

3
Mechanical
Calculating
Machines

3.1 INTRODUCTION

The development of automatic computation really begins with the invention and development of mechanical devices to automatically perform the four standard arithmetic functions. By devising a system in which mechanical levers, gears, and wheels could replace the facilities of human intellect, the early pioneers in these devices paved the way for complete automation of the process of calculation. Needless to say, the early efforts were very crude, not because the inventors lacked the intelligence to construct better devices, but because the technical abilities of the workmen and the materials available were often not up to the demands put upon them by these new machines. There was also the problem of inventing new techniques in order to get mechanical devices to produce some of the motions required of them when doing simple arithmetic.

Almost every mechanical calculating machine has to have six basic elements in its design:

A Set-up Mechanism: The device by which the number is entered into the machine. In the very early designs this was actually part of the selector mechanism, but the more sophisticated designs required that it be a separate device.

A Selector Mechanism: The device which selects and provides the proper mechanical motion in order to cause the addition or subtraction of appropriate amounts on the registering mechanism.

A Registering Mechanism: The device, usually a series of wheels or disks, which could be positioned to indicate the value of a number stored within the machine.

A Carry Mechanism: The device which would ensure that, if a carry were generated because one of the digits in the result register advanced from 9 to 0, then that carry was propagated to the next digit or even across the entire result register if necessary.

A Control Mechanism: A device to ensure that all gears were properly positioned at the end of each cycle of addition to avoid inadvertently obtaining a false sum as well as jamming the machine.

An Erasing Mechanism: A device which would reset the registering mechanism to store a value of zero.

Individual machines may not have contained each of these items as a separate device. Indeed many of the early machines required an operator to move each digit of the register manually in order to reset its value to zero. An examination of the Leibnitz multiplying machine, to be described in detail a little later on, will show an early version of each of these components.

It used to be thought that Pascal invented the first true adding machine to contain a carry mechanism; however, the investigative work of Professor Bruno Baron von Freytag Loringhoff in the 1950s and 1960s showed that honor belonged to Wilhelm Schickard. It is quite possible that further investigation will reveal a yet earlier device, but such a suggestion is unwarranted at this time. A popular legend has it that the monk Gerbert (later Pope Sylvester II), whom we have already met in the discussion on the abacus, developed some form of early calculating device. It is almost certain, however, that this refers to Gerbert's abacus rather than an actual mechanical device. It seems far-fetched to believe that a much cruder technology would allow anything to be produced which could match the sophistication of the Schickard or Pascal machines.

3.2 *WILHELM SCHICKARD (1592–1635)*[1]

Wilhelm Schickard was Professor of Hebrew, Professor of Oriental Languages, Professor of Mathematics, Professor of Astronomy, Professor of Geography,

---

[1]Some of the material in the following section has appeared in an article by the author, "From Napier to Lucas," in *Annals of the History of Computing,* 5, No. 3 (July 1983), 279–96.

and, in his spare time, a Protestant minister in the German town of Tübingen during the early 1600s. He has been compared to Leonardo da Vinci in that both had far-ranging interests and enquiring minds. Besides being an excellent mathematician who developed some methods that were still in use well into the nineteenth century, he was a good painter, a good enough mechanic to construct his own astronomical instruments, and an engraver skilled enough to provide some of the copper plates used to illustrate Kepler's great work *Harmonices Mundi*.

It is known that Schickard and Kepler not only knew each other well but that they also collaborated on several occasions. It was one of these joint efforts that resulted in Schickard's producing the first really workable mechanical adding machine. Kepler and Schickard were both born in the same town, were both interested in mathematics and astronomy, and both had associations with Tübingen University. It was only natural that they saw each other whenever possible, and wrote back and forth discussing the problems each was attempting to solve. When Kepler's mother was accused of being a witch and thrown into jail, Kepler returned to Tübingen to help in her defense and, while there,

Figure 3–1. Wilhelm Schickard. (Courtesy of Baron von Freytag Loringoff.)

was known to have associated with Schickard. As was mentioned in Chapter 2, Kepler and Schickard were known to have discussed John Napier's various inventions as early as 1617. During Kepler's stay in Tübingen he shared with Schickard some results he had obtained using Napier's "bones" and logarithms. This seems to have inspired Schickard to consider the design of a machine which would incorporate both a set of Napier's "bones" and a mechanism to add up the partial products they produced in order to completely automate the multiplication process.

On September 20, 1623, Schickard wrote to Kepler saying (in translation):

> What you have done in a logistical way (i.e., by calculation), I have just tried to do by mechanics. I have constructed a machine consisting of eleven complete and six incomplete (actually "mutilated") sprocket wheels which can calculate. You would burst out laughing if you were present to see how it carries by itself from one column of tens to the next or borrows from them during subtraction.[2]

Kepler must have written back asking for a copy of the machine for himself because, on February 25, 1624, Schickard again wrote to Kepler giving a careful description of the use of the machine together with several drawings showing its construction. He also told Kepler that a second machine, which was being made for his use, had been accidentally destroyed when a fire leveled the house of a workman Schickard had hired to do the final construction.

These two letters, both of which were found in Kepler's papers, give evidence that Schickard actually constructed such a machine. However, the drawings of the machine had been lost and no one had the slightest idea of what the machine looked like or how it performed its arithmetic. Then some scholars who were attempting to put together a complete collection of Kepler's works were led to investigate the library of the Pulkovo Observatory near Leningrad. While searching through a copy of Kepler's *Rudolphine Tables*, they found a slip of paper which had seemingly been used as a bookmark. It was this slip of paper which contained Schickard's original drawings of the machine. One of these sketches is shown in Figure 3–2. Little detail can be seen, but with the hints given in the letters it became possible to reconstruct the machine.

The reconstruction was done by Professor Bruno Baron von Freytag Loringhoff, now retired from the post of Professor of Philosophy at the University of Tübingen. The Baron was able to figure out the details of the machine because, among other things, he is an expert on the techniques used by seventeenth-century clockmakers. This reconstruction was featured on a stamp issued by West Germany in 1971 to honor the 350th year of its invention.

In the stamp illustration, the upper part of the machine is set to show the number 100722 being multiplied by 4. The result of this multiplication would

---

[2]As quoted by Dr. Baron von Freytag Loringhoff in an unpublished lecture given at the Los Alamos Conference on the History of Computing, June 10–15, 1976.

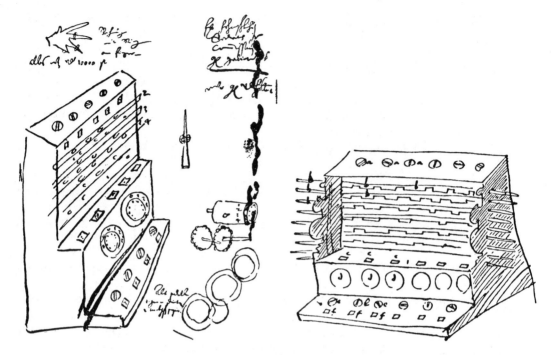

Figure 3–2. A copy of Schickard's drawing of his machine sent to Kepler in a letter. (Courtesy of Baron von Freytag Loringhoff.)

be added to the accumulator using the lower portion of the machine. The upper part is simply a set of Napier's "bones" (multiplication tables) drawn on cylinders in such a way that any particular "bone" may be selected by turning the small dials (marked a) in Schickard's drawing. Moving the horizontal slides would expose different sections of the "bones" to show any single-digit multiple of the selected number; the fourth multiple is shown exposed in the stamp illustration. This result could then be added to the accumulator by turning the large knobs (marked d), and the results would appear in the small windows just above (marked c). The very bottom of the machine contains a simple aide-memoire. By turning the small knobs (e) it was possible to make any number appear through the little windows (f), and this eliminated the need to have pen, ink, and paper handy to note down any intermediate results in the computation.

The mechanism used to effect a carry from one digit to the next was very simple and reliable in operation. As shown in the drawing, every time an accumulator wheel rotated through a complete turn, a single tooth would catch in an intermediate wheel and cause the next highest digit in the accumulator to be increased by one. This simple-looking device actually presents a host of problems to anyone attempting to construct an adding machine based on this principle. The major problem is caused by the fact that the single tooth must

Figure 3–3.   Schickard's calculator, from a West German stamp issued to commemorate the 350th year of its construction.

enter into the teeth of the intermediate wheel, rotate it 36 degrees (one tenth of a revolution), and exit from the teeth, all while only rotating 36 degrees itself. The most elementary solution to this problem consists of the intermediate wheel being, in effect, two different gears, one with long and one with short teeth, together with a spring-loaded detente (much like the pointer used on the big wheel of the gambling game generally known as crown and anchor) which would allow the gears to stop only in specific locations. It is not known if Schickard used this exact mechanism, but it certainly works well on the reproductions constructed by von Freytag Loringhoff.

The major drawback of this type of carry mechanism is the fact that the force used to effect the carry must come from the single tooth meshing with the teeth of the intermediate wheel. If the user ever wished to do the addition 999,999 + 1, it would result in a carry being propagated right through each digit of the accumulator. This would require enough force that it might well do damage to the gears on the units digit. It appears that Schickard was aware of this weakness because he constructed machines with only six-digit accumulators even though he knew that Kepler undoubtedly needed more figures in his astronomical work. If the numbers became larger than six digits, he pro-

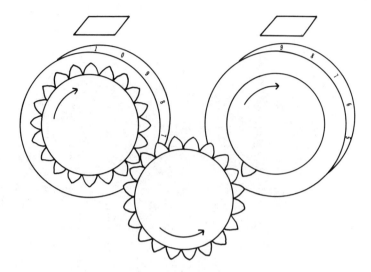

Figure 3–4. The Schickard carry mechanism.

vided a set of brass rings which could be slipped over the fingers of the operator's hand in order to remember how many times a carry had been propagated off the end of the accumulator. A small bell was rung each time such an "overflow" occurred to remind the operator to slip another ring on his finger.

Although we know that the machine being made for Kepler was destroyed in a fire, there is some mystery as to what happened to Schickard's own copy of the device. No trace of it can be found in European museums. It may well turn up one day in some dusty forgotten corner of an old building, but the most likely situation is that it has simply been lost. This is particularly likely in that Schickard and all his family died during one of the great plagues that swept Europe. As he left no living heirs, the machine was probably taken by someone who could not understand its workings and found its last use as firewood in some family kitchen.

3.3 BLAISE PASCAL (1623–1662)

The next major attempt to design and construct a calculating machine is credited to the great French mathematician and philosopher Blaise Pascal. The fact that he was not the first to construct such a device in no way reduces the magnitude of Pascal's achievement because his machine was entirely different from Schickard's and it is almost certain that Pascal would not have known of Schickard's machine, much less have actually seen it in operation.

Figure 3–5. Blaise Pascal, from a French stamp issued in his honor.

Blaise Pascal came from the area of Clermont in southern France, west of Lyon. The Pascal family was one of the noble houses of the area. The life history of Pascal is full of little stories which undoubtedly grew up around him because of his fame in later years. His family servants report, for example, that Blaise was seen to walk out of second story windows and gently float to the ground! He did not attend school in the usual sense of the word, but was educated entirely by his father, Etienne Pascal, whose library served as the boy's schoolroom. After having been taught the elementary skills of reading and writing, Blaise was essentially left to develop his own education by reading through his father's library.

Etienne was a reasonable mathematician in his own right. It is to him, rather than to Blaise, that we owe the curve known as Pascal's Limacon. Etienne realized that there was no future for his boy in the field of mathematics and made sure that he did not waste his time on the subject. Blaise, like most boys who have been told not to read certain books, made a point of giving up his play time to secretly read mathematical works. When Blaise was 12 years old, Etienne found that he had mastered some aspects of mathematics but, without proper training, he had invented his own terminology for angles, lines and circles (calling them by names such as "rounds" and "bars"). Etienne relented and made sure the boy had proper instruction. Whenever Blaise had done particularly well in his other work, Etienne would teach him some more mathematics as a reward.

While Blaise was still young, the family moved to Paris where they lived off the investments Etienne had made in government securities. The Thirty

Years War had caused the French government to run out of money and they eventually defaulted on some of their bonds and lowered the interest rate on others. When Cardinal Richelieu declared that the interest rate would be lowered, Etienne put up such a protest that he only avoided being imprisoned by going into hiding. Several of his friends intervened with the Cardinal but to no avail, and Etienne was not allowed to come out of hiding. When he eventually was reinstated in the Cardinal's good graces, he was sent off to Rouen and given the job of "Commissioner deputed by His Majesty for the Imposition and Collection of taxes in Upper Normandy." Being a tax collector is not a popular job, but it kept the Pascal family out of financial trouble and enabled them once again to enjoy the delights of associating with the upper echelon of French society.

It was in Rouen where Blaise finally got down to the writings and inventions which have made him famous in literature, philosophy, and mathematics.

Both he and his two sisters showed great talents at an early age. In fact it was partly Richelieu's impression of some poems written by one of the sisters that enabled the father to return to public life. When still in his mid-teens, Blaise wrote a mathematical paper on conic sections, and sent it off to Paris so that it could be the subject for one of the evening discussion groups at the Mersenne Academy. This was not such a bold step as it might appear, for Etienne was a member of several Paris academies and Blaise had been introduced to most of the famous scientists of the day when his father had taken him along during visits to the French capital. When some of these scholars were impressed by the contents of the paper, Etienne gave up attempting to limit Blaise's mathematical study and encouraged him to learn as much as he could.

The daily grind of adding up long columns of tax figures gave Blaise the impetus to design something which would relieve some of the tedium. When he was only 19 years old, he managed to design the first of his many calculating machines. He hired a group of local workmen and, showing them his carefully done drawings, asked them if they could make the instrument. What they produced was quite unworkable because they were more used to constructing houses and farm machinery than they were delicate instruments. This led Blaise to train himself as a mechanic, even spending time in a blacksmith shop to learn the basics of constructing metal parts. He experimented with gears made out of ivory, wood, copper, and other materials in an attempt to find something which would withstand the strain encountered.

Although he produced about 50 different machines during his lifetime, they were all based on the idea incorporated in his first machine of 1642. The device was contained in a box small enough to easily fit on top of a desk or small table. The upper surface of the box, as can be seen in Figure 3-6, consisted of a number of toothed wheels above which were a series of small windows to show the results. In order to add a number, say 3, to the accumulator, it was only necessary to insert a small stylus into the toothed wheel at the position marked "3" and rotate the wheel clockwise until the stylus encountered

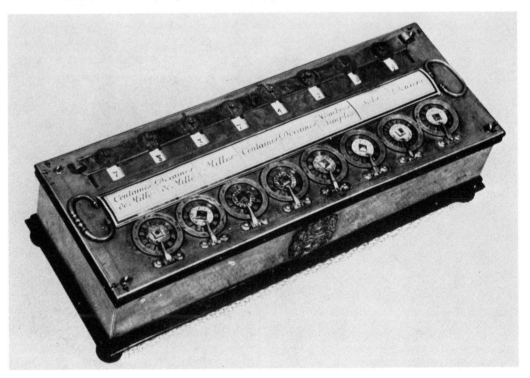

Figure 3–6. Pascal's calculating machine. (Photograph courtesy of IBM Archives.)

the fixed stop, in much the same way that you would dial a telephone. The windows through which the results were read actually consisted of two separate sections, with a brass slide to cover the section not in use at the moment. The upper window was for normal addition while the lower window, which displayed the nines complement of the number held in the accumulator, was used for subtraction. This arrangement was necessary because, due to the internal construction of the machine, it was not possible to turn the dials backward in order to do a subtraction.

Pascal seems to have realized right from the start that the single-tooth gear, like that used by Schickard, would not do for a general carry mechanism. The single-tooth gear works fine if the carry is only going to be propagated a few places but, if the carry has to be propagated several places along the accumulator, the force needed to operate the machine would be of such a magnitude that it would do damage to the delicate gear works. Pascal managed to devise a completely new mechanism that was based upon falling weights rather than a long chain of gears.

As can be seen from the drawing of the internal workings of Pascal's machine, the entire mechanism is quite complex, but the essentials can be seen

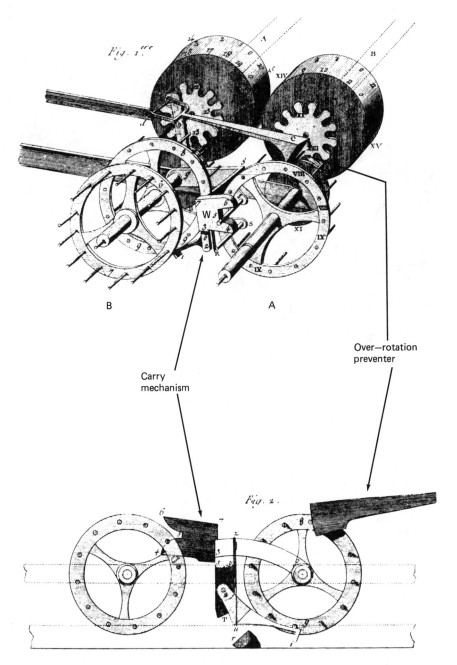

Figure 3–7. The internal workings of Pascal's machine.

from the drawing of the carry mechanism. If the wheel marked A was connected to the units digit of the accumulator and the one marked B was connected to the tens digit, then any carry would be propagated from one to the other by the device marked W between the two shafts. W is a weight which is lifted up by the two pins attached to wheel A as it rotates. When the wheel rotates from 9 to 0, the pins slip out of the weight, allowing it to fall, and in the process the little spring-loaded foot, shown in black, will kick at the pins sticking out of wheel B, driving it around one place. This gravity-assisted carry mechanism was placed between each pair of digits in the accumulator and, when a carry was generated through several digits, could be heard "clunking" all the way down the line.

This carry mechanism, which would have been the pride of many mechanical engineers 100 years after Pascal, eliminated any strain on the gears. However, it did have the drawback that the wheels turned in only one direction, and this meant that it was only possible to add and not to subtract with the machine. As mentioned earlier, the subtraction problem was solved by simply adding the nines complement of the required number, a process which limited the use of the machine to those with a better than average education.

Pascal attempted to put the machine into production for his own profit. This was not a successful venture, but it did result in a large number of units surviving to the present day. They are all slightly different in that they have different numbers of digits in the accumulator or slight differences in their internal mechanisms. None of the surviving models functions very well, and it is doubtful if they functioned perfectly even in Pascal's day. The mechanism, although ingenious, is rather delicate and prone to giving erroneous results when not treated with the utmost care. Some of them will, for example, generate extra carries in certain digits of the accumulator when they are bumped or knocked even slightly.

It is quite possible that, had he continued to experiment with the machine, the problems with its delicate nature would have been removed. However, one night in 1650 he experienced a dream which profoundly affected the rest of his life. It was such a strong religious experience that he gave up his connections with the mathematical and scientific world and retired to a life of religious contemplation and philosophical writings. Three years later he returned, for a short period, to a life of science. On November 23, 1654, four runaway horses almost resulted in his being thrown off a bridge at Neuilly. It was only the "miracle" of the horses' traces breaking at the last moment which saved his life. He took this as a sign that God would rather have him return to a life of contemplation, which he did for the remainder of his days. As far as we know, he never again considered the problems of constructing a calculating machine.

Pascal did not live an entirely happy life. By the time Etienne Pascal died in 1651, the Pascal fortune had been reduced to the point that, although Blaise was able to live in reasonable comfort, he was always concerned with finances. He began to take what little money he had and donate it to the poor. The year before he died he sold all his belongings, including his library, and rewrote his will so that all his assets would be donated to hospitals in Paris and Clermont. On August 19, 1662, at the age of 39, he finally succumbed to a very painful illness which had bothered him most of his adult life. A post mortem examination showed that he had been suffering from a brain lesion and large deformities of the stomach and intestines. Although not a very nice thing for Blaise, his health problems were to the general benefit of mankind. Some of his best work in philosophy and mathematics were produced when, unable to stop the pain in any other way, he would concentrate so deeply on a difficult problem that he could forget about his physical condition for a few hours.

3.4 GOTTFRIED WILHELM LEIBNITZ (1646–1716)

Gottfried Wilhelm Leibnitz (sometimes spelled Leibniz or even Lubeniecz) was born in Leipzig on July 1, 1646. Figure 3–8 shows Leibnitz at the height of his career. His father, a professor of moral philosophy, only lived until the boy was six years old, but he and his library were a great influence on young Leibnitz's

Figure 3–8. Gottfried Wilhelm Leibnitz.

early education. When his father died, young Gottfried (who by that time had learned some Latin) was allowed to have free run of his father's library. At the age of 15 he entered the University of Leipzig to study law and, when he was 20, he applied for the degree of Doctor of Laws. Leipzig refused to grant him the degree because of his youth so he left for Nuremberg where the University of Altdorf was so impressed with his ability that it immediately awarded him the degree and offered him a professorship. Wanting a job with a little more action in it, he refused the offer and took a job as an advisor to the Elector of Mainz, one of the most famous statesmen of his day.

It was while he was in service to the Elector of Mainz that he was required to dream up a plan to take the minds of the French generals away from the seizure of German states. His "plan" was to divert French attention from Germany to Egypt, as part of a larger campaign for a united Europe to conquer the non-Christian world. In an attempt to convince the French to go along with this scheme, Leibnitz travelled extensively through Europe and actually resided in Paris for several years. During these travels he managed to meet most of the famous men of his day. This resulted in his being made a member of the Royal Society and, later, a member of the French Academy.

Exactly when Leibnitz became interested in the problem of mechanical calculation is not certain. It is known that, when he heard that Pascal had invented a mechanical adding machine, he wrote to a friend in Paris asking for details of its construction. We don't know if Leibnitz ever actually saw one of Pascal's machines, but we do know that, at least in his early years, he did not completely understand the workings of the device. In Leibnitz's notes is a series of suggestions and drawings for an attachment to be placed on top of Pascal's device in order to enable it to perform multiplication. The drawing in Figure 3–9 shows a cleaned up version of Leibnitz's diagram.

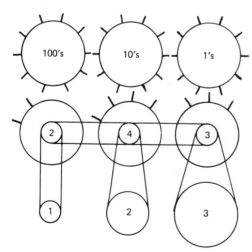

Figure 3–9. A drawing of Leibnitz's first multiplying machine.

Pascal's machine had a number of wagon-wheel-like devices which had to be turned in order to add a number to that already held by the machine. The top row of wheels shown in the drawing were to fit over Pascal's wheels and, by means of another series of wheels (the lower two sets in the drawing), they were to be turned enough to add the required partial products to the accumulator in Pascal's machine. The set-up for the lower two sets of wheels was to be easily changeable; that pictured here is for the product 243 times 123. This whole attachment was to be movable so that it would first be used to add a partial product to Pascal's units wheel; then it would be moved to the left so that its rightmost digit was driving Pascal's tens digit, and so on.

Although it was an interesting idea, the device could not have worked because you could not rotate more than one wheel of Pascal's machine at any given instant. Presumably Leibnitz either found this out, or the pressure of other work caused him to put the idea aside until it no longer had any relevance, for he never seems to have continued in this line of thought.

The machine for which Leibnitz is most famous, his mechanical multiplier, was actually lost to us for about 200 years. Lots of records existed to prove that he had actually constructed a machine, but the actual device seemed to have vanished. It appears that, sometime in the late 1670s, the machine was given to a Mr. A.G. Kastner at Göttingen for overhauling and that somehow it was later stored in the attic of one of the buildings of Göttingen University where it remained for the next 200 years. In 1879 a work crew was attempting to repair a leaking roof and accidentally found it lying in a corner.

The workings of the machine are based upon one of Leibnitz's inventions, the stepped drum, as illustrated in Figure 3–10.

A result wheel, shown at the end of the square shaft, could be rotated to any of ten different positions to register the digits 0 to 9. In order to add a quantity, say 8, to the result indicated on the wheel, it was only necessary to cause the square shaft to rotate 8 steps. This was done by having the small gear on the shaft mesh with 8 teeth on the large drum below the shaft. The small gear could slide up and down the square shaft so that, depending on its position, it would interact with a different number of teeth on the major drum. Leibnitz's machine had eight of these mechanisms so that, when a number was registered on the machine by setting the small pointers (which controlled the position of the gears on the square shafts), a turn of a crank would cause all eight stepped drums to rotate and add the digits to the appropriate counters. To multiply a number by five, you simply turned the crank five times. The actual machine was constructed in two layers in order to solve multiple-digit multiplication. For example, to multiply by 35 the following steps were required:

- The number to be multiplied was set up by moving the gears along the square shafts so that the pointers indicated the desired number.
- The crank was turned five times.

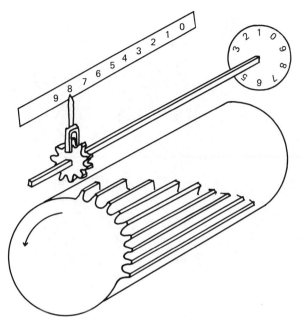

Figure 3–10. A drawing of Leibnitz's stepped drum mechanism.

- The top layer of the machine was shifted one decimal place to the left.
- The crank was turned another three times.

One of the biggest problems when attempting to design this type of machine is how to deal with the possibility of a carry being generated from one digit to the next when the first digit rotates from the 9 position through to the 0 position. Leibnitz only partially solved this problem. Although it appears complex, the diagram of the full mechanism is really quite simple when explained and shows the actual full workings of the machine. The diagram shows two digit positions of the machine, the stepped drums being denoted by the digit 6. The gears in front (labeled 1, 2, and 3) are really just part of the drive mechanism and can be ignored. The more complicated mechanics, consisting of the levers, star wheels, cogs, and pentagonal disks (12, 11, 10, and 14) are all part of the carry mechanism.

When a carry was needed, the small lever (7) would interact with the star wheel (8) and partially turn the shaft so that one of the points of the star (11) would assume a horizontal position (note the two different positions the star wheels could assume). Now the lever (12), which turns once for each turn of the addition crank, would be in a position to give the wheel a little extra push, causing it to flip over to the next digit—that is, add the carry to the next digit.

Note that this does not complete all the requirements of the carry mechanism, for this carry could in turn cause another carry in the next higher digit.

Figure 3–11. The Leibnitz stepped drum mechanism as contained in the Edmondsons Circular Calculating Machine.

There is no way that this simple mechanism can be used to ripple a carry across several digits. Note the two different positions of the pentagonal disk (14); it can have a flat surface uppermost (which would be flush with the top cover of the machine and thus not noticeable to the operator) or it can have one of its points projecting above the top surface. This disk is so arranged that whenever a carry is pending the point is up, and when the carry has actually been added into the next digit the point is down. Thus an operator who turned the crank to add a number into the register would note a ripple carry by the projection of one or more of these points from the top of the machine. The operator would then reach over and give the pentagonal disk a push, which would cause the carry to be registered on the next digit and the point to slide back down into the mechanism. If that carry in turn caused another carry, further pentagonal disks would push their points through the slots in the top of the machine to warn the operator that he had to give the machine a further assist.

We know that Leibnitz started to think about the problems involved in designing such a machine sometime about 1671. In January of 1672 he happened to be in London and was able to demonstrate a wooden model (which did not work properly) to the members of the Royal Society. Leibnitz promised to make some technical changes and bring his machine back when it was properly functional. Robert Hooke (famous for Hooke's law dealing with the properties of springs) was quite caustic about how useful Leibnitz's machine might be and indicated that he could produce a better one. He did, however, inspect the wooden model very carefully and even asked Leibnitz if he could take it apart. Hooke never made anything even close to this kind of machine, but the

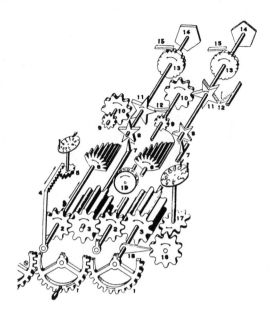

Figure 3–12. The full Leibnitz mechanism. (From the drawing by L. L. Locke in "The Contributions of Leibnitz to the Art of Mechanical Calculation," *Scripta Mathematica*, Vol. I, 1932.)

interest of the Royal Society members did spur Leibnitz into thinking about some substantial alterations he could make to the mechanism. The Secretary of the Royal Society did not invite Leibnitz to the next meeting but suggested that, when a proper working model was available, they would like to have it demonstrated. Several letters remain in existence between the Secretary of the Royal Society and Leibnitz concerning the progress of the machine over the next two years.

Leibnitz was plagued by the same types of problems that were faced by Pascal and others—poor workmen and poor materials with which to work. The final machine was only put together because Leibnitz had found, during his stay in Paris, a French clockmaker named Olivier, who was both honest and a fine craftsman. No one really knows for sure, but it is assumed that Leibnitz simply explained the problems to M. Olivier, and then let the clockmaker get on with the real construction work. The final version of the machine, which is now housed in the Landesbibliothek in Hannover was put together in the summer of 1674.

As previously mentioned, the machine consists of two basic sections; the upper one contains the set-up mechanism and the result register, while the lower part contains the basic Leibnitz stepped-gear mechanism. When the multiplicand digits have been entered into the set-up slides, the handle on the front is turned once for every time that the multiplicand should be added to the answer dials. The large dial on the top right of the machine would have a pin set into it at the position indicated by the multiplier digit (for example, 5) and, after five turns of the front handle, it would bring this pin up against the stop

Figure 3–13. The Leibnitz calculating machine. (Photograph courtesy of IBM Archives.)

to be seen at the top of the dial, thus preventing the operator from adding the multiplicand to the result too many times. After a single digit of the multiplier had been processed, the crank at the far left of the machine would be turned once to shift the top section of the machine over by one digit place so that the next digit of the multiplier could be considered. Thus, this machine was simply the mechanical version of the common shift-and-add procedure used for multiplication on many digital computers.

The knowledge that a new calculating machine was available spread rapidly through the scientific circles of Paris, where Leibnitz happened to be living while performing his diplomatic functions. Eventually Etienne Perier, the eldest nephew of Blaise Pascal, contacted Leibnitz and requested to examine the machine. Through this contact, Leibnitz gained access to some of Pascal's unpublished mathematical papers which he used for his own private study and, in return for this kindness, he helped Perier to edit them for publication.

Leibnitz is more widely known for his work in mathematics and philosophy than for his invention of a calculating machine. It is interesting to note, however, that the principle of the stepped-drum gear was the only really workable solution to the problems involved in constructing calculating machines until about 1875 when Baldwin (U.S.A.) and Odhner (Russia) produced two inventions which resulted in a true variable-toothed gear. The first real commercially available calculating machine was put on the market by the Frenchman Thomas de Colmar in 1820. It very closely resembled Leibnitz's design but had a proper carry mechanism which would deal with the case of a ripple carry. It is unlikely that Thomas de Colmar knew of Leibnitz's machine in detail, but the Leibnitz drum was famous enough that there is no doubt where the basic ideas came from.

Leibnitz died on November 14, 1716. His last years were marred by disease, filled with controversy (not the least with Newton over the invention of calculus), and embittered by neglect. Although he was tolerant of differences of opinion and charitable in his judgments of others, he made a great many enemies because he was very impatient of contradiction in small matters, fond of money to the point of covetousness, and protective of his own pride. None-theless, he holds the position, perhaps more than any other post-Renaissance figure, of a man of almost universal genius. People like him are often very difficult to get along with, and there was an almost audible sigh of relief from his contemporaries when he finally died. An eyewitness tells us that "he was buried more like a robber than what he really was, the ornament of his country."[3] His secretary was the only mourner attending the funeral!

3.5 SAMUEL MORLAND (1625–1695)[4]

Samuel Morland was the son of an English clergyman who, because of the political turmoil surrounding the taking of power by Oliver Cromwell, did not get a chance to attend university until he was much older than most young men seeking higher education in his day. Not wishing to become a clergyman, the usual profession for someone with a B.A. in Morland's day, he took up the study of mathematics and, in 1649, he was elected as a fellow of Magdalene College, Cambridge, just in time for him to sign Samuel Pepys' enrollment forms in 1650. Morland and Pepys later become good friends, and it is from Samuel Pepys' *Diary* that we get some of the personal background information about Morland.

In 1653 Morland was fortunate enough to be selected as a "gentleman admitted to Whitelocke's table" in the party of Bulstrode Whitelock who was being sent as ambassador to Queen Christina of Sweden to arrange a commercial treaty between the two countries. Queen Christina was a great patron of the sciences, who encouraged the greatest scientists and philosophers in Europe to attend her court. Men like Salmasius, Grotius, and Descartes were often to be found in person and others, like Pascal, would send the Queen copies of their latest papers or inventions. It is not surprising then that Whitelocke reports that, during the eight months he spent in Sweden, the majority of the time was spent in "disputations in Latin among the young men who were scholars."[5] One of the things that was likely to have been discussed was the copy of Pascal's adding machine which he had, in 1652, sent as a gift to the Queen. She was known to have kept this machine on hand as a curiosity to be shown to visiting dignitaries. Whitelocke reports that Morland was

> . . . a very civil man and an excellent scholar; modest and respectful; perfect in the Latin tongue; an ingenious mechanist.[6]

[3]*Encyclopedia Britannica,* article on Leibnitz, 11th edition (1911), 16, 387.

[4]Some of the material in this section has been published by the author in "From Napier to Lucas," *Annals of the History of Computing,* 5, No. 3 (July 1983), 279–96.

[5]B. Whitelocke, *Journal of the Swedish Embassy* (London, 1855), vol. II, p. 354

[6]H. W. Dickinson, *Sir Samuel Morland, Diplomat and Inventor* (Cambridge: W. Heffer and Sons Ltd., 1970), p. 8.

Figure 3–14. Samuel Morland.

This last remark indicates that, even before Morland began the inventive phase of his career, he was both interested in, and capable of, fine mechanical work.

    The year after his return from Sweden, Morland was again sent on a diplomatic mission, this time to Italy as an envoy to the Duke of Savoy. On the trip to the Duke's Court, it is known that he stopped off at the court of Louis XIV for at least one month. Although not accomplishing anything of diplomatic value while in Paris, he would likely have made contact with the scholars and mechanics who worked there, a fact which will become significant when we consider the developments attributed to Rene Grillet. It is only reasonable to suppose that any well-educated man who had made a study of mathematics, was known to be interested in mechanical devices, and who had almost certainly seen and discussed one of Pascal's adding machines during the previous year, would take the opportunity of investigating the matter more thoroughly when he was in the French capital. It is highly unlikely that Morland ever met Pascal for, although he was still alive at the time, he had retired to a life of religious contemplation by the time Morland was in Paris. If any meeting did take place, no record of it appears to exist. Morland is known to have again stopped in Paris on his return journey about one year later. His connections with France and the French court were further cemented when, in 1657, he married Susanne de Milleville, daughter of Daniel de Milleville, Baron de Bois-say. These connections were obviously kept up, for there are records of frequent trips to France by either Morland or his wife. Samuel Pepys (who also had a French wife) indicates that Morland attended the French church in London, and he translated at least one technical work on fortifications from the French into English. By 1681 he had gained enough of a personal reputation in France that he was appointed as a consultant for the water supply of Versailles. Thus, although no records appear to exist to verify the fact, Morland must have been known to another inventor of calculating instruments, Rene Grillet who held the position of clockmaker to Louis XIV.

Morland, who had managed to work himself up into sensitive positions in the diplomatic service of Oliver Cromwell, had, in reality, been a spy for the exiled King Charles. When Charles returned to the throne, Morland was given several honors and some small pensions for his service. Finally free from the need to hold down a job, he proceeded to turn his mechanical ability to use in the invention of several devices ranging from calculating machinery to barometers, speaking trumpets, and water pumps.

Morland invented three different kinds of calculating instruments; one of them has already been discussed in Section 2.5.2, while the other two were a simple adding machine and a mechanical version of Napier's "bones." Although these latter two machines were both invented in the middle 1660s, it was not until 1673 that Morland published a small book, *The Description and Use of Two Arithmetic Instruments,* which described both machines and the types of operations they could perform.

The adding machine consisted of a simple set of wheels, each of which could be rotated by a small stylus. If it was desired to add 4 pounds to a sum already registered on the machine, you simply put the stylus into the hole at the position marked 4 on the dial corresponding to the units digit of the pounds register (upper right-hand dial) and then rotated it in a clockwise direction until the stylus was at the top of the dial. The result of the operation could be seen through the small window at the 12 o'clock position on each dial. There was no proper carry mechanism incorporated in this instrument. Instead, a number of small auxiliary dials were constructed above each of the major dials and, every time the major dial was turned from 9 through 0, a small tooth would advance the auxiliary dial by one position. When the addition was complete, the auxiliary dials would indicate how many carries should have been added to the next major dial, and this operation could be performed by hand. This partial carry mechanism might well have been motivated by the fact that a fancy carry mechanism like Pascal's was very complex from a mechanical point of view and not always reliable in its operation, while a single-tooth mechanism such as Schickard's might require a motive force sufficient to damage the

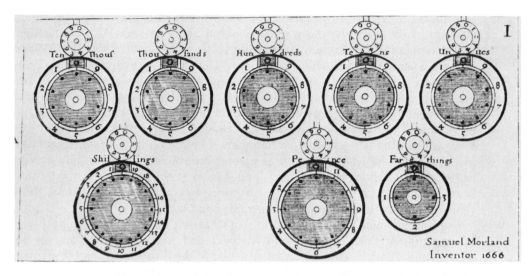

Figure 3–15. Morland's adding machine, as illustrated in his 1673 book.

wooden gears. Morland's adding machine was, on the other hand, both simple in construction and reliable in operation as long as the operator remembered to add the carries forward at the end of the normal adding operation.

Morland designed this instrument for the addition of pounds, shillings, pence, and farthings, but he had the foresight to position the nondecimal dials on the lower portion of the device so that the upper part could be used for the addition of any five-digit decimal numbers. It was small enough to be easily carried in a pocket; the surviving examples are about 4 in. by 3 in. by 0.25 in. thick.

Morland offered the device to the public by way of an advertisement in the *London Gazette* of April 16, 1668. Few of the machines were sold, however, because the general impression was similar to the one held by Samuel Pepys who, on March 14, 1668, went to dinner at Lord Hinchingbroke's house and later remarked in his diary:

> . . . and there, among many other things my Lord had Sir Samuel Morland's invention for casting up sums of £.s.p which is very pretty but not very useful.[7]

In the book Morland wrote describing the instrument, he indicated that additional secondary carry wheels could be added to the instrument so that the number of times the primary carry wheels had progressed from 9 to 0 could be automatically registered. He was careful to point out that the numbers registered on these secondary carry wheels should be added to the digit two places

---

[7]*Samuel Pepys' Diary* (London: G. Bell & Sons, 1926), p. 472.

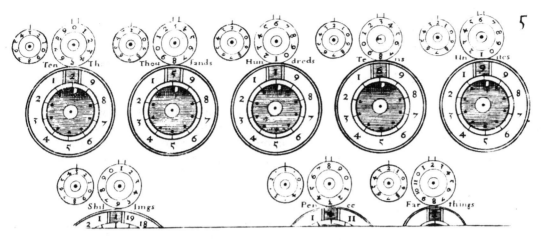

Figure 3–16. Morland's modified adding machine, as illustrated in his 1673 book.

to the left! The proposed layout of the device, as indicated in Morland's own diagrams, is shown in Fig. 3–16. As far as the author is aware, no instruments of this design were actually constructed or, if they were, none have survived to modern times. Morland was obviously aware that his single-tooth carry mechanism was strong enough to advance two successive carry wheels, but would not take the strain of propagating a carry from one end of a register to another.

Morland's second calculating machine was designed as an aid to multiplication and division using the principles involved in Napier's "bones." It consisted of a flat brass plate with a perforated, hinged gate, a series of circular disks with numbers engraved near their edges, and several semi-circular pins upon which the flat disks could be placed. The disks were simply a circular version of Napier's "bones" with the products being set down around the edge of the disk in such a way that the two digits of a number would be placed at the opposite ends of a diagonal. For example, the illustration of one of his disks

Figure 3–17. Morland's version of Napier's "bones," as illustrated in his 1673 book.

shows his version of Napier's "bone" for the number 3; the product of 4 × 3 = 12 is shown highlighted by an arrow, and adjacent digits represent the product 3 × 3 = 9 and 5 × 3 = 15. The large digits engraved in the middle of the disk indicate which "bone" is being represented; the upper digit identifies this side of the disk and the lower digit indicates which "bone" can be found engraved on the underside.

To find the single-digit products of a given number, for example, 1234, the disks representing these digits would be removed from the upper pins and placed over the semi-circular pins on the lower portion of the instrument, as shown in Figure 3–18. The hinged gate would then be lowered over the disks, and the key (marked G–H) would be turned until the small pointer (marked E–F) indicated that the proper multiple would be showing through the windows in the hinged gate. The act of turning the key would, through an elementary rack-and-pinion mechanism, rotate the disks under the gate and move the pointer along the product indicator. The digits of the required product could

Figure 3–18. Morland's multiplying machine (gate open), as illustrated in his 1673 book.

Figure 3–19. Morland's multiplying machine (gate closed), as illustrated in his 1673 book.

then be found by adding together the pairs of digits showing through each gate window (4 × 1734 = 6936 as shown in Figure 3–19). Both photographs were meant to show the same number (1234), but Morland's engraver misread a 2 for a 7 in the closed gate position of Figure 3–19.

The machine came complete with 30 disks for ordinary multiplication and a further five special disks (marked with the letters Q/QQ) used for finding square and cube roots.

The adding machine and the multiplying machine make a fine pair because, not only do they complement one another in the operations they perform, but the process of using the modified Napier's "bones" to perform multiplication requires that the user add up the partial products as they are generated. As Morland states in his book:

> . . . if any person have the Curiosity, and is willing to goe to the Expence; the Adding Instrument being joined to the Multiplying Instrument, performs Addition, Subtraction, Multiplication, and Divisions; as likewise the Extraction of the Square and Cube-roots, etc. without the help of Pen and Ink, or exposing the Operator to any difficulty or uncertainty.[8]

3.6 RENÉ GRILLET[9]

Very little is known about René Grillet or his accomplishments; the major reference work about French clockmakers simply notes his existence with no details as to his life or work. Even such basic facts as the dates of his birth and death appear to be unknown. It is known that he once held an appointment as clockmaker to Louis XIV, and at least one source claims that, after constructing a calculating machine, he took it on a tour of country fairs, charging a silver collection to see it operate.[10] The machine has been the subject of speculation for some time, and the author even encountered one individual who claimed that the calculator invented by Leibnitz was none other than Grillet's machine which had been taken by Leibnitz during the latter's stay in Paris.

The external form of Grillet's machine has, in fact, been known for some time. In 1678 he published a short description of the machine in the *Journal des Scavans*, one of the leading scientific publications of the day. Unfortunately the text of that article does very little to enlighten us as to the mode of operation of that machine. After telling his readers that the idea stemmed from the "rulers" of M. Neper (sic), mentioning that M. Pascal had invented an admirable

[8]Samuel Morland, *The Description and Use of Two Arithmetic Instruments* (London, 1673), p. 11.

[9]Some of the material in this section has already appeared in an article by the author "From Napier to Lucas," *Annals of the History of Computing*, 5, No. 3 (July 1983), 279–96.

[10]See F. A. P. Barnard, *Report on the Processes of the Industrial Arts and Apparatus of the Exact Sciences* (New York: Van Nostrand, 1869).

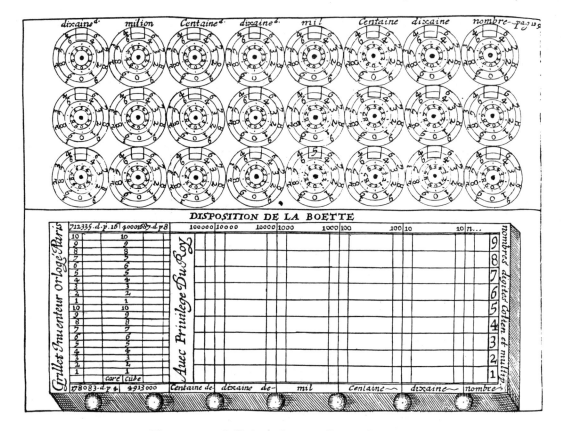

Figure 3–20. Grillet's machine, as illustrated in his 1673 book.

machine for doing arithmetic and that M. Petit had given us a *cylindre arithmetique* (Napier's "bones" engraved on a cylinder), Grillet simply says that his device combines the wheels of Pascal with the cylinder of Petit to provide a wondrous machine which would perform all the arithmetic operations. The rest of the article was simply devoted to where one could go in order to purchase his creation.

The diagram obviously shows a box with 24 sets of wheels in the lid, each of which consists of several concentric circles, while the bottom of the box appears to contain a set of Napier's "bones" engraved on cylinders, reminiscent of those produced by Gaspard Schott (see Section 2.6.2). The fact that Grillet wanted to keep the workings of the device a secret, combined with the fact that none of his machines appear to have survived to the present day, means that we had no idea if the wheels in the lid contained a carry mechanism, either of the complex variety like Pascal's, the single-tooth mechanism of Schickard, the simple-minded approach like Morland's, or whether they were just individual dials to be turned by hand in order to do away with the need for pen, ink, and scratch paper when doing simple arithmetic.

Our one clue to the internal operations of Grillet's machine comes from a manuscript that once belonged to Charles Babbage and only came to light in 1977. The manuscript is now in the Crawford Library in Edinburgh together with most of Babbage's private library. The manuscript starts out:

> Usage de la machine d'arithmetique de l'invention de Sieur Grillet—Horlogeur a Paris (Usage of the arithmetic machine invented by Mr. Grillet—clockmaker of Paris)

The manuscript came to the Crawford Collection from the sale of books held upon the death of the famous French mathematician Michel Chasles (1793–1880). The Chasles catalogue still exists but shows no record of anything under the name Grillet. It does, however, record the manuscript under the heading Gaillet, together with a note indicating that it dates from sometime in the seventeenth century. At the time the manuscript was acquired by the Crawford Library, the librarian simply accepted the misspelled Chasles classification and, for all practical purposes, the manuscript was lost for 100 years.

The manuscript is written entirely in French and consists of 18 handwritten pages, plus four extra pages of pen-and-ink diagrams, the majority of which are simple geometric drawings and have nothing at all to do with this manuscript. The pertinent diagrams, however, are virtually identical with those used by Grillet in the 1678 paper. The text, while never describing the hardware in detail, gives enough examples of its use to clearly show the mechanical workings of the device. The organization of the machine was rather simple, with no connection at all between the groups of wheels on the lid. Its use was limited to being a substitute for pen and ink when doing elementary addition and subtraction. The lower part of the instrument is a set of Napier's "bones" engraved on cylinders in the style of Schott. The only addition to Schott's mechanism was the inclusion of the square and cube root cylinders on the left-hand end of the machine. For reasons not explained, Grillet's "bones" were drawn with the nines multiples at the top of the cylinder rather than the bottom as was the practice of all other makers of Napier's "bones."

The diagram on the top of the box, showing the 24 sets of circles, is actually a partial x-ray view of the construction. Of the concentric circles shown, the outer two are actually underneath the lid while the innermost ones are on top. The small square at the 12 o'clock position of each circle is a small window through which the digits engraved on the lower plates can be viewed. For example, the fourth circle from the right in the lower line indicates a five showing through the window. The two sets of figures which were capable of showing through the small windows are actually tens complements of one another. This allowed the operator to more easily perform both addition and subtraction. The actual manipulation of the dials is almost the same as that used with Morland's adding machine, which is not surprising since Grillet's court position would have made it certain that, even if Morland did not know Grillet, Grillet would have known about Morland and his work.

To perform an addition or subtraction on the lid dials, the operator would set up the first number on the upper line of wheels, the second number on the middle line of wheels, and then perform the operation mentally, setting down the digits of the answer on the lower line of wheels. The lid would, of course, have found its main use in adding up the partial products generated by the set of cylindrical Napier's "bones," and the manuscript devotes several pages to a careful description of this process. After a brief mention of the fact that, when a wheel is rotated past the zero position, the operator must either add or subtract one from the adjacent wheel on the left, the subject is not mentioned further. The examples all deal with the simple case where no carry is ever required, and there is no mention at all of a carry possibly generating one or more further carries. The last few pages of the manuscript deal with division, the addition and subtraction of fractions, and the extraction of square and cube roots, all of which are given the briefest of mention and illustrated by only elementary examples.

Although not a very sophisticated machine, Grillet's device, with its eight-digit capacity in the adding mechanism, would have been more useful during multiplication than Morland's combination of circular "bones" and five-digit adding machine. To do justice to both men, it should be pointed out that Morland's machine had the more useful mechanism for Napier's "bones" while Grillet's had the larger capacity adding mechanism.

This simple device would have been quite useful in a society where the only material usually available for recording intermediate results was a quill pen and liquid ink. It at least made it possible for someone to carry a pocket-sized device to perform the four standard arithmetic operations without the need to resort to pen and ink. This is, after all, one of the reasons why we carry the small credit-card-sized pocket calculators.

3.7 COMMERCIALLY PRODUCED MACHINES

3.7.1 The Thomas Arithmometer

It has already been noted that the first commercially produced calculating machine to have any real degree of reliability and usefulness was done by M. Charles Xavier Thomas de Colmar in France. He took the basic Leibnitz mechanism and, applying some modern engineering and design practice, produced a machine he called an "arithmometer" in the early 1820s. Although based on the Leibnitz stepped-drum gears, the arithmometer incorporated several features which made it easier to use. For example, M. Thomas reversed the operating motion (during a multiplication operation) of the result registers, so that the result registers moved to the left over the top of the stepped-gear mechanism rather than attempting to move the stepped-gear mechanism under the result registers. These changes, together with the improvements introduced because of better manufacturing techniques for the gears, resulted in a machine which was basically reliable in operation even if it was large enough to cover a complete desk and often required two men to move it safely from place to place.

Arithmometers remained in production until about the start of the First World War. They were produced in several standard models, some with six, seven, or even eight figures in the set-up mechanism and twice that number of digits in the result register. Several special machines were constructed having 16-digit set-up mechanisms and a 32-digit product register. It had many rivals, some with quite sophisticated features, but they were all really based on the Leibnitz stepped drum and, because of this, were usually quite awkward machines, both in their physical size and in their ease of use. Individual machines were produced before M. Thomas started up his firm, but he ranks as the first to actually create an industry which manufactured mechanical devices to aid in calculation. He was the acknowledged leader in this field for most of the

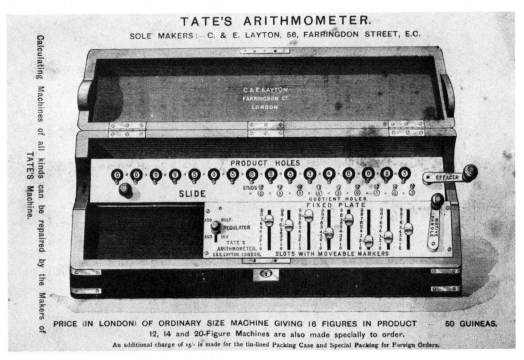

Figure 3–21. The Tate arithmometer, a commercial machine much like the Thomas arithmometer, as illustrated in one of their advertisements.

Figure 3–22. Edmonson's circular calculating machine, an early commercially produced calculator based on the Leibnitz stepped drum.

nineteenth century, being awarded the Chevalier of the Legion of Honor for his achievement.

3.7.2 The Baldwin–Odhner Machines

The big breakthrough in the design and production of desktop calculators came when new mechanisms were perfected which would allow the designers to replace the Leibnitz stepped drum with a more compact, and usually lighter weight, mechanism. The whole purpose of the stepped-drum gear was to have some device which would allow the result register to be turned through a variable number of positions (0 to 9) depending on the set-up mechanism which held the number being manipulated. In effect the Leibnitz drum provided a gear with a variable number of teeth, the number of teeth in use being determined by the position along the drum of the next gear being driven off this shaft. It was realized that before the existence of a true variable-toothed gear—

one that would literally change the number of teeth that were projecting from its surface—there could be no significant reduction in the size and weight of the resulting calculator.

There were several attempts to produce a working variable toothed gear during the late 1700s and early 1800s, but none of these succeeded because neither the workmen nor the materials were available to implement the ideas. The first properly constructed variable-toothed gear was created, essentially simultaneously, by Frank S. Baldwin in the United States and T. Odhner, a Swede working in Russia. The actual mechanisms were very similar to each other, and the machines constructed from them were known by the generic term "Baldwin Machines" in America and "Odhner Machines" in Europe.

As can be seen from Figure 3–23, a small disk contained a number of movable pins which could be extended from the outer edge of the disk. The number of pins protruding was controlled by a lever attached to a circular device running through the middle of the pins. When the lever was moved, the cam-like deformation of the circular control strip would cause the pins to move either into or out of the disk.

A calculator based on this device would have, as its input, the levers of these disks. If you wanted to register the number 52, one lever would be moved so that five pins were projecting from the edge of the disk and another so that

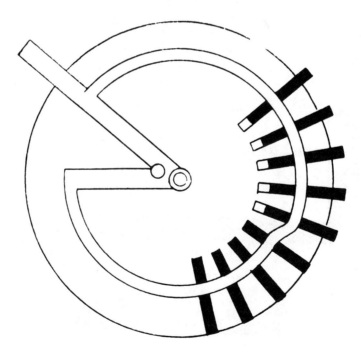

Figure 3–23.   An illustration of the variable toothed gear.

two pins were projecting from the disk mounted to the right of the first. To add this number into the result register, the whole group of disks would be rotated about their common central shaft, and this would cause the result register digits to increase by as many positions as there were pins sticking out of the edge of each disk.

The real benefit of these variable-toothed gears was not only in their ease of use and general reliability, but in the fact that they were constructed from essentially thin, flat disks. This meant that many of them could be mounted, side by side, on a common shaft in only a few inches of space. The resulting decrease in the size of a calculating machine was quite dramatic. Rather than taking up almost the entire surface of a desk, a four-function calculator now had become something which would sit easily on the corner of a desk and thus a practical addition to many offices. The rapid increase in the popularity of these machines can be seen from the fact that one of the major manufacturers, the Brunsviga Co., produced their first crude model in 1885 and were able to boast that they had produced over 20,000 machines by 1912. Although the Brunsviga Co. was one of the major manufacturers, it was by no means alone

Figure 3–24. The Brunsviga "Dupla" machine.

in the field, and the total number of these machines in use may well have been ten times the Brunsviga figure.

3.7.3 Key-Driven Machines

There was still a major problem to be overcome before the general business world was to adopt the mechanical calculator for office use. For applications such as adding up invoice amounts, the operations of setting levers to register the appropriate amounts and then pulling a lever or turning a crank to actually cause the addition to be performed were just too time-consuming for high-volume business offices.

It had long been known that the energy involved in pushing a lever to put a number into the set-up mechanism of a machine was actually sufficient not only to set up the number but also to cause the addition to be performed. Unfortunately all attempts to combine the set-up operation with the actual addition had failed for one of two different reasons. The first was the fact that, once the result register had been put into high-speed motion by a quick key stroke, it was very difficult to stop it before the result wheels turned too far and registered an incorrect result.

The second reason involved a problem that only became apparent when people were actually attempting to use the machines. When an operator wished to add the number 52 to the result register, it was possible to put fingers on both the 5 key and the 2 key (in the tens and units column, respectively) and

Figure 3–25.   An early comptometer.

push them both at the same time, rather than pushing first the 2 key and then the 5 key in separate operations. Because the two wheels for the units and tens digits of the result register would be in operation at the same instant, it became necessary to design a mechanism for propagating a carry between them in less time than it took the keys to return to their normal operating position after they had been pushed. The time interval for carry propagation was further restricted by the fact that one carry might cause another, and so on down the line. It was not until some mechanism could be found which would cause a carry to be added to an adjacent result wheel in less than 1/150 of a second that the key-driven machines became a practical reality.

The man who made the comptometer function was Mr. Dorr E. Felt. Felt became quite well known, partly because the company manufacturing his comptometer was very successful and partly because he loved to collect, display, and lecture on mechanical computing devices. His company kept an historical archive which documented the changes made in his and other calculating machines from their earliest beginnings. Felt had an idea that he thought would work for a key-driven machine and, not being able to afford the cost of having a metal model constructed, decided to make one out of wood. As he tells the story:

> I went to the grocery and bought a macaroni box to make a frame of. I went to the butcher and bought skewers to make the keys of, and to the hardware store and bought staples, and to the bookstore and bought rubber bands to use for springs. I went to work to make a calculating machine, expecting to have thousands in use in ninety days. I began on Thanksgiving Day, because it was a holiday, and worked that day, and Christmas and New Year's, but I didn't get it done in three days. It was a long time before I got it done.[11]

His first model was actually finished on New Year's Day of 1885, and he managed to produce the first fully working comptometer in the autumn of 1886. By combining the action of entering a number with the action of actually adding it to the result register at the same time, Felt was able to speed up the addition operation by an order of magnitude above the times available with other mechanical calculators. As noted above, this speedup of the mechanical action led to problems of inertia and momentum which had never been faced by previous designers. It was only by using advanced engineering skills that combined lightness with strength of the parts that the comptometer became a successful machine.

From this point on there were no really new designs produced for desktop calculating machines. Of course there were many engineering improvements which made them both smaller and more reliable, but the basic design always involved at least one of the three forms just discussed.

[11]Dorr E. Felt, "Mechanical Arithmetic or The History of the Counting Machine," *Lectures on Business*, no publisher noted, p. 17.

Figure 3-26. Felt's "macaroni box" machine, as illustrated in the *Handbook of the Napier Tercentenary Celebration,* 1914.

Some special machines were produced which had a built-in multiplication table, stored as a series of rods protruding from a metal base. The length of each rod indicated the result of a multiplication by the digit associated with its base. For example the mechanism for 5 would have a sequence of rods of length 5, 10, 15, 20, . . . , two digits being represented by two rods of the appropriate length. When a multiplication was being performed, the mechanism would add to the result register an amount equal to the lengths of the rods in use; which rods were used was dependent on the number currently in the set-up mechanism. These special machines were typically quite expensive and, again, large and cumbersome to use. It was really only the larger science-oriented institutions that purchased such a device.

FURTHER READING

BARNARD, F. A. P. (1869). *Report on the Processes of the Industrial Arts and Apparatus of the Exact Sciences.* New York: Van Nostrand.

DICKENSON, H. W. (1970). *Sir Samuel Morland, Diplomat and Inventor (1625–1695).* Cambridge: Newcomen Society.

FLET, D. E. (?) "Mechanical Arithmetic or The History of the Counting Machine," *Lectures on Business,* no publisher noted.

GRILLET, RENÉ (1673). *Curiositez Mathematiques.* Paris.

——. (1678). "Nouvelle machine d'Arithmetique," *Journal de Scavans,* pp. 164–66.

HAMMER, F. (1958). "Nicht Pascal, sondern der Tübinger Professor Wilhelm Schickard erfand die Rechenmaschine," *Büromarkt,* No. 20.

HOFFMAN, J. E. (1974). *Leibnitz in Paris.* Cambridge: Cambridge University Press.

HORSBURGH, E. M. (1983). *Handbook of the Exhibition of Napier Relics and of Books, Instruments, and Devices for Facilitating Calculation.* Edinburgh: Tomash Publishers. (Originally published in 1914.)

IBM DEUTSCHLAND (1970?). *Rechenuhr nach Wilhelm Schickard.*

JACOB, L. (1911). *Le Calcul Mecanique.* Paris: Gauthier-Villars.

LAST, J. (1962). "Digital Calculating Machines," *The Charted Mechanical Engineer,* December, 572–79.

LENARD, P. (1933). *Great Men of Science.* (trans. from the German by S. Hatfield). London: Bell & Sons.

LOCKE, L. L. (1933). "The Contributions of Leibniz to the Art of Mechanical Calculation," *Scripta Mathematica,* 1, 315–21.

MORLAND, S. (1673). *The Description and Use of two Arithmetic Instruments.* London.

MURRAY, F. J. (1948). *The Theory of Mathematical Machines.* New York: King's Crown Press.

STEINMANN, J. (1962). *Pascal.* (trans. from the French by Martin Turnell) New York: Harcourt Brace Jovanovich.

TARDY, H. L. (1971–72). *Dictionnaire des Horlogers Francais,* 2 vols. Paris.

TURCK, J. A. V. (1921). *Origin of Modern Calculating Machines.* Chicago: Western Society of Engineers.

VON FREYTAG LORINGHOFF, B. (1957). *Eine Tübinger Rechenmaschine aus dem Jahre 1623, Heimatkundliche Bätter für den Kreis Tübingen.* 11. Jahrgang, Nr. 3 (Juli).

——. (1973). *Prof. Schickard's Tübinger Rechenmaschine von 1623 im Tübinger Rathaus.* Druckerei Tübinger Chronik.

——. (1976). *Wilhelm Schickard.* Unpublished lecture given at the Los Alamos Conference on the History of Computing, June 10–15, 1976.

VON MACKENSEN, L. (1969). "Zur Vorgeschichte und Entstehung der ersten digitalen 4-Spezies Rechenmaschine von Gottfried Wilhelm Leibniz," *Studia Leibnitiana,* Supp. II, pp. 34–68.

WHITELOCKE, B. (1855). *Journal of the Swedish Embassy* (new edition), London.

WOLF, A. (1935). *A History of Science and Technology in the 16th and 17th Centuries.* London: Allen and Unwin.

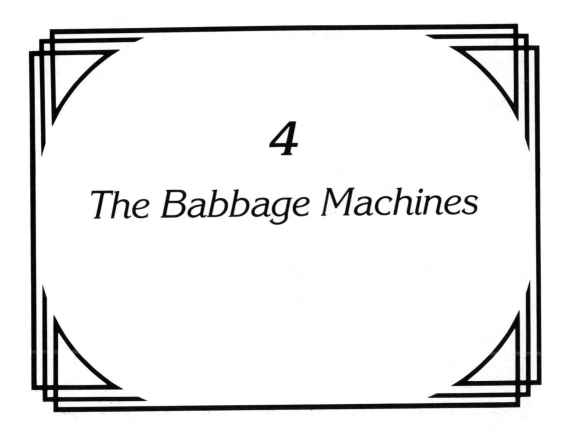

4

The Babbage Machines

4.1 *THE LIFE OF CHARLES BABBAGE (1791–1871)*

Charles Babbage, perhaps more than any other person, can be considered to be the grandfather of the computer age. The level of technology he had available to him was, by today's standard, crude enough that we have to limit his relationship to that of being a grandparent, but his ideas were so far in advance of his time that they would have fit easily into the early computer work being done by people like Konrad Zuse and Howard Aiken in the 1940s. It will be instructive to briefly examine the life of this remarkable gentleman before venturing into a description of the machines he produced.

Babbage's early life is a bit of a mystery. It used to be thought that he was born in Devon in 1792, but his baptismal records were found a few years ago and these seem to indicate that he was actually born in London in 1791. His father was a wealthy banker and the family were able to live in considerable comfort. Charles inherited about 100,000 pounds from his father, and this enabled him to live a life of study and research without the need to worry about

Figure 4–1. Charles Babbage in his late 30s.

holding down a job. Because of this freedom from day-to-day financial concerns, his scientific life was extremely productive. Although he is known today primarily for his work on automatic computation, he was also an excellent mathematician, one of the leading members of the Royal Astronomical Society, a founder of the Royal Statistical Society, and published occasional research papers in the fields of optics, atmospheric observations, electricity and magnetism, the operation of life insurance companies, cryptology, geology, metal working, taxation systems, the operation of lighthouses, and the design of diving bells. In addition he published several books, one of which (*On the Economy of Machinery and Manufactures*) is now recognized as one of the pioneer works in the area we now call "operations research."

Charles showed an intense interest in the workings of mechanical things from his earliest youth. In his own writings about his younger years he states:

> My invariable question on receiving any new toy, was "Mamma, what is inside of it?" Until this information was obtained those around me had no repose, and the toy itself, I have been told, was generally broken open if the answer did not satisfy my own little ideas of the "fitness of things."[1]

This interest was not confined to mechanical items but also extended to all facets of his life. He once attempted to cause the devil to appear in order to confirm the truth of several Biblical statements concerning Satan's existence. When, much to his relief, nothing happened, he resolved to confirm the existence of God by a different type of experiment. As Babbage himself wrote:

> I resolved that at a certain hour of a certain day I would go to a certain room in the house, and if I found the door open, I would believe in the Bible; but that if it were closed, I should conclude that it was not true. I remember well the observation was made, but I have no recollection as to the state of the door.[2]

After obtaining his elementary education at a boarding school, during which time he used to sneak out in the middle of the night in order that he and another boy might study mathematics by the light of forbidden candles, his father decided that he should attend Cambridge University. In order to give Charles some advice as to what to expect, a Cambridge tutor was invited to the house. As Charles recalls:

> The advice of the Rev. Doctor was quite sound, but very limited. It might be summed up in one short sentence: "Advise your son not to purchase his wine in Cambridge."[3]

Babbage's time in Cambridge was spent studying mathematics. He soon found that he knew more than his tutor in this area and consequently spent the majority of his time reading the papers of the great European mathematicians and holding meetings with other advanced students in his rooms. These meetings led to Babbage's collaborating with John Herschel (the son of the great astronomer and later himself to become Astronomer Royal) and George Peacock (later Dean of Ely) to produce an English version of a French calculus text by LaCroix. They not only produced a fine translation, but added considerably to the text and included notes to explain the more difficult sections. This book became the standard English-language text on calculus during the first part of the last century and helped reform the teaching of mathematics throughout the

---

[1] Charles Babbage, *Passages from the Life of a Philosopher* (London: Longman and Co., 1864), p. 8.

[2] Ibid., p. 13.

[3] Ibid., p. 25.

entire English-speaking world—not a bad achievement for three young under-graduates!

While at Cambridge he took the time to become involved in many different social activities; in fact, his social life was so active that it is a wonder he had time for any formal studies at all. He was a regular member of two groups, one that specialized in playing chess at all hours of the day and night and another for whist. He could often be found in a small boat on the river Cam but also kept a sort of open house in his rooms for students who wanted to participate in interesting discussion groups. When it became obvious that he had a few hours to spare in his week, he would help form a society under almost any pretext. Two of the most famous were the Cambridge Ghost Club, which spent its time collecting evidence as to the existence of ghosts, and a club known as "the extractors." This latter organization, although basically a Sunday morning discussion group, had four simple rules:

1. Every member must communicate his address to the Secretary at least once every six months.
2. If this communication was delayed beyond 12 months, it would be taken for granted that his relatives had shut him up as insane.
3. Every effort legal and illegal shall be made to get him out of the madhouse (hence the name "extractors").
4. Every candidate for admission shall produce six certificates to be kept on file—three that he is sane and three that he is not.

When Babbage left Cambridge, he looked for a lectureship at a university, but was never able to obtain such an appointment because they were usually under the control of government ministers and, at that time, he had no influence in these circles at all. He moved to London and began his life of study and research. In later years he was elected as the Lucasian Professor of Mathematics in Cambridge (the same position once held by Newton). Being quite disgruntled with his former lack of recognition by the University, he wrote a letter to them which, in essence, indicated just what they could do with this honor. Before the letter was mailed, a number of friends talked him out of such a rash act, and he agreed to accept the position. He only rarely travelled back to Cambridge, and even then it was simply to participate in some formal activity or to be an examiner for a special mathematical prize.

The Lucasian professorship was the only public honor ever given to Babbage in England. He was, however, well known and respected on the continent. He was elected as a member of at least 15 European scientific societies and even named commander of the Italian Order of St. Maurice and St. Lazarus. It is not entirely strange that he should have been given several honors in Italy for he went there as often as his other commitments would allow.

While in Italy he was impressed with the smoke rings which would occasionally blow from the top of Mount Vesuvius. This prompted him to do various experiments with short blasts of air from a funnel, which in turn led to his proposing that burning hydrogen could be fired into the air to form flaming rings for fireworks displays.

Having studied Vesuvius for several weeks, he decided that any proper scientific study should include a trip into the crater. The fact that the mountain was then erupting was of no concern to him. He hired a group of men to carry him in a chair up the side of the mountain in order that he could save his strength for the descent into the crater. He managed to spend the best part of a day inside the crater taking temperature and air pressure measurements while having to dash out of the way of streams of lava and minor eruptions that were occurring every 10 to 15 minutes. When his guides, who refused to accompany him into the crater, finally pulled him out, he found that his thick boots had been entirely destroyed by the heat and fell to pieces when he attempted to remove them. Only Victorian England could have produced men who felt they were immortal enough to risk their lives in such endeavors.

One example of Babbage's thoroughness in his scientific work is exemplified by the work he did to determine the best way of publishing mathematical tables. In 1826 he published his own set of logarithm tables, considered the most accurate set published to that date. Not willing to content himself with simply producing a correct set of logarithms, he experimented with different typefaces in order to improve their readability and thus reduce still further the chance of errors being made. As a further experiment in improving readability, he had one page of the tables printed on 140 different tints of paper in ten different colors of ink plus a further set printed on specially prepared papers in various metallic inks, giving a total of 13 different inks on 151 different colors of paper. This experiment, which resulted in some later editions of his tables being produced using black ink on yellow paper, left nothing to chance for, besides the more obvious choices of inks and papers he even tried such combinations as black ink on black paper, red ink on red paper, yellow ink on yellow paper, and so on. These sheets were later bound into 21 volumes, the last of which consisted of gold, silver, and copper printing on vellum and various richly colored papers.

The creation of the British railway system was a project which Babbage just could not resist. Besides inventing the "cow catcher," which was a standard fixture on the front of all steam trains, he spent a full six months engaged in taking observations of the vertical and lateral movements of the different types of cars. This project, for which he invented several different types of recording devices, was instrumental in the decision to standardize on the broad track, rather than narrow gauge, system. His inventive mind can be seen once again in action when, while helping out in a different experiment, he found himself left behind when his car was decoupled from the engine. Noting that a strong breeze was blowing, he simply erected a sail and his car ". . . gradually acquiring greater velocity, finally reached and sailed across the whole of the Hanwell viaduct at a very fair pace."[4]

All these scientific pursuits did not seem to interrupt his very hectic social life. He became a well-known member of London society, and invitations to his evening parties were eagerly sought after by all members of the London elite. He in turn was invited to be a guest in most fashionable houses, and copies of his correspondence still exist to show that he often had to turn down several invitations for the same evening. His guests were always treated to displays of scientific or technical items. These were anything from pieces of his latest attempt to construct a calculating machine to fancy buttons made from metal with a diffraction grating etched into the surface. Another source of amusement for his guests was the fact that he had the first house in London to have been equipped with an air conditioning system. This system, which obtained the cool air from ice stored in the attic, was of Babbage's own design.

His social activities gradually diminished as he became older and developed a cantankerous attitude to life. He became quite famous for his dislike of street musicians and openly campaigned for their abolishment. He even went so far as to secure the Liberal Party nomination for the riding of Finsbury so that he could take his campaign to the electorate. He was, of course, not elected. In their turn, the musicians would harass Babbage at any opportunity, often gathering to play on the street outside his house. In one of his writings he mentions:

> I have very frequently been disturbed by such music after eleven and even after twelve o'clock at night. Upon one occasion a brass band played, with but a few and short intermissions, for five hours.[5]

His objections were not only to the noise generated by these people, but included the street nuisances which accompanied them. He took particular dislike to the fact that:

> [it] not unfrequently gives rise to a dance by little ragged urchins, and sometimes by half-intoxicated men, who occasionally accompany the noise with their own discordant voices. . . . Another class who are great supporters of street music consists of ladies of elastic virtue and cosmopolitan tendencies, to whom it affords a decent excuse for displaying their fascinations at their own open windows.[6]

These "ladies of elastic virtue" were also known to gather in front of the Babbage house in the hope of causing him as much embarrassment as possible. Toward the end of his life he even had to endure his neighbors inviting:

[4]Ibid., pp. 325–26.
[5]Ibid., p. 338.
[6]Ibid., p. 339.

. . . musicians, of various tastes and countries, to play before my windows . . . even with the accompaniment from the lips of little shoeless children, urged on by their ragged parents to join in a chorus rather disrespectful to their philosophic neighbor.[7]

These occurrences were by no means rare. In one case over a hundred people followed him through the streets shouting abuse.

Although not appreciated by London's lower classes, his scientific reputation was well known on both sides of the Atlantic. He was invited to spend a year lecturing in the United States and made arrangements to sail on the steamship *Arctic* in October of 1853. About a month before he was due to sail the pressure of work on his calculating machines forced him to cancel the booking. This was rather fortunate because on that trip the *Arctic* was struck by a smaller vessel off the coast of Newfoundland and sank with the loss of almost all aboard. He never again considered going to North America.

It is very difficult to consider Babbage's life without some discussion of the calculating machines he designed. Thus it is time to consider each of them in detail. Although the story of these machines (the difference engine and the analytical engine) revolves around the contributions of Charles Babbage, it is also appropriate to consider the development of these machines in toto. Thus the remainder of this section, while concentrating upon the work of Babbage, will also attempt to outline some of the background that led up to his work and the developments that followed from it.

4.2 THE NEED FOR ACCURACY[8]

The late eighteenth century saw the start of the large-scale publication of mathematical tables. These tables spanned the whole spectrum from simple addition and subtraction tables to tables of logarithms of over 20 digits. Whatever the content of the tables, two factors were always present: The tables were intended to reduce the labor of calculation, and the tables were always full of errors.

Because of the inherent difficulty of some of the calculations he might be called upon to perform, it was not uncommon to find a scientist of the time having a private library of over 125 volumes of tables of different kinds. Indeed Babbage's own large private library contained over 300 volumes of tables of one kind or another. A survey done in 1835 of one scientist's library (it is likely that the scientist was Babbage although this was never made clear) showed it to contain 140 volumes of arithmetical and trigonometrical tables alone. Of

---

[7]Ibid., p. 349.

[8]Some of the material in Sections 4.2 through 4.6 has previously appeared in an article by the author entitled, "The Difference Engines," *The Computer Journal*, vol. 19. No. 1, and is reproduced here by courtesy of the British Computer Society.

these a sample of 40 volumes was taken and found to contain over 3,700 known errors.

The task of preparing a new set of tables was of such magnitude that few were prepared to begin such a project, and even fewer to carry it through to completion. After the Revolution, the new French government decided that it would publish, primarily for prestige reasons, a new set of mathematical tables. The best French mathematicians were called upon to contribute toward this project. A Mr. Prony was set in charge and told to devise the procedure by which the tables would be produced. He used three sets of people: six of the most famous French analysts to produce the formulae used in the computation, ten qualified mathematicians who very carefully computed the required constants for the formulae, and over 100 men who actually did the arithmetic. It is interesting to note that most of Mr. Prony's workforce came from the ranks of unemployed hairdressers, the fashion for powdered wigs having died out with the Revolution! Each number was computed at least twice to ensure accuracy, the different computations being done in different parts of France to prevent collaboration between the two groups. After all this effort and care in checking the results, the tables still contained errors!

The process of calculation was not the only source of errors in the tables which managed to survive long enough to be published. A number of errors were also introduced into a table during the process of setting it into type. Babbage decided early on in his career that he would publish a truly error-free set of tables. These were finally printed in 1827 and were, in fact, the most accurate set of tables produced until that time. They were not recalculated, but were simply copied from previous publications. To ensure accuracy he had the tables checked against four different sets of tables which he knew had been independently calculated; they were then set in type and proofread three times against the aforementioned tables. As a final check they were again proofread, by a different set of people, against another previously published table. All of these precautions resulted in his finding 32 errors in the manuscript and a further eight errors after they were set in type.

The vast majority of tables were not subject to anything like as severe a check on their accuracy as Babbage's tables were. For example, one of the most famous sets of multiplication tables (Dr. Hutton's tables of 1781) contained all the products of A times B ($0 <= A <= 100$, $0 <= B <= 1000$) and was found to have 40 errors on just one page. Similarly the first edition of the *Nautical Ephemeris for Finding Latitude and Longitude at Sea* was found, by one seaman, to contain over 1000 errors.

The ordinary process of checking different sets of tables for the same value, to eliminate errors, was not without hazards. In 1825, for example, it was found that there were six common errors in apparently *independent* sets of logarithm tables. A further check showed these same errors present in over 20 different sets of tables which had been published in Britain, France, Germany, Italy, Holland, and, remarkably enough, China.

The mathematicians of the late eighteenth century were well aware of the fallibility of their tables, and several studies had the purpose of finding a method to remedy the situation. The technique most often used was simply to publish a table of errata, which, however, was not always successful because some of the errata were known to contain a higher percentage of errors than the original tables! The only foolproof method of cutting out the inaccuracies arising during the process of computation would be to eliminate humans from the process by substituting a mechanical device to perform the arithmetic.

4.3 THE METHOD OF DIFFERENCES

The method of differences, although once the main tool of all table makers, has now fallen into disuse. The method was used to eliminate the difficult operations of multiplication and division, replacing them with simple addition, when constructing tables of polynomial function values. If a function, such as $F(x) = 2x + 3$ is evaluated for successive values of x, and then the differences noted between each adjacent value of $F(x)$, one finds:

$$x = 1 \quad 2 \quad 3 \quad 4 \quad 5 \quad 6 \quad 7 \quad 8 \quad 9 \ldots$$
$$F(x) = 5 \quad 7 \quad 9 \quad 11 \quad 13 \quad 15 \quad 17 \quad 19 \quad 21 \ldots$$
$$\text{differences} = \quad 2 \quad 2 \quad 2 \quad 2 \quad 2 \quad 2 \quad 2 \quad 2 \ldots$$

If the function were slightly more complex, say $F(x) = x^2 + 2x + 3$, then it would have been necessary to obtain the differences of the differences (or second differences) before a constant value was found. For example:

$$x = 1 \quad 2 \quad 3 \quad 4 \quad 5 \quad 6 \quad 7 \quad 8 \quad 9 \quad \ldots$$
$$F(x) = 6 \quad 11 \quad 18 \quad 27 \quad 38 \quad 51 \quad 66 \quad 83 \quad 102 \ldots$$
$$\text{First differences} = \quad 5 \quad 7 \quad 9 \quad 11 \quad 13 \quad 15 \quad 17 \quad 19 \ldots$$
$$\text{Second differences} = \quad 2 \quad 2 \quad 2 \quad 2 \quad 2 \quad 2 \quad 2 \ldots$$

In general, if the polynomial to be evaluated had a term of x^n, then it would require the nth differences to be taken before a constant difference would be obtained. If one has to evaluate a polynomial for many values of x, such as when computing tables, it is easier to do it by adding the constant difference to the difference above, then adding that difference to the one above it, and so on, until the value of the function is reached. This results in a procedure in which only additions are performed rather than the many multiplications which would be required if the function itself were to be evaluated for each value of x.

Although all polynomials have a constant difference, functions such as logarithms and the trigonometric functions do not, in general, have this property. Thus in order to take advantage of the method of differences when producing tables of these functions, it is necessary to approximate the function with a polynomial and then actually evaluate this polynomial.

A difference engine is simply a machine which is capable of both storing a series of numbers and performing additions with them. The numbers will represent the function value, its first difference, second difference, third difference, and so on. By causing the machine to add the lower differences to the upper ones and finally to the function value, it is possible to generate successive values of the function. The first reference to such a device appears in a book published by Mr. E. Klipstein in Frankfurt in 1786. The title of this work translates as *Description of a Newly Invented Calculating Machine,* and it actually was a description of how to use a mechanical calculating machine that had just been invented by J. H. Muller, a Captain of Engineers in the Hessian Army. The book contains a small appendix in which Muller describes a much more ambitious calculating machine which he could construct if only someone would provide the finances. This machine was to be a difference engine operating from a constant third difference. The device was designed to print out its results on a piece of paper placed under the machine. Muller figured that it was capable of one addition per second and that a table of the cubes of the integers from 1 to 100,000 could be produced by "a common laborer" in about 10.5 days. Although it appears that his plea for financial aid was never answered, Muller certainly deserves recognition as the person who first published the basic suggestion of a machine designed to implement the method of differences.

4.4 BABBAGE'S DIFFERENCE ENGINE

Charles Babbage, as has been previously noted, had a passion for accuracy. He was continually being distressed by the errors he found in the mathematical tables available in his lifetime. His passion for accuracy spilled over into most other aspects of his life, and he was able to combine it with his great inventive genius to produce a number of worthwhile inventions. One of these was, of course, a difference engine.

In his book, *Passages from the Life of a Philosopher,* he states that the idea of a difference engine came to him, while still a student at Cambridge, in 1812 or 1813 when

> One evening I was sitting in the rooms of the Analytical Society, at Cambridge, my head leaning forward on the table in a kind of dreamy mood, with a table of logarithms laying open before me. Another member, coming into the room, and seeing me half asleep, called out, "Well Babbage, what are you dreaming about?" to which I replied, "I am thinking that all these tables (pointing to the logarithms) might be calculated by machinery."[9]

[9]Babbage, *Passages,* p. 42.

It is almost certain that Babbage had no knowledge of Muller's proposal for a difference engine made slightly more than a quarter of a century previously. Other matters pressed upon Babbage and he put aside the idea of calculating tables by machinery for a few years.

In the early 1820s, spurred by his experience at publishing his tables of logarithms, he again took up the challenge of attempting to design a working machine to both compute and print a set of mathematical tables. The mechanism had to be able to set the type for the printing of the tables for, as Babbage had found to his cost, it was possible to introduce many errors in going from the manuscript to the final galleys of print. Being of moderate independent means, he was able to devote full time to this exercise and, by 1822, was in a position to show a working model of a difference engine to his friends. He had constructed a machine which was capable of working with six-figure numbers and capable of evaluating any function having a constant second difference.

Babbage wrote to Sir Humphrey Davy, president of the Royal Society, on July 3, 1822, and described the machine as "producing figures at the rate of 44 per minute, and performing with rapidity and precision all those calculations for which it was designed."[10] The main purpose of this letter was to seek the aid of the Royal Society in a petition to the government for financial aid in the construction of a full-scale difference engine.

The Royal Society was asked by the government to look into the project and so appointed 12 of its members to prepare a report. By May of 1823 they were able to send a letter to the Lords of the Treasury stating that "they consider Mr. Babbage as highly deserving of public encouragement in the prosecution of his arduous undertakings."[11] This report was not entirely unanimous; a certain Dr. Young was of the opinion that any money given to Babbage would be better used by investing it and using the dividends to pay human calculators.

By July of 1823 the Chancellor of the Exchequer agreed to advance 1,500 pounds (about $7,500 at the 1823 rate of exchange) for the project, and Babbage agreed to put up between 3,000 and 5,000 pounds out of his own private fortune. This was not a stroke of generosity on his part but rather his contribution to what he thought would be the total cost of the detailed design and construction of the machine. He assumed the government would reimburse him upon completion of the project. It was thought that the machine would be ready for practical use in two to three years.

Babbage quickly found out that it was one thing to make a few model parts in a basement workshop in order to demonstrate his ideas, and quite another to make machinery sufficiently advanced to execute the many highly complex movements required of his full design. He set about to examine all the major

---

[10]C. R. Weld, *History of the Royal Society* (Cambridge: Cambridge University Press, 1848), pp. 370–71.

[11]Ibid., p. 372.

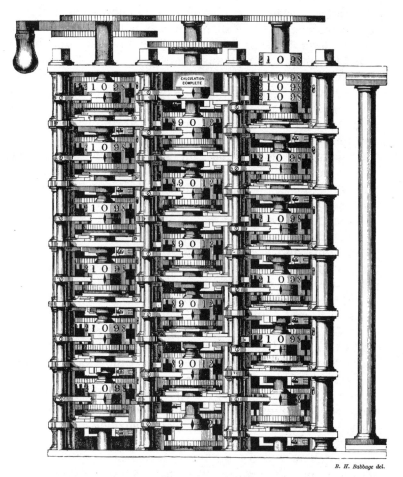

B. H. Babbage del.

Impression from a woodcut of a small portion of Mr. Babbage's Difference
Engine, No. 1, the property of Government, at present deposited in the
Museum of King's College, Somerset House.

It was commenced 1823.
This portion put together 1833.
The construction abandoned 1842.
This plate was printed, June, 1853.

Figure 4–2.   A woodcut illustration of Babbage's first Difference Engine, 1833.

manufacturing workshops and came to the conclusion that, before he could
attempt to construct a difference engine, he had to spend some of his resources
in attempting to advance the art of construction itself. During the next few
years he would carefully design each part, and then design and construct the
tools for making this part. The twofold operation would, as often as not, suggest
alternate and often simpler mechanisms for either the object or the tools needed

to create it, and the whole process would be repeated for this new version. By this process Babbage managed to advance the toolmaking trade faster than it had ever been known to move before. The training he gave to the men working for him was in time disseminated throughout other British workshops and, even though Babbage never managed to complete his full design, the money advanced by the British government was well repaid by the advancement in the art of mechanical toolmaking.

The constant effort of design, toolmaking, and redesign soon took its toll. In October of 1827 (four years after starting the construction) Babbage's health broke down. His doctors advised him to go to a warmer climate to recover, so he moved to Italy for a time. While there, he had a chance to go over his accounts and discovered that he had spent 3,475 pounds. He therefore set about petitioning the government to recover the 1,975 pounds that he had put out of his own pocket. Unfortunately the Chancellor of the Exchequer had forgotton about his verbal agreement to refund the money that Babbage had spent, and it required the intervention of several of his influential friends to get the government to act. After requesting the Royal Society to make another report on the progress of the difference engine, and receiving one which highly praised all Babbage's efforts, the Chancellor of the Exchequer agreed to advance a further 1,500 pounds. A further appeal by some of Babbage's friends to the Duke of Wellington (then Prime Minister) resulted in an additional 3,000 pounds and the suggestion that Babbage show evidence of his progress.

These financial troubles were a constant source of concern to Babbage. He was always very scrupulous in all his dealings, getting all his accounts audited by the committee of the Royal Society before presenting them to the government. Unfortunately this procedure introduced long delays between the expenditure for materials and the release of money from the Treasury. He managed to keep the project moving by spending his own money and then attempting to claim it back. There were, however, several work stoppages due to lack of personal funds and long debates by government ministers on the future of the project. During these enforced periods of idleness, some of which lasted up to four years, he had to let most of his engineering staff go and then, when more money was forthcoming, hire and train new personnel.

It was during one of these breaks in production that Mr. Clement, who was the chief mechanic for Babbage and had been kept on through thick and thin, made some demands concerning the working conditions in a new fireproof building which had been constructed to house the partially completed engine. Babbage refused to agree to Mr. Clement's demands and the two men broke off their association. This was particularly unfortunate because, under British law, mechanics possess the right of property to all tools they have constructed, even if the cost of their construction has been paid by their employers. Mr. Clement exercised his right and removed all the tools Babbage had designed to help in the construction of his dream. He also removed, but later returned, all the mechanical engineering drawings Babbage had made. In fairness to Mr. Clement, he did attempt to come to some settlement, but Babbage refused to have any further dealings with him, even if it meant losing all his tools.

It was during the absence of all his engineering drawings that Babbage, while attempting yet another modification of the design, conceived the idea of his famous analytical engine. He realized at once that, if he was ever to construct such a machine, it would require a much more sophisticated arithmetic mechanism than that present in the design for the difference engine. Accordingly he set about further experimentation with mechanical adding devices. After designing and testing over 20 different mechanisms, he produced one which he thought could not be improved. He informed the government that, in his opinion, it would take less time and money to construct a new difference engine to his improved design than it would to finish the old one.

The news of yet another redesign was not received warmly. Rather than come to an immediate decision on the future of the difference engine, the ministers asked Babbage to wait for their further deliberations. During these deliberations a general election was called, the government lost its majority, and Babbage had to start all over again in dealing with a new group of ministers. After further delays, this time lasting a total of nine years, an appeal was made to the Prime Minister to decide one way or the other. As a result of this appeal Babbage received a letter on November 3, 1842, informing him that Sir Robert Peel had decided to abandon all government support but offering to let Babbage keep all the drawings, tools, and parts of the machine which then existed. However, honoring his original agreement of over 20 years ago, he reminded the government that the machine was their property and that they should be responsible for its future. The partially completed machine and its drawings were then given to the Museum of King's College, London, where they remained for another 20 years, after which they were removed to the South Kensington Science Museum where parts of them are now on display.

After a final accounting, it was determined that the project had cost the British taxpayer a total of 17,000 pounds (about $84,000 at the 1842 exchange rates) while Babbage had contributed a further 20,000 pounds (about $100,000 in 1842) from his own resources.

Although Babbage's descriptions of the machine are difficult to follow, a popular description was written by Dr. Dionysius Lardner which indicates, in general terms, how the machine would have looked and its mode of operation. The entire mechanism would have been about 10 ft high, 10 ft wide, and 5 ft deep. It was to be composed of seven vertical steel axles, each of which would carry 18 brass wheels about 5 in. in diameter. Each vertical axle would represent one of the six orders or differences while the seventh axle would store the value of the function being computed. These values were represented on the axles by the positions of the 18 brass wheels. Each wheel was engraved with the digits from 0 to 9 around its circumference and thus, by simply turning the wheels so that they displayed their various digits, any 18-digit number could be represented on each vertical axle. The units digit was to be stored on the lowest wheel, the tens on the next, and so on. Babbage decided on this vertical arrangement of the numbers because the friction generated by the gears and wheels was less than it would have been for a horizontal arrangement of the numbers.

Behind the first set of vertical axles, which contained, besides the number wheels, the mechanism for dealing with a carry from one digit to the next, was a second set of vertical axles supporting the mechanism which could perform the addition of numbers from one column to the next. Behind these were yet another set of seven axles which served to engage and disengage the adding mechanism, as and when required.

The engine was to operate in four distinct cycles, each one corresponding to a quarter turn of the drive wheel. The first cycle caused the numbers represented by the first, third, and fifth difference axles to be added to the numbers stored on the result, second, and fourth difference axles, respectively. The second cycle took care of any carries which may have resulted from the first cycle additions. The third cycle caused the addition of the second, fourth, and sixth differences to the first, third, and fifth while the last cycle again took care of any carries generated.

The system was designed with several fail-safe devices to protect the machine and to stop it from generating errors. If one of the wheels got slightly out of place, it was forced back into its exact position by a system of springs and pins. If the malfunction was severe enough to prevent this automatic readjustment, then the machine would simply lock up and prevent any further computations from taking place until after the difficulty had been found and corrected.

There were a number of ingenious additions to the basic system which would allow the computation of tables which did not have a constant difference. For example, to calculate a table of logarithms, it was necessary to approximate the logarithm function by a polynomial, evaluate this polynomial for about 100 values, then determine a new polynomial for the next portion of the table. The mechanism could be set so that, after a predetermined number of calculations, a bell would ring to inform the operator that it was time to reset the difference wheels for the new polynomial. There were also several adjustments which would enable the device to add any difference, any number of times, to a difference of any other order. This enabled computations of tables which did not have a constant difference but whose fourth difference, say, was some form of geometric series, or tables of astronomical data which fitted observed phenomena but whose analytic solution was not known. A series of comparison units were attached to each axle which would be able to detect when any column contained a specific value. These would then cause an automatic change (positive or negative) in the constant, sixth, difference wheels, or ring a bell informing the operator that it was time to make the change.

Another remarkable property of the machine was that it could be used to compute the rational roots of certain functions. These functions were subjected to transformations to ensure that the roots were all integers; then the engine was set to produce a table of values for this transformed function. When the function had imaginary roots, its value at the root would cause the first difference to be zero. The ringing of the first difference bell would warn the operator that it was time to stop computing, and the pair of imaginary roots could be found by inspecting the other axles.

Although 18-digit numbers were sufficient for most computations, Babbage foresaw that there could be troubles with accumulating round-off errors. Consequently he made sure that the addition mechanism would correctly round off the eighteenth digit whenever necessary. There was also an adjustment which would allow two columns to act in unison to enable numbers up to 30 digits to be used when required. This latter adjustment would, of course, reduce the machine to operating on a constant third difference.

The printing mechanism was to consist of a series of camlike devices attached to the wheels representing the final result. These acted against levers, each of which was raised to one of ten different positions corresponding to the digits 0 to 9. The other end of each lever moved an arm containing ten steel punches, one for each digit, which were to be driven into a copper or lead plate to leave an impression which could then be used to cast a sterotyped plate for the printing presses. The copper or lead plate was automatically shifted up one place with each turn of the drive wheel.

In 1849, while working on the plans for his analytical engine, Babbage took time off to draw up a complete set of plans for his new improved difference engine. These plans were the most complex set of mechanical drawings that had ever been produced up to that time, covering over 1000 square feet of paper. He presented the plans to the government in the hope that they might one day decide to have it constructed. The Chancellor of the Exchequer, however, described the plan as "indefinitely expensive, the success problematical, and the expenditure incapable of being calculated."[12]

Thus the difference engine was put to rest. It is an irony of history that only a few years were to elapse before the British government was to finance the construction of a difference engine designed in Sweden.

4.5 THE SCHEUTZ DIFFERENCE ENGINE

As mentioned earlier, Dr. Dionysius Lardner wrote a popular article for the *Edinburgh Review* describing Charles Babbage's attempt to construct a difference engine. A Swede, George Scheutz, who, as editor of a Stockholm technical journal, made it his business to keep informed on such matters, saw at once

[12]Charles Babbage, *Passages From the Life of a Philosopher* (London: Longman, Green & Co., 1864), p. 108.

that the machine Dr. Lardner described would be a great help to virtually every branch of science. Dr. Lardner's article was designed to be read by the general public and was therefore only a general description of what a difference engine would do, and not how it was designed. Scheutz was fascinated by the concept and rather than writing to Babbage for details of the construction, set out to design one for himself.

He started out by designing the basic components of a machine and then constructed several models in wood, pasteboard, and wire. After verifying that his design was practical, he was forced, through pressure of work, to set aside the construction of a proper machine. In the summer of 1837 his son Edvard returned from the Royal Technological Institute where he was an engineering student. Having been inspired by his father, Edvard set about the construction of a working machine from metal. Toward the end of October the Scheutzes were in a position to see that the construction of a fully working model was beyond their financial means. Accordingly they made application to the Swedish government for a grant to aid them in their work, but, perhaps because of the British experience in these matters, they were refused.

The Scheutzes continued to spend what time and money they could afford and, by 1840, had completed a small machine which operated from only the first difference, with each of the two registers capable of holding a five-digit number. By 1842 they had extended it to a machine capable of dealing with three orders of difference. Finally, in 1843, the printing device was attached and the whole mechanism was submitted to the Royal Swedish Academy of Science for its approval.

Although the machine was well received by the Academy, and a certificate issued by them recommending the device, no orders were forthcoming for a complete machine. This preliminary model was put aside and remained a conversation piece for the next seven years.

In 1851 George Scheutz, encouraged by friends, again asked his government for a grant to enable the full machine to be constructed. The Swedish minister, again following the British example, referred the request to the Swedish Royal Academy which produced a very favorable report and the suggestion that money be made available. However, the government again decided that no public funds were available for the project. Later that same year a member of the Diet (the Swedish Parliament) put forward a motion which would supply the Scheutz team with a grant, but only after His Majesty the King had, on due examination, given it as his opinion that the machine was complete and answered its purpose. The inventors now tried to obtain the money in advance and, toward the end of 1851, the government relented and advanced the money on the condition that a number of the Scheutz family's friends guarantee to return it if the machine was not finished to the King's satisfaction before the end of 1853.

The difference engine (actually called a tabulating machine by the Scheutzes) was complete in October 1853. It differed slightly from the initial model. Various improvements were incorporated to enable it to do computations in the sexagesimal as well as the decimal scale. These changes, which were to prove valuable in calculating hour- and angle-related tables, were set up in working drawings by Edvard Scheutz, and the final machine was constructed by the engineering firm of Bergstrom in Stockholm. In a spirit of generosity not often found in the public domain, the Royal Academy suggested to the King that, as expenses had been heavy, a second grant, equal to the first, should be awarded. His Majesty agreed and, by 1854, the Scheutzes had produced the world's first fully operable nontrivial difference engine—and had been partially compensated for their expenditure by the government's princely grant of the equivalent of 560 pounds (about $2,800 in 1854).

Back in London, an engineer named Brian Donkin came to hear of the progress being made in Sweden. Mr. Donkin had a long association with Babbage and his ordeal. In fact, he had been on both the committees of the Royal Society which judged Babbage's progress and had been one of the three members of the Royal Society who audited all of Babbage's accounts. In 1854 Mr. Donkin was instrumental in having the Swedish machine shipped to London and bringing it to the notice of the Royal Society. Babbage, after inspecting it, gave his unreserved praise to both the machine and its inventors. The Scheutzes in return never concealed their admiration of Babbage for his original idea of a difference machine.

Figure 4–3.   The Scheutz Difference Engine.

No. 2. $u = x^4 - 6x^3 + 11x^2 - 6x$		No. 3. $u = x^4 - 72x^3 + 1798x^2 - 18072x$	
x	u	x	u
0	0	0	0
1	0	1	16345
2	0	2	29512
3	0	3	39897
4	24	4	47872
5	120	5	53785
6	360	6	57960
7	840	7	60697
8	1680	8	62272
9	3024	9	62937
10	5040	10	62920
11	7920	11	62425
12	11880	12	61632
13	17160	13	60697
14	24024	14	59752
15	32760	15	58905
16	43680	16	58240
17	57120	17	57817
18	73440	18	57672
19	93024	19	57817
20	116280	20	58240
21	143640	21	58905
22	175560	22	59752
23	212520	23	60697
24	255024	24	61632
25	303600	25	62425
26	358800	26	62920
27	421200	27	62937
28	491400	28	62272
29	570024	29	60697
30	657720	30	57960
31	755160	31	53785
32	863040	32	47872
33	982080	33	39897
34	1113024	34	29512
35	1256640	35	16345
36	1413720	36	00000
37	1585080		
38	1771560		
39	1974024		
40	2193360		
41	2430480		
42	2686320		
43	2961840		
44	3258024		
45	3575880		
46	3916440		
47	4280760		
48	4669920		
49	5085024		
50	5527200		

Figure 4–4.   A sample table as computed by the Scheutz Difference Engine.

After residing in London for almost a year, showing the machine to the scientific community and hoping to find a buyer for it, the Scheutzes shipped it to Paris to be exhibited in the Great Exhibition then being held. The jury, composed of men from all over Europe, unanimously awarded it the Exhibition's Gold Medal. This award brought it to the attention of Professor B. A. Gould of the Dudley Observatory in Albany, New York. He, in turn, managed to convince a local philanthropist to purchase the device for $5,000 and present it to the Observatory. After serving a semi-useful life in the Observatory, it was sold to a Dr. Dorr E. Felt, the inventor of the comptometer, for his private collection of calculating devices. The Swedish Difference Engine Number 1, as it is officially called, now finds a home in a Chicago museum.

The general organization of the components was similar to that envisaged by Babbage. It was constructed so that each register could contain a 15-digit number. These were represented by a series of 15 circular silvered brass rings aligned in a horizontal row. There were five rows of rings, four for the four orders of differences and one for the final result. The entire mechanism was mounted on 15 vertical steel axles. The most interesting aspect of the construction was that the figure rings were not actually attached to the steel axles, rather they simply sat on small platforms with the axles running through them. This method of construction did away with the need for special devices to stop the figure rings from rotating too far, and the friction between the ring and its supporting platform stopped any excess rotation.

Figure 4–5 shows a model made by the Scheutzes to demonstrate the workings of their machine. The steel axle (marked A) and the platforms (marked B) upon which the numbered rings (marked C) rest are all easily seen. A bit of imagination will reveal that the rings (C) were turned by the trigger pieces (D), which came into gear with the cogs (E) whenever the revolving shaft brought the tailpiece (F) of the trigger (D) in contact with the rising piece (G) on the ring. The circular ring (C) had a projection which, when a carry was generated by the ring turning from 9 to 0, contacted the lever (H) which set up the mechanism so that the next set of rings would be moved one place.

The printing mechanism was identical to Babbage's, both of them having been modeled on the mechanism used to control the striking of the hours in chiming clocks. It was positioned at the top and slightly behind the main calculating part of the engine. Although the machine was capable of computing with 15-figure numbers, the typesetting mechanism would round off each number to eight figures before creating the mold from which the type was cast. The principle employed by Babbage of first adding the even orders of difference to the odd, then vice versa, was repeated in the Scheutz design.

When being worked by an experienced operator, the Scheutz machine could generate 120 lines of a table per hour. In one experiment it generated logarithms of the numbers from 1 to 10,000 in just under 80 hours, including the time taken to reset the differences for the 20 different approximating polynomials used.

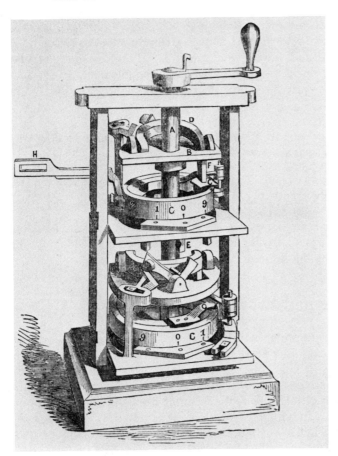

Figure 4–5. The register mechanism of the Scheutz Difference Engine.

In the middle 1850s the British Register General, the man responsible for the collection and publication of vital statistics, decided that it was time to produce a new set of tables for the insurance industry. It was found that the required tables could, for the most part, be easily approximated by polynomials. This naturally led to the decision to use a difference engine in the calculations. The Register General arranged for the British government to put up 1,200 pounds (about $6,000 in those days) toward the cost of constructing a calculating machine. He had the support of the Astronomer Royal in this application, no doubt because the Astronomer Royal wished to have access to the same type of facilities as were available at the Dudley Observatory. Mr. Donkin's engineering firm agreed to the price of 1,200 pounds for constructing a second difference engine according to the Scheutz design.

This Swedish Difference Engine Number 2 was, in most respects, identical to the previous one. It consisted of just over 4,000 separate pieces (only about 1000 pieces were actually used in the mechanism, the rest being nuts, bolts, screws, and links in the drive chain), and weighed about 1000 pounds. Of all the early difference engines, this one was given the most use. During its working life it computed and stereotyped over 600 different kinds of tables. Although it undoubtedly eased the production of these tables, it was not without its faults. As Mr. W. Farr, the editor of the resultant *English Life Tables*, noted:

> The machine required incessant attention. The differences had to be inserted at the proper terms of the various series, checking was required, and when the mechanism got out of order it had to be set right. . . . [I]ts work had to be watched with anxiety, and its arithmetical music had to be elicited by frequent tuning and skillful handling, in the quiet most congenial to such productions.[13]

This second Swedish engine was eventually given to the South Kensington Science Musuem where it joins Babbage's early models in a display of nineteenth-century calculating equipment.

4.6 OTHER ATTEMPTS AT DIFFERENCE ENGINES

There were many other attempts, both professional and private, to construct difference engines. For example, a Mr. Alfred Decon of London was inspired by Lardner's description of Babbage's work in exactly the same way Scheutz had been. Mr. Decon managed to construct a small model, now lost, capable of storing three orders of differences with the numbers being kept to 20 digits. Because the machine was intended simply as a model, he did not incorporate any form of printing mechanism. He built the device entirely for his own satisfaction and, as far as can be deduced, it was only shown to a few friends. It is entirely possible that this model was later given to, or purchased by, Charles Babbage, because he indicates he owned such a model but does not give enough details to firmly fix it às being the Decon machine.

Another Swede, Martin Wiberg, redesigned the Scheutz machine and, in so doing, managed to reduce its size and weight. His device was first used to publish a set of interest tables in 1860. He was not happy with the style of these tables and spent the next two years redesigning the print mechanism. In 1875 he published a set of tables of seven-place logarithms of the numbers from 1 to 100,000 together with logarithms of trigonometric functions, all produced on his difference engine. Wiberg's machine eventually ended its days in the possession of the Academy of Sciences in Paris.

Mr. G. B. Grant, who eventually became the founder of the American gear-cutting industry, was engaged in the late 1860s in computing a series of tables

---

[13]W. Farr, *Tables of Lifetimes, Annuities and Premiums* (London: H. M. Stationery Office, 1864), preface.

for "cut and fill" problems when he first thought of the possibilities of a machine to do the same job. He had, at that time, not heard of any of the previous attempts and, after experimenting for a short time, gave up the idea. Grant, who was a student at the time, was encouraged by his professors and, with the help of Mr. J. N. Bachelder, who was in charge of the Scheutz machine at the Dudley Observatory, was able to design and build a small model. Grant's professors managed to arrange for a sum of $10,000.00 to be used in building a full-scale machine which, when completed, was to be given to the University of Pennsylvania. This machine, which weighed over a ton, stood 5 ft high by 8 ft long, and contained 15,000 parts, was displayed at the Philadelphia Centennial Exhibition of 1876. It drew praises from the Exhibition's judges as being the finest machine of its kind. A machine to Grant's design was sold to The Provident Mutual Life Insurance Company where it was used to produce tables similar to those computed by the Office of the Registrar General in Britain. Grant's original machine was given to the Smithsonian Institute, but now appears to have been lost.

The only other large-scale design was proposed by the French mechanical genius, Leon Bollee. Bollee's youth was highlighted when, at the age of 18 (in 1887), he designed and built the first machine which could directly multiply two numbers together, rather than arriving at the product by repeated addition. Bollee later turned his attention to the developing automobile industry. After his untimely death, however, there were discovered among his papers the complete plans for a difference engine capable of operating to 27 orders of difference, by far the most extensive machine of its type ever envisaged.

Although Grant's was the last "large" difference engine actually constructed, the technique did not die out. Several other individuals and teams in different countries constructed small difference engines in order to prepare various types of tables. The next major step, however, had to wait until the period between the First and Second World Wars. During this time the manufacturing techniques had been perfected to the point where many different kinds of desktop calculating machines were available on the open market. It did not take long for scientists to realize that these machines, with slight modifications, could become the modern version of Babbage's engine. In 1931 Dr. L. J. Comrie, then superintendent of His Majesty's Nautical Almanac Office, recognized that the National Accounting Machine (produced by the National Cash Register Co.) would provide an ideal basis on which to construct a new difference engine.

The basic National device consisted of an adding machine with a 12-column keyboard and six separate registers designed for accumulating subtotals. The features which made the machine so valuable were that (1) any number set on the keyboard could be entered into any of the six registers, (2) numbers already stored in the registers could be transferred to any of the others, and (3) the machine would print the result of each computation. The National had a movable carriage which contacted various "tab-stops," which would activate

Figure 4–6. The National accounting machine.

or deactivate the different registers. Thus, as the carriage moved from left to right, the stops would engage the correct registers to cause the first difference to be added to the function value and the result printed; the next stop would add the second difference to the first and the result would be printed, and so forth. Comrie's description of this mechanism before the Royal Statistical Society made it clear that, almost 100 years after Babbage's failure, an efficient, inexpensive difference engine was at last available.

4.7 BABBAGE'S ANALYTICAL ENGINE

The last section dealt mainly with the idea of a difference engine and the problems that Charles Babbage had in attempting to construct such a machine. Although the difference engine is an important development in the story of computation, it was Babbage's ideas for another machine—the analytical engine—that signal a new concept in computing, namely a computing machine being directed by an external program.

If you recall from the last section, Babbage was hard at work attempting to construct his difference engine when lack of money forced him to break off the project until further government grants could be obtained. It was during this time, and after a disagreement about working conditions, that Mr. Clement, Babbage's chief mechanic, resigned and made some demands concerning the uncomfortable working conditions in a new building that had been constructed to house the workshops. Babbage refused to agree to Clement's demands and the two men broke off their association. Mr. Clement exercised his rights and removed all of Babbage's tools as well as all the engineering drawings Babbage had produced.

Babbage may have been prevented from doing any further actual construction on his difference engine, but he used this opportunity to rethink the entire system. In attempting to determine how he could add more flexibility to his design, he conceived of the possibility that the digits on the result wheels might somehow be fed back into the last order of differences. This strange arrangement would allow for the automatic calculation of tables whose functions had no elementary analytical solution. In order to implement this change in control structure, the machine had to be redesigned so that the mechanical registers were arranged in a circular shape.

The more he played with this new circular design concept, the more he began to realize that the mechanical registers were really all identical. Rather than being limited to simply adding a quantity to their immediate neighbor, they could be thought of as a storehouse of numbers. Furthermore, these numbers could be passed from one register to another with arithmetic processes going on between any two of them.

These new ideas for a calculating machine appear to have arisen about late 1834 for, in May of 1835, Babbage wrote a letter to a Mr. Quetelet in which he said that he had

> . . . for six months been engaged in making the drawings of a new calculating engine of far greater power than the first. I am myself astonished at the power I have been enabled to give to this machine; a year ago I should not have believed this result possible.[14]

Babbage continued to design new, and redesign older, components of this new machine, yet no large component was actually constructed. Instead Babbage preferred simply to develop his concept of the Analytical Engine as an

[14]Weld, *Royal Society*, p. 386.

academic exercise, while still keeping in mind the practical difficulties of actually constructing his device. Many detailed plans give evidence of his concern that some particular component could be produced without undue difficulty.

The constant changes in design, some of which continued to be made right up to the end of his life, make it very difficult to describe the eventual detailed form of his analytical engine. However, by about 1840 the design had progressed to the point where the major components were fixed and only minor changes were introduced from that point on. If we take the design as it existed at that time, it can best be described by reference to one of Babbage's own diagrams, an overhead view of the analytical engine design as it was in 1840.

This diagram is a view of his machine from above, each circle representing one column of gears and wheels which would hold a number in much the same way as was earlier described for the difference engine. This diagram shows over 200 individual columns of gear trains and number wheels, but a lot them were used only for detailed control mechanisms and can be ignored when attempting to understand the basic concept of the machine. The machine can be thought of in three basic sections, "the store," "the mill," and the "control barrel." The store is the equivalent of our modern memory; the mill cor-

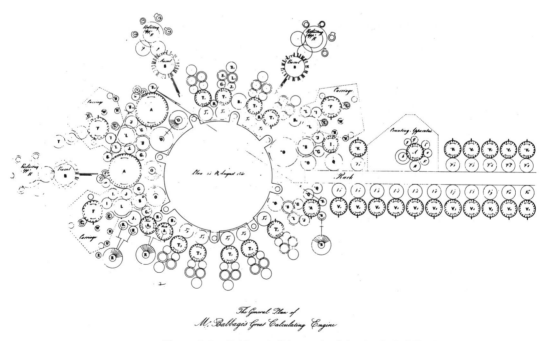

Figure 4–7. Babbage's lithograph of the Analytical Engine.

responds to the arithmetic unit, and the control barrel is a primitive micro-program control unit.

The store was simply a modified version of the individual registers from his difference engine. Each column of mechanical registers (labeled V in the drawing) could store a number by means of a series of gears, each of which could rotate to ten different positions to store the individual digits of the number. This diagram shows a store with 16 register columns (each of which could store two numbers), but the design was open-ended in that additional columns of registers could be easily incorporated into the design. It appears, from some of his other writings, that Babbage actually intended his machine to have 50 register columns, which would give his memory a total capacity of 100 numbers, each of 40 decimal digits. In another source, however, he comments about the design of his machine having 1,000 variables, each of 50 decimal digits. The numbers could be passed to and from the mill by means of a simple gear rack, represented by the long parallel lines extending to the right in the diagram.

The mill consisted of a very complex arrangement of gears and linkages, all distributed around a central circle. In its most elementary form it consisted of two major accumulators (marked A and 'A) and the associated gearing to perform carry operations from one digit to the next. A third accumulator (marked "A) is located just below where the rack joins the mill. It was designed to help with the housekeeping jobs that were necessary during operations such as multiplication and division. The nine smaller "table axes" (marked T1, T2, ..., T9), clustered around the central mill gears, were for use in multiplication and division operations. When the machine was to do a multiplication of x times y, the nine single-digit multiples of x (x, $2x$, $3x$,...,$9x$) were stored on the nine table axes, and then these partial products were added to the result register as required by the digits in y. During multiplication the two main accumulators could be linked together to act as one double-length register to hold the product. Division was performed in an analogous way.

The control barrels (marked B) were very much like large, robust music box barrels but, instead of storing a tune, their studs were the basic microlevel machine instructions. The barrels were able to move back and forth, and their studs would push on different sets of control rods (in the part of the machine marked "Reducing Appr") to engage or disengage the levers and gear trains that were necessary to implement different instruction steps. Each of the three control barrels was capable of not only containing sets of studs to control different gear trains, but also of being coded to automatically rotate to a new position to implement subsequent microsteps in the instruction. Thus the control barrels approximated our own idea of a machine microcode in which each microinstruction contains both the basic machine operations to be performed and the address of where the next microinstruction is to be found.

The last major structure contained in the diagram (marked "Counting Apparatus") was a simple counter register, like the ones in the difference engine, which could be used to count the number of times a particular operation had been performed. The intention was to use this counter in much the same way that loop counters are used in modern computer languages.

Babbage indicates that the basic cycle time of the analytical engine was dependent on the type of operation that was being done. It would, for example, take about 2.5 seconds to transfer a number from the store to one of the registers in the mill, while an addition to a number already in the mill would require about 3 seconds. The extra time for the addition was to allow any carries to be propagated from one digit to the next in the register. Although rather slow by modern standards, these times would have resulted in a huge increase in computational ability in Babbage's day. Even just over one hundred years later, when Howard Aiken constructed the modern mechanical machine known as the Harvard Mark I (see Chapter 6, "The Mechanical Monsters"), addition times were still about 0.3 of a second. A later modification to the analytical engine design called for the individual registers to hold 50 digits each and the machine speed to be increased to the point where additions and subtractions could be done in one second while multiplications and divisions would take about one minute each.

One of the most important, and difficult, parts of the analytical engine is the mechanism for dealing with the problem of a carry which is generated when adding one number to another. For example, 9 + 1 will result in a zero in the units place and a carry of one to the tens place in the result register. These elementary carry mechanisms had been solved by Babbage in some of his early design efforts, but the more complex problem of "ripple" carries (e.g., 99999 + 1) still required the machine to take one addition cycle for each digit that the carry had to ripple through. He solved this problem with what he called an "anticipating carriage." This mechanism would sense when any digit was storing a 9 and, should a carry be generated further down in the register, it could be passed through the register to the next non-9 digit.

The anticipating carriage was developed using the idea of "chain" which Babbage used not only in this mechanism, but also in other parts of the control equipment of the analytical engine. "Chain" can best be thought of as a long rod, made up of many independent segments, which is capable of being moved by a force exerted at one end. As long as all the segments are in place, the force will push one segment against the next and the whole rod will move.

If, however, you remove a segment from the middle of the rod, then when you push on the left-hand end, only the leftmost portion of the rod will move

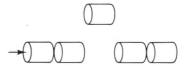

Figure 4–8. A drawing of Babbage's idea of "chain."

because the missing segment isolates the right-hand part of the rod from the motive force. If each of the rod segments can be moved in or out of alignment by some action of the machine, what you end up with is, in effect, a large AND gate where the force applied to one end of the rod is transmitted to the other end if, and only if, all the segments happen to be in alignment. It takes a fair amount of skill in visualizing mechanical apparatus to see exactly how "chain" was used to implement the anticipating carriage mechanism, but the underlying principle can be shown more easily by illustrating the electrical analogue of Babbage's mechanical apparatus.

If, in Figure 4–9, the boxes each represent a single digit of a number being stored in an accumulator then, whenever an addition to this number is done, some digits may advance from 9 to 0 and generate a carry which must be propagated to the next higher digit. If any digit did generate a carry, the three-position switch associated with that digit would be moved so that it made contact at point A. If any digit was currently storing a 9, and thus any carry coming into it should cause the counter to advance to 0 and the carry to be passed on to the next higher digit, the switch was set to make contact at position B. When the addition was finished, a single pulse along the top "carry" wire will cause all appropriate carries to happen at one time, regardless of how long any ripple carries may be. Babbage, of course, did not use such electrical devices, but circuits similar to this were incorporated in the early electrical accounting machines manufactured by Herman Hollerith. Anyone wishing a detailed account of the actual mechanical workings of the anticipating carriage should consult the excellent article by Bromley noted in the references at the end of this section.

Had the 1840 version of the analytical engine ever been constructed, it would have stood about 15 ft high, the mill would have been about 6 ft in diameter, and the store would project for about 10 to 20 ft (depending on the number of registers) from the side. The tolerances required of the individual components would be in the order of plus or minus 1/500 of an inch for each component. These were obtainable in Babbage's day, but only at considerable cost.

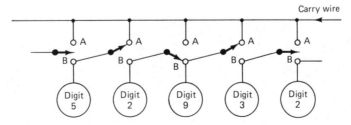

Figure 4–9.   The electrical circuit diagram analogous to the anticipating carriage.

Babbage himself never wrote a complete description of the workings of the analytical engine. However, while on a trip to Italy, he described the details of the machine to a group of interested individuals in Turin and this inspired a military engineer, L. F. Menabrea, to write down the outline of its operation. This basic description was later published in a Swiss periodical. One of Babbage's friends, Ada Augusta Countess of Lovelace (the daughter of the poet Byron) translated this article into English and added an extensive set of comments and notes which provide us with a wealth of detail as to exactly how the computer was to function.

The program for the Analytical Engine was to be stored on a series of punched cards, an idea Babbage had obtained from the workings of the automatic Jacquard loom, in which the pattern woven into the fabric was controlled by a series of punched cards. These cards were formed into a program by attaching them together into a long chain with bits of ribbon. The card reader would read a card (containing an instruction like V6 * V3) and then the microprogram barrels would cause the machine to execute the microsteps involved in implementing the instruction. Loops were possible because the cards could contain an instruction such as "if the counting apparatus contains a num-

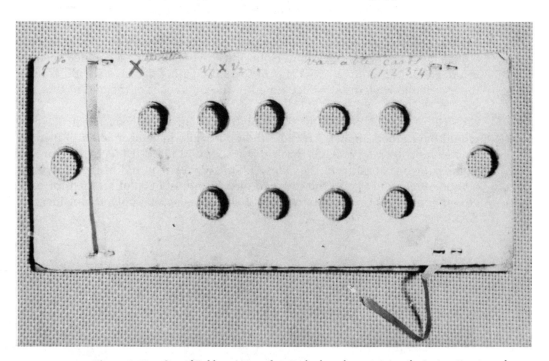

Figure 4–10. One of Babbage's sample punched cards containing the instruction to multiply the contents of the storage location V6 by the contents of storage location V2. (Photograph courtesy of the Science Museum, London.)

ber less than N then back up the chain of punched cards O places and start over again." Other control functions, such as "skip forward N cards," gave the machine as much flexibility as was required for performing any of the computations that Babbage may have required.

The above description of a program is somewhat simplified from the real state of affairs. Babbage actually envisaged that there would be multiple card readers, one reading the operation to be executed, others reading the variables on which this operation was to be performed, and still others for loading constants in various registers or reading tabular values such as logarithms and trigonometric function values. Each of these card readers could be made to advance or back up its card chain independently of the others. This independent control allowed for such things as creating a loop of operations to be performed on several different sets of registers or using different constants in the calculation.

As an example of the type of programming needed for the analytical engine, consider the steps needed to calculate values for the formula:

$$a(b + c)/(d - e)$$

The cards which controlled the actions of transferring numbers between the store and the mill (called directive cards) were to simply contain the number of the store register to, or from, which a number was to be transferred, together with some indication as to the direction in which the transfer was to be accomplished. For example, $'N$ would indicate a transfer from store register N to the mill, while N' would cause the machine to transfer a number from the mill to store register N. If the following initial assignments to store registers had already been made:

$$a \text{ was stored in V1}$$
$$b \text{ was stored in V2}$$
$$c \text{ was stored in V3}$$
$$d \text{ was stored in V4}$$
$$e \text{ was stored in V5}$$

then the following sequence of directive cards:

$$'2,'3,6','6,'1,7','4,'5,8','7,'8,9'$$

combined with the operation cards being tied together in the order:

$$+, *, -, /$$

would result in the machine performing the following sequence of operations:

$$V2 + V3 = V6$$
$$V6 * V1 \ = V7$$
$$V4 - V5 = V8$$
$$V7 / V8 \ = V9$$

In order to obtain a table of this function, the value in V9 would be printed out, the values of V1 to V5 incremented, and the sequence of Jacquard cards on each reader backed up to the beginning to start the evaluation of the next function value.

Three mathematicians asked Babbage how he intended to deal with formulae which required logarithms or other values from tables. His reply is interesting in that it shows he not only could design mechanical solutions to such a problem, but that he was also aware of the effects that a machine like the Analytical Engine would have on the future development of mathematics:

> . . . at the time that logarithms were invented, it became necessary to remodel the whole of the formulas of trigonometry in order to adapt it to the new instrument of calculation: so, when the Analytical Engine is made, it will be desirable to transform all formulas containing tabular numbers to others better adapted to the use of such a machine. This, I replied, is the answer I give to you as mathematicians; but, I added, that for others less skilled in our science, I had another answer, namely: That the Engine might be so arranged that wherever tabular numbers of any kind occurred in a formula given it to compute, it would call for the required logarithm (say log 1207) by stopping and ringing a bell to summon the attendant who would find written at a certain part on the machine "wanted log of 1207." The attendant would then fetch from tables previously computed by the Engine [a Jacquard card containing] the logarithm it required, and, placing it in the proper place, would permit the Engine to continue its work. The next step of the Engine on receiving the tabular number (in this case log 1207) would be to verify the fact of its being really that logarithm. In case no mistake had been made by the attendant, the Engine would use the given tabular number and go on with its work until some other tabular number were required when the same process would be repeated. If, however, any mistakes had been made by the attendant and a wrong logarithm had been accidentally given to the Engine, it would have discovered the mistake, and have rung a louder bell to call the attention of its guide, who, on looking at the proper place would see a place above the logarithm he had just put in with the word "wrong" engraven upon it. By such means it would be perfectly possible to make all calculations requiring tabular numbers without the chance of error.[15]

Babbage kept to the idea that the analytical engine was simply an academic exercise. Except for some small experimental pieces, none of it was ever constructed during his lifetime. After Babbage died, his son (Major Henry P. Babbage) managed to get the firm of R. W. Monro to help him in constructing the mill from one of the later designs. The actual construction was completed in 1906 when the mill was used to calculate and print the first 25 multiples of π to 29 decimal places just to prove that it worked. The mill is now in the

---

[15]H. P. Babbage, *Babbages Calculating Engines* (London: E. & F. N. Spoon, 1889) p. 308. (Reprinted by Tomash Publishers, Los Angeles, 1982.)

Figure 4–11. The mill from Babbage's Analytical Engine, as finally constructed under the direction of H. P. Babbage. (Photograph courtesy of the Science Museum, London.)

Science Museum, London, together with some of the other early Babbage machines.

4.8 PERCY LUDGATE (1883–1922)

It appears that one other mechanical analytical engine was designed, if not actually constructed, about the year 1908. Percy Ludgate was an Irish accountant who did all his work on calculating machines in his spare time. He claims:

> I have myself designed an analytical machine, on different lines from Babbage's, to work with 192 variables of 20 figures each. Complete descriptive drawings of

the machine exist, as well as a description in manuscript, but I have not been able to take any steps to have the machine constructed.[16]

Unfortunately all Ludgate's drawings and manuscripts appear to have vanished forever. The only thing we know is that his machine was to be quite different from Babbage's. It appears that it was to be quite small, only 8 cu ft, but would have been capable of multiplying two 20-digit decimal numbers together in about 6 seconds.

It was to be, like Babbage's machine, entirely mechanical in operation but may well have been designed to be powered by an electric motor. The number storage facility was not like Babbage's but rather was to consist of a number of rectangular boxes from which a series of rods could be extended. A single number would be stored on one box, the length of the rods extending from the box denoting the number, one digit per rod. The control was to be done by punching instructions on a paper tape which could later be read by his machine's control unit. The control unit could also take its commands from a special keyboard. The above information all comes from a short description of the machine published in the *Scientific Proceedings of the Royal Dublin Society* in 1909. The description does not contain any diagrams or detailed explanations of the inner workings of the machine so, barring the miracle of his drawings being found, we will likely never know any more about either this man or his machine.

FURTHER READING

ARCHIBALD, R. C. (1947). "P. G. Scheutz and E. Scheutz: Biography and Bibliography," *Mathematical Tables and Other Aids to Computation, 2*, 238–45.

———· (1947). "Martin Weiberg, his Tables and Difference Engine," *Mathematical Tables and Other Aids to Computation, 2*, 371–73.

BABBAGE, C. (1827). *Tables of the Logarithms of the Natural Numbers from 1 to 108000.* London: J. Mawman.

———· (1838). *The Ninth Bridgewater Treatise.* London: John Murry.

———· (1864). *Passages from the Life of a Philosopher.* London: Longman and Co.

BABBAGE, H. P. (1889). *Babbage's Calculating Machines.* London: E. Spoon and Co. (reprinted in 1983 by Tomash Publishers).

BARNARD, F. A. P. (1869). *Report on the Machinery and Processes of the Industrial Arts.* New York: D. Van Nostrand.

BAXANDALL, D. (1926). *Catalogue of the Collections in the Science Museum.* London: H. M. Stationery Office.

---

[16]P. E. Ludgate, "Automatic Calculating Machines," *Handbook of the Napier Tercentenary Celebration* (Edinburgh: Royal Society of Edinburgh, 1914) p. 127. (Reprinted by Tomash Publishers, Los Angeles, 1982.)

BROMLEY, A. G. (1982). "Charles Babbage's Analytical Engine, 1838," *Annals of the History of Computing, 4* (No. 3), 196–219.

BUXTON, L. H. D. (1933). "Charles Babbage and His Difference Engines," *Transactions of the Newcomen Society, 14,* 43–65.

(1892). *Catalogue of the Scientific Collections, South Kensington Museum.* London: H. M. Stationery Office.

CHASE, G. C. (1952). "History of Mechanical Computing Machinery," *Proceedings of the A.C.M.,* pp. 1–28.

COMRIE, L. J. (1928). Untitled article, *The Observatory, 51,* (April).

————— · (1932). "Mathematical Tables," *Monthly Notices of the Royal Astronomical Society, 92* (No. 4).

————— · (1936). "Scientific Applications of the National Accounting Machine," *Supplement to the Journal of the Royal Statistical Society, 3* (No. 2).

————— · (1946). "The Application of Commercial Calculating Machines to Scientific Computing," *Mathematical Tables and Other Aids to Computation, 2* (No. 16).

D' OCAGNE, P. M. (1905). *Le Calcul Simplifie.* Paris: Gautheir-Villars.

————— · (1915). "On the Origin of Machines of Direct Multiplication," in *Napier Tercentenary Memorial Volume,* ed. C. G. Knott. London: Longmans, Green for the Royal Society of Edinburgh.

FARR, W. (1864). *Tables of Lifetimes, Annuities and Premiums.* London: H. M. Stationery Office.

GRANT, G. B. (1871). "On a New Difference Engine," *American Journal of Science, Third Series, 2* (No. 8), 113–17.

(1876). *Handbook of Scientific Apparatus; South Kensington Museum Science Handbook.* London: H. M. Stationery Office.

HUTTON, C. (1781). *Tables of Products and Powers.* London: Board of Longitude.

JACOB, L. (1911). *Le Calcul Mecanique.* Paris: O. Doin.

KLIPSTEIN, P. (1786). *Beschreibung seiner Neu Erfundenen Rechenmaschine.* Frankfurt.

KNOTT, C. G., ED. (1915). *Napier Tercentenary Memorial Volume.* London: Longmans, Green for the Royal Society of Edinburgh (reprinted in 1983 by Tomash Publishers).

LARDNER, D. (1834). Untitled article, *The Edinburgh Review, 120* (July), 263–327.

LUDGATE, P. E. (1909). "On a Proposed Analytical Machine," *Scientific Proceedings of the Royal Dublin Society, 12* (No. 9), 77–91.

————— · (1915). "Automatic Calculating Machines," in *Napier Tercentenary Memorial Volume,* ed. C. G. Knott. London: Longmans, Green for the Royal Society of Edinburgh.

(1946). "Manual of Operation," *The Annals of the Computation Laboratory of Harvard University, 1.*

MORRISON, P., and E. MORRISON (1961). *Charles Babbage and His Calculating Engines.* New York: Dover Publications.

(1855). "New Calculating Machine," *London Illustrated News,* June 30.

RANDELL, B. (1982). "From Analytical Engine to Electronic Computer: The Contributions of Ludgate, Torres, and Bush," *Annals of the History of Computing, 4* (No. 4), 327–41.

SCHEUTZ, G., and E. (1857). *Specimens of Tables Calculated, Stereomoulded and Printed by Machinery.* Privately published, London.

VAN SINDEREN, A. W. (1980). "The Printed Papers of Charles Babbage," *Annals of the History of Computing,* 2 (No. 2), 169–85.

WELD, C. R. (1848). *History of the Royal Society,* 2 vols. Cambridge: Cambridge University Press.

WILKES, M. V. (1956). *Automatic Digital Computers.* London: Methuen & Co.

WILLIAMS, M. R. (1976). "The Difference Engines," *The Computer Journal,* 19 (No. 1), 82–89.

———·(1981). "The Scientific Library of Charles Babbage," *Annals of the History of Computing,* 3 (No. 3), 235–40.

WOMERSLEY, J. R. (1946). "Scientific Computing in Great Britain," *Mathematical Tables and Other Aids to Computation,* 2 (No. 15).

5

The Analog Animals

5.1 INTRODUCTION

It is quite obvious that there are two basic methods of representing numerical quantities inside a calculating machine, the analog and the digital. What is not quite so obvious, in this era of the digital computer, is that the analog methods have some very real advantages over digital ones, particularly when attempting to design mechanical components for registers and the types of accumulating devices used in problems involving integration.

There is also a very fine line between what is considered an analog device in one application and a digital device in another. For example, the use of a simple rotating disk or drum, such as those used for the final result register in the Pascal and Morland calculators, is very little different from the rotating dials used on a typical natural gas meter; yet the former is clearly a discrete digital device while the latter is a continuous analog representation. The basic difference is that the Pascal wheel is constrained by built-in stops to halt only at certain discrete positions while a gas meter readout can assume any position in its 360-degree cycle of rotation. Some of the more advanced digital machines, such as those produced by Charles Babbage or Howard Aiken, had quite sophisticated checks built into them to ensure that the wheels used to store the results of an operation were very carefully constrained to stop in only one of ten possible positions.

The analog calculating instruments and machines actually go back in history much further than the digital ones. This is not very surprising because a lot of the very early calculating instruments were intended to aid in such problems as determining the future motions of the stars and planets, both for astrological and navigational purposes. It is very much easier to construct an analog model of the motions of the heavens, and observe its behavior, than it is to deduce the basic mathematical equations of motion for such a system. And one must know these mathematical equations before embarking on a digital solution to the problem.

A great many analog devices were developed between about 400 B.C. and mid-nineteenth century, when developments in both mathematics and calculating machines allowed the digital calculations to be produced more rapidly (and more accurately) than could be done by analog methods. Typical of these devices is the astrolabe and its various derivatives, including the navigational sighting instruments and the early planetarium devices known as "Orreries."

Another class of such instruments, which were only abandoned as major calculating devices in the late 1960s and early 1970s, were the automatic integrating machines. These were used for such projects as finding the solutions to differential equations and modeling the behavior of very complex systems such as the ocean tides or large power grids. These machines ranged from the early combinations of wire and pulleys used on the ocean tides projects, through the very complex mechanical differential analyzers, to the electronic analog computers, a few of which are still being used for specialized applications today.

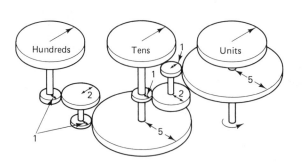

Figure 5-1. A diagram of an analog gas meter readout mechanism.

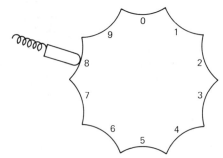

Figure 5-2. A diagram of a digital wheel register with detents.

5.2 THE ASTROLABE

A tiny but precocious babe
Was playing with an astrolabe
Her younger brother did prefer
A large interferometer.[1]

The astrolabe is a device used to perform many different astronomical observations and calculations. It has been claimed, in some of the older treatises, that it can perform over 1000 different observational and calculational tasks. Its history is quite clear from about the time of the rise of the Arabic Empire, but the earlier history is clouded in myth and conjecture. The ancient Babylonians had an advanced ability to make accurate observations of the heavens; they had a highly developed calendar system, divided the circle into 360 degrees, had developed the concept of the zodiac with 12 signs, and seem to have made some elementary star maps. Nothing, however, has been found to indicate that they produced an instrument like an astrolabe, but it is likely that they laid the groundwork for production of the instrument by the Greeks at their famous school in Alexandria. The earliest surviving example of an astrolabe dates from 1062 A.D., but the writings of Ptolemy imply that the techniques were known by Hipparchus of Bithynia (ca. 180–125 B.C.). The fundamental concept necessary to create an astrolabe is the ability to construct a projection, or map, of the celestial sphere upon a plane, usually assumed to be the plane of the equator of the earth. This so-called "stereographic" projection was mentioned by Ptolemy in his book *Almagest*, which was written in the first century after Christ. Later Greek authors such as Theon of Alexandria (ca. 430 A.D.) and John Philoponus (ca. 625 A.D.) wrote small books which accurately describe the instrument; thus it must have been in common use in the first centuries of the Christian era.

The traditional form of the device consists of a number of metal plates, engraved with what looks like the lines of a spider web, which fit inside an outer shell called "the mother." On top of the metal plates is placed a fretwork cutout, called "the rete," having a large circle together with a sequence of dagger-like points. The spider web engraving on the plates is a stereographic projection of the heavenly sphere as it would appear from some particular latitude on the surface of the earth, together with a map of the earth showing such items as the equator and the tropic of cancer. The large circle on the rete is a representation of the zodiac (really just a map of the sun's position in the heavens at different days of the year), while the dagger points indicate positions of some of the more prominent stars.

[1]As quoted by C. F. Jenkins in *The Astrolabe* (Oxford: Oxford University Press, 1925), preface.

Figure 5–3. An astrolabe.

By rotating the rete over the engraved plates it is possible to do such computations as:

- work out the position of the sun and principal stars for any hour of a given day of the year
- find the latitude of the observer, even during the day when the stars were not visible
- calculate how many hours of daylight there would be between sunrise and sunset on any given day of the year

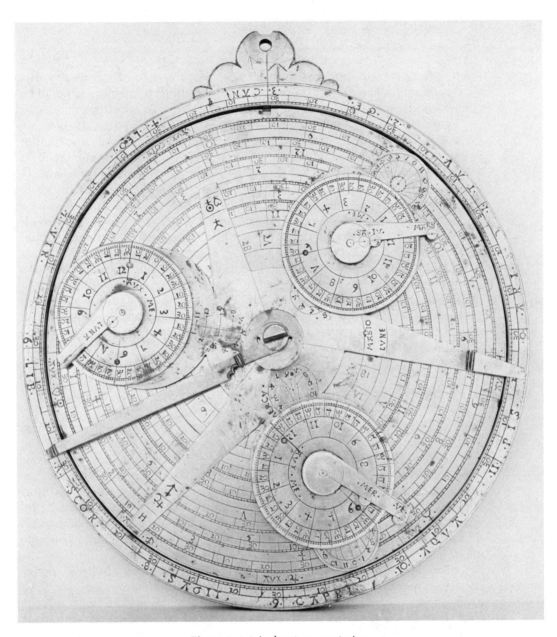

Figure 5–4. A planetary equatorium.

- calculate the hours of twilight at both sunrise and sunset for any given day of the year (important when considering how many hours of work to allocate to field hands, for example)
- find the time, both day and night

Finding the position of the sun and stars at any given hour of a given day was very important when casting horoscopes. The positions of the planets could be determined by a similar instrument called a planetary equatorium.

Without some knowledge of the heavens and the way they look to observers on different parts of the earth, it is difficult to describe the construction and use of an astrolabe in any detail. Two very easily obtained references do go into these matters: (1) the paper by J. D. North (see references) is easily obtained from almost any library, and (2) for those people interested in very early historical descriptions, the work written by Geoffrey Chaucer (the man who wrote the great English classic, *The Canterbury Tales*) entitled *A Treatise on the Astrolabe* is, again, easily found in any library having one of the many volumes of Chaucer's collected works. Chaucer's description is the earliest known to be written in English. When he wrote it, about 1392, almost all such works were done in Latin. He likely wrote it in English because it was intended as a tutorial for his "lytle sonne Lowis" (little son Lewis) who was then about ten years old. The work was clearly intended for the person not yet developed in the sciences because it was given the subtitle *Bred and Mylke for Childeren* (Bread and Milk for Children).

5.3 THE ANTIKYTHERA DEVICE

The next major step in creating an analog device is to incorporate some form of drive mechanism. It used to be thought that sophisticated gearing, involving such items as differential gears like those found in an automobile, did not occur until about the middle 1500s. In 1959 a preliminary description of a very remarkable device was published which put the date of such sophisticated gear work back all the way to the start of the Christian era. The object, usually referred to as the Antikythera device, is in such a bad state of preservation that it took about 15 years of detailed investigation before its true function became clear.

The device was first discovered in 1900 when a group of Greek sponge fishermen had to take shelter from a storm blowing up in the Aegean Sea. They dropped anchor off the small island of Antikythera, about half way between Crete and the Greek mainland. When the storm had died down, they sent divers over the side on the off chance that there might be sponges available. Rather than finding sponges, they found a wreck of a large Greek ship full of marble statues and other artifacts. The wreck was dated as being about the time of Christ and appears to have been on its way from Rhodes to Rome when it, too, was likely caught in a storm. The Greek government raised all the statues and artifacts, among which were a number of fragments of a bronze statue of the god Hermes. Several months later, one large lump of encrusted bronze was determined to be not a part of the statue, but appeared to be some collection of gears that had once been inside a wooden box. Unfortunately the action of the sea water had so encrusted the fragment that no details were visible of the mechanism and the remains of the box had long ago disintegrated.

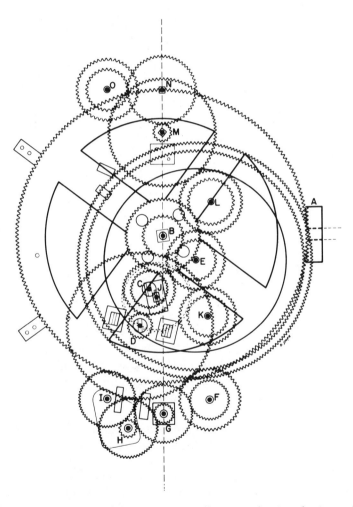

Figure 5–5. The Antikythera Device—two diagrams showing the internal gearing arrangements. (Photographs courtesy of the American Philosophical Society, originally appeared in "Gears From the Greeks," *Transactions*, 64, part 7.)

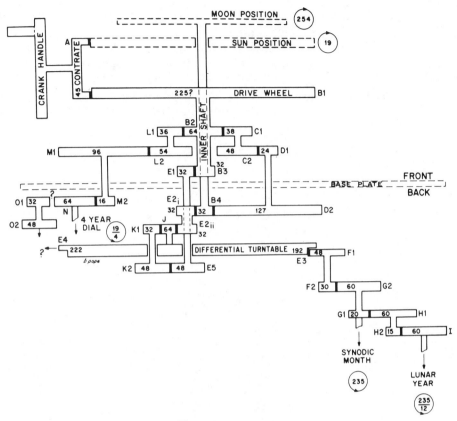

Figure 5–5. (cont.)

The object remained in the Greek National Archaeological Museum until it was noticed by Professor De Sola Price of Yale. He happened to be an expert on ancient clockwork mechanisms, so it caught his interest enough that he arranged for special cleaning, X-ray photographs of the interior, and special gamma ray photographs to reveal the sections that were impossible to see in any other way.

From other evidence aboard the ship it was determined that the vessel was on its way from Rhodes to Rome when it met with disaster. Knowing that the source was likely Rhodes, scholars were able to refer back to the works of the Roman philosopher Cicero who, when on a visit to Rhodes, reported seeing a device which reproduced the motions of the sun, moon, and the five visible planets. Even if it is not the same mechanism Cicero described, this Antikythera device is obviously something very similar. It had a wooden case, about 1 ft. high, 8 in. wide, and 4 in. deep, with a crank extending from its side. The front and back of the case appear to have had dials which were meant to represent the position of the sun and moon for each day in the lunar calendar.

Unfortunately so much corrosion has gone on that exact determinations of the functions of each dial may never be made.

Inside the case were about 30 different gears all very neatly made from a bronze alloy. The very remarkable thing about the gearing is that it seems to contain a sophisticated set of gears called an epicyclic differential turntable. This consists of a single large gear which could be rotated in different directions by two smaller meshing gears which turned at different rates. As mentioned earlier, complex gearing of this type, similar to that found in the differential of an automobile, did not reappear in Europe until 1575.

It appears that we will never know who made this device, why it was made, or why it was being shipped from Rhodes to Rome. Indeed it may well be that it did not originate in Rhodes because some evidence of later solder repairs indicates that it was not brand new when it sank. It does, however, give us firm knowledge that mechanical analog devices are much older than is generally recognized. Even though the techniques for constructing these astronomical computers died out for the next 15 centuries, it is obvious that men of genius were capable of producing mechanical analog machines from very early times.

5.4 TIDE PREDICTORS

One of the most obvious problems that concerned scientists and tradespeople over the ages has been that of attempting to predict the rise and fall of the ocean tides. It was of considerable importance to the people engaged in maritime commerce because they tended to become annoyed when, after an apparently successful trading voyage, the ship tore its bottom out by attempting to enter a harbor when the tides were not high enough to adequately cover the rocks and other hazards on the ocean bed. Of course, most seamen would have some notion of the state of the tides, but accidents were common enough that a considerable effort was made to devise instruments and tables which would accurately indicate the times of high and low tide at particular ports.

We now know enough about the dynamics of the gravitational interaction of the sun, moon, and earth that it is possible to calculate the state of the tides from first principles for almost all of the simple harbor/ocean systems. Some, because of the nature of the interaction of certain tide runs and complex estuaries, still defy complete analysis but are easily computed by Fourier sequences based on past tide records. This was, obviously, not always the case. In the Middle Ages, for example, it was known from simple observations that the tides were somehow based on the positions of the sun and moon, but the exact mechanism remained a complete mystery.

Figure 5–6 shows a fifteenth century device used to calculate the times of high and low tides for several European ports. The two pointers, having pictures of the sun and moon, were set to represent the positions of these bodies

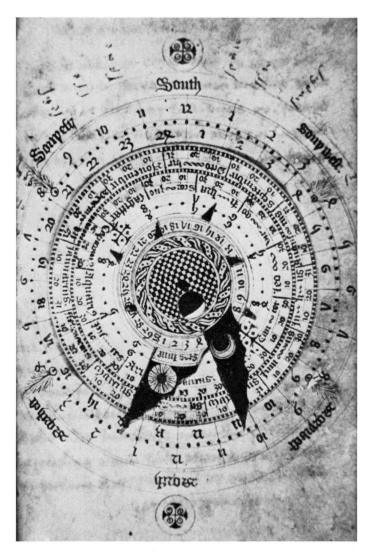

Figure 5–6. A fifteenth century tide predictor. (Photograph courtesy of the Curators of the Bodleian Library, Oxford.)

in the sky. A very ingenious check system was incorporated into the instrument to allow the user to verify the correctness of the settings. The hole visible in the central portion of the device would, depending on the settings of the two pointers, show a light-colored portion ranging from a thin crescent to a full circle. If this representation of the phase of the moon matched the actual moon in the sky, the user could be assured that the pointers had been set correctly for the present conditions. Knowing one other item of information, called the "aspect" of the port, the user could read the approximate time of high tide from the other scales on the device. Although only approximate, this tide predictor must have saved a number of ships from disaster.

It is, of course, possible to take measurements of tides for one particular site and, provided sufficient historical data are known, to predict mathematically the tide actions into the future. It was not until the middle of the 1800s that the subject of harmonic analysis was sufficiently developed to enable the computation of a series of cosine coefficients which would yield a formula precise enough to be used as a tide predictor. Eventually the great Scottish physicist Lord Kelvin, under the sponsorship of the British Association, was able to construct a method of obtaining the coefficients for a formula of the form:

$$y = A \cos(u) + B \cos(v) + C \cos(w) + \ldots$$

He then set about constructing an analog machine to evaluate this formula.

Each of the pairs of gears visible in the lower portion of Figure 5–7 is of an appropriate size to cause the upper gear to turn an amount proportional to one of the coefficients A, B, C, ... in the formula. Connected to each of the upper gears is a rod which would move up and down as the gear rotated. This up-and-down motion was the mechanical analog of the cosine function, the amplitude of the movement being determined by the gear ratios on the machine. A thin wire connected each of these rods to a pulley in such a way that, as the rod moved up and down, the pulley would be raised or lowered. A wire, fastened at one end of the machine and threaded through the pulleys, was then attached to the pen of a chart recorder at the far end. As the pulleys rise and fall the vertical portions of the wire are lengthened or shortened, and the pen moves up or down on the chart, tracing out the function which is twice the sum of the cosine functions being generated by the gears. As long as one knows the gear ratios to use for a particular site, the computation of the tides was simply a matter of turning the drive wheel and making sure that enough paper was in the chart recorder.

Kelvin's instrument could deal with a tide predictor formula having at most 12 cosine terms. Two other analog tide predictors were later constructed in the United States, both based upon the same principle, which would deal with a formula having 17 and 37 terms. The 37-term machine was constructed by the U.S. Coast and Geodetic Survey, which started the project in 1905. It was finished in time to be used for tide prediction work for the year 1911. In its final form it stood about 7 ft. high, 11 ft. long, and weighed almost 2500 pounds. By using a 37-term formula, it could calculate the height of the tides to the nearest 0.10 ft. for each minute of the year. This machine was in constant use until the mid-1960s, when it was replaced by a program that ran on an IBM 7094 computer. As a comparison, the computer program had to call upon a cosine subroutine some 20,000,000 times in order to do tide prediction for one site for one year. Quite a different order of computational effort from simply

Figure 5–7. Lord Kelvin's tide predictor, as illustrated in the "Handbook of the Napier Tercentenary Celebration," 1914

turning the crank and letting the mechanical analog equipment perform a simple simulation of the same task.

5.5 DIFFERENTIAL ANALYZERS

One of the problems that has vexed applied mathematicians over the years has been that of calculating the area under a given curve. This area, more formally known as the integral of the given function, or

$$\int f(x)dx$$

is quite easy to calculate for elementary functions that can be integrated analytically, but can be almost impossible if the function, $f(x)$, is either not known in analytic form or, if it is known, is not well behaved.

A number of simple expedients were often used to gain some idea of the numerical solution to such problems, the simplest of which required only a good eye, some fine quality paper, and an accurate balance. If you plot the function on good quality paper of very even thickness and cut out the resulting area between the X axis and the value of the function, then the weight of this piece of paper is proportional to the area under the curve. All that is required is to cut out a unit area from the same paper, find the weight of the unit area and the weight of the piece of paper whose boundaries are the function values, and a simple division will yield an approximation to the area under the curve. The accuracy of this method is obviously limited by three factors—your skill at cutting, the even quality of the paper, and the sensitivity of the balances used. Although full of potential sources of error, the method has been, and in some cases still is, used to obtain quick estimates of the integrals of certain functions.

Mechanical methods of performing the same type of estimates were first devised about 1825, but had to wait until almost the end of that century before they became reliable enough to be used in any serious way. It was Professor James Thomson, the brother of Lord Kelvin, who devised a mechanical arrangement of a rotating disk, a sphere, and a cylinder that would perform elementary integrations. This was an extension of earlier work, but it does rank as one of the first really workable integrating devices.

The basic idea is that the disk, which is capable of rotating about an axis perpendicular to its plane, will cause a sphere, which is movable along the radius of the disk, to rotate; this rotational movement will be passed to the cylinder, which is in contact with the sphere. If the sphere is located in the center of the disk then it will, of course, not move; but if it is located between the center and the edge of the disk, friction will cause the sphere to revolve, and this motion will in turn cause the cylinder to rotate. The amount of rotation of the cylinder is a function both of the movement of the disk and the position of the sphere on the disk's radius.

If the disk rotates by some amount Qdx, and the sphere is positioned at a point Y units from its center, then the point of contact between the disk and

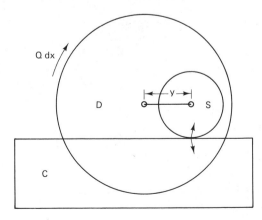

Figure 5–8. The disk-sphere-cylinder integrator.

the sphere will move through a distance of $QYdx$. If the radius of the cylinder is R, then the total angle turned by the cylinder is $QYdx/R$. Thus the total angle turned through by the cylinder actually measures:

$$\int Ydx$$

It is quite easy to construct a mechanism such that, given a graph of $Y = f(x)$, you can have two pointers, one to run along the X axis of the graph and the other to follow the curve of Y values. Such a mechanism will control the amount of rotation of the disk so that the value Qdx will always equal the pointer's position on the X axis and the position of the sphere will always be the corresponding Y value. Thus you simply trace out the graph with the pointers and then read the value of the integral by noting how much the cylinder has rotated.

ROLLING-DISC PLANIMETER

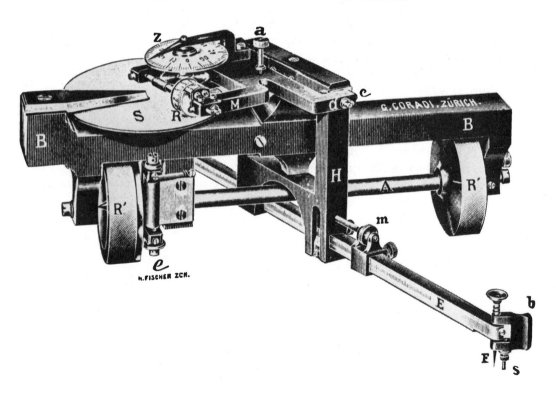

Figure 5–9. A planimeter, from a set of drawings made about 1910.

In most simple planimeter instruments the sphere was replaced by a rotating disk, but the principle of operation remained exactly the same. About the beginning of this century several different companies manufactured elementary planimeters for use by applied mathematicians and engineers when attempting to calculate integrals.

The big drawback to incorporating this type of integrating device into any automatic calculating machinery was the fact that it relied simply on friction to drive the result wheels. If any tension was put on the result wheels, the contacts between the wheels and the rotating disks would slip, thus making the results invalid. The final solution to this problem was to devise some form of system to use the rotating result cylinder to control, but not actually drive, the gears and wheels used in the next stage of the process. The resulting system has been implemented in several different ways by different groups of people, but the first one to actually construct a working machine was Vannevar Bush at MIT.

Bush's idea was actually attempted by Lord Kelvin but, because of problems in obtaining accurate machining, it had to wait until the 1930s when better techniques were available. The concept is remarkable in its simplicity. Sailors had been using a rotating capstan to haul up heavy equipment for centuries. Bush took the same principle to construct his power amplifier. A string was wound around a spinning shaft and, when you gently pulled one end of the string to tighten it, the shaft grabbed the string and pulled the other end with a considerable force. The control end of the string was attached to the output cylinder of the integrator, and the other end was used to drive a series of gears that transmitted the results to another part of the mechanical computation process.

Bush's involvement with constructing a working differential analyzer, as the resulting machine was called, began when he was attempting to solve some differential equations associated with a power network. He found that, after working for several months on one equation, it was simpler to spend his time in the design and construction of a special analog machine than it was to continue in the fruitless effort to solve the equations analytically. He actually constructed three different machines, a simple breadboard scheme to show that his ideas would work, a production-scale machine (ca. 1930) that incorporated his torque amplifiers, and a later machine which replaced the mechanical interconnections by electronics but kept the mechanical integrators. This last machine, known as the Rockefeller Differential Analyzer #2 (or RDA2 for short), was finished just before the start of the Second World War and was extensively used, as was his earlier mechanical version, for the calculation of ballistic firing tables by the armed services.

The mechanical version had three basic types of units: integrators, gears for constant multiplication, and differential gears for doing addition and subtraction. The various units were connected together for a particular problem by setting the gears on a series of long rotating shafts which would pass the

Figure 5–10. Vannevar Bush and the mechanical differential analyzer. (Photograph courtesy of the MIT Museum.)

analog values, represented by rotation of the shaft, from one part of the machine to another. One had to be skilled with wrenches and hammers when programming this particular device.

The mechanical differential analyzers took a long time to set up for a particular differential equation, and one had to make sure that the operators, who sat at the integrator tables alongside the device, were very careful to move the Y-axis pointers along the preplotted curve as the machine's internal motion caused it to consider the different X-axis values. Once set up, the differential analyzers seldom had to be changed in any real way. The usual problems of ballistics, for example, involved solving the same differential equation over and over again so that all one had to do was to be careful that the internal mechanism was kept in alignment. This was not always an easy task, but these machines were a big step above the usual methods of solving differential equation by hand.

At least five different copies of Bush's machines were made in the years before World War II. Perhaps the two most famous were the one constructed out of meccano by D. R. Hartree and A. Porter of Manchester University and the copy produced at the Moore School of Engineering in Philadelphia. The Hartree machine was smaller and much lighter than Bush's, but it did show that useful work could be done by machines built from children's construction sets. The Moore School machine, which used plate glass for the basic rotating disk, was, like the one at MIT, used extensively for war-time ballistic calculations. Other copies of this type of machine were known to have been made in Germany, Norway, and Leningrad.

One of the most interesting stories concerns a machine built prior to World War II in Norway. It is one of the earliest incidents of computer sabotage. After the German invasion of Norway, it came to the attention of one of the senior people that the Germans intended to ship the machine to Germany to aid in their own war-related computations. The next day this senior man vanished over the border into Sweden and with him went some of the vital parts of the torque amplifier. The machine sat idle for the rest of the war!

The Norwegians were rather good at this sort of thing. They had developed a punched card system for use in the government census and tax bureaus which the Germans intended, among other things, to use for recruiting work parties. One night a group of local resistance fighters scaled the building and let themselves down, through sky lights, into the main data center. They planted explosive charges in all the equipment and also did a great deal of damage to the card files. Needless to say, the Germans were also denied the use of this equipment in any of their future plans.

As mentioned previously, the differential analyzers found their main use as calculators for ballistic firing tables. The second MIT machine was used for one particular job which, although never mentioned in any of the usual reference sources, made a major contribution to the war effort. The British asked the MIT people to produce a set of ballistic tables quite unlike any that had been seen before. The request came to the director of the MIT installation from very high government officials and, although he did not at the time realize exactly what the differential equations represented, he set up the machine to solve a ballistic trajectory of very much greater range and height than any gun could produce. A few weeks later he was informed that his tables were obviously wrong, and an investigation showed that he had simply forgotten to take into account the curvature of the earth under this very long flight path. The tables were recalculated and the director heard no more about the project. In hindsight the trajectory was obviously that of the German V2 rockets. This implies that the British either had radar of a very much longer range than has been admitted, and hoped to predict the impact site of the V2 warhead once a launch had been detected, or more probably they were attempting to work backward from the impact site in an attempt to pinpoint the V2 launch sites. The fact that they were able to tell the MIT people that the original tables were in error, and request them to be redone, shows that they were capable of tracking the V2 for at least part of its flight. Like the material on the Colossus machines, some information on this project may one day become available when the British Official Secrets Act is allowed to lapse on this material.

Unfortunately almost all of the differential analyzers are no longer with us. The advent of electronic analog, and later digital, computers made the mechanical devices completely useless. Bush's original machine, for example, was given to Wayne University (later Wayne State University) in 1954, and they broke it up for scrap value in the early 1960s. A few of the large integrators have been salvaged and are on display at places like the MIT Museum, and sections of Hartree's meccano machine have been kept by the Science Museum in London. Nowhere, to my knowledge, has a fully working mechanical differential analyzer been preserved.

FURTHER READING

BUSH, V. (1931). "The Differential Analyzer," *Journal of the Franklin Institute, 212* (No. 4), 447–88.

——(1971). *Pieces of the Action.* New York: William Morrow and Co.

—— and S. H. CALDWELL (1945). "A New Type of Differential Analyzer," *Journal of the Franklin Institute, 240* (No. 4), 255–326.

CARSE, G. A., and J. URQUHART (1914). "Planimeters," in *Handbook of the Napier Tercentenary Celebration,* ed. E. M. Horsburgh. Edinburgh: Royal Society of Edinburgh.

COLLINS, A. (1970). "The Great Brass Brain," *Datamation,* Nov. 15, pp. 33–36.

HORSBURGH, E. M. (1914). *Handbook of the Napier Tercentenary Celebration.* Edinburgh: Royal Society of Edinburgh. (reprinted in 1983 by Tomash Publishers)

JENKIN, C. F. (1925). *The Astrolabe—Its Construction and Use.* Oxford: Oxford University Press.

NORTH, J. D. (1974). "The Astrolabe," *Scientific American,* January, pp. 96–106.

PRICE, D. J. (1955). *The Equatorie of the Planetis.* Cambridge: Cambridge University Press.

PRICE, D. De SOLA (1975). *Gears from the Greeks.* New York: Science History Publications.

ROBERTS, E. (1914). "Tide-predicting Machine," in *Handbook of the Napier Tercentenary Celebration,* ed. E. M. Horsburgh. London: Tomash Publishers.

6

The Mechanical Monsters

6.1 INTRODUCTION

The decade starting in the late 1930s saw a number of different groups construct working calculators with some type of automatic control system. The special electronic machines, such as ENIAC, will be dealt with in the next chapter while here we concentrate on devices based on mechanical, electromechanical, or relay technology. The initial designs of some of the entirely electronic machines were influenced to a considerable degree by these mechanical giants and, although they left no direct descendants in the computing field, they were vital as stepping stones toward the electronic stored program computer.

The story of these mechanical machines can be divided into four basic lines: (1) work done in Germany by Konrad Zuse, (2) the Bell Telephone Laboratories production of a series of computers based on relay technology, (3) the projects undertaken by Howard Aiken at Harvard, and (4) the efforts of IBM in the design of both small- and large-scale mechanical and electromechanical computing equipment. Although these different projects, with the exception of the war-enforced isolation of Konrad Zuse, shared ideas and even technicians, it is worth considering each of them as a separate line of development. The interrelationships between them will be highlighted, and a glance at the chronological table at the back of this book will help to indicate the progress at any given time of each of these lines of equipment. It should also be kept in mind that, by the mid-1940s, progress in the design and construction of purely electronic equipment was very rapidly sounding the death knell for these, the dinosaurs of the computing age. However, the newer electronic techniques were not available to everyone who wanted to experiment with an automatic computing machine, so various groups, particularly in Europe and Japan, continued to rely on electromechanical technology to construct their machines up to the mid-1950s.

6.2 THE ZUSE MACHINES

6.2.1 Konrad Zuse

Konrad Zuse holds a special place in the history of computation because it was he who first managed to construct an automatically controlled calculating machine. It was not electronic, and it did not have a stored program, but it was capable of being automatically controlled by an external reader, which would take the instructions to be executed from a punched tape.

Zuse was born in Berlin in 1910 and after childhood dreams of becoming a famous designer of moon rockets or a great city planner, he studied civil engineering at the Technische Hochschule Berlin-Charlottenburg and began his working career as a design engineer in the aircraft industry. It was while he was still a student that he became aware of the tremendous amount of labor required to produce the calculations necessary for the design and analysis of structures.

Zuse very soon learned that one of the most difficult aspects of doing a large calculation with either a slide rule or a mechanical adding machine is keeping track of all the intermediate results and using them in their proper place in later steps of the calculation. His first attempt at automating the calculation process was simply a scheme to get around this "housekeeping" problem. He designed a series of special forms upon which a calculation could be done without the possibility of confusing intermediate results. These forms contained preprinted boxes in which the numbers could be written; boxes horizontally adjacent should have their contents multiplied together, while those boxes vertically adjacent would have their contents added. This situation is most easily seen in the diagram shown in Figure 6–2. His thinking about the design of these calculating-plan forms soon led him to the realization that, if the numbers were entered into a mechanism which could link together me-

Figure 6–1. Konrad Zuse, circa 1970. (Photograph courtesy of Konrad Zuse.)

chanical calculators in the way indicated by his forms, then the calculations could be done automatically.

The next step in the development of Zuse's ideas involved his consideration of a device which would have an arm capable of moving over the surface of a table, much like today's flatbed plotters. This arm would be used to read and write numbers, in the form of punched cards, into the various boxes of Zuse's calculating-plan forms. The arithmetic was to be done by a mechanical calculator while the movement of the arm was to be controlled by a mechanism which would be following a series of coded instructions from the calculating-plan form. Zuse suddenly realized that, once you had the instructions coded for the control mechanism, there was no longer any need for the calculating-plan form at all and it had become nothing more than a series of boxes acting like a memory. Thus, by 1934, Zuse had realized that an automatic calculator

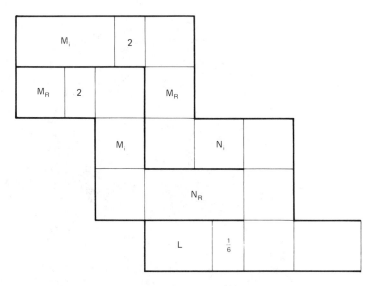

Figure 6–2. Zuse's calculating-plan boxes for evaluating the formula L/6 [N$_i$ (2M$_i$ + M$_R$ + N) $_R$ (M$_i$ + 2M$_R$)].

only required three basic units: a control, a memory, and a calculator for the arithmetic.

6.2.2 The Z1

Zuse was not familiar with the detailed design of mechanical calculators. This proved to be an advantage in that he did not attempt to produce a calculator based on the known and proven technology of his day, but rather thought things out from first principles. He decided that any memory unit should be based on a binary mechanism rather than on the rotating ten-position wheel used in most mechanical calculators and tabulating equipment. His mechanical memory was to be designed around a very simple system in which a small pin rested in a slot cut out of a strip of metal. This pin could be pushed from one side of the slot to the other in order to represent either a binary one or a zero. The pin in turn caused the reading mechanism to move to either the right or left depending on which end of the slot the pin happened to be residing.

With the help of several of his friends he set up a small workshop in the living room of his parents' apartment in Berlin, and began to construct a mechanical memory. By 1936 he had progressed to the point where he was able to apply for a patent on the idea. He left his job at the Henschel Aircraft Company and, much to the consternation of his parents, decided to continue with his design of calculating equipment in their living room. By 1937 he had produced a mechanical memory capable of storing 16 binary numbers, each of 24 bits. One year later he had finished the construction of the first of his computing machines. It was originally called the V-1, which stood for Versuchs-modell-1 (experimental model 1) but, after the war, he changed the designations on all his machines to the letter Z to avoid confusion with the rockets developed by his friend Wernher von Braun.

The Z1 was entirely mechanical in construction. Its basic component was a mechanical gate cunningly constructed from a series of sliding plates connected together by various rods. The unit illustrated in Figure 6–3 was typical in that a back-and-forth motion was applied to the plate marked d, and this motion would be passed through to the plate marked f if, and only if, the two smaller plates (marked b and c) were in the appropriate positions. The positions of plates b and c were the inputs to the gate which determined if the "signal" could travel from plate d to f.

The arithmetic unit constructed from these mechanical gates was designed to work with binary floating point numbers, and an additional unit managed to convert his floating point binary notation to and from decimal to facilitate the input and output of data. There were actually two separate arithmetic units, one for the 16-bit mantissa and one for the 7-bit exponent.

Control of the Z1 was by means of instructions punched on tape. While most people attempting to construct a tape-controlled machine used the punched paper tape normally found in the telex industry of the day, Zuse used discarded 35mm movie film which he punched with a hand punch. The sug-

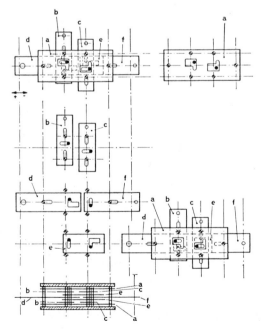

Figure 6–3. Zuse's mechanical logic gate. (Courtesy of Konrad Zuse.)

gestion for using movie film was made by his friend Helmut Schreyer who had previously worked as a movie projectionist and thus knew of the device which would move film through a projector in a series of discrete steps, a necessary feature in the control mechanism. The input of data was handled by a simple four-decimal-place keyboard while the output was shown on a four-decimal-place electric lamp display.

Although the machine functioned, as Zuse put it, "after a fashion," the mechanical design did not lend itself to being produced by amateurs in the living room of a small apartment. The memory worked well and was the basis of the memory units in later machines, but the design of the arithmetic unit presented serious problems, most of which were caused by the complexity of routing signals from one place to another. The movement of signals in an electrical machine is a simple matter of running a wire from one point to another, but when the signals are represented by sliding metal plates it is very difficult to make them go around corners.

6.2.3 The Z2

Even before the Z1 was finished, Zuse had already begun design work on a relay-based arithmetic unit to overcome the signal routing problem. His friend Helmut Schreyer, a graduate student at the time, constructed a model of part

Figure 6–4. Schreyer (left) and Zuse (right) working on the Z1 in Zuse's parents' living room. (Photograph courtesy of Konrad Zuse.)

of Zuse's machine using vacuum tubes. This small model was demonstrated at the Technical University in Berlin in 1938, but because it was impossible, in prewar Germany, to obtain all the necessary parts for a machine containing about 1,000 vacuum tubes, Zuse abandoned that line of research and continued with the development of the relay-based Z2. Schreyer continued to be interested in the use of vacuum tubes as part of a calculating device and actually constructed some experimental circuits. He was later to use this material in his Doctoral dissertation, "The Tube Relay and the Techniques of its Switching" in 1941.

The Z2 was designed to function with the mechanical memory of Z1 while all the rest of the device was to be based on relays. Normal relays were beyond Zuse's limited financial means for, although they only cost the equivalent of about $2.00 each, there would be a need for several thousand of them. With some help from Schreyer, Zuse managed to find a source of secondhand relays, and he and his friends began rebuilding them for use in the Z2.

The Z2 was almost finished when, in 1939, Zuse was drafted into the German armed services. Several of his friends used what influence they could to get him out of the army so that he could continue with his experiments, but it was almost a full year before the army took any notice and, when they did, it was only so that Zuse could go back to his old profession as an aircraft engineer. While Zuse was away in the army, Schreyer continued to experiment with electronic analogs of Zuse's equipment. In attempting to duplicate the memory system, Schreyer came up with the idea of using small neon lamps driven by a series of vacuum tubes. This system, which is described further in the section dealing with computer memories, also led to the construction of a prototype arithmetic unit which could deal with numbers up to 10 bits long. The device, which required about 100 vacuum tubes, was unfortunately destroyed in an air raid.

After his release from the army, Zuse left Schreyer to the experimentation on electronics and contented himself with spending his free weekends away from the Henschel Flugzeugwerke in an attempt to finish the Z2. When he had the relay-based arithmetic and control units functioning, he put them together with the mechanical memory and set up a demonstration for the Deutsche Versuchsanstalt für Luftfahrt (German Aeronautical Research Institute). The Z2 functioned well for the demonstration and, with constant care and patience, could be made to perform calculations. The hybrid mechanical/relay machine was, however, not reliable enough to be put to any practical use. Its one major contribution was to convince the people from the DVL that automatic computing machines could be constructed from relay technology. Because they were inspired by the demonstration of the Z2, the DVL agreed to finance Zuse in the construction of a much more ambitious machine which he called the Z3.

Although the DVL agreed to back his project, they did not provide him with any laboratory facilities or technicians. He was forced to continue working out of his own home using what help he could get from friends like Schreyer.

The work was interrupted when he was again drafted, this time to the eastern front, but only spent a very short time in the army before the influence of his friends and the DVL managed to have him returned to Berlin.

6.2.4 The Z3

The Z3 was very much a machine in the spirit of the Z1 and Z2. It was controlled by punched tape, again using discarded movie film, while the input and output were via the same four-decimal-place keyboard and lamp display. The entire machine was based on relay technology, about 2,600 of them being required, 1,400 for the memory, 600 for the arithmetic unit, and the rest as part of the control circuits. They were mounted in three racks, two for the memory and one for the arithmetic and control unit, each about 6 feet high by 3 feet wide. The control panel sat on a small table with the 35mm film reader at its side.

One of the major drawbacks to the use of relays is the fact that the current going through the contacts will cause sparks to be given off each time the relay

Figure 6–5. A photograph of the rebuilt Z3. (Photograph courtesy of Konrad Zuse.)

contacts are opened or closed. This sparking causes a lot of wear and corrosion of the contact points and is the main cause of failure in relays. Zuse overcame this problem by having a revolving drum to which all power connections were made. The drum, part of which can be seen under the right-hand cabinet in the picture of the Z3, contained various metal coatings on its surface, and carbon brushes made contact with these as the drum rotated. All signals passing through a set of relay contacts would first be routed through this drum in such a way that a small delay would ensure that the relay had closed its contacts before any current was passed through them. This meant that no sparking would occur at the relay contacts, but rather at the carbon brushes making contact with the drum. The carbon brushes could be easily replaced when they wore down.

The 64-word memory was, like his earlier machines, floating-point binary in organization but this time it had a word length of 22 bits: 14 for the mantissa, 7 for the exponent, and 1 for the sign. All the floating-point numbers were kept in a normalized form in which the mantissa was shifted to the left until the leftmost bit was a 1, the exponent being adjusted accordingly. Zuse realized that there was no real need to store this leftmost "1" if it was going to be present in all numbers, so the mantissa was always shifted one more place to the left and the missing "1" was always reinserted by the arithmetic unit (except, of course, for the number zero). This technique is still in common use today on machines with a short word length, but very few people realize that its origins go all the way back to 1941.

Like his earlier machines, the arithmetic unit consisted of two separate mechanisms, one each for the exponent and mantissa, which would operate in parallel. It not only had the circuitry to perform the four standard arithmetic operations but it included facilities for calculating square roots and had special hardwired instructions to multiply a number by −1, 0.1, 0.5, 2, or 10. It also continued the practice of having special units to automatically convert numbers between binary and decimal notation in order to ease problems of reading and writing data.

The Z3 might best be compared in speed to the Harvard Mark I discussed later in this chapter. Although the Mark I was finished some two and a half years later than the Z3, it was no faster. The Z3 could perform three or four additions per second and multiply two numbers together in 4 to 5 seconds. The floating point representation of numbers in the Z3 made it more flexible than the Mark I's fixed point scheme, but the Mark I could deal with 23 decimal digits as compared with the Z3's more modest four-decimal-digit accuracy (although because of its floating-point memory it could represent numbers up to 10^{12}, but only with four-digit accuracy).

Started in 1939, the Z3 was operational by December 5, 1941. The total cost of materials was 25,000 RM (about $6,500 at the time). It was never used for any large problems because its limited memory would not enable it to hold enough information to be clearly superior to the manual methods for solving a system of linear equations, which was the problem that had motivated the DVL to fund the project. It remained in Zuse's house until being destroyed in an air raid in 1944. The Z1 and Z2 count as working versions of an automatically controlled calculating machine, but the Z3 was the first machine in the world that could be said to be a fully working computer with automatic control of its operations. There was, of course, no internally stored program and no way to easily implement conditional branch instructions, but both of these were several years away from being developed anywhere in the world. The achievements of Konrad Zuse are remarkable when you consider that he was cut off, because of the war, from all the developments in machine technology taking place in other countries. It is truly outstanding when you consider that he was also ignorant of the earlier work of Charles Babbage and out of contact with the people in Germany who were making modifications to the more traditional accounting machines. It was not until almost the end of the war, when he was shown a picture of the Harvard Mark I and realized the paper tape readers must be controlling a calculator like his own, that he even knew of any other development work along these same lines.

6.2.5 The Z4

The DVL had always considered the Z3 a prototype machine so, when it was complete, Zuse started on the improved version, the Z4. It was essentially the same as the Z3 except that it had a longer word length (32 bits) and reverted to the mechanical memory system. The Z4 was almost complete when, due to continued air raids, it was moved from Berlin to Göttingen where it was installed in the laboratory of the Aerodynamische Versuchsanstalt (Experimental Aerodynamics Institute). It was only there for a few weeks before Göttingen was in danger of being captured and the machine was once again moved, this time to Bavaria, where Zuse hid it in the basement of a house in the small town of Hinterstein, just before the area was captured by North African troops of the French Army. It was completely impractical to consider doing any further development work on computers at that time, so the team of 12 people that had been working with Zuse disbanded, each person following his own plans for coping during those very troubled times. Zuse, together with Wernher von Braun, the famous rocket engineer, went into hiding but both were persuaded to give themselves up to American troops when they arrived upon the scene.

In 1948 Zuse was taken to London to be interrogated by an executive of the British Tabulating Machine Co. (later known as ICL). The two men did not speak each other's language well and, no matter how hard he tried, Zuse could not convince the man from BTM that he had done anything of importance. In fairness to the BTM man, it should be remembered that very few people in the world at that time would have been able to comprehend Zuse's machine and even fewer would have been able to see any future in the computer industry.

The Z4 was removed from its hiding place and refurbished; some addi-

Figure 6–6. A reconstruction of the Z4 with the memory unit open for display. (Photograph courtesy of Konrad Zuse.)

tional tape control facilities were added to give it a conditional jump instruction, and it was taken to Switzerland where it was installed in the Federal Polytechnical Institute (ETH) in Zurich in 1950. As set up at the ETH, the machine still retained its mechanical memory. It could store 1,000 words in a mechanism which took up less than a cubic meter of space. Had Zuse continued with relay technology for the memory, it would have required at least 32,000 relays, the equivalent space of a very large room. In 1950 the Z4 was the only computer operational in Europe and one of only a few in the entire world. It was used by the Institute of Applied Mathematics at the ETH until 1955 when it was moved to the French Aerodynamic Research Institution near Basel, where it continued to give acceptable service until 1960.

The Z4 had a very interesting lookahead feature incorporated into its control and memory sections. The program tape was always read two steps ahead of the instruction that was currently being executed. This lookahead allowed three different speedup techniques to be implemented:

1. The next two instructions could be executed in reverse order if it would not affect the calculation and would increase the speed of the machine because intermediate results would be more readily available.
2. Two memory operations could be executed ahead of time in order that the slow speed of the mechanical memory would not degrade the performance of the machine.
3. It allowed the control unit to save a number which it was about to store back into the memory if that number would be needed by one of the next two instructions.

Such speedup techniques were, of course, necessary on a mechanical machine of this nature if it were to compete with the more traditional forms of calculating machines such as a modified accounting machine.

6.2.6 The Other Zuse Machines

Besides constructing the Z1 to Z4 machines, Zuse was also responsible for the development of two special-purpose computers for the Henschel firm. Henschel manufactured a special type of flying bomb called the HS 293. It was released from an airplane and then guided to the target by radio control. Although never used extensively, this weapon caused considerable problems with Allied shipping in the Mediterranean Sea.

One of the problems that arose during the construction of these bombs was that small deviations in the wing and control surfaces would cause difficulties with controlling the device. Zuse constructed a special calculator which would measure 100 points on the surface of the craft, convert these readings from analog to digital form, then calculate the expected deviations from the required aerodynamic properties of the craft. The wings and control surfaces were then adjusted to compensate for the deviations. The machine had a fixed program stored on rotating switches, much like a music box stores its tune. The actual operational part of the device was made from about 800 relays.

This special-purpose process control computer worked for almost two years from 1942 to 1944 when it was destroyed in an air raid. A replacement model was designed and constructed, but the war had progressed to the point where Henschel could no longer construct the flying bomb, so the new unit never was used in a productive capacity.

After the war, Zuse formed a company, the Zuse Kommandit Gesellschaft which was better known as Zuse KG. One of his first projects was to produce another relay-based, punched-tape driven, machine for the Leitz Optical Company. This was very similar to the refurbished Z4 in that it had a conditional branch instruction which could cause it to exit from loops. This machine, known as the Z5, was the forerunner of 42 more relay-based machines, called Z11s, which were in production until the mid-1950s. In 1956 Zuse began to design a vacuum-tube-based computer, the Z22, of which the first, of an eventual 50 machines, was delivered in 1958. A transistorized version was soon produced and well over 200 machines were built and delivered before a series of mergers and takeovers resulted in Zuse KG becoming part of the computer division of the giant industrial firm of Siemens.

Besides being an innovator in the design and construction of computers of all kinds, Zuse was also a leader in the field of software design. In the period immediately after the war, he occupied his time in the design of one of the world's first algorithmic languages, the Plankalkul. This language again shows his very early grasp of the fundamental problems of computer science because it contained variables, assignments, conditional and looping statements, structures, subscripts, and procedures with parameters. The only fundamental facilities any of today's major languages has beyond Zuse's initial concept are pointers and recursion. The description of the Plankalkul is beyond the scope of this book; however, it was a fundamental step in the creation of programming systems and should be studied by people with an interest in this area.

6.3 THE BELL RELAY COMPUTERS

6.3.1 The Situation

By the start of the twentieth century the electromagnetic relay had developed to the point where it could be put to use in commercial devices. It was soon one of the major devices incorporated into the telephone switching networks springing up around the world. The use of the relay by the telephone companies resulted in two things which were to aid in the development of computers: first the technical expertise in the use of relay technology was concentrated in research labs large enough to undertake very large projects and, secondly, the production of relays reached the stage where very reliable relays, of a standard design, could be easily obtained by both the professional engineer and the amateur experimenter.

The design of any piece of electrical apparatus, such as telephone transmission lines, involves extensive calculation and manipulation of numbers which have imaginary parts (involving the square root of minus one). These so-called "complex numbers" can be awkward to use when attempting calculations on an ordinary desktop mechanical calculator because the operator has to keep track of two different results, one for the real and one for the imaginary part of each number. In the late 1930s the problems involving calculation with complex numbers for the design of new telephone equipment began to hamper the growth of the Bell Telephone Company, and their research labs began to examine any mechanism which showed promise of alleviating this bottleneck.

In 1937 George Stibitz, a mathematician with the Bell Telephone Laboratories, rescued some relays out of a pile of scrap at the Labs and took them home so that he could experiment with them in his spare time. Stibitz had observed the similarity between binary numbers and the circuit diagrams involving telephone relays and, when the weekend left him with some spare time, he started playing with his ideas. He cut strips from a tin can and nailed them to a piece of wood to provide a primitive on/off switch while some batteries and a few flashlight bulbs provided an output device. He wired the relays together to form a circuit to add together two single-bit binary numbers, and the primitive input and output devices were hooked to either end.

Stibitz took the simple model into the Bell Labs to show his colleagues. In the summer of 1938 the head of Stibitz's group, Dr. T. C. Fry, had just been told about the problems the company was having in dealing with its calculating load, and he asked Stibitz if his toy could deal with complex numbers. Stibitz

Figure 6–7.   George Stibitz, 1979. (Photograph courtesy of AT&T Bell Laboratories.)

Figure 6–8. Stibitz's experimental circuit, the "model K" (for kitchen). (Photograph courtesy of AT&T Bell Laboratories.)

had already considered the types of circuits he would need for complex numbers and was able to quickly sketch out the basic concept. After a period of consideration, the Bell company decided to undertake the construction of Stibitz's ideas.

6.3.2 The Complex Number Calculator

The project got underway in earnest in late 1938 when S. B. Williams was appointed to oversee the entire project. Although Stibitz had the ideas, he was not an engineer and needed help with the design and drafting of workable relay circuits. By early 1939 Stibitz and Williams had managed to complete the design of what was to become quite a large and powerful calculator. Construction started in April of 1939, and it was complete enough for simple trials by the end of the year. Fully operational on January 8, 1940, the calculator remained in daily use at Bell Labs until 1949.

The Complex Number Calculator, composed mainly of standard telephone relays, could add, subtract, multiply, and divide complex numbers. It was not like a modern computer with a stored program, but was rather more like a large and sophisticated desktop calculator. There were three operating stations within the Bell Labs building, each of which was a standard teletype. An operator could request that an arithmetic operation be done simply by typing it in on the teletype, the answer would be printed on the same teletype moments later. Although there were three operating stations, only one could be actively using the machine at any given instant. There was a simple interlock mechanism, like the busy signal of a telephone, to ensure that only one person at a time was actually using the machine.

One of the great claims to fame for the Bell Complex Number Calculator is the fact that it was not only the first machine to service more than one terminal, but that it was also the first machine to be used from a remote location. On September 11, 1940, the American Mathematical Society held one of its meetings at Dartmouth College in Hanover, New Hampshire. Stibitz decided to use this meeting as the forum for a paper describing the calculator and

Figure 6–9. An operator using the Complex Number Calculator circa 1940. (Photograph courtesy of AT&T Bell Laboratories.)

wanted to have a demonstration of the machine in action as the final part of his presentation. A teletype was set up in the meeting area and connected, via special telephone lines, to the calculator at Bell Labs in New York. Conference participants were asked to enter problems and the machine returned its answers in less than one minute. This demonstration caused quite a stir among the assembled mathematicians. Participants in this meeting clearly remember both John Mauchly (one of the developers of ENIAC) and Norbert Weiner (a prominent mathematician) spending a lot of time experimenting with the system.

The machine was composed of about 450 ordinary telephone relays and ten crossbar switches, of the type normally to be found in a telephone exchange. The operations it performed were really limited to multiplication and division of complex numbers, but it was possible to ask for the results of successive operations to be accumulated in a register. If you wished to add or subtract a value from the accumulated total, multiplying it by either 1 or -1 would cause the desired operation to be performed. The operating stations printed their results with eight decimal places, but the internal registers would always work with ten decimal places to ensure accuracy.

Stibitz had, at first, intended the internal registers to be able to deal with numbers where the decimal point could be located between any two digits. He soon realized that this design would be impractical with the facilities available to him, so he eventually settled on a scheme in which all numbers inside the computer were in the range $+1$ to -1. The human operators had to scale all their inputs into this range and then remember to expand the results to the correct order of magnitude. Although this process was awkward for the operators, it very much simplified the design and construction of the machine.

The internal relay registers held all their numbers in the "plus three binary-coded decimal" form. Each decimal digit was represented by four binary bits according to the following scheme:

0	0011	5	1000
1	0100	6	1001
2	0101	7	1010
3	0110	8	1011
4	0111	9	1100

This strange coding scheme was chosen because it led to a simplification of part of the arithmetic unit. If plus three BCD code is used, rather than ordinary BCD, then it turns out that fewer relay-based circuits are required to deal with problems such as carry operations between digits, taking the complement of a number, and determining the sign of a number.

Although the Complex Number Calculator was an outstanding success as a first system, Bell Telephone Laboratories had spent about $20,000 on its design and construction, and they felt that it was not financially feasible to at-

Figure 6–10. The arithmetic unit of the Complex Number Calculator. (Photograph courtesy of AT&T Bell Laboratories.)

tempt the construction of another machine. This was unfortunate because Stibitz had made some suggestions, such as a floating-point number system, which would have made the machine even more useful. Stibitz and Williams returned to their normal jobs with Bell under the assumption that they had seen the end of their association with computing machinery. The increasing political tensions and the dawn of the Second World War were soon to change all that.

6.3.3 *The Relay Interpolator*

When the United States became involved in the Second World War, George Stibitz was co-opted by the National Defense Research Council to help out with some of the war work. One of the projects undertaken by the NDRC was the construction of an automatic aiming device for antiaircraft guns. The object of this project was to construct a device which, as the gunner turned knobs to track an airplane across the sky, would automatically aim the gun far enough ahead of the airplane so that the chance of a hit being scored would be improved over manual aiming of the gun.

The initial design for such an aiming device called for extensive calculations in order to predict how the mechanism would function. Stibitz, deciding that simulation would be a better way of predicting the actions of a gun director, constructed a device which would simulate the arbitrary motions of a target airplane. The idea was that this simulator would be controlled by a punched paper tape and that *it* could be used for testing the gun director instead of having a large number of aircraft tied up making test flights over the gun range. The problem of producing the large quantity of punched paper control tape was solved when Stibitz suggested that a relay-based calculator be constructed, tested, and used to produce the punched tape in less time than it would take to do the required calculations by hand.

Bell Telephone Laboratories was commissioned to construct the machine. In later years it was formally called the Model II Relay Calculator but, because it was used to do linear interpolations and smoothing operations on data read from paper tape, it was initially christened the Relay Interpolator. It was finished, and fully operational, in September of 1943.

In its final form the Interpolator consisted of five separate units: (1) a group of five registers, each of which could store a five-digit number, (2) an arithmetic circuit to perform addition, (3) a master control unit, (4) ordinary teletype paper tape readers used for input of data, and (5) teletype printers for listing results. The machine was capable of executing 31 different instructions which were invoked by commands punched on paper tape, the machine reading and executing one command before going on to read the next. For most jobs the control tape was in the form of a paper tape loop so that the same series of instructions could be performed over and over again on data being read in from other paper tape readers. Although only really capable of addition, the arithmetic circuits were used for subtraction by adding complements of numbers.

Stibitz was anxious to make this machine as reliable as possible. Because it had about 500 relays, it was thought that at least one of them would fail from time to time and thus produce incorrect answers without any means of knowing that this had occurred. The major design feature which allowed for self-checking was the use of the bi-quinary system of coding for the numbers held in the registers. This system, which was used in all subsequent machines de-

THE BI-QUINARY CODING SCHEME

Digit	Bi-quinary coding	
0	01 00001	
1	01 00010	
2	01 00100	
3	01 01000	
4	01 10000	(1 = relay set)
5	10 00001	(0 = relay not set)
6	10 00010	
7	10 00100	
8	10 01000	
9	10 10000	

signed by Stibitz, consisted of making the registers essentially decimal in nature, with each digit being stored in seven relays using bi-quinary notation. This notation divides the relays into two groups, the first group consisting of five relays used to indicate values from zero to four, the second group of two relays used to indicate the presence or absence of a value of five.

Although this scheme is wasteful of relays when you compare it to the binary coding of digits (which would require only four relays for a single digit), it has the advantage that one, and only one, relay is set in each group for the coding of any given digit. This allowed the machine to self-check each digit of a number whenever it was involved in an operation. It is, in fact, a more powerful checking device than the parity checking schemes used in later computers.

The final machine consisted of 493 relays mounted in two racks each 2 ft wide by 5 ft high. The input-output equipment sat on a separate table at the end of the room in which it was housed. It became operational in September of 1943 and quickly accomplished the initial calculations for which it had been designed. Although it was intended as a special-purpose machine, its range of computational tasks were expanded, and it remained in use throughout the rest of the Second World War. After the war was over, the NDRC donated it to the U.S. Naval Research Laboratory where it continued to lead a productive life until it was finally shut off for the last time in 1961.

6.3.4 The Model III and IV

The third of Stibitz's relay computers grew out of the same project as the Relay Interpolator and was, in fact, being designed in 1942 even before the Relay Interpolator was complete. In order to decide if the antiaircraft gun director was actually tracking an aircraft correctly and aiming the gun so that the shells would burst just in front of the airplane, it could either be tested out with a real airplane and live ammunition or an attempt could be made to simulate the situation and calculate where the shell would have been when it exploded. It was, of course, the latter situation which was decided upon and a mathematical model was created for it.

A bomber was flown down the gun range and photographs were taken, at one-second intervals, of the indicators showing angular height, azimuth, and range of the airplane and elevation, angle of train, and fuse settings of the gun. From this data it was possible to calculate where the shell would have been at the instant it detonated. Unfortunately, each test run resulted in a series of calculations which required about one week to do by hand. This held up the development of the antiaircraft director project to such an extent that it looked like the war would be over before the device was ready for action. Again a special relay calculator was constructed to help solve the problem. In later years it became known as the Model III, but it was usually referred to as the "Ballistic Computer" because of its use in the simulation of the ballistic flight of a projectile.

The technology employed in the Ballistic Computer was of the same type that was so successful in the Relay Interpolator. The storage was doubled from the five registers available in the Relay Interpolator to ten for the Ballistic Computer, but the bi-quinary storage mechanism and the method of performing additions and subtractions were retained because of their reliability. A new unit for doing multiplication and division was designed and integrated into the arithmetic unit. Multiplication was done by the addition of partial products, much as we do it today with paper and pencil, while division was done by subtraction of the partial products. The list of partial products was generated by a special unit which essentially consisted of a multiplication table, like a set of Napier's "bones," implemented from relays. There was nothing really new in this idea for, as we have already seen, this was the same scheme used by Charles Babbage in the analytical engine.

There were four paper tape readers attached to the machine: one for reading information about the airplane's position, one for information about the aiming of the gun, one which generally held a long loop of tape containing tables of ballistic functions, and the fourth for reading the tape containing the instructions which the machine was to execute.

If, during a calculation, the machine needed a number from one of the ballistic tables, it could be instructed to hunt the long loop of tape in the table reader until it found the required value. The standard teletype paper tape readers were modified so that they could move the paper tape either forward or backward, and a special "hunter" circuit was created to scan the loops of tape searching for a particular value. The hunter circuit was designed so that, if it decided it could find the proper value faster by searching the tape in the opposite direction, it would simply cause the paper tape reader to reverse the direction of tape movement. People who remember the machine claim that it was almost human in its action of starting to read a table tape, stopping and suddenly skipping backward along the tape to the requested value.

A typical calculation for one shell would require about 40 multiplications and 20 or 30 additions and subtractions; this would take the Ballistic Computer about 2½ minutes to accomplish, the actual time for a single multiplication being about 1 second. Although not what we would call fast by modern standards, it was very reliable in operation, often being loaded up with enough tape to keep it in operation for 24 hours or more. A special bell was set up over the bed occupied by the machine's supervisor and, if the checking circuits detected an error, the bell would summon the luckless army sergeant to correct the problem before he could resume his night's sleep.

When construction was finished in June of 1944, the machine consisted of 1300 ordinary relays plus an additional 35 multicontact relays used in the multiply/divide unit. These were mounted in five separate frames, each about 3 ft wide by 5 ft high. The input/output and control equipment was actually in a building adjacent to the one in which the main equipment was housed.

In 1948 the Model III was moved to the laboratory of the Army Field Forces Board in Fort Bliss, Texas, where it remained in service until 1958. After the move, it was modified to have 14 internal registers rather than 10.

A second Ballistic Computer, this one known officially as Bell Laboratories Relay Calculator Model IV (or Error Detector Mark 22 by the Navy) was constructed for the ordnance group at the Naval Research Laboratories in Washington, D.C. This machine, completed in March of 1945, was used for the same type of calculations as the Army's Ballistic Computer. The only real dif-

Figure 6-11.   The Bell Model III. (Illustration from a paper by E. G. Andrews, 1952.)

ference from the Model III was the incorporation of some circuits to aid in calculations involving trigonometric functions of negative angles which were required for aiming guns from the rolling deck of a ship at sea. It remained in active service in the United States Navy until 1961.

6.3.5 The Model V (The Twin Machine)

Because of success with the small Relay Interpolator and the Ballistic Computer, the United States government decided to back the design and construction of a much larger relay-based computing system. The main reason for needing larger machines was the growing backlog of computations which were needed by the people producing artillery firing tables, a subject discussed in more detail in the section dealing with the ENIAC. In 1944 the government gave a contract to Bell Telephone Laboratories to produce two identical machines; one was to be used at the National Advisory Committee for Aeronautics at Langley Field, Virginia, while the other was destined for the Ballistic Research Laboratories at the U.S. Army Proving Grounds in Aberdeen, Maryland. The first of these was delivered to Langley Field in July of 1946 while the second, and not quite identical, machine remained under test at Bell Laboratories until February 1947. There is a small dispute over the exact dates these machines were delivered. E. G. Andrews, for example, suggests that they were delayed about six months from the dates just indicated. These machines were known as the Bell Laboratories General Purpose Relay Calculators, or Model V for short.

The Model V was actually two machines in one. It could be split in half with each half working on a separate problem or, for larger calculations, both halves could work together. Each Model V was an order of magnitude more complex than any of the previous Bell products. Each machine consisted of two arithmetic units, four problem input stations (each of which had twelve paper tape readers), and two output stations (each with a teleprinter and a paper tape punch). The initial design called for a machine with six arithmetic units and ten problem input stations, but only the versions with two arithmetic units were ever constructed. Stibitz's ideas on how to implement floating-point numbers were at last incorporated into a relay-based machine. The registers, while still employing the bi-quinary coding scheme, were divided into two separate parts, one for holding a seven-digit mantissa and the other an exponent in the range -19 to $+19$. Each machine had 44 such registers, 30 of which were available for storing numbers while the other 14 were for internal functions in the arithmetic and control units. Each floating point register required 62 relays in order to implement its full abilities.

The four-problem input stations (the Langley machine actually had only three) were designed so that one station could be used to control each half of the machine while the remaining two could be kept ready, loaded with paper tapes, for the next problem to be solved. This design eliminated, to a large

Figure 6–12. The Bell Model V. (Photograph courtesy of AT&T Bell Laboratories.)

extent, the lengthy set-up time which had reduced the efficiency of both the Ballistic Computer and the Relay Interpolator. Each input station had 12 paper tape readers whose jobs were divided as follows:

1. One reader would read a "problem definition" tape containing the code numbers of the tapes in the other eleven readers. The machine would check these code numbers by reading the first few inches of each tape just to make sure no errors had been made in loading tapes.

2. Five of the readers were used to mount tapes containing machine instructions. Any of the five could assume control over half of the machine or pass control to a specific section of tape on another reader.

3. The last six readers were used for ordinary data tapes and long loops of table values which might be needed in the calculation.

The paper tape punch in the output station could be used to punch out intermediate results which could then be fed back into the machine via one of the data tape readers. After it was finished with its job of checking the problem definition tape code numbers, the first reader could be used for an additional data tape if the problem were complex enough to require the extra data.

Each of the two Model V machines contained about 9,000 relays and about 50 pieces of miscellaneous teletype equipment; it weighed in at about 10 tons and required 1,000 sq ft of floor space to accommodate it. Part of the increase in size and complexity from the earlier models was due to the large array of input/output equipment, but this machine also had a much more sophisticated control and arithmetic unit than anything Bell had made before.

The arithmetic unit was interesting in that it did not really have any arithmetic circuitry; rather it looked up the answer to any addition problem in a large hardwired addition table. This CADET (Can't Add, Doesn't Even Try) architecture was actually reasonably efficient and was copied in several subsequent electronic computers, the IBM 1620 Model I being a notable example from the early 1960s. Subtraction was done, as in the earlier machines, by simply adding the complement of the required number. Multiplication was done by simple repeated addition, while both the division and square root operations were implemented by repeated subtraction. The instruction times were slowed down a bit because of the need for checking the accuracy of the results at each stage of the operation, but were not totally unreasonable for their day. Both addition and subtraction required 0.3 of a second each, a multiplication took 0.8 seconds, division 2.2 seconds, and taking a square root needed 4.3 seconds. Rather than cause the machine to waste time by searching down long paper tape loops of tables for frequently used functions, a series of five hardwired tables was incorporated into the arithmetic units. These tables contained critical values of sin, cos, arctan, log, and antilog functions and, if other values were needed, the machine could interpolate them from these tables in about 15 seconds.

The control unit was also larger and had more options than any of the previous Bell machines. The usual operating mode was to use two of the input stations to drive the machine on two individual problems and have the two spare problem stations loaded with tapes ready to go. The machine contained automatic switching equipment to transfer control from one station to another when the first calculation was complete. While running on an individual problem, the control mechanism had instructions which could discriminate on the sign of any register and then switch control from one paper tape to another. This allowed for the programming of loops and for a primitive type of subroutine system.

Programming for the machine would have been familiar to modern programmers because the instructions, rather than being coded as a single row of punches as in the earlier Bell machines, were actually punched out as a series of letters in the six-hole-wide paper tape. A typical instruction might have been:

$$BC + GC = A$$

which would have been interpreted by the Model V as "add the contents of register B to the contents of register G and put the result into register A." The optional C in the instruction meant to clear the registers to zero when the operation was complete. This rather complex command structure meant that the machine required almost two seconds to read, decode, and begin the execution of each instruction on the control tape. This implied that the speed of the machine was not determined by the slowness of the arithmetic elements, but rather the speed at which the instructions could be understood. It quite literally often took six times as long to read an instruction as to execute it.

Although this was one of the slowest of the early machines—with, perhaps, the exception of the Harvard Mark I—it was by far the most reliable. The extra trouble taken to design a failsoft system around the bi-quinary coding scheme proved worthwhile time and time again. If a speck of dust got trapped in a relay contact and caused an erroneous result then, as soon as it was found and removed, the machine would take up the calculation from the point at which it had been interrupted without any effort. In one week at the Ballistic Research Laboratory the Model V was used for useful production for 167 out of a possible 168 hours, most of it unattended. During the first four months of operation at the BRL the machine produced one wrong answer due to incorrect wiring in the machine as delivered by Bell. Several wrong answers were produced when people deliberately interfered with the mechanism, but none were ever found to be caused by an undetected malfunction of the machine. The machine at Langley Field averaged about 22 hours of productive computing in each 24-hour day. When a fault did occur, it usually only took 15 to 30 minutes to find and correct the problem before productive work could continue.

The high degree of reliability was not only because the hardware was well designed, but because care had been taken in the way the program tapes were prepared. The instruction tape was punched twice by two different people, and then these would be compared by a special machine that punched out a third tape to actually control the machine. The comparison device was sophisticated enough to do some simple translation of numerical information from decimal to the internal floating-point format of the Model V during its operation of comparing the two tapes. This not only helped to reduce the error rate in the program tapes, but allowed for a more convenient form of numerical notation for the human operators.

Development costs were never made public by Bell, but the actual construction costs were about $500,000 for each of the two machines.

After the War, the Model V used by the Ballistic Research Laboratory was moved to Fort Bliss and, when the Army no longer felt it was productive, it was given to the University of Arizona. The machine used by the National Advisory Committee on Aeronautics was donated to the Texas Technological College in 1958 but the truck moving it was involved in an accident and the machine destroyed. It ended its days as a series of spare parts for the one in Arizona.

6.3.6 The Model VI

After the war Stibitz had already left his position with Bell, but that did not prevent Bell from constructing one more version of the Stibitz-inspired machines. The Model VI was really a modified Model V. Only one of these machines was ever made, and it was installed in the Murray Hill location of the Bell Telephone Laboratories in November of 1950. It was used mainly to do the same sort of work that the old Complex Number Calculator had been doing during the previous ten years.

The main difference between the Model V and the Model VI was that the latter could deal with 10-digit rather than 7-digit numbers, it had only one arithmetic unit, and it contained facilities for up to 200 hardwired subroutines to be incorporated into the control mechanism. This not only eliminated the need to read control tapes to obtain instructions for common subroutines but it also speeded up the machine because it eliminated the time-consuming reading and decoding process. A secondary advantage, discovered afterwards, was that it also greatly improved the coding accuracy of the programmers.

The hardwired subroutines were implemented with technology which came directly from their number 5 cross-bar telephone dialing system. It consisted of some 80 air core coils, each of which could trigger a circuit when a pulsed current flowed in any of several wires threaded through the coil. A subroutine was programmed by threading a wire from a numbered pulse terminal, through a set of coils, to a common ground. A pulse from the terminal would excite the appropriate circuits in the machine. There were six possible levels of subroutines. The first was invoked by an instruction punched on paper tape, and this could invoke others at lower levels. The last level would invoke individual instructions built into the machine.

The Model VI, like the Model V, would automatically initiate a second trial if an error was detected while executing an instruction. If the second attempt failed, the machine would automatically produce a trouble report on punched paper tape and switch to another problem. Because relay problems were often intermittent in nature, this system worked quite well, and most problems were overcome on the second try.

In the late 1950s the Model VI was donated to the Polytechnic Institute in Brooklyn, New York, and the Institute in turn donated it in 1961 to the Bihar Institute of Technology in India where it still resides as an historical display.

Although only a few individuals have been named in this account of the developments that took place at Bell Labs, over 20 engineers actually took part in the design and construction of Models I through VI. This expertise was put to good use when these engineers, and the people they in turn trained, took jobs throughout the developing computer industry. Bell Labs also made use of this expertise when they constructed relay-based equipment to automatically record and bill subscribers for their detail-billed and bulk-billed telephone calls. This relay-based accounting equipment was used for many years but was finally replaced by standard commercial electronic computers when the growing volume of calls demanded higher speeds from the accounting equipment.

6.4 THE HARVARD MACHINES OF HOWARD AIKEN

6.4.1 Introduction

There was another sequence of machines being produced, at the same time as those of Zuse and Stibitz, under the guidance of Howard Aiken at the Computational Laboratories in Harvard University. Unlike Stibitz's machines at Bell Laboratories, Aiken's designs were not all based on one form of technology, such as the relay, but used whatever technology was available at the time. The Harvard machines span the whole range from the almost entirely mechanical, through the use of the electromagnetic relay, to the incorporation in the last model of electronic elements such as magnetic ferrite core memories. As with the Bell Laboratories machines, the initial ideas were present before the outbreak of the Second World War, but it was the war which provided the impetus for their eventual development.

6.4.2 The Harvard Mark I

At the time he started these machines, Howard Aiken was a professor of applied mathematics at the Graduate School of Engineering, Harvard University, but our story actually begins earlier when he was still a graduate student in physics at the same institution. Some of the research problems that interested Aiken involved nonlinear differential equations whose solutions could not be obtained by the standard analytical procedures. If Aiken had attempted to solve the equations by means of numerical methods, the labor would have been enormous. He decided that he required a calculating machine whose power was at least an order of magnitude above anything available at the time. Aiken, through contacts at Harvard, was aware of the existence of the IBM-sponsored, punched card based, Thomas J. Watson Astronomical Computing Bureau at Columbia University. He was familiar with the types of calculations which could be done by using standard punched card accounting equipment, but realized that, in order to have a powerful calculating machine, a large number of individual punched card machines would have to be hooked together and be controlled

Figure 6–13.   Howard Aiken. (Photograph courtesy of the Harvard University Cruft Photo Laboratory.)

from one central unit. Aiken knew about Charles Babbage and very likely obtained some of his central control ideas from reading Babbage's works.

Aiken suggested his ideas to several people in various firms that constructed calculating machines but no one seemed very interested. Finally, in 1937, with the help of some astronomers at Harvard and from Wallace Eckert at the Thomas J. Watson Astronomical Computing Bureau, he managed to convince IBM that, with financial help from the United States Navy, it should undertake to construct a large-scale computing machine. IBM agreed to Aiken's proposal not because management thought there was a market for such a device, but rather for the publicity and good will that such a project would generate. Design and construction of the machine began in 1939 at the IBM plant in Endicott, New York. Although Aiken was the driving force behind the project, he was usually careful to point out that the IBM engineers had made substantial contributions and that three of them (B. M. Durfee, F. E. Hamilton, and C. D. Lake) should be considered, with him, as co-inventors. The machine required several years of construction effort before it became operational at Endicott in January of 1943. It was then moved to the prepared site at Harvard where it was demonstrated to be operational in May of 1944. In the summer of that same year, T. J. Watson, president of IBM, presented the computer to Harvard as a gift from IBM. It was officially called the Harvard-IBM Automatic Sequence Controlled Calculator, but it soon became known as the Mark I. At the presentation ceremony T. J. Watson felt that Aiken's speech did not give enough credit to the efforts of IBM and their engineers. This slight, whether imagined or real, was to result in a falling out between the two men which was to last the rest of their lives.

The basic design called for the construction of a machine whose registers were built from standard IBM mechanical accounting machine registers, each of which was a self-contained adding machine; that is, each register, rather than being a simple storage mechanism, was a complete accumulator and simple arithmetic unit in its own right. Numbers could be transferred out of one register and added to another without involving any other arithmetic units than

Figure 6–14.   The Harvard Mark I, July, 1944. (Photograph courtesy of the Harvard University Cruft Photo Laboratory.)

those which were an integral part of the two registers involved. The Mark I was to be given its sequence of instructions via specially constructed punched paper tape readers. Numbers were transferred from one mechanical register to the next by means of electrical signals.

There were 72 of the mechanical registers in the machine, each capable of storing 23 decimal digits plus one digit for the sign (0 for plus and 9 for minus). The position of the decimal point was fixed for any particular computation, but could be changed, via plugboard settings, to be between any two digits in the register. It was usually set to be between the 15th and 16th decimal positions.

Each register was constructed from the standard IBM accounting machine register mechanism of the day. There were 24 wheels, each of which could be rotated to ten different positions to store a digit from 0 to 9. These wheels had a large hole in the center, through which ran a continually rotating shaft. The shafts from all registers were connected to a main drive shaft which ran the length of the machine and this, in turn, was powered by a 5 hp motor which resided behind the main units. If a pulse appeared on a signal wire, signaling that some quantity was to be added to a particular digit, it would cause a magnetic clutch to "grab" the rotating shaft and, as long as the signal was present, the wheel representing that digit would be caused to rotate. Thus a signal lasting two pulse-time units would cause the wheel to rotate two steps, adding two to that particular digit.

If it was required to add the contents of one register to the contents of another, the wheels storing the first number would be rotated and electrical brushes would sense the position of each wheel and cause signals of the appropriate length to be sent to the second accumulator. These signals would cause the magnetic clutches of this accumulator to grab the rotating shaft for enough time to add the required amounts to each wheel. All this would take place in the time taken for the main drive shaft to move through one half a rotation. The second half of the rotation was used to perform the carries generated by the addition, in much the same way that Babbage and Scheutz did it almost a century earlier.

Facilities existed for splitting or joining some registers so that half-, full-, or double-length arithmetic was possible. The background noise of the continuously rotating drive shafts, together with the clicks and clacks of the magnetic clutches grabbing and releasing, resulted in the machine room having a very impressive busy feeling.

Besides the mechanical accumulators, the Mark I contained 60 constant registers, the numbers in which were set by means of switches on an external panel, three paper tape readers used to read long loops of tabular information, a large 24-channel paper tape reader for the control tape, two standard IBM card readers, a card punch, and two electric typewriters for printing results. The instructions were punched on wide strips of paper tape which were simply made from uncut standard IBM accounting machine card stock. The holes were

MECHANICAL DRIVE SYSTEM

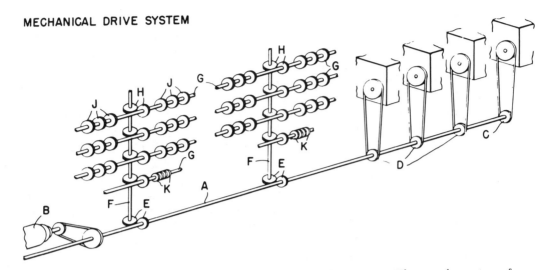

Figure 6-15. The Harvard Mark I mechanical drive system. (Photograph courtesy of the Harvard University Cruft Photo Laboratory.)

sensed by the then standard IBM method of wire brushes making contact with a brass roller through holes in the tape. Data for a particular problem was usually read through the card reader while the results went to either the card punch or the typewriters. If a problem required only one or two data items, these data were often set up on the special bank of constant switch registers. However, as it took setting 24 switches to represent each number, this was not done if there were any more than a few numbers.

Each accumulator, constant register, input/output unit, and switch register was given a unique number which was used as part of the instructions punched on the control tape. Each instruction occupied one complete row of 24 punch positions in the following format: The number represented by the first eight bits was that of the unit which supplied the data, the second eight bits represented the unit number destined to receive the result, while the third group of eight bits specified the operation to be performed. All the numbers were punched in binary.

The basic cycle time was established by the fact that the control tape reader was attached to the same drive shaft that powered the accumulators. The 200 rpm rotation of this shaft meant that the elementary operations of reading the next instruction from the tape, adding, subtracting, clearing a register, or transferring a number from one register to another each took about 0.3 second. Special arithmetic units were set up to do multiplication, division, and to calculate specific values of $\sin(x)$, 10^x, and $\log(x)$. An additional mechanism interpolated between two tabular values so that it was always possible to obtain trigonometrical values. These special devices were used only when it was impossible

Figure 6–16.   The Mark I paper tape readers. (Photograph courtesy of the Harvard University Cruft Photo Laboratory.)

to avoid them because their operation time was nontrivial: sin(x) took a full minute, 10^x needed over 61 seconds, while a logarithm required 68.4 seconds. Although the process was time-consuming, it should be remembered that these values were all obtained by series approximations and were accurate to 23 decimal places—which is more than can be said for some modern computers. Multiplication and division were quite fast, considering the mechanical nature of the design. Multiplication took at most six seconds, and often less, while division could need 16 seconds, but usually required only 10. This variable length of time stemmed from the fact that the multiplication was done by the addition of partial products and, when the multiplier has some zeros in its digits, they can be skipped over very rapidly. Finding the product of two numbers was really a three-step process requiring three different instructions to be punched into the control tape. The first instruction would send a number off to the multiply unit, which would then generate all the single-digit multiples of the number, much like assembling the set of Napier's "bones" which would be required.

The second instruction would cause the multiplicand to be sent to the unit, which would then select out the required single-digit multiples (the rows of Napier's "bones") and add them up with the appropriate decimal place shifts. The third instruction would indicate a transfer from the multiply unit's result register to one of the standard registers in the machine. The most time-consuming part of this process was the calculation of the single-digit multiples, and it was often the case that other operations would be coded between steps 1 and 2 on the control tape so that they could be done in parallel with this phase of the multiplication. Division operated in a similar way to multiplication and, like it, required three individual steps on the control tape. Other operations could be carried out in parallel with the first phase of the division operation in the same way that it would be done with multiplication.

When it was first constructed, the machine had very little capability for modifying its sequence of instructions based on results obtained during the calculation. It was capable of choosing from different algorithms for the calculations required by its special function units, the choice depending on the value of the function argument, but the only way of changing from one sequence of programmed instructions to another was to halt the machine and let the operators change the control tape. It did have the ability to test when the contents of a register became greater than a certain limit, but when the only possible outcomes are either to continue with the calculation or to halt the machine, it made unattended operation impossible.

In later years, three large boxes, known as the Subsidiary Sequence Mechanism, and three more control tape readers were added to give the programmers more flexibility in the control of the machine's operations. With these additions control could be transferred between the paper tape readers depending on whether the contents of registers were positive or negative. The Subsidiary Sequence Mechanism was a large series of plugboard panels which allowed for up to ten often used subroutines to be "wired" into the machine. These wired subroutines, which were invoked from the main sequence control tape, could run up to 22 instructions long.

The initial configuration of the Mark I was a 51-ft-long series of panels, 8 ft high, with two other 6-ft-long panels extending from the back of the machine at right angles. It was a very impressive-looking device because IBM, anxious to make this a showcase of their engineering ability, had done it up properly with very good looking cabinets, the majority of which had glass fronts. Internally there were over 750,000 different parts, most of which were either binary switches, relays, decade (ten-position) switches, rotating wheels for the registers, or simple cams used for timing pulses. There were over 1400 ten-position rotary switches on the front of the machine, mainly in the panel incorporating the 60 constant registers. Although only 51 ft long, the Mark I contained over 500 miles of wire to carry the power and digital signals from unit to unit.

When, in May of 1944, the Mark I was set up and working at Harvard, it

Figure 6–17. The Mark I from a different vantage point, July, 1944. (Photograph courtesy of the Harvard University Cruft Photo Laboratory.)

was immediately enlisted in the war effort. Aiken, who was a commander in the United States Naval Reserve, was put in charge of the computation project of the Navy's Bureau of Ships, and the machine was entirely devoted to military uses until after the war. Responsibility for the machine was later shifted to the Navy's Bureau of Ordnance, but this resulted in little change as far as Aiken and his crew were concerned. One of Aiken's young assistants, Lieutenant Grace M. Hopper, was to continue her association with both the Navy and the computing industry and made fundamental contributions to the development of the first compilers and to the later United States Navy standardization of COBOL. She has been promoted through the ranks and, in the mid-1980s, when she attained the rank of Commodore, she became the oldest serving officer in the United States Navy. Her voice is still being heard in the design of languages to be used by the military in the 1980s.

After the war, the Mark I spent its time doing work such as computing mathematical tables of Bessel functions. However, even with its added control readers and the Subsidiary Sequence Mechanism, it was overtaken in both speed and ease of use by the increasing number of electronic computers. It remained in active use until 1959 when it was dismantled, some of the parts being kept for display at Harvard, the IBM headquarters in New York, and at the Smithsonian Institute in Washington, D.C.

The Mark I design was to influence the designers of more advanced machines, such as the ENIAC. In fact, the Mark I probably had more impact as a design model than it did as an actual machine. The Harvard log books show that almost everyone who was involved in the design and development of computing machines visited the Harvard Computational Laboratories at one time or another to inspect the machine for themselves. It was only with the advent of suitable devices which could act as random access computer memories that the fundamental architecture of computing machines moved away from the basic ideas incorporated in the Harvard-IBM Mark I.

Because IBM did all the early development work and designed all the special features of the control units without regard to the eventual selling price of the machine, it is impossible to gauge the actual development costs of the project. Perhaps IBM might one day put an accountant to work with their old

Figure 6–18. Grace M. Hopper U.S.N. (Photograph courtesy of Grace Hopper.)

records to total up what will undoubtedly be a very large expenditure on development. The actual hardware incorporated into the Mark I, together with the construction charges, came to between $400,000 and $500,000.

6.4.3 The Harvard Mark II

Aiken was well aware that the basic ideas of automatically sequenced computing machines were not limited to one form of hardware implementation. When he first proposed that such a machine be constructed, it was in very general terms and, only when IBM agreed to back his plan, did it firm up into the reliance on IBM tabulating machine components. He was familiar with the history of people attempting to construct calculating machines, particularly the efforts of Charles Babbage. As a consequence he was well aware that an attempt to construct a machine using too high a level of untested technology would likely get him into the same kind of trouble that Babbage found when attempting the construction of his own machines.

When he was asked, in later years, why he chose the slower electrically controlled mechanical components over the possibilities of making an entirely relay-based machine, Aiken reportedly indicated that what he wanted was a calculating machine and he was willing to work with anyone's technology as long as they paid the bills. Aiken had actually first approached the Monroe Co., who made a line of traditional mechanical desktop calculators, about constructing his machine and it was only when they turned him down that he found IBM would be interested. Had Monroe actually agreed to Aiken's proposal, the Mark I would likely have been made from purely mechanical components.

Aiken's technological flexibility is illustrated by the fact that, in early 1945, the Navy asked him to design and construct another machine for use at the Naval Proving Ground in Dahlgren, Virginia. This machine, known as the Mark II, was designed entirely from electromagnetic relays. It was finished to the point where it could run some realistic test problems by July of 1947. The Mark II was considerably faster than the Mark I. The replacement of the entirely mechanical register mechanism of the Mark I by a relay-based system was one source of greatly increased speed, but other areas also contributed to the increased performance. Because he had Navy backing, and could obtain materials that were generally in short supply, Aiken used a specially designed high-

Figure 6–19.   The Harvard Mark II front panel, January, 1948. (Photograph courtesy of the Harvard University Cruft Photo Laboratory.)

speed relay. This relay had six-pole, double-throw contacts, operated at 100 volts DC, required six watts to keep the contacts made, and could make or break the contacts in less than 0.01 seconds. About one third of the relays had special mechanical locks which would keep them closed without the magnets being energized. This saved on power costs, provided a secure form of storage even with the power off, and, most importantly, it also reduced the heat dissipation problems of a large machine. Mark II was not cheap—the special relays cost $15.00 each and it used just over 13,000 of them.

The Mark II, like the Bell Telephone Laboratories Model V which was being constructed about the same time for other branches of the armed services, could be split into two separate machines to work on two different, but smaller, problems. Each half of the machine contained 50 registers for storing numbers, two multiplication units, one addition unit, two separate paper tape readers for the instruction tapes, and an additional four tape readers for data tapes. A numerical register could hold a 10-digit floating-point number with an exponent in the range -15 to $+15$. The digits were stored via binary-coded decimal (BCD) techniques. An additional relay provided an indication of the sign. There were a number of hardwired subroutines which were designed to allow $1/x$, $1/sqrt(x)$, $ln(x)$, $exp(x)$, $cos(x)$, and $arctan(x)$ to be calculated automatically. Rather than construct a special divide unit, that operation was done by the two-step process of using the built-in subroutine to obtain the reciprocal of the divisor and then using the multiplication unit to multiply the numerator by this reciprocal to obtain the final result.

Although there were multiple arithmetic units which could be used in parallel to perform several different operations at once, it was seldom the case that this facility could be used over long periods of time because of the difficulty of organizing the program tapes. The difficulty lay in the fact that the machine was designed to read an instruction from the control tapes, decode it, and begin its execution without checking that any of the required operands were actually available. There were no interlocks, in the way we would think of them today, to prevent the machine from attempting to use a result before it was available. Instead the rather clever control system took care of this situation.

The control system would read an instruction from the control tape and, although there were only eight possible instructions that it could find on the tape, it depended on the current state of the machine as to the meaning of each of these eight commands. Each second was divided up into a number of time periods, and an instruction would mean different things if executed in a different time period. This required that some operations, say a multiplication, could be initiated only during certain time periods, and any reference to the result register of that unit could also only take place during certain periods. The instructions, and their associated time periods, were chosen so that there was no possibility of accessing a value before it was available. In each second of time there were four periods when a multiplication could be started, eight periods when an addition or subtraction could be done, and 12 times when it was possible to transfer information from register to register. This scheme worked well but was difficult to program unless the operator was willing to accept a loss of machine efficiency while it waited for the appropriate time period to arrive.

The Mark II was considerably faster at arithmetic than the Mark I, 125 milliseconds being required for addition, 750 milliseconds for multiplication, and between 5 and 12 seconds being required to execute one of the built-in functions, depending on the function required and the value of its argument.

The multiplication unit used an interesting algorithm. When the multiplicand had been sent to the unit, it would automatically calculate five different multiples of the number; 1,2,4, and 5 times the multiplicand were generated by special circuits to do direct multiplication, while the 3 times multiple was generated by adding together the 1 and 2 times multiples. When the multiplier was sent to the unit, it would select the required multiple, depending on the digits present in the multiplier, and, after appropriate shifts, either add or subtract them from the result register. The idea of generating only the first five multiples, and then using complementary subtraction to effectively add the sixth through ninth multiple seems to have been unique to this machine.

6.4.4 The Harvard Mark III and Mark IV

After the war, Aiken continued to develop his machines at the Harvard Computational Laboratory, although the funding was always provided by outside agencies. He was much more concerned with the ease of use of his machines than with any thoughts of creating an ultra-high-speed computer. In the tests he did on the Mark I and the Mark II he found that increasing the speed of a machine by a factor of ten only resulted in a factor of two or three in increased throughput, while a decrease in the error rate in the control and data tapes resulted in large gains in productivity. Thus Mark III and IV were designed more for accuracy and ease of use than for any dramatic increase in speed. Aiken used to boast that his Mark III was the slowest all-electronic machine in the world because it took 12.75 milliseconds to do a multiplication.

Mark III, finished in September 1949, used eight magnetic drums (each 8 in. in diameter, 40 in. long, and rotating at 7,000 rpm) as the main storage elements for data, while instructions were stored on another drum (16 in. in diameter, 30 in. long, rotating at 1730 rpm). It was the first of Aiken's machines to incorporate what we would now think of as an internally stored program. The drum could accommodate about 4000 instructions for one program. Aiken also had an interpretive system which would allow a mathematician to use the machine by means of what he called a mathematical button board. The board had buttons labeled in simple mathematical notation which, when pressed, would automatically produce the appropriate commands and subroutines on a program tape for the Mark III. Although interesting, this innovation was not used in any very extensive way.

The innovation which was to be more important in the future of computing machines was part of the Mark III's control system. Mark I and Mark II suffered from the fact that their paper tape programs were not very flexible from the point of view of allowing modifications to the program. This was solved in Mark III, not only by having an internally stored program, but by having the address of the quantity to be worked on stored in a register before actually invoking an instruction. This allowed the program to modify these addresses to ease the tasks of stepping through long arrays of data or to do indirect addressing of operands. This indirect addressing feature not only made for easier programming for loops, but resulted in a much more flexible machine for all types of tasks.

Although slow, the Mark III was a reasonable design. It had a total data storage of 4,350 16-bit numbers. These were divided between the data storage drums in such a way that 4,000 numbers would reside on six of the drums while the remaining 350 were divided between the seventh and eighth drums. The arithmetic unit could only access numbers stored on these last two drums; the others had to be "paged" (20 numbers at a time) from the other six drums. This "paging" of numbers from the backing drum was quite slow because the data had to be routed through an intermediate relay register, but this was partially compensated for by the fact that 20 numbers at a time were paged from the "slow" to the "fast" drums.

The technology of the Mark III was divided between electronic and electromechanical, with the final machine consisting of over 5,000 vacuum tubes and 2,000 relays. After the Mark III was shipped from Harvard to its permanent home at the Naval Proving Ground in Dahlgren, Virginia, in March of 1950, it suffered from rather severe reliability problems. Most of these were traced to components failing because of repeated heating and cooling cycles when the machine was switched off over the weekend. ENIAC, as described in a later chapter, had gone through the same types of problems a few years earlier, but this had not been publicized and the Dahlgren people had to learn about this type of failure the hard way.

The Mark IV incorporated many of the features of the Mark III, with the exception that ferrite magnetic cores were used to construct 200 registers. This helped to increase the speed of the Mark IV to the point where, while still not one of the fastest machines available at the time, it would perform the calculations required of it by the United States Air Force. It was finished in 1952 and, although it remained at Harvard, it was used extensively by the Air Force and for other general engineering and scientific calculation.

After finishing the Mark IV, Aiken retired from the business of designing and constructing new computing equipment. The rest of his time at Harvard was devoted to the training of what were to become the second generation of computer scientists in America.

Figure 6-20. The Harvard Mark IV, October, 1958. (Photograph courtesy of the Harvard University Cruft Photo Laboratory.)

In 1961 Aiken resigned from his teaching duties at Harvard and set up a firm called Aiken Industries in Florida. Even the pressures of business did not keep him from the classroom for he continued to teach part time and to help in organizing university computer centers until his death in 1973.

6.5 THE IBM CALCULATORS

6.5.1 The Punched Card Systems

The mechanical calculating machines produced by companies like IBM before it got into the computer business actually comprise several different series of equipment rather than one unified development. From the time that Herman Hollerith produced some of the first punched card accounting machines about the turn of the twentieth century, that type of equipment was marketed in various forms and under various names throughout the world. In Europe the line of tabulating machines and punches was called Hollerith equipment while in North America the line took on the name of the principal supplier, IBM.

The concept of using punched card equipment to aid in computational tasks, rather than accounting-oriented problems, was developed in several places at different times. By 1928 the German firm of Deutsche Telephonwerke of Berlin was attaching Hollerith punches to various types of mechanical calculating machines in order to obtain punched card copies of both final and intermediate results. This was done with at least two different types of equipment, the Astra, a key-driven adding machine, and a Mercedes bookkeeping machine.

The first use of Hollerith tabulating equipment for large-scale scientific calculation was done by L. J. Comrie, who was head of the National Almanac Office in London, England. Comrie devised a way for Fourier series calculations to be carried out on several standard types of punched card accounting machines, and used this to calculate the motions of the moon for the years 1935 to 2000. These calculations were based on Brown's "Tables of the Moon" and, when E. W. Brown visited Great Britain in 1928, he was shown the computations in progress. This resulted in Brown's taking the technique back to the United States with him and discussing it with his friend Wallace J. Eckert, a mathematician and astronomer.

In 1929 Columbia University had talked Thomas J. Watson into founding the Columbia University Statistical Bureau as a center for processing large statistical surveys. Watson, the head of IBM, made sure that the Bureau was well equipped with all the standard units of IBM's punched card tabulating and accounting machines. About a year later, Wallace J. Eckert started a campaign to convince Watson that much more than simple statistical surveys could be accomplished if only IBM would be willing to donate the equipment and fund the project. Eventually the Statistical Bureau was expanded and its name changed to the "Thomas J. Watson Astronomical Computing Bureau." Now, Eckert could work on some of the same types of astronomical calculation problems as Comrie had done in London.

With Comrie working on one side of the Atlantic and Eckert on the other, it was not long before the standard line of punched card accounting equipment was modified to further facilitate large-scale calculation. In 1932 Comrie managed to persuade the Hollerith firm to modify their equipment so that the contents of one register, which previously had been limited to taking part in addition operations, could now also be transferred to other mechanical registers in the machine (IBM equipment was modified in the same way about ten years later). This modification enabled the plugboard wired program to be set up to simulate Babbage's Difference Engine. The simulation involved the same two-step mechanism as had the original, first the even order differences were added to the odd order differences, then vice versa. When the modified Hollerith machine was finally wired up this way, it was capable of producing about 1000 lines of a table per hour. Again Babbage's Difference Engine was resurrected in a different form.

Having at last a very large and powerful Difference Engine did not satisfy the need for the production of scientific tables. There were always special cases of tables which could not be easily produced via the standard method of differences. The commercial community also had need for a machine which would help in areas such as the production of gas and electricity accounts where a reading from a meter had to be multiplied by a rate to produce the final bill. In 1935 IBM started to manufacture a multiplying punch, called an IBM 601, to satisfy the needs of both types of user. It was essentially a relay-based arithmetic unit which could multiply two numbers together in about 1 second. These machines, because of their ready availability, formed the backbone of most of the scientific and commercial calculation until the advent of the electronic computer. IBM eventually supplied over 1500 of them to their various customers.

The multiplying punch rapidly evolved into several different models and submodels, the 602, 602A, 603, 604, and the 605, each with increasing abilities when it came to performing arithmetic. The IBM 604 multiplying punch was first delivered in 1948 and was the first of this series of machines to rely on vacuum tube technology rather than the relay. There were eight internal reg-

Figure 6–21.   The 603 multiplying punch, circa 1946. (Photograph courtesy of IBM archives.)

isters, but these were usually used in pairs to give four working registers, each with a capacity of eight decimal digits. The 604 could be "programmed," by means of two large plugboard panels, to read a card, perform up to 60 different arithmetic steps, and punch the results into the same card when it reached the machine's punching station about 80 milliseconds after it was read. Information could also be stored in the internal registers in order that a running total could be punched into the last card through the device. Eventually about 4000 of these machines were produced.

The technique of programming via plugboards has been gone for so long that it perhaps needs a few words of explanation. The IBM 604 plugboard contained 60 groups of terminals, each consisting of three places in which a plug wire could be inserted. Each of these groups was called a "program level" and, after the information had been read from a card, electrical pulses would be emitted from program levels 1 through 60 in sequence. If a plug wire were inserted in a particular program level, it would carry the pulse to whichever functional unit happened to be connected to the other end of the plug wire. When an electrical pulse was routed to a functional unit, it would operate on the data that happened to be in the central "bus" register at the time. For example, to transfer a number from one storage register to another during program level 5, two wires would be run from the program level 5 terminal, one to the function unit causing the number to be put out on the central bus, and another to the unit which would cause a register to store the number currently on the bus. Functional units were available which would cause the number to be shifted left or right before sending it to the bus, add or subtract it from a register, or cause a multiplication or division to take place using the special multiplication/quotient register. The content of a register could be tested for its sign and, depending on the outcome, the pulse on the next program level could be suppressed.

When the 604 multiplying punch was announced in 1948, Northrop Aviation approached IBM with a request to connect this arithmetic unit to one of the standard tabulating machines rather than IBM's usual arrangement of using their reproducing gang punch for reading and punching cards. Northrop realized that their need for scientific calculation was based on having printed results rather than punched cards as the output medium, and the tabulating machine could print the results on standard accounting machine printer paper.

IBM managed to combine the 604 with a 407 tabulating machine and added another unit consisting of 16 electromechanical storage registers each of which could hold a ten-digit number. Up to five of these storage units could be attached to a 604, giving a potential total of 80 registers. The result was a machine which could no longer be controlled by the plugboard unit incorporated in the 604 but would take sequences of instructions from punched cards read in through the tabulating machine's card reader. The operations could be changed by rewiring the plugboard but, in the standard wiring, each instruction consisted of four sections, three of which specified the register numbers which held the two operands and the register which was to receive the result, while the fourth section indicated the operation to be performed. The operands could come from either one of the machine's registers or be constants read from the punched cards. Instructions were executed one at a time as the cards containing them were read. Programs were typically stacks of punched cards several feet high because it was not possible to create control loops like those made out of paper tape on some of the other machines. One of the employees of Northrop eventually found a mechanism to reduce the number of cards necessary for a program; in one case it reduced a program from a deck of cards a yard high to one only 7 inches high.

With these facilities, Northrop found that it could solve at least one aspect of its accounting and calculation problems without investing in the effort to develop an electronic computer. IBM later marketed a combination of the newer 605 multiplying punch and the 407 tabulator as the Card Programmed Calculator, or CPC for short. The product was not very successful from the point of view of sales volume—only about 200 were ever produced—but for those firms which needed only limited calculating ability it proved so successful that a number of them were still in use in the early 1960s.

IBM later brought out a successor to the 604, the 626. It was essentially the same type of machine as the 604 with improved speed and control functions. It could, for example, do about 1000 calculations per minute, its arithmetic facilities were improved so that it could multiply an eight-digit number by a 32-digit number, and the control was modified to provide 14 special pro-

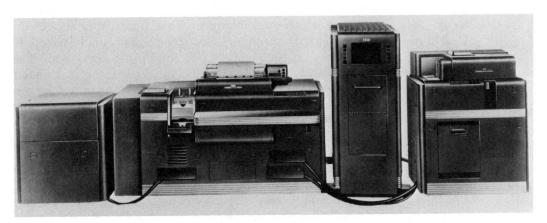

Figure 6–22.   The IBM Card Programmed Calculator. (Photograph courtesy of IBM archives.)

Figure 6–23. A typical IBM punched card accounting/calculating installation. In the front row, from left to right, are an interpreter, a sorter, and a statistical machine (essentially a sorter capable of accumulating and printing totals). Along the extreme left hand side of the room are tabulating machines and the right rear corner appears to have a 600 type multiplying punch showing behind a collator. (Photograph courtesy of IBM archives.)

gram steps which could either be suppressed or caused to loop, depending on the information fed in from the input cards.

IBM had little competition in supplying the needs of the calculating community with punched card equipment. Although Remington Rand supplied a line of similar equipment which used the same size of punched card (3.25 in. by 7.375 in. by 0.0067 in.), their machines used a coding scheme in which 90 digits could be represented on each card in two rows of 45 digits each. The holes in the Remington Rand cards were circular rather than the rectangular holes that were standard with IBM. This system was not as convenient for use as the IBM 80-column punched card, so the vast majority of scientific users opted for IBM equipment rather than any of their competitor's products.

When used for calculational purposes, the typical installation would consist of a group of four or five of the standard business accounting machines; the calculating process was done by passing decks of cards from one machine to the next, with each machine contributing something to the process. As long as facilities were available for counting, sorting, and searching cards for specific values, together with some means of performing the four standard arithmetic operations and printing the results, it was possible to do almost any calculation. The machines most often used, along with their abilities, are summarized in the following table:

Machine	Operation							
	count	sort	search	print	+	−	*	/
sorter	X	X	X					
collator		X	X					
tabulator	X			X	X	X		
multiplying punch (601–604)				X	X	X	X	X

In general, the punched card method of doing a large calculation allowed for slightly greater speed than using an electrically driven desk calculator but, more importantly, it allowed for increased accuracy because of the need for fewer human interventions in the process. With the results being printed out on one of the tabulating machines, there was no need to set up elaborate human proofreading schemes, a large source of error in earlier work.

6.5.2 The Large IBM Calculators

The first calculator of any size with which IBM was connected was the Harvard Mark I. As mentioned earlier, the Mark I was a joint effort between Howard Aiken of Harvard University and the design engineers and technicians at the IBM Endicott Labs. With the success of this venture, IBM went on to develop their own large relay-based computer for use in their New York office. They were able to gain some additional experience constructing large calculators when, during the Second World War, they were asked by the United States Army to produce what became known as the IBM Pluggable Sequence Relay Calculator.

IBM made two of the PSRCs during the period 1944–1945 for use by the ballistics people at the Aberdeen Proving Ground. The following year they manufactured five more, three of which went to the Naval Proving Ground at Dahlgren and the final two to the T. J. Watson Scientific Computing Laboratory at Columbia University in New York (formerly the T. J. Watson Astronomical Computing Bureau). The PSRCs were based on relay technology and used the standard IBM control technique of having their operations controlled by plugboard wires augmented by a special series of 96 control relays. These relays were controlled by data fed from punched cards and were used to connect or disconnect various plugboard wires so that the plugboard program could be slightly modified by reading in a different set of control cards.

The arithmetic units of these machines could do the four standard arithmetic operations as well as calculate square roots. Because of a conscious effort to implement parallel operations, the unit was almost ten times as fast as the IBM 602 multiplying punch which it resembled in its level of technology. The standard register, of which there were 30, was six decimal digits long, but there were several of 12 digits just so that the results of multiplication could be accumulated.

Although not a very large calculating machine, it was not one of IBM's standard product lines and so has been generally considered as one of the special-purpose war-time calculators rather than just a modification of their multiplying punch.

6.5.3. The Selective Sequence Electronic Calculator

The one really big mechanical monster produced by IBM was known as the Selective Sequence Electronic Calculator, but was usually known as the SSEC within the IBM organization. It was one of IBM's showpieces and, as such, was placed behind large windows on the ground floor of IBM's main office building in New York. The machine naturally attracted considerable interest from the passing pedestrians who would refer to the calculator as "Poppa." It was, by a substantial margin, the largest and most complex of the electromechanical computers. IBM unveiled the device in January of 1948 but it was actually running test programs for several months before that time.

Figure 6–24.   The IBM SSEC. (Photograph courtesy of IBM archives.)

Figure 6–25. A different view of the IBM SSEC. (Photograph courtesy of IBM archives.)

When the design of this machine was being considered, the ENIAC had already been shown to work as a reliable vacuum-tube-based calculating instrument, and the IBM engineers had already obtained some experience of electronic design with the latest version of their multiplying punch. There was, therefore, some question as to which technology should be used to construct what was to be a showpiece machine. In the end the design settled on was a hybrid of vacuum tube and relay technology, the vacuum tubes being used where speed was essential and the relays where their slower speed could be tolerated. More importantly, their lower cost and more trouble-free operation would help keep down the cost of both the construction and maintenance of SSEC. About 13,000 vacuum tubes were used to construct the arithmetic unit and eight very high-speed registers, while 23,000 relays were used in the control structure and 150 registers of slower memory. Although 13,000 vacuum tubes approaches the number used in the construction of ENIAC, they were actually used in a more efficient way in SSEC. Where ENIAC required ten tubes to represent each digit of its accumulator, the SSEC's binary-coded decimal (BCD) memory scheme allowed IBM's engineers to use only four tubes per digit of memory.

Like most of the other mechanical monsters, the SSEC was controlled by instructions punched on paper tape, although it was possible also to have instructions issued from a few internal registers in the machine. There were 66 special paper tape readers any one of which could be used to control the machine. This gave it much more flexibility than similar machines which could only transfer control between three or four control tape readers. The arithmetic unit, being made from vacuum tube technology, was faster than any of the other mechanical monsters. A typical addition time would be about 0.004 seconds. It was seldom possible to use this high-speed arithmetic for anything other than a short period of time; because of the slow paper tape control mechanism it could only keep up a sustained rate of about 50 instructions read and executed each second. Since it was very difficult to program the SSEC, it tended to be used for problems involving extensive sets of data solvable by a single program.

The SSEC was probably the first machine ever to be used in a commercial service bureau. During the last few years of its life it was leased almost constantly by the United States government for various calculations, notably ones for the Atomic Energy Commission. One of these calculations took the machine a full six months to complete. It was also used by Wallace J. Eckert to tabulate the positions of the five outer planets every 40 days for the period 1653 to 2060. This job required that the SSEC perform about 5,000,000 multiplications and a further 7,000,000 additions and subtractions, which it did without error.

In 1951 IBM developed the first of its electronic stored program computers, the 701. As the SSEC was meant to be not only a useful calculator but also a showpiece of IBM's technical ability, it could not be allowed to exist when the much more powerful 701 was to be available to commercial customers sometime in 1952. Thus, "Poppa" was finally switched off and dismantled in August of 1952 after about four and one half years of productive use. No one would ever again attempt to construct a mechanical monster on such a large scale.

FURTHER READING

AIKEN, H. H., and G. M. HOPPER (1946). "The Automatic Sequence Controlled Calculator," *Electrical Engineering*, 65, 384–91, 449–54, 522–28. (reprinted in Randell)

ALT, F. L. (1948). "A Bell Telephone Laboratories Computing Machine," *Mathematical Tables and Other Aids to Computation*, 3, 1–13, 69–89. (reprinted in Randell)

ANDREWS, E. G. (1951a). "Use of the Relay Digital Computer," *Electrical Engineering*, February, pp. 158–63. (reprinted in the *Annals of the History of Computing*, 4, (No. 1), 1982, 5–13.

——(1951b). "A Review of Bell Laboratories Digital Computer Developments," *Proc. of the Joint AIEE-IRE Computer Conference*, Philadelphia, Dec. 10–12, 1951.

BAURER, F. L. (1976). "Between Zuse and Rutishauser—The Early Development of Computing in Central Europe." Lecture given at the Los Alamos Computer History Conference, June 10–15, 1976. (reprinted in Metropolis et al.)

BERKLEY, E. C. (1961). *Giant Brains, or Machines that Think.* New York: Science Editions, Inc. (originally published in 1949)

BOWDEN, B. V. (1953). *Faster Than Thought: A Symposium on Digital Computing Machines.* London: Pitman and Sons Ltd.

CERUZZI, P. E. (1981). "The Early Computers of Konrad Zuse, 1935–1945," *Annals of the History of Computing, 3* (No. 3), 241–62.

CESAREO, O. (1946). "The Relay Interpolator," *Bell Telephone Laboratories Record, 23,* 457–60. (reprinted in Randell)

COMRIE, L. J. (1928–29). "German Calculating Machine Enterprise," *Transactions of the Office Machinery Users Association.*

——·(1946). "The Application of Commercial Calculating Machines to Scientific Computing," *Mathematical Tables and Other Aids to Computation, 2* (No. 16).

DAVIS, H. M. (1949). "Mathematical Machines," *Scientific American, 180* (No. 4) April, 29–39.

DESMONDE, W. H. (1966). "The Zuse Z3," *Datamation,* September, pp. 30–31.

Electronics (1980). *The 50th Year Issue of Electronics.* New York: McGraw-Hill, April 17.

Engineering Research Associates (1950). *High Speed Computing Devices.* New York: McGraw-Hill.

GOTLIEB, C. C., and J. N. P. HUME (1958). *High Speed Data Processing,* London: McGraw-Hill.

HOLBROOK, B. D. (?). "Bell Laboratories and the Computer," *Bell Laboratories Computing Science Technical Report #36.*

JULEY, J. (1947). "The Ballistic Computer," *Bell Telephone Laboratories Record, 24,* 5–9. (reprinted in Randell)

LAST, J. (1962). "Digital Calculating Machines," *The Charted Mechanical Engineer,* December, pp. 572–79.

LIDA, S. L. (1953). "IBM Computing Machines," *Proceedings of the Symposium on Industrial Applications of Automatic Computing Equipment,* Kansas City, January 8, 9.

MALIK, R. (1970). "Only Begetters of the Computer," *New Scientist, 16* (July), 138–39.

METROPOLIS, N., HOWLETT, J., and G. C. ROTA (1980). *A History of Computing in the Twentieth Century: A Collection of Essays.* New York: Academic Press. (reprints of the lectures given at the Computer History Conference held in Los Alamos, June 10–15, 1976)

PANTAGES, A. (1967). "Computing's Early Years," *Datamation,* October, pp. 60–65.

POORTE, G. E. (1951). "The Operation and Logic of the MARK III Electronic Calculator," *Proc. of the Joint AIEE-IRE Computer Conference,* Philadelphia, December 10–12.

RANDELL, B. (1973). *The Origins of Digital Computers—Selected Papers.* New York: Springer-Verlag. (reprints of many of the early papers dealing with the invention of the computer)

SCHUSSEL, G. (1965). "IBM vs RemRand," *Datamation,* May, pp. 54–66.

SHELDON, J. W., and L. TATUM (1951). "The IBM Card Programmed Electronic Calculator," *Joint AIEE-IRE Computer Conference,* New York, December 10–12. (reprinted in Randell)

Speiser, A. P. (1980). "The Relay Calculator Z4," *Annals of the History of Computing, 2* (No. 3), 242–45.

Stibitz, G. R. (1967). "The Relay Computers at Bell Labs," *Datamation*, April and May, pp. 35–49.

Wilkes, M. V. (1950). *Report on a Conference on High Speed Automatic Calculating Machines*, University Mathematical Laboratory, Cambridge, England.

——. (1956). *Automatic Digital Computers.* London: Methuen and Co. London

Zuse, K. (?). *Method of the Automatic Execution of Calculations with the Aid of Computers*, a German patent application, a translation of excerpts. (reprinted in Randell)

——·(1962). *The Outline of Computer Development from Mechanics to Electronics*, a translation of excerpts. (reprinted in Randell)

——·(1976). "Some Remarks on the History of Computing in Germany," a lecture given at the Los Alamos Computer History Conference, June 10–15, 1976. (reprinted in Metropolis et al.)

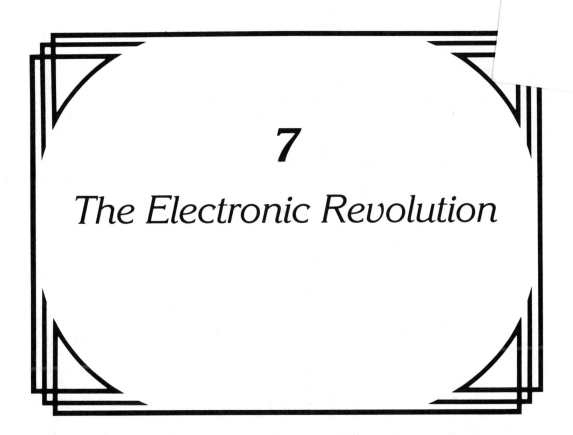

7
The Electronic Revolution

7.1 INTRODUCTION

Today we tend to think of the computer as an electronic device but, as we have seen in earlier chapters, there were many automatic computing devices based on mechanical or electromechanical technology. When the development of electronic devices reached the stage where reliable components started to become available, people began to consider their use in computing machines. The Second World War spurred the development of electronics from what was essentially a small-scale analog industry concentrating on radio circuits to its status as one of the leading technologies of our day. About that time it occurred to several different people that this developing technology could be used as basis for a calculating machine, but the expense of setting up the necessary research and development facilities meant that only the truly inspired, or the very foolish, would attempt any actual construction.

The Eckles-Jordan flip-flop circuit was invented just after the First World War, but digital electronics was first used—other than for small-scale or experimental devices—by Dr. C. E. Wynn-Williams, in 1932. He constructed a binary counter from a series of thyratrons for use in counting events in physics experiments being done in Cambridge at the Cavendish Laboratories. By the time of the outbreak of the Second World War, this technique had been adopted by many different people, and the electronics and engineering journals of the day contained many different papers describing the circuits that had been designed for this application. The war spurred the development of digital electronic techniques, not only for such projects as the development of radar and the counters needed for the atomic energy investigations, but also for the construction of coding and deciphering machines as well as electronic calculators.

The very first serious attempt at the construction of electronic circuits for calculation was done by Zuse and Schreyer, as described in Chapter 6. Schreyer managed to produce electronic devices for both memory and arithmetic units but was prevented from actually constructing an electronic computer by the more pressing needs of the German war-time economy.

The next step was taken by a professor at Iowa State University (then known as Iowa State College), John Vincent Atanasoff, and one of his graduate students, Clifford Berry. Working essentially alone, they managed to produce the world's first working electronic digital calculator during the period from 1940 to 1942. This machine was very limited in its ability, and was never used for any really large practical calculations because Atanasoff left his university position to help the U.S. Naval Ordnance Laboratory with its war effort, and Berry graduated and joined an engineering firm. By the time the war was over, there was no point in following up on Atanasoff's ideas because they had been superseded by the developments that had taken place at the Moore School of Engineering during the development of the ENIAC.

This chapter describes the three main steps to the development of digital electronics which were to lead, ultimately, to the construction of the first electronic digital stored-program computer. These three penultimate steps [the Atanasoff-Berry computer (the ABC), the Electronic Numerical Integrator and Computer (ENIAC) produced in the Moore School, and the Colossus designed in Britain] were the seed bed from which the modern electronic computer sprang just after the end of the Second World War.

7.2 JOHN ATANASOFF, CLIFFORD BERRY, AND THE ABC

John Vincent Atanasoff was an American of Bulgarian heritage who was destined to play a key, if controversial, role in the development of the electronic computer. He, like Charles Babbage, never completed the machine he was working on, but his efforts did have an influence on one of the designers of the first large electronic machines, the ENIAC. The controversy surrounding Atanasoff's early work has not been helped by the fact that he, at first, deliberately kept himself in the background of the publicity surrounding the devel-

Figure 7–1. John Vincent Atanasoff circa 1935. (Photograph courtesy of Dr. Atanasoff.)

opment of the computer. This may well have been because he was aware of his own obstinate nature and, like a lot of very creative people, seemingly preferred to work alone or with the few people that were capable of making him feel at ease.

The other main figure involved in the development of the ABC (the Atanasoff-Berry computer) was Clifford Berry, Atanasoff's graduate student during the late 1930s and early 1940s when the majority of the work was being done at Iowa State College (later to become Iowa State University). Berry evidently did a great deal of work on the ABC and, although the concept was clearly first thought of by Atanasoff, he deserved roughly equal credit for the actual detailed design and construction. Unfortunately the controversy as to the influence the ABC was to have on subsequent developments cannot be put to rest by reference to Berry because he apparently became mentally unbalanced and took his own life in 1963. Atanasoff never accepted the suicide verdict and did his best to check out Berry's death but was unable to shed any further light on the mysterious incident.

It was in the late 1930s that Atanasoff realized he needed some help in finding solutions to large and complex sets of equations that were arising as part of his research interests. Iowa State College did not have access to the same type of facilities that were available in places like the T. J. Watson Astronomical Computing Bureau at Columbia University, so he had to cast about for some way of obtaining calculating help on a much smaller, but local, scale.

The Department of Mathematics happened to have leased a small IBM tabulating/accounting machine which seemed like it might be able to provide some slight help with the arithmetic, so Atanasoff proceeded to learn the intricacies of the plugboard wire control mechanism. He soon found that was not capable of performing all the tasks he would like to have available, so he took the direct path of attempting to modify the machine so that it would more nearly suit his purpose. When the local IBM salesman learned about what he was attempting, Atanasoff received a letter telling him that, as the machine was not owned by the college but only leased from IBM, he must stop all modifications immediately and restore the tabulator back to its standard operational condition. Thus, his one hope of obtaining some mechanical, semiautomatic help with the calculations was removed.

Having an inventive turn of mind, and being a person who never let the lack of either money or equipment stand in his way, he began to consider how he might possibly construct something in his own laboratory which could help with his calculating needs. His experience with the mechanical IBM Tabulating machine had convinced him that mechanical devices were unlikely to be successful in yielding the calculating speed he required, so he turned his thoughts to electronic devices. Unfortunately, what little digital electronic expertise existed in 1937 was certainly not in Iowa State College, so he had to start right from scratch in not only producing the design for actual circuit elements but even in coming up with the concept that it would be possible to design such circuits.

After a particularly frustrating evening in his laboratory, during which time he was faced with one conceptual problem after another, he realized that what he needed was to get away from the problem for a few hours and relax. He left the laboratory with the intention of going for a drink. In 1937 Iowa was a dry state, so his drink required that he drive about 200 miles to the Mississippi River and cross it into the state of Illinois. The long relaxing drive, combined with a drink or two at the far end, put him back in the mood to reconsider his whole problem. He began to think about how he could design a device to store the coefficients of his equations.

While he was still a child, his mother had given him a book which had discussed number systems in different bases and, remembering this book, he came to the realization that an electronic device would likely be easier to design if all the numbers were stored in binary notation. During the rest of that evening he was able to sketch out the design of a memory system consisting of a large number of capacitors, each of which could store one binary bit, and some of the elementary circuitry which would be needed to control the logic and arithmetic functions of the machine. Thus, some of the basic steps in the creation of the electronic computer owe their existence to the friendly and relaxed atmosphere of a roadside bar.

The basic ideas for an electronic calculator were set down, likely on the bar napkins, during the winter of 1937–38, but it was almost two full years before Atanasoff and Berry could show a working prototype machine. They verified their basic ideas on a series of small breadboard circuits and, by December of 1939, were confident enough of their design to proceed with the

Figure 7–2. Clifford Berry and the ABC. (Photograph courtesy of Dr. Atanasoff.)

construction of a full-scale machine. Up until 1941, when he received a $5,000 grant to help finish the construction, his total working outlay was based upon a $650 grant from the State College. Atanasoff used $200 of this grant for materials and the other $450 to pay Clifford Berry a small salary.

By 1942 the team had almost produced a working electronic calculator which, although it was a special-purpose device for solving systems of equations, incorporated an electronic regenerative memory and used vacuum tubes for the basic control circuit elements. At this point United States involvement in the Second World War was beginning to demand that highly trained technical people join the war effort unless they were already in special war-protected occupations. This meant that Atanasoff abandoned his development of electronic calculating machines to take up a position with the Naval Ordnance Laboratory in Washington, and his machine never did become fully operational.

The ABC demonstrated a number of features which were to have a great influence over calculator design in the next few years. Other than Helmut Schreyer, who was working on electronic design of calculating instruments

Figure 7–3. The ABC with the drum capacitor memory cover removed. The two large metal objects in the foreground are a binary card reader/punch of Atanasoff's own design while the object in front of the drum near the control panel is an IBM card reader. (Photograph courtesy of Dr. Atanasoff.)

with Konrad Zuse, the ABC or its 1939 prototype was the first machine to demonstrate the use of electronic techniques in digital calculation, and the first machine to incorporate a regenerative memory. Unlike the work of Schreyer, which was essentially unknown because of the war, the ABC work managed to influence John Mauchly of the Moore School of Engineering, and this in turn had a huge influence on the rapid development of electronic computing machines.

As it was left in 1942, the ABC consisted of an arithmetic unit, constructed from about 300 vacuum tubes, which was capable of only performing the operations of addition and subtraction. Because of the special-purpose nature of the machine, there was no need for multiplication and division operations. Another 300 vacuum tubes were used for various control and memory regenerating circuits. The memory consisted of a large number of capacitors mounted on two rotating drums. These gave enough storage to keep 30 numbers on each drum, each number being stored in 50 bits. The capacitors would only store their information for about the length of time it took for one rotation of the drum so the memory had to be refreshed (regenerated) on each revolution.

7.3 THE ENIAC

7.3.1 Introduction

Although there were several large-scale electromechanical computing machines designed and operational before ENIAC, it is undoubtedly the case that this machine, and the people involved in its design and construction, were the direct cause of a huge advance in the construction and use of electronic computing devices. For this reason the story of ENIAC deserves to be told in more detail than that of some of the other machines.

7.3.2 The Place and the Problem

The Moore School of Electrical Engineering of the University of Pennsylvania, Philadelphia, was founded in 1923. By the early 1930s it had formed a connection with the U.S. Army Ordnance Department Ballistic Research Laboratory at the Aberdeen Proving Ground in Maryland. This connection grew gradually during the 1930s and, by the time the Second World War had started, the Moore School had become a major source of technical and computational help to the Ballistic Research Laboratory.

The first major joint project between these two groups started with the proposal, by the Moore School, to construct a differential analyzer similar to the one that Vannevar Bush had produced at MIT. The Moore School suggested that, if the Ballistic Research Laboratory would provide the initial funding for the design of the device, they would undertake to construct two machines, one for the Moore School to be used in general scientific computation and one for the Ballistic Research Laboratory to be used in solving problems involving ballistic trajectories. Vannevar Bush cooperated with the staff of the Moore School, to the point of even lending them his chief designer, in order to get the design phase underway and, by 1934, the differential analyzer was operational. This successful project cemented the growing relationship between the two groups and was a factor in building up the confidence of one group in the other's ability to carry out a large-scale project.

In order to grasp the importance of the connection between these two groups, it is necessary to enquire into the types of work being done by the Ballistic Research Laboratory. The U.S. Army Ordnance Department was charged with the responsibility for preparing the very complex ballistic firing tables used by artillery men to accurately aim their weapons. One of the best illustrations of the importance of these tables is the story (perhaps apocryphal) of the large German railway gun which was being test fired during the First World War. Some elementary estimates had been made as to the range to be expected from certain combinations of gun elevation and amounts of propellant. The gun was positioned so that there was adequate room ahead of it to allow for error in these range estimates. When the gun was actually fired, the shell went almost twice as far as had been predicted—in fact it went completely out of the artillery range and into a small farming community. The reasons for this error were several, but one of the main ones was the fact that the artillery men had neglected to take into account that the drag imposed on the shell by its passage through air was very much reduced at the high altitudes reached by the trajectory. Needless to say, this type of error was not condoned during experimental firings of guns and made the accurate use of artillery impossible during battle conditions.

Given a particular type of gun, firing a specific shell, with a known charge of propellant, at a known elevation, the actual computation of the trajectory required that a solution be found to several different differential equations. Each gunner would need a ballistic table containing the solutions to about 3,000 different trajectories and, if the table were for a very long-range gun, it would have to consider extra factors such as air pressure, humidity, and wind speed to obtain the trajectory with any accuracy. The calculations for a single trajectory would take a skilled person, working with an electrically driven desk calculator, about 20 hours to produce the results. If the calculations for the trajectories were done on a machine such as the differential analyzer constructed at the Moore School, it would only take about 20 minutes of actual machine time per trajectory, but that was only after the differential analyzer was properly adjusted and set up for the specific problem. The differential analyzer required constant attention and careful adjustment because, like any mechanical analog device, it suffered from accuracy limitations due to slippage and backlash problems in the gearing.

At the start of the Second World War the need for more and better trajectory tables became acute. The Ballistic Research Laboratory was using their copy of the differential analyzer full time and, in 1940, took over the one at the Moore School in order to increase their ability to cope with the problem. The Moore School also took over the task of training groups of women to help out by doing some of the calculations on desk calculators. These women, several hundred of whom were eventually trained, were given a three-month intensive course in the required areas of mathematics and operational skills. This calculational help was still not sufficient, and the production of adequate ballistic tables fell further and further behind.

7.3.3 The People

By 1940 the Moore School was the center for the construction of several electronic projects which were to be used for the development of radar. For example, several people who were to become important contributors in the development of ENIAC (Arthur Burks, Joseph Chedaker, J. Presper Eckert, and Kite Sharpless) were involved in the construction of an amplifier with a wider band width than anything which had been produced to that time. Later Chedaker, Eckert, and Sharpless were to become involved in the production of electronic circuits used as counters and in the development of the mercury delay line, again used in radar work. Burks, who was joined by a new staff member, John Mauchly, later went on to radar-related antenna analysis projects for the Signals Corps.

There were a large number of people who, at one time or another, made a contribution to the ENIAC project. Two people, at least in the early days, stand out as the main driving force behind the Moore School end of the project: J. Presper Eckert and John Mauchly.

Eckert, known as "Pres" to his friends, was a very bright young student at the Moore School who had developed a deep knowledge of electronics. He was appointed to be a laboratory instructor for a government-sponsored course in electronics which was being held in the Moore School in 1941. This course was intended to train people in the basic techniques of electronics in order to build up a pool of expertise for use during the war effort.

Mauchly was professor of physics at Ursinus College near Philadelphia when the war broke out. He had some knowledge of electronics but, because of the war effort, he enrolled in the government electronics course at the Moore School. Once there, he found that the laboratory exercises assigned to the students were so elementary that there was no need for him to actually complete that portion of the course. Thus, he and Eckert used to sit in the laboratory and discuss other aspects of electronics while the rest of the students worked on their assignments. When the Moore School had some staff positions become vacant because men were called to active service, Mauchly was approached and quickly agreed to join the school.

While Eckert had the expertise in electronics, Mauchly's training had introduced him to several areas that required large amounts of calculation. One of these was his lifelong interest in the possibilities of predicting the weather by extensive statistical calculations.

In December of 1940, Mauchly met Atanasoff at a meeting of the American Association for the Advancement of Science. This led to Mauchly's visiting Iowa State College during the summer of 1941 and talking with Atanasoff and Berry about the calculator they then had under construction. This visit led to continued discussions with Eckert, and anyone else who would listen, about the use of electronics for performing calculations. In August of 1942 Mauchly finally put his ideas down in a short paper entitled "The Use of High Speed Vacuum Tube Devices for Calculating" in which he compared the advantages that electronic techniques would have over the then current level of mechanical technology. He was able to indicate that the use of electronics should make it possible to increase the rate of solving trajectories from one every 15 to 30 minutes on the differential analyzer to one every 100 seconds on an electronic device. Unfortunately no one seemed very interested in Mauchly's ideas and, when the report was needed a year later, it could not be found.

By early 1943 the production of ballistic tables had fallen so far behind schedule that the Ballistics Research Laboratory was searching for any and all means of speeding up the process. Lieutenant Herman H. Goldstine, an assistant professor of mathematics at the University of Michigan before the war started, was given the responsibility of making sure no stone was left unturned in an attempt to speed up the production of the tables. He was well acquainted with the Moore School and heard of Mauchly's interest in electronic calculators. In March of 1943, Goldstine approached John Brainard, the administrative head of the Moore School, and, when Brainard endorsed Mauchly's ideas, Goldstine started some preliminary discussions with the people at the Ballistics Research Laboratory. All this discussion culminated in a meeting being arranged between the Moore School and the Ballistic Research Laboratory people for April 9, 1943. When Mauchly could not locate any copies of his earlier report, he and Eckert attempted to reconstruct it from the shorthand notes made by his secretary the summer before. At 1:00 a.m. on April 9, they had it finished and Mauchly, Eckert, and Brainard went off to the Aberdeen Proving Grounds for the meeting that same morning.

The Moore School delegation presented the idea of constructing a device they called an "Electronic Numerical Integrator," a title they had chosen because of the Ballistic Research Laboratory's interest in numerical integration. Mauchly, however, stressed that the device was to be of more general use than simply replacing the integrating functions of the differential analyzer. A colonel at Aberdeen approved the project and, because of its more general nature, suggested that they add the words "and Computer" to the title of the project. Thus was born the project known as ENIAC.

7.3.4 The Machine

The report prepared by Mauchly was somewhat sketchy in nature, so the first job was to add some flesh to the bones. This was not done without some considerable criticism being leveled at both the Army and the Moore School during the process. A large number of responsible engineers voiced concern over the plans because it was turning out to be the most complex bit of electronic equipment ever put together. The only thing of even the same order of magnitude of complexity was the telephone network which, when taken as a whole, was larger but could not really be compared to ENIAC as a design for a single piece of equipment. Not only would ENIAC have to be about 100 times larger than the largest single piece of electronic equipment assembled before that time, but it would have to set new standards in reliability. In order for the machine to function for 12 hours without failure, it would have to operate with only one chance in 10^{14} of a malfunction in any of its circuits. Some calculations done at the time seemed to indicate that the machine could be expected to be operational about 50 percent of the time; the wags openly suggested that this meant it would produce correct results only every other millisecond!

Actual work was started on May 31, 1943, with Mauchly dealing with the conceptual design and Eckert with the design of individual circuits. Chedaker was put in charge of the actual construction team (which consisted mainly of factory women and telephone linemen moonlighting after their regular shift), while Burks and Sharpless acted as senior engineers. About one month later the government actually signed the formal contract for:

> . . . research and experimental work in connection with the development of an electronic numerical integrator and computer. . . .[1]

Goldstine was appointed as the representative of the Ballistics Laboratory to make sure that the development team was able to obtain all the materials it required.

Although Eckert was one of the younger members of the team, he had considerable experience behind him because of his earlier work on radar projects. He realized that the organization of such a construction project required a very firm set of guidelines for both the design and actual construction of the equipment. He was able to impose a discipline upon the team which resulted in very little time being wasted following up ideas which led to dead ends. Eckert was insistent that each part of the machine be designed in a simple, straightforward manner. The whole thrust was to get the project moving. If the choice had to be made between an elegant engineering solution to a problem

---

[1] H. H. Goldstine, *The Computer from Pascal to Von Neumann* (Princeton: Princeton University Press, 1972), p. 152.

and a brute force, ugly solution which was known to work, the choice was invariably the latter.

Eckert decided that the design of the ENIAC should obtain the necessary reliability by careful design of the circuits rather than by the use of ultra-reliable components. There was also the question of expense, the common 6SN7 tube cost only about $0.50 while the ultra-reliable tubes used in the undersea telephone repeater stations cost almost $100 each. Eckert went to a "worse case" design philosophy. For example, he would build a test circuit and, if the tubes in this circuit operated successfully at plate voltages of between 100 and 400 volts, he would design the system to operate at 200 volts so that the whole system would be guaranteed to function even if the conductivity of different tubes varied by factors of two. If the design called for a certain resistor to be able to withstand a power level of 0.25 watts, he used resistors whose ratings were at least 0.5 watts. This resulted in the system's becoming operational without the lengthy testing of individual components before they were incorporated into the circuits. Reliability was enhanced by using only a few basic types of circuit and having these mounted on plug-in units for ease of servicing.

When the design had progressed to the point of actual construction, the age-old problem of the need for more and better facilities had resulted in an expansion of the initial idea to one almost twice the original size. By the time ENIAC was complete, the design had expanded from one containing 5,000 vacuum tubes to one which contained 18,000 vacuum tubes of 16 basic types, 1500 relays, 70,000 resistors, 10,000 capacitors; it was 8 ft high, 3 ft wide, almost 100 ft long, weighed 30 tons, and consumed 140 kilowatts of power. When the Army agreed to the project they had established a budget of $150,000, but this, like the rest of the project, grew until the final accounting showed a total expenditure of $486,804.22.

The construction team had lots of experience with earlier work on radar projects and drew on this for some of their designs, but most of the electronics was patterned after the simple designs used in the pulse-counting circuits of electronic counters. Many of the electronic circuits which performed the basic arithmetic operations were simply electronic analogs of the same units used in mechanical calculators and the commercial accounting machines of the day. For example, the mechanical calculators would store a decimal digit by having a wheel turn to one of ten possible positions, whereas the ENIAC stored a decimal digit by having ten vacuum tube flip-flops connected together in the form of a ring with one of the flip-flops (say the sixth) in a conducting state to represent that digit (6 in this case). If two pulses were sent into this ring counter, the conducting state would transfer to the eighth flip-flop. When the conducting state had passed completely around the ring, a carry pulse would be emitted which would cause the next highest ring counter to advance one place. The basic unit on the machine was an accumulator which consisted of ten ring counters plus a special circuit to indicate the sign of the 10-digit number being stored. Each flip-flop required one double triode vacuum tube (a 6SN7), so a

Figure 7–4. A general view of the ENIAC. (Photograph courtesy of IBM archives.)

single accumulator would need 100 tubes just to store the ten digits of its one number. With all the other associated electronics, an accumulator actually required 550 vacuum tubes.

The complete ENIAC consisted of a large number of individual units arranged, in a horseshoe shape, around the outside walls of a large room in the Moore School. The units were of seven different types:

1. Accumulators. There were 20, which acted as both a memory for a single 10-digit signed number and as an arithmetic unit capable of adding or subtracting another number from the one currently being stored; they were essentially electronic versions of the mechanical registers used in the Harvard Mark I.
2. Multiplication unit. The electronic circuits were essentially a hardware version of a single-digit multiplication table which could be applied repeatedly to determine any desired product.
3. A combined division and square root unit.
4. Three function tables which could, by setting a large number of switches, store tables of values for use by the machine.

5. An input unit connected to a card reader (120 cards per minute).

6. An output unit connected to a card punch (100 cards per minute).

7. The master programmer which controlled the sequence of operations.

Each unit consisted of ranks of electronic vacuum tubes and relays behind front panels which contained switches, indicator lights, and the plug sockets for the interconnection of these basic units. There were a total of 40 front panels, each about 2 ft. wide, and individual functional units each required one or two of these depending on the complexity of the electronics.

ENIAC was cooled by forced air. Two 12 hp blowers pumped about 600 cubic feet of air per minute through each panel. The largest source of heat was the vacuum tubes, but the main reason for the cooling fans was to ensure long life for the resistors, which would be damaged by heat buildup. In addition to the forced air cooling, each panel had a thermometer and adjustable dampers to enable the operators to regulate the temperature by hand. There was also a thermostat on each panel so that, if it went over 120 degrees, the entire machine would be automatically shut down. Because of the need to open the panels for servicing, it was possible to disable the temperature-sensing devices, and this led to the one major disaster to befall the ENIAC. A technician mistakenly left the safety switch disabled one day and, as the machine grew hotter, two oil-filled capacitors ruptured and the resulting fire destroyed two units before it could be brought under control.

Of the vacuum tubes used in the machine, the rectifiers in the power supplies were the most unreliable with one out of 150 failing every week or so. Of the main 18,000 logic tubes, there would be one failing every two or three days. In general, tube life seemed to average about 9,000 to 10,000 hours. About two thirds of the tubes were mounted in 700 removable units, some with up to 28 tubes each. This enabled service personnel to simply remove an entire faulty unit, plug in a new one, and take the old unit to the shop bench for trouble shooting.

The individual functional units were capable of being connected to any of the others by means of two sets of cables which ran the entire length of the machine. One of these sets of cable buses consisted of the lines which were intended to carry data, while the other carried a sequence of pulses which would stimulate a given unit into action. A unit was normally inactive until it received an activation pulse along one of the program cables. When it received an activation pulse, it performed one of several different jobs depending on the setting of the switch registers on the front of the unit. These switch settings enabled the unit (say an accumulator) to perform tasks such as:

- determine which digital buses should be used in receiving or transmitting information

- determine whether the unit was to receive or transmit a number during this activation

- determine if the reception or transmission was to be a once only event or if the action was to be repeated a given number (1–9) of times
- determine, for the action of transmitting a number, if the memory was to be reset back to zero after the action was complete or if it was to retain the number itself

After completing a given action, the unit would send out a special pulse, on one of the program lines, to activate the next unit in the sequence of units required to perform the computation.

Numbers were transmitted from one unit to another along the numerical buses; up to five for input and two for output could be attached to any given accumulator as long as only one of these connections was active at any given time. One of the output ports was used to transmit the number currently being held in the accumulator while the other was used to transmit the nines complement of this number. This ability to transmit the nines complement of a number removed any necessity to implement specific subtraction hardware. The numerical buses consisted of cables of 12 wires each, ten being used to

Figure 7–5.   A close-up view of some of the ENIAC panels, the digit busses, program busses, control switches and indicator lamps. Pres Eckert is changing a switch setting. (Photograph courtesy of the Sperry Corporation.)

carry the pulses which represented the 10-digit number, one of the remaining wires was used to carry the sign indication, and the last wire was a common ground connection. To represent a digit, say 7, on a given wire of the bus, 7 pulses were sent down the wire in rapid succession, each pulse lasting about 2 microseconds with a 10 microsecond delay between them. A positive sign was represented by an absence of pulses, while a series of nine pulses represented a negative sign, a system that was compatible with nines complement arithmetic. The program buses were constructed identically to the numerical buses in order to achieve a greater degree of standardization of components. Any of the 11 wires in a program bus could be used to control the individual units in a way which will be discussed later.

When an accumulator was adding a number to another already in its internal register, it simply caused the decade counters to move along one position for each digit pulse received on the wire of the numeric bus which corresponded to the digit involved. All ten digits of the number would be added in parallel and this meant that an anticipatory carry mechanism, similar to the one described in the section on Charles Babbage's analytical engine, was required. Each accumulator had the ability, via the setting of the front panel switches, to either add an incoming number to the number already stored, clear its register to zeros before accepting the number, or clear its register to zeros except for one digit which would contain a five. This last option enabled the accumulator to round off any incoming numbers to any desired number of significant figures. If it became necessary to work with more than ten significant figures, two accumulators could be hooked together to function as one large accumulator of 20-digit capacity.

The activation pulses were sent from one unit to the next by means of the program bus wires. Each accumulator was capable of being connected to any of 99 possible program wires. The precise action of the accumulator was, as mentioned earlier, controlled by the front panel switches, of which there were two for each of the 11 possible program wire connection ports. Only eight of these program connection ports had the ability to cause the unit to repeat the reception or transmission of information a given number (1–9) of times.

The multiplication unit was capable of being connected to any of 24 program wires. Each of these 24 program connection ports had a series of switches which could be set to change the action of the unit. These changes could involve (1) indicating which numeric buses were to be used to receive the two numbers to be multiplied together, (2) indicating to which numeric bus the result should be sent, and (3) specifying the number of digits to be retained in the final product. The actual multiplication was done by forming a number of partial products which were then added together to give the final product, much the same way as it is done with a set of Napier's "bones" or when multiplying two numbers together using pencil and paper. This scheme resulted in the multiplication unit being about 4.5 times faster than one based on repeated addition. Two 10-digit numbers could be multiplied together in just under three milliseconds to create a 20-digit product, which would normally be reduced back to ten digits before being sent off down a numeric bus.

The combined division/square root unit was the slowest part of the electronic sections of the machine. It performed its operations by the standard shift and subtract algorithm. Because of its slow speed, it was often the case that the other operations could be carried out in parallel with a division. In that case, a special interlock mechanism ensured that the final pulse, directing the activation of the next program step, would not be sent until both parts of the parallel operations had been completed.

It is interesting to compare each of ENIAC's functional units with those of the Harvard Mark I. In almost every case it is possible to see that the ENIAC's unit was simply the electronic analog of the Mark I's electromechanical mechanism.

Because there was no form of memory, as we now think of it, incorporated into ENIAC, it was difficult to obtain standard function values for use during a computation. This difficulty was sometimes overcome by reading them, as needed, from cards. A more common method was to use the three so-called function tables. Each function table could contain 208 6-digit numbers or 104 12-digit numbers. The individual numerical entries had to be set up on a series of switches on the front of the function units. If a two-digit number (00 to 99) was transmitted to the function table, it would cause the preset value for that argument to be sent back on one of the numeric buses. The function tables could be set up so that, instead of transmitting back one value, they would send back three adjacent values which could then be used to interpolate any required intermediate value of the required function. This explains the fact that, although they could only be interrogated for 100 separate values, they were actually required to be able to store 104 different 12-digit numbers.

These function tables could also be set to repeat the transmission of a value up to nine times in succession. This feature was occasionally used to multiply a value by repeated additions. The main use, however, was to store the values of the ballistic "drag" functions needed for calculating trajectories.

The input equipment consisted of a card reader which would transmit eight numbers, each of ten digits, from a card to a special buffer unit constructed out of relays. This buffer could be interrogated at any time during a computation, and its contents would be sent out on a numeric bus for use by another unit. The card reader could also be activated, at any time, by a program pulse in order to refill the relay registers from a new card. A further two relay registers in the input unit could be set, via switches, to act as a sort of mini function table. The card punch was similarly buffered by a series of eight relay registers. The decision to construct these units out of relay technology rather than vacuum tubes was made because it was cheaper and because it was realized that the speed of the card reader and punch were such that there was no need for a very high-speed buffer. It also meant that these units required an interlock mechanism, like the one used in the division/square root unit, to prevent the machine from attempting to access the relay buffers before the input or output operation had been completed. The punched card machines were the greatest source of unreliability in the ENIAC, with card jams, breakdowns in the punches, and problems with the bearings being the major sources of trouble. This suggests that the project may have had a poor maintenance program for the mechanical equipment as these were, normally, very reliable devices.

Because of the greatly increased internal speed of the ENIAC over that of an electromechanical machine, it was obvious that any attempt to devise a control mechanism based on instructions punched into paper tape would have been impractical. The control of the machine was done by the master control unit. It was, in every way, the heart of the machine, because it was the device which controlled the loops and the switching of the machine from one series of program steps to another. The unit basically consisted of ten electronic switches, each of which could assume six different positions. With each switch was associated an electronic counter which could be used to control the stepping of the switch from one position to the next, or in special cases it could be stepped by a series of special stepper lines controlled by the accumulators. The counters could count the number of program pulses which had been received on a particular program bus and, when the counter reached a predefined value (set on a series of front panel switches), the associated electronic switch would advance to the next position (clearing the counter in the process). This would cause the incoming program pulses to be routed to a different set of program lines, which would in turn initiate a new sequence of operations in the computation. As long as the electronic switches were not stepped to the next position, the system would route the incoming program pulse (which had been generated by the last unit in the sequence of calculations) over to the unit which performed the first computation in that sequence. The result was a calculation loop which would only be abandoned when the master programmer counters reached the predetermined value specifying the end of the loop.

The use of the special lines to step the master programmer switches enabled a loop to be performed a variable number of times, rather than having the upper limit on the iteration counter always fixed. These special stepper lines were often used to step the master programmer switches when the accumulators encountered numbers of certain signs or magnitudes arising during the calculations. The master programmer switches could also be reset back to their starting positions by another set of special reset lines controlled from the accumulators or from other stepper switches. Thus it was possible to set up "subroutines" of steps that could be invoked in the proper sequence by the master programmer unit. Indeed, the individual "subroutines" were capable of operating so much in parallel that it was possible to have co-routines or even two separate problems running at the same time.

The master programmer contained an initiating unit to supply the clock pulses and an initial program pulse to start a computation. The clock could be set to run automatically or to deliver a single series of clock pulses, equivalent

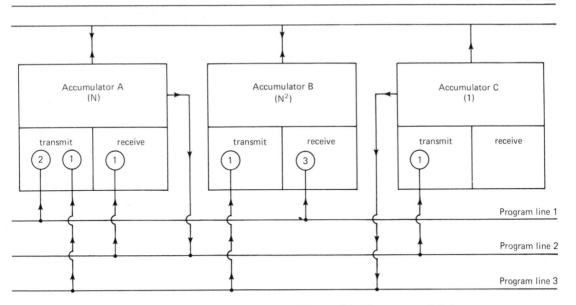

Figure 7–6. A simple ENIAC wiring to produce a table of integers and their squares.

to one addition time, to allow a wired up program to be run a single step at a time for debugging purposes. The indicator lights on the front of each panel would show the number currently being stored in each register so that a program could be debugged by systematically examining this information.

In order to gain an appreciation of the way the ENIAC was "programmed," it is instructive to examine a trivial problem and note the way the ENIAC was wired to compute the solution. If it was required to produce a deck of cards, each card containing the number N in the first ten columns and the number N^2 in the next ten columns, then the diagram in Figure 7–6 shows the essentials of the method used to wire together the different units of the ENIAC to obtain the desired card deck. Some liberty has been taken by not showing the wiring to and from the master programmer and the input/output units, but the careful study of this diagram will illustrate the basic principles of the machine.

If accumulator A currently contains the number N and accumulator B contains the number N^2 (both of which have already been punched on cards), then to obtain (N + 1) and $(N + 1)^2$, for the next output card, the following process was initiated:

- A program pulse appearing on program line 1 (the pulse being generated by the card punch unit) would cause accumulator A to transmit its contents (twice because of the switch settings) onto the numeric bus shown at the top of Figure 7–6. This same pulse would be picked up by accumulator B and put into a state in which it was ready to receive three numbers from the numeric bus.

- After accumulator A has done its task of transmitting its contents twice onto the data bus (the two numbers being received by accumulator B and being added to the number already stored there), it emits a program pulse onto program line 2.

- The pulse on program line 2 is picked up by accumulator A (putting it in a mode to receive a number to be added to its register), and it is also picked up by accumulator C which is made to transmit the constant "1" (one) onto the numeric bus. This constant is added to accumulator A (because it was just put into receive mode), and it is also added to accumulator B (because it was still waiting for the last of the three numbers it was told to receive).

- At this point, accumulator A is storing the number $(N + 1)$, while accumulator B is storing $N^2 + 2N + 1$ which is the same thing as $(N + 1)^2$.

- As soon as accumulator C has transmitted its contents to the numeric bus, it places a pulse on program line 3 which will cause accumulators A and B to transmit their contents (on data buses not shown on the diagram) over to the card punch. When the card punch has finished doing its job, it will place a pulse on program line 1 to restart the whole process in order to compute $(N + 2)$ and $(N + 2)^2$.

The number of accumulators available on the ENIAC was the limiting factor in most calculations. Although there were 20 accumulators, four of these were required during a multiplication (two to hold the numbers to be multiplied and two others to accumulate the partial products) and a further four were required for use during a division, so that only 12 could be counted on to store intermediate results during a computation. It was often necessary to punch out intermediate results and have these fed back into the machine at some later stage of the process. The numerical technique employed in solving a particular problem was often determined by the number of accumulators that happened to be available at any given stage, rather than any consideration for efficiency.

Multiplication and division were so time-consuming that they were avoided whenever possible. If a number had to be multiplied by a single-digit integer, it was often done by repeated addition (using the iterative transmission feature of the accumulators) rather than using the special multiplication unit. If a number had to be multiplied or divided by some small power of ten, it was generally done by simply transmitting the number from one accumulator to another by a special plug which would shift the order of the digital lines around to accomplish the multiplication or division by, in effect, moving the position of the decimal point. Whenever possible, difference methods needing only additions, such as those used by Babbage, were employed in order to avoid the use of the multiplication or division units.

Although Mauchly had visions of creating an electronic computing machine in 1942, it was not until 1943 that any real action took place. By January of 1944 the basic design had been worked out to the point where actual progress could be made on the main machine, as opposed to simply constructing test circuits. In July of that year, two accumulators, a power supply, and a signal generator had been constructed and were shown to work by performing some very elementary calculations. As with all the early machines, it is rather difficult to say when ENIAC was complete and working properly. Because of the highly parallel nature of the basic units, the machine just continued to work better and better as further units were added to the two original accumulators. By the spring of 1945 the ENIAC was functioning very well and, although it was considered as still being under test, it had actually run many production programs for the ballistic people, the scientists of the Moore School, calculations for the Los Alamos atomic energy people, and it was even wired up to do some work on a number theory problem during the Thanksgiving holiday weekend of that year. After remaining in the Moore School for about one year, it was dismantled and shipped to the Ballistics Laboratory at Aberdeen, Maryland, where it was reassembled by the Moore School engineers. The war was already over and, although there was no longer a critical need for ballistic tables, the ENIAC was soon put into full production working on a variety of problems. For a few years, ENIAC was the only large-scale, electronic, digital computer in daily use.

The vacuum tubes used in the ENIAC were found to be very stable devices once they had reached their final operating temperature, but they had a high failure rate during their warmup period. For this reason the Moore School never turned the machine off unless it was absolutely necessary. When the machine had been operating in Aberdeen for several months, a call was put in to the Moore School stating that the ENIAC was having severe reliability problems. The machine was nonfunctional about 50 percent of the time and it was sometimes the case that the faults would take all day to trace down and correct, leaving no time at all for production work. An investigation showed that someone in authority at Aberdeen had decided it was impossible to have the machine left on over night because of the cost of the electricity and the cost of a guard to watch over it in case of fire. When this difficulty had been corrected, and the machine was allowed to run continuously, the reliability problems vanished and the ENIAC gave good service for the next ten years. There were periods, during that time, of up to three days when no maintenance was necessary, but this was the exception rather than the rule. On average, the machine burnt out one tube every two days but it only took about 15 minutes to find and replace a defective unit.

In later years some enhancements were made to the basic ENIAC. A magnetic drum storage unit was attached in order to allow for storing more intermediate results. In 1952 a core memory was added, again to allow for the storage of intermediate results and to act as a high-speed buffer for the input/output units. This core memory could store 100 words of ten digits each. The access address was provided by two decade counters already in an accumulator; in effect it was a fancy version of the old switch set function table. The core memory operated at what, for that time, was a very fast cycle time of 16 microseconds. The 100 words of core storage required a cabinet about 2 ft 6 in. long, 2 ft wide, and 7 ft high!

The ENIAC was never intended to be a computer with an internally stored program. Indeed, although it was developed shortly afterwards, the idea of an internally stored program was not even known when Mauchly made his first tentative suggestions about constructing an electronic calculating machine. It is a strange twist of fate, therefore, that the ENIAC actually did most of its work while operating as a stored program computer. In 1947 Richard F. Clippinger, head of the Computer Laboratory at the Ballistics Laboratory, was able to show that the ENIAC could be converted to operate as a stored program computer by wiring it up to perform 99 different very elementary computations and having each of these initiated by one of the 99 possible program lines. This essentially made it into an electronic computer with 99 available instructions. The machine was modified, at the suggestion of N. Metropolis of Los Alamos, by the addition of a converter unit which took pairs of decimal digits and, depending on the number represented, sent a pulse down one of the 99 possible program lines to invoke one of the 99 possible "instructions." The portable, switch-set function tables were now useful as a programming device. The switches were set so that they represented the program of instructions required, and the main sequence mechanism of the ENIAC would now simply step along the function tables and have them send pairs of digits to the converter unit. This unit would in turn energize the appropriate program line to perform the required instruction. Although there were 99 different program lines available, there were initially only 60 different instructions available under the standard wiring arrangements, but this was increased to 92 about a year later. Each function table could hold 600 two-digit integers so the ENIAC ended up with a program space of 1800 instructions for any one program.

The introduction of a standard wiring scheme and "programs" stored on the function tables resulted in the basic speed of the ENIAC being slowed down quite a bit. However, this was more than balanced by a tremendous gain in the speed at which ENIAC could be set up to perform a computation. Under the old scheme, where the whole wiring had to be stripped off and the program, data, and control lines reconnected, it could often take several days to set up ENIAC to perform a complex computation. When ENIAC became "programmable" with a standard wiring that was never changed, it was only a matter of an hour or two to change the settings on the function table switches in order to set up a new problem. Thus, what you lost in brute force execution speed, you more than regained in the number of productive computing hours which became available.

The ENIAC was shut off for the final time on October 2, 1955. It has been conjectured that, during the ten years of ENIAC's useful life at the Aberdeen Proving Grounds, this machine did more arithmetic than had been done by the whole human race prior to 1945. A few small pieces of ENIAC, including several of the front panels, are now on display in the Smithsonian Museum in Washington, D.C.

7.4 THE COLOSSUS MACHINES

7.4.1 The Enigma

In the years between the two world wars, the Germans developed a machine to convert ordinary language into coded form for secret transmission via either radio or telephone lines. This machine, known as "Enigma," came in two versions, one for commercial use and one for use by the military. The commercial machine was the first to be put into production and was available for purchase by interested companies by about 1927. Simply owning one of these machines was not sufficient for breaking a coded message, because the device had a number of different settings and one had to know the settings on the machine which generated the code in order to convert the coded message back into plain text.

The Enigma came in a small wooden box and resembled a portable typewriter in that it had the 26 letters of the alphabet inscribed on a typewriter-style keyboard. In the lid of the box were 26 small flashlight bulbs, each labelled with a different letter of the alphabet. Inside the box were three rotating wheels with 26 possible electrical contacts on each flat side of a wheel, the contacts on one side being joined to the contacts on the other by a series of wires running through the thickness of the wheel. These connections were not made in any regular way, that is, two adjacent contacts on one side were usually connected to nonadjacent contacts on the other. Thus any electrical signal being put into a contact on one side of the wheel would appear at a contact in some other position on the opposite side of the wheel. When an operator pressed one of the typewriter keys, the rightmost wheel would turn $1/26$ of the way around, the key pressed would cause a voltage to be passed into one of the contacts on the side of the wheel, the voltage would then be passed through the wheel to a different contact on the other side, and that would then make contact with the next wheel in line. In this way the voltage would be passed from wheel to wheel. A series of further connections would cause the voltage to be passed back through the wheels again, and finally it would cause one of the 26 lamps to light. Which lamp lit was determined by the positions of the wheels, the electrical signal path being different when the wheels were in different positions within the mechanism or when they were rotated relative to each other. The letter illuminated by the lamp was sent as the code for the letter whose key had been pushed. Because the wheels rotated part of the way around with each push of a letter key, the same letter struck twice in succession would, most of the time, produce two different letters for the coded message. To decipher a coded message, the operators had to set up their sequence of wheels in exactly the same positions as they were for the start of the encoding procedure. They would then simply type in the coded text and the plain message would be displayed, letter by letter, on the lamp board.

In order for the sender and receiver of a message to be working with the same code, they both had to start with the wheels set in identical positions. For commercial use, a lot of companies simply had a standard setting used for a month at a time, which was communicated to branch offices by mail or special delivery service. Each of the wheels could be started in any of 26 possible rotational positions, and wheels could be interchanged into any of six possible combinations within the machine. The military version of the machine contained a small plugboard which would allow up to six pairs of letters to be interchanged with others in each coding scheme. This resulted in over 100 billion possible different ciphers which were dependent on the initial setting of the machine. When the military first began using Enigma, they tried to change the settings every few days, based on a table which was good for the next month. As they became more familiar with the machine, they changed the initial settings at least once per day. Eventually the daily key was only used by the coder to create a three-letter group at the start of each message which would communicate the initial setting of Enigma for the following message. Thus, in its ultimate form, the Enigma was used with a coding scheme which was unique to this message and quite possibly would never be used again. Because of the enormous number of possible initial settings for an Enigma, the German military were not concerned that their code would be broken even if one of the coding machines accidently fell into unfriendly hands.

On July 15, 1928, the German military began to use Enigma code on one of their radio stations and Polish radio operators alerted their Cipher Bureau to this fact. The Polish Cipher Bureau simply purchased a commercial copy of the Enigma, modified it with the military plugboard, and started to see if they could use it to break the code. They initially had little success with the decipherment and the project was abandoned until 1932. At that time the Polish mathematician Marian Rejewski was assigned to again study the situation to see if he could find any clues which would help in the decipherment of the military messages. After a great deal of effort, he made some initial headway on determining the pattern of initial settings being used by the Germans. More people were put on the job and, within a short period of time, the Poles were managing to decipher about 75 percent of all the German messages. As the years went by, the Poles constructed various machines to aid them in their decipherment task and, just as quickly as the Poles figured out a better method of breaking the codes, the Germans found better methods of doing the coding. On July 25 and 26, 1939, when it became obvious that war was going to break out, the Poles called a meeting of British, French, and Polish intelligence agencies and informed their allies of what they had been doing. It came as a distinct surprise to the others that the Poles had managed to crack the German code, for they too had been trying for several years with little or no success. The Poles gave the British a Polish-built copy of the German military Enigma, described the electromechanical machines they had been using (called *bombas* [bombs] because of the ticking noise they made) to aid in the decipherment of Enigma codes, and also presented the British with enough statistical material about the German coding schemes that the British were, from that time on, able to break a large percentage of the German Enigma coded messages.

After the start of the war, the Germans still believed that the Enigma was secure, but just to be sure they started using a very much more complex device of the same type. They called this new coding machine a *Geheimschreiber* (secret writer). It resulted in the British adding a number of people to its decoding group in an attempt to use the Polish techniques to decipher the codes produced by this new machine.

The British government Code and Cipher School was located outside London at a place called Bletchley Park. It is unfortunate that we do not know more about the work that went on in Bletchley Park because it seems that one of the very first large-scale electronic calculating machines was developed there to aid in the decipherment project. The British government still considers the wartime code-breaking work a state secret and, other than a few bits and pieces of information and a few fuzzy pictures of the equipment being used, remains completely silent on the details of the men, methods, and equipment used to break the German codes.

It is known that the British rapidly constructed several new versions of the electromechanical Polish *bombas* machines and, adapting the Polish name to English, called these devices "bombs." This has led to some confusion as to the true role of Bletchley Park in the war effort, but the only thing these "bombs" destroyed was the German Air Force message security. Changes in the German military Enigma, such as increasing the number of code wheels in the Navy version, soon led to the "bombs" becoming too small and slow to be of any use in deciphering German secret messages and new methods had to be found.

One of the big problems in attempting to piece together information about the code-breaking activities at Bletchley Park, other than the fact it is still bound by the British Official Secrets Act (the penalties for breaking it are quite severe so the people involved have mainly remained silent), is the fact that, although there were a lot of people at work at Bletchley, they were all on a "need to know" basis as far as information was concerned. If there was no need for you to know anything about a particular machine or procedure, then steps were taken to ensure that, even if you worked in the next building, you did not even know the machine existed, let alone how it worked. This means that, although some people are willing to discuss their war-time experiences at Bletchley Park, they all have a biassed view of what was really taking place. Any coordinated description of the genesis and development of the electronic machinery will likely have to wait until the British government opens its secret files.

7.4.2 Alan Turing (1912–1954)

Alan Turing was a British mathematician who had a great deal to do with the construction and use of various pieces of equipment at Bletchley Park. Because of his influence in subsequent developments in the field of computer science, it is worth a small digression to consider his life story. Turing studied mathematics at King's College in Cambridge, entering there in 1931 and quickly distinguishing himself as a first-rate scholar. After graduation he remained there, as a Fellow of the College, during which time he produced his famous paper "On Computable Numbers with an Application to the Entscheidungsproblem" which was the first to show that there exist classes of problems having no algorithmic solution. His publications became known to others in the world of mathematical logic and, in 1936, he went to spend a year at Princeton, during which time he got to know men like von Neumann, Courant, Einstein, and Lefschetz. Although only intending to spend one year in America, he managed to get King's College to agree to extending his leave for a further year and thus did not arrive back in Britain until the summer of 1938. Upon the outbreak of the Second World War, he was appointed as a temporary civil servant in the Department of Communications of the British Foreign Office where his training in mathematical logic was immediately put to use in their code-breaking efforts.

Several stories about Turing will give some idea of the personality of this remarkable man. He was frequently bothered by hay fever when he cycled from his lodgings (an Inn three miles from Bletchley Park) to his office so, quite unconcerned about what anyone thought, would cycle the distance wearing his government-issued gas mask. Several of his colleagues report that the bicycle he used had the habit of slipping the chain off the hub gear during his ride to and from work. Unlike most people, who would have taken the bicycle in for repair, Turing noted that the breakdown always happened after x rotations of the pedals and would count the number of times his pedals had gone around so that he could dismount from the bicycle before the chain fell off. He later added a small mechanical counter to the pedals so that he could think of other things while going to and from work and not have to be counting all the time. A later mathematical analysis of the problem showed him that it only occurred after so many thousand chain links had passed over the gears, and this led to the discovery that a slightly deformed chain link would catch with one slightly bent gear tooth and cause the chain to come off.

Although he had an active mind, it was not a very practical one. He was, at one time, convinced that the Germans would invade Britain. Because of this,

Figure 7–7.   Alan M. Turing, aged 39. (Photograph by Elliot & Fry, courtesy of the National Physical Laboratory.)

he converted all his money into silver bars which he transported in a baby carriage to the woods behind Bletchley Park and buried in two separate places. He not only injured his back in the process but, after the war, was completely unable to locate them again.

Turing evidently made a number of fundamental contributions to the work of breaking the German codes. These were in both the areas of creating hardware (suggesting modifications to the "bomb" electromechanical relay machines) and in the area of procedures to be used in the code-breaking process. We are, once again, denied knowing the exact details of Turing's contributions and the extent to which they contributed to the breaking of both the *Geheimschreiber* and modified Enigma code schemes, but the very high regard in which he is held by the people with whom he once worked, together with the fact that the King awarded him an OBE after the war, indicates that his contributions were of the highest importance. Additional information can be found in the excellent biography prepared by Hodges, noted in the reference section at the end of this chapter.

7.4.3 The Robinsons

By the middle of 1942 the number of people working at Bletchley Park had increased to the point where several different sections, or "huts" as they were called (because of the fact that they were housed in temporary buildings) were formed. These "huts" tended to work independently on different problems, or on different approaches to the same problem, with only the heads of the different "huts" in contact with each other. Some of the people who were taken on at this time—for example, Donald Michie, I. J. Good, and W. Tutte—continued in the fields of mathematics and computer science after the war was over and were still active in the 1980s.

Because the "bombs" were now too slow to deal with the problems at hand, and different code-breaking techniques were being developed, there was a need for bigger and better machinery to aid the human decoders. The General Post Office, telephone division, had a large research department at a place known as Dollis Hill in northwest London. Mr. T. H. Flowers was the head of a group of 50 people at Dollis Hill doing research into telephone switching problems. Because of their expertise, the Flowers' group was commissioned to build several different pieces of machinery, designed mainly by people like Turing and his co-workers, for use at Bletchley Park. Very few of the Dollis Hill people had any idea of the eventual use to be made of their equipment; the group designing a photoelectric paper tape reader was told, for example, that it was to be used in a new type of telegraph system.

In late 1942 a new member of staff, M. H. A. Newman, arrived at Bletchley Park. He found that he was not much good at the task he had been given, but was able to see that, given enough resources, it should be possible to automate at least part of the process. Newman was put in touch with Dr. C. E. Wynn-Williams who had been working in the Cavendish Laboratory where, as early as 1931, he had constructed a binary counter out of a series of vacuum tubes. By 1942, Wynn-Williams had gained a lot of experience in constructing all sorts of sophisticated laboratory control equipment incorporating relays, vacuum tubes, and automatic printers. Winn-Williams agreed to design a machine which would perform the functions envisaged by Newman and, with the help of several engineers at Dollis Hill, had the machine complete by April of 1943. Because of the rather unusual, for that time, nature of the machine, it was immediately christened the "Heath Robinson," after a cartoonist of the time who was well known for designing strange and wonderful machines.

The Heath Robinson was a combination electronic and relay-based machine. The high speed accumulators were implemented in vacuum tubes while the slower functions, even including some of the high-order digits of the accumulators, were constructed out of relays. Because it is still covered by the British Official Secrets Act, the exact function of the Heath Robinson is not clear. It is known that it was automatic in its operation, and results were produced upon an elementary form of line printer. The machine was not a general-purpose computer but was specialized to perform some type of boolean operations on information it would read from two endless loops of punched paper tape. The tape loops were usually about 1000 characters long and, presumably, must have contained copies of intercepted coded messages and potential matching decode data. These were read by two specially constructed paper tape readers which operated at 2000 characters per second. The first Heath Robinson was not very reliable. It was not well constructed, due to the haste with which it was needed, and the result was a constant set of problems for the people at Bletchley Park. The machine did, however, prove that it was possible to construct high-speed electronic devices which would help the decoding process, and at least two other Robinsons, named "Peter Robinson" and "Robinson and Cleaver" after two well-known stores in London, were constructed.

7.4.4 The Colossus

Flowers, who had not been a part of the Heath Robinson project, was called in as an electronics expert in an attempt to redesign part of the Robinson machinery in order to make it more reliable. Seeing that a simple patch job was unlikely to be successful, he suggested that a completely new all-electronic design be done which would use about 1500 vacuum tubes. This was more vacuum tubes than had been used in any other single project up to that time and was only exceeded by the ENIAC developments in the United States, when it had several functioning accumulators, about a year after Flowers' machine was operational. Flowers was unable to get the approval of the Bletchley Park people to construct such an innovative machine, so he took his ideas to the head of the Dollis Hill Research Station and they started on the project in the sure knowledge that it would eventually be accepted and prove useful in the war effort. In less than a year the machine had been designed, constructed, moved to Bletchley Park, and was in operation by December of 1943.

Luck was with Flowers because the first job that was attempted on the new all-electronic machine was done in only 10 minutes. At a time when the Robinsons could not produce enough output to enable the decoding of large numbers of messages, the new machine was hailed as the salvation of all their problems. It was quickly named "Colossus." Although the exact jobs it performed are still considered secret, it was known to have used biquinary registers for storing numbers, an internal clock to synchronize operations, a five-step binary shift register, and was controlled by means of a plugboard and wires. The photoelectric readers were improved versions of those found on the Robinson machines.

Flowers, attempting to anticipate demand, asked the Bletchley Park people to give him advance warning of any requirement for additional copies of the Colossus. Although never getting any such warning, he quietly saw to it that the Dollis Hill people started constructing some of the more time-consuming components which might be required. Suddenly, in March of 1944, he was told that Bletchley Park would require lots more of these machines, and could they please have them by June 1st! Flowers' foresight enabled him, through a huge effort on the part of the Dollis Hill people, to get one of the new Mark II Colossi installed and functional in Bletchley Park on June 1, 1944, just five days before the Allies invaded Europe. This was, of course, the reason behind the rush to get additional Colossi functional by June 1.

Before the end of the war, several more Colossi were in use at Bletchley Park. It may be that as many as ten were fully functional by the time the war was over, each being a slight improvement over its predecessor. By utilizing parallel circuitry, the effective speed of the Colossus was increased to deal with operations on 25,000 characters per second. Nothing is known as to the eventual fate of these machines, but they were presumably kept in use for other code-breaking activities of the British government. It is known that at least one group of British RAF radio technicians were moved, after the war was over, to northern Iran in order to intercept coded Russian radio messages. Thus it seems likely that the Colossi continued to be used for code-breaking functions until they were replaced by more modern computers.

The Colossi were special-purpose machines, but only to the extent that they were designed to perform boolean functions, at high speed, on data read from paper tape. The fact that all the standard arithmetic operations can be performed by a sequence of boolean commands meant that, in principal, the Colossi could also be used for accomplishing arithmetic jobs. This was demonstrated, after the war, by having one of the Colossi wired up to do multiplication of base 10 numbers. The plugboard wiring job was so complex that it was not worth using the Colossus in this mode, but it at least showed that the scheme was possible. Another fact that makes the Colossus look very much like a forerunner of the modern computers is that they were capable of conditional branching; that is, they were capable of executing one of several different plugboard wired "programs" depending on results so far generated within the machine. The exact form taken by this conditional branching facility is not known because of the conditions imposed by the Official Secrets Act.

The Americans must have also had some type of mechanical, electro-mechanical, or electronic help in their decoding efforts during the war. The code schemes of both the German and Japanese military were complex enough that it was necessary to have some type of check on the permutations and combinations of various coding machine settings before a proper decoding could be attempted. The United States, like Great Britain, still considers the detailed code-breaking methods a secret and will not discuss the existence of any possible code-breaking machines constructed during the war years.

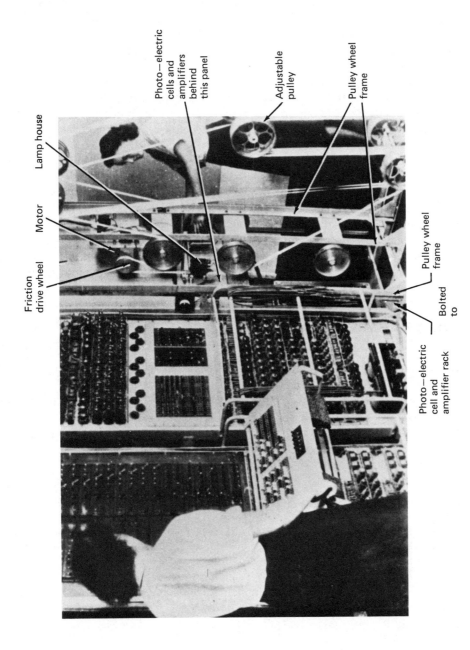

Friction
drive wheel

Motor

Lamp house

Photo—electric
cells and
amplifiers
behind
this panel

Adjustable
pulley

Pulley wheel
frame

Pulley wheel
frame

Bolted
to

Photo—electric
cell and
amplifier rack

Figure 7–8. The Colossus. (Photograph courtesy of the British Public Record Office.)

There are one or two hints that some machines may have been constructed in America. Alan Turing is known to have visited the United States at least once during the war and to have met men like Claude Shannon, and toured the facilities at Bell Labs. The efforts at war-time secrecy are well illustrated by the fact that George Stibitz recalls Turing showing very little interest in the Bell Labs relay computers; this would be most unusual of a man who had been involved in the construction of essentially similar devices at Bletchley and who, according to a report in a book written by his mother, spent the entire trip back to Britain in a storm-tossed navy vessel reading technical specifications of electrical and electronic devices. It is known that the purpose of Turning's visit to Bell Labs was to discuss a machine to encode voice transmissions. However, the visit may also have involved some secret talks with Sam Williams, the man who helped Stibitz construct his relay computers, because it is thought that Williams produced a secret, relay-based machine for use on unspecified problems during the war. Although the United States probably used some devices to help with its code-breaking efforts, the people who should be knowledgeable in these matters (even if they won't admit it) acknowledge that the Colossi were far in advance of anything available in the States at the time.

FURTHER READING

AUERBACH, I. L. (1952). "A Static Magnetic Memory System for the ENIAC," *Proceedings of the ACM Conference,* May 2 and 3, p. 213.

BRAINERD, J. G. (1976). "Genesis of the ENIAC," *Technology and Culture, 17* (No. 3), July, 482–91.

BURKS, A. W. (1947). "Electronic Computing Circuits of the ENIAC," *Proceeding of the IEEE, 35,* 756–67.

Electronics. (1980). A McGraw-Hill magazine, entire April 17 issue.

GARDNER, W. D. (1982). "The Independent Inventor," *Datamation, 26* (No. 10), 12–22.

GOLDSTINE, H. H. (1972). *The Computer from Pascal to von Neumann.* Princeton: Princeton University Press.

———— · and GOLDSTINE, ADELLE (1946). "The Electronic Numerical Integrator and Computer (ENIAC)," *Math. Tables and Other Aids to Computation, 2,* 97. (Reprinted in Randell.)

GOOD, I. J. (1976). "Pioneering Work on Computers at Bletchley," Lecture given at the National Physical Laboratory, Teddington, England, on April 28, 1976. (Reprinted in Metropolis et al.)

HARTREE, D. R. (1946). "The ENIAC, an Electronic Computing Machine," *Nature, 158* (Oct. 12), 500.

———— · (1947). *Calculating Machines, Recent and Prospective Developments.* Cambridge: Cambridge University Press.

HODGES, A. (1983). *Alan Turing: The Enigma.* New York: Simon & Schuster.

MAUCHLEY, J. W. (1942). *The Use of High Speed Vacuum Devices for Calculating*, Aug. (Reprinted in Randell.)

———· (1975). "On the Trials of Building the ENIAC," *IEEE Spectrum*, April, pp. 70–76.

METROPOLIS, N., and J. WORLTON (1980). "A Trilogy of Errors in the History of Computing," *Annals of the History of Computing*, 2 (No. 1), pp. 49–59.

MILLINGTON, R. (1976). "What Did You Do in the War, Daddy?" *Computing Europe*, June 3, p. 10.

PANTAGES, A. (1967). "Computing's Early Years," *Datamation*, October, pp. 60–65.

RANDELL, B. (1973). *The Origins of Digital Computers*. New York: Springer-Verlag.

RANDELL, B. (1976). "The Colossus," Lecture given at the Los Alamos Computer History Conference, June 10–15, 1976. (Reprinted in Metropolis et al.)

REJEWSKI, M. (1981). "How Polish Mathematicians Deciphered the Enigma," *Annals of the History of Computing*, 3 (No. 3), July, 213–240.

STEVENSON, W. (1976). *A Man Called Intrepid*. New York: Harcourt.

TURING, S. (1959). *Alan M. Turing*. Cambridge: Heffer.

WINTERBOTHAM, F. W. (1974). *The Ultra Secret*. New York: Harper.

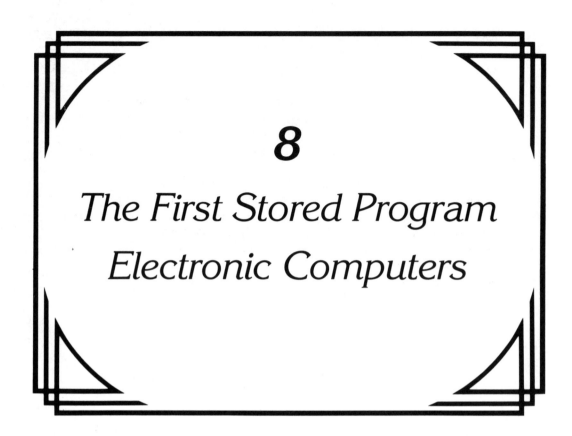

8

The First Stored Program

Electronic Computers

8.1 THE GENESIS OF THE IDEAS

Up to this point, all the different calculating machines described were programmed by either some form of instructions on punched tape or by a complex hardwired interconnection of the machine's basic components. The advent of the true stored program computer was on the horizon, but during the time of the Second World War most technical groups were so busy with war-related work that they didn't have the time or resources to look around for possible future developments.

The question of who actually invented the concept of the stored program has caused more controversy than perhaps any other in the history of computing science. The debate has been carried on both in print and at various public meetings, sometimes with a degree of bitterness that is not usually found in what is, after all, a purely academic question. Part of the reason for there being a debate at all is the fact that two groups of people with basically different values—academicians and entrepreneurs—were involved in the actual production of the stored-program computer. This was complicated by the usual human problem that one person's memory of a sequence of events can be totally different from another's, even if they were both involved in the same situation. The view has been further clouded over the years because some of the computer companies were involved in extensive legal battles over patents and manufacturing rights.

The place in which the idea was generated is not in any doubt: It was at the Moore School and it was the team working on the construction of ENIAC that first came up with the idea of the stored program. We have already met most of the principal individuals involved in the invention: John Mauchly and Pres Eckert of the Moore School, and Herman Goldstine the liaison officer with the Ballistic Research Laboratories were introduced in the section dealing with the development of ENIAC. The one other major individual was the brilliant mathematician John von Neumann, and it is appropriate that some of his background and reasons why he was associated with the Moore School should now be described.

John von Neumann was born in Hungary just after the turn of the century. He came from a wealthy banking family and was privately educated until he was 11 years old. When he entered into a formal school setting, his teachers recognized his unusual mathematical talents and convinced his parents to have him continue with private education under the direction of university professors. By the time he was 19, he was publishing his own papers on mathematical subjects. He spent several years at different universities—in Berlin, Hamburg, and Princeton—and, in 1933, he was made the youngest member of the newly opened Institute for Advanced Study at Princeton University. He was equally at home in the realms of physics, pure and applied mathematics, game theory, and numerical analysis. When he died in 1957, his collected writings were published and required six large volumes. He has to rank as one of this century's most brilliant mathematicians and undoubtedly among the ranks of leading mathematicians of all time. At the outbreak of World War II, he was called to take an active part in a number of scientific projects then being undertaken, the most famous of which was the development of the atomic bomb. He had the ability, often found in mathematicians, of absorbing enormous amounts of material in a very short time, except that von Neumann seemed to excel all others when it came to this type of mental effort. His ability to organize and systematize a body of knowledge was legendary, and there are many stories of how he was able to solve problems in a few minutes that others had worked on for months with no progress being evident.

Herman Goldstine, in his book *The Computer from Pascal to von Neu-*

mann, clearly indicates that he has an almost reverent regard for von Neumann and his abilities. He details for us several examples of von Neumann's actions which helped create this legend. One of the typical episodes is related as:

> Von Neumann had an uncanny ability to solve very complex calculations in his head. This was a source of wonderment to mathematicians and physicists alike. It is possible to illustrate this quality of him by an amusing anecdote: One time an excellent mathematician stopped into my office to discuss a problem that had been causing him concern. After a rather lengthy and unfruitful discussion, he said he would take home a desk calculator and work out a few special cases that evening. Each case could be resolved by the numerical evaluation of a formula. The next day he arrived at the office looking very tired and haggard. On being asked why, he triumphantly stated he had worked out five special cases of increasing complexity in the course of a night's work; he had finished at 4:30 in the morning.
>
> Later that morning von Neumann unexpectedly came in on a consulting trip and asked how things were going. Whereupon I brought in my colleague to discuss the problem with von Neumann. We considered various possibilities but still had not met with success. Then von Neumann said, "Let's work out a few special cases." We agreed, carefully not telling him of the numerical work in the early morning hours. He then put his eyes to the ceiling and in perhaps five minutes worked out in his head four of the previously and laboriously calculated cases! After he had worked about a minute on the fifth and hardest case, my colleague suddenly announced out loud the final answer. Von Neumann was completely perturbed and quickly went back, at an increased tempo, to his mental calculations. After perhaps another minute he said, "Yes, that is correct." Then my colleague fled, and von Neumann spent perhaps another half hour of considerable mental effort trying to understand how anyone could have found a better way to handle the problem. Finally, he was let in on the true situation and recovered his aplomb.[1]

Stories such as these show that von Neumann was a remarkable man in his ability with mental calculation but, perhaps more important, he had an equal facility with organizing information and a dedication to the production of written reports which gathered together all known aspects of a particular topic.

Von Neumann's abilities quickly made him an important consultant in many different areas of war-time science and technology, and he was well known and respected in the highest government scientific and technical circles. In January of 1944 he was in need of large-scale calculating help in the solution of a very difficult series of problems, so he wrote to one of the government offices in charge of coordinating projects in applied mathematics to enquire what facilities were available. At this time the construction of the

---

[1] Herman H. Goldstine, *The Computer from Pascal to von Neumann* (Princeton: Princeton University Press, 1972), pp. 181–82.

ENIAC was just getting started and it was unknown whether it would work or not, so von Neumann was told to contact Howard Aiken, George Stibitz, or the Thomas J. Watson Astronomical Computing Bureau at Columbia University. A few months later von Neumann was accidentally to find out about ENIAC while he was on one of his consulting visits to the Ballistic Research Laboratories. Herman Goldstine also happened to be there and, as Goldstine relates:

> I was waiting for a train to Philadelphia on the railroad platform in Aberdeen when along came von Neumann. Prior to that time I had never met this great mathematician, but I knew much about him of course and I had heard him lecture on several occasions. It was therefore with considerable temerity that I approached this world famous figure, introduced myself, and started talking. Fortunately for me von Neumann was a warm, friendly person who did his best to make people feel relaxed in his presence. The conversation soon turned to my work. When it became clear to von Neumann that I was concerned with the development of an electronic computer capable of 333 multiplications per second, the whole atmosphere of our conversation changed from one of relaxed good humor to one more like the oral examination for the doctor's degree in mathematics.[2]

Soon after, von Neumann arranged to visit the Moore School and talk with Eckert and Mauchly about their machine.

If we now return to examine the situation at the Moore School during the first half of 1944, we should be able to see how all the pieces of the puzzle fit together. As described in the earlier section dealing with the ENIAC, by January of 1944 the basic design of ENIAC had been created and construction work had started on the actual machine. In July, just before von Neumann's first visit, two accumulators had been constructed and shown to work up to expectations. Once the basic design features had been fixed, the pressures upon Mauchly and Eckert had shifted from their shoulders to those of the actual construction team, leaving the two major design people time to consider other things besides the ENIAC. It was well known, of course, that these types of machines actually executed a series of stored commands because, although not obvious in the case of ENIAC, the paper tape control mechanisms for the Zuse, Aiken, and Stibitz machines were nothing more than a form of read-only memory containing the program instructions. This form of control had to be abandoned for ENIAC because the very high electronic speeds were well above what could be usefully used when reading instructions one at a time from paper tape. The ENIAC progress report of December 31, 1943, portions of which are reprinted in Nancy Stern's[3] book, make it quite clear that no attempt had been made to "make provision for setting up a program automatically." This would have created extra complications in the machine's design, and the fact that

---

[2]Ibid., p. 182

[3]Nancy Stern, *From ENIAC to UNIVAC* (Bedford Mass.: Digital Press, 1981).

ENIAC was designed primarily for ballistics problems meant that it would need to have the external wiring changed only infrequently.

By January of 1944, there was enough time for Mauchly and Eckert to consider the problem of how to implement a device to store and quickly access the sequence of instructions that might be needed in any future electronic computing machines. Eckert wrote a three-page document describing a "magnetic calculating machine" in which the instructions could either be stored magnetically on special alloy disks, when the program would only be needed temporarily, or etched permanently on disks when the program was to be kept available for repeated use. Thus the initial concept of a stored program computer appears to have had its tentative beginnings in late 1943 or early 1944.

When von Neumann learned of the ENIAC during the summer of 1944, he promptly took a deep and lasting interest in the activities at the Moore School. Starting in September of 1944 he became a regular visitor to the ENIAC project and, although he was too late to participate in the design of the ENIAC, he took an active part in discussions concerning a new machine, eventually to be called EDVAC, which was capable of storing its instruction tape internally within its memory and issuing its instructions at electronic speeds which were comparable with those available in the rest of the machine. In October 1944 the Army Ordnance Department granted a Moore School request that just over $100,000.00 be added to the ENIAC project budget in order to do some proper research and development work on EDVAC. This request had been made in the previous August by Herman Goldstine but it likely required the influence of John von Neumann before it was taken seriously.

From this point on von Neumann took an active part in the discussions concerning the design of EDVAC, even to the point of writing letters to the group when he could not actually be present. It is undoubtedly the case that he made many major contributions to these discussions but it is also true to say that the germ of the stored program idea existed before von Neumann became involved with the project, and, even after he was a regular participant in the design discussions, they also involved all the other members of the ENIAC team. Eventually it was von Neumann's genius for organizing material and his penchant for producing reports which led him to write down the results of all these design meetings in a document which he called *First Draft on a Report on the EDVAC* in June of 1945. It was this document which first described, in detail, the concept of the stored program digital computer.

As the name implies, the report was seemingly designed only as a draft of a more complete description, but it was circulated to the Moore School staff and to several others not directly associated with the EDVAC project. Because von Neumann is listed as the only author, he has become associated with the concept of the stored program to such an extent that subsequent computers based upon this idea were often referred to as "von Neumann machines." Needless to say, several other members of the Moore School staff were annoyed to find little or no mention of their own contributions in this document, and this has led to some of the hostile battles which still rage today about who actually was responsible for what in EDVAC's design. This conflict, together with other ones involving patent rights, were to lead to both Eckert and Mauchly leaving the Moore School in 1946 and forming their own firm to design and manufacture electronic computers.

Once the idea of the electronic computer was known, and the end of the Second World War allowed people to consider projects not directly related to war work, there were so many enquiries about the developments at the Moore School that a special course was planned for the summer of 1946 so that interested parties could come and learn first-hand about these developments. The course was called "Theory and Techniques for the Design of Electronic Digital Computers," and it attracted 28 people from both sides of the Atlantic. Twelve of the people came from various armed forces installations, nine from different universities, four from various industrial installations such as G.E. and Bell Labs, and three from the National Bureau of Standards. Most of these groups either had, or were soon to have, serious computer development projects underway.

This course was the turning point in the spread of information about the electronic digital computer. Many of the people who came were under the impression that it would discuss the ENIAC developments and were surprised when the lecturers spent a lot of their time discussing the "new" design for EDVAC. In fact the course was a very informal affair with the speakers often changing their topics in order to fit in with what had been discussed earlier. Several sessions were abandoned all together, and it would seem that the "course" took on an aspect of a seminar and discussion group rather than a set series of lectures.

The first group to show any rapid development of computer projects were the English. M. V. Wilkes, from Cambridge University, D. R. Hartree (who had been one of the lecturers), and David Rees, from Manchester University, were soon to put into practice what they had learned at the Moore School lectures. They all returned to England and engaged in computer construction projects at their respective institutes, all of which were to result in functional machines some time before anyone else managed to duplicate their efforts.

As we have seen, the techniques for producing electronic devices to perform arithmetic and to control the flow of information inside a machine were all well known by the time the Moore School lectures were held in the summer of 1946. What was not known was how to construct a large capacity, reliable electronic memory. As this memory was to be fundamental in the creation of a stored program computer, it is only reasonable that, before taking a closer look at any of the early computer projects, we examine the different kinds of hardware devices which were used to create the memory for some of these new machines.

8.2 COMPUTER MEMORY SYSTEMS

8.2.1 Introduction

Probably the most important aspect of the development of modern computers was the production of devices to serve as memory systems for the machines. From the earliest days of the construction of the stored program computer, the main memory design was the controlling factor in determining the rest of the machine's architecture. It was certainly the case that the construction of large reliable storage devices was one of the main stumbling blocks in the creation of the early machines.

It was recognized very early on that a computer's memory should have a number of properties:

- it must be possible to erase the contents of the memory and store new data in place of the old
- it must be possible to store information for long periods of time
- it must be inexpensive to construct because it would be needed in large quantities
- it must be possible to get at the information being stored in very short periods of time because there is no point in producing high-speed electronic arithmetic and control units if you cannot get at the instructions and data with the same high speeds

None of the early devices was able to completely satisfy all of these requirements, but magnetic core memory came as close as any. It should be noted that it was only from about 1975, when large-scale integrated circuits became available, that memory systems satisfying all these requirements were produced.

The early pioneers in the design of memory systems suggested many different approaches to the problem and used almost every conceivable physical property of matter in their operation. Some of the more obvious solutions, such as the magnetic drum storage, occurred to many people at the same time, and it is often not possible to assign a definite date or inventor to any given system. The various groups working on computer design in the late 1940s and early 1950s were very free about exchanging information. It was often the case that a particular design would be suggested by one group and actually constructed by another. The shortages introduced by the Second World War were also responsible for novel ideas as to how to create a memory device. The materials with which to manufacture items such as magnetic memories were either very expensive or just not available at any price, and the technology was not yet fully worked out even though the Blattnenphone magnetic tape–voice recorder had been in use in Germany from the 1930s. A. D. Booth, then at Birkbeck College in London, admits that while travelling to Germany as part of official delegations at the end of the Second World War, he "liberated" items such as magnetophone magnetic wire for use in his own laboratory.

The most obvious candidate for a memory device was the simple relay. It had already proven its usefulness in the large electromechanical calculators, such as the Harvard Mark II and the relay calculators at Bell Labs. It also had the advantage of being readily accessible. It was never used on a large scale because, being a mechanical device, it could only change its state between 100 and 200 times a second, and this was just not compatible in speed with the vacuum tube, which could change its state about 1,000,000 times a second. Another, but not so important, reason for the lack of use of relays was that the physical size of the resultant memory unit and the power it would consume were beyond what could be tolerated by most institutions attempting to construct a machine. Despite all these objections, some mechanical and electromechanical devices were used experimentally as computer memories.

The actual devices which were constructed (some for test purposes only) can be divided into six basic categories:

1. thermal devices
2. mechanical devices
3. delay lines of different types
4. electrostatic storage mechanisms
5. rotating magnetic memories
6. stationary magnetic memories

Each of these will be examined in turn.

8.2.2 Thermal Memories

The idea of a thermal memory was tried (experimentally) by A. D. Booth who, through the lack of other suitable material being available in Britain after the Second World War, was forced to experiment with almost every physical property of matter in order to construct a working memory. The device was never put into production because of the inherent unreliability of the system.

Booth's thermal memory consisted of a small drum whose chalk surface was capable of being heated by a series of small wires. These wires would locally heat a small portion of the surface of the drum and, as the drum rotated, these heated spots would pass in front of a series of heat detectors. When a hot spot was detected, it was immediately recycled back to the writing mechanism which would copy it onto a clean (cool) part of the drum. The back of the drum was cooled (erased) by a small fan so that, by the time the drum had rotated to bring the same area under the heating wires again, a fresh surface was available to receive the recycled information.

Heaters

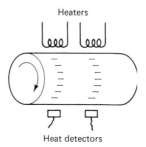

Heat detectors

Figure 8–1. A diagram of Booth's experimental thermal memory.

8.2.3 Mechanical Memories

Mechanical memories, other than relays, were first produced on a large scale by Konrad Zuse, whose system has already been discussed in Section 6.2. The main problem with mechanical or electromechanical memories is that the access time is several orders of magnitude slower than the internal working speeds of an electronic computer. This did not stop the experimental production of various devices, either because they were destined to be attached to a slow machine anyway or, more commonly, the early workers were unable to acquire the necessary materials to experiment with the more sophisticated systems.

A. D. Booth was, as mentioned earlier, particularly hampered by the lack of suitable material being available in post-war Britain. He did, however, have the offsetting advantage of being able to work closely with his father, a very fine mechanical engineer. This cooperation led to the production of experimental mechanical memories of several different kinds, two of which deserve mention if only to indicate the level of ingenuity which went into their construction. The first, shown in Figure 8–2, consisted of a series of rotating disks, each of which had a number of small holes near the outer edge. Each hole contained a tiny pin which was allowed to slide back and forth through the hole and, as the disk rotated, a solenoid was used to push the pins so that they protruded from one side of the disk or the other. A small brush made electrical contact with those pins which were sticking out of one edge of the disk. It was this brush which enabled it to read the binary number stored by the pin positions.

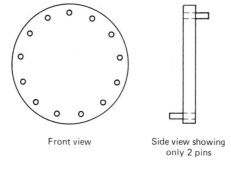

Front view

Side view showing only 2 pins

Figure 8–2. A diagram of a single disk from Booth's disk-pin memory system.

By putting a number of such disks together on one shaft, it was possible to produce either a serial storage unit (where one number is stored on each disk and the readout is done bit by bit as the disk rotates) or a parallel storage unit (where one number is stored on the corresponding positions of a series of disks and the readout of all the bits of a number takes place at the same instant). Figure 8–3 shows a working version of Booth's disk-pin storage device which was constructed along these lines and, although only 8 in. long and 2 in. in diameter, is capable of storing 50 numbers, each of 21 binary bits (in parallel mode in this particular unit). This device had an average access time of about 0.25 second.

There are obvious problems in the construction of this type of memory, the most difficult being not the actual construction of each piece but simply assembling the unit when the pieces were finished. The problems of engineering the disk-pin memory prompted the design of a simpler system which was easier to manufacture. Figure 8–4 shows a disk with a number of very fine wires extending out from its edge. This disk was made to rotate inside a hole cut from a thin sheet of insulating material, with some of the tiny wires riding on top of the sheet and some below it. A small section of the sheet was set to act as a guiding vane (marked G in the diagram), which was capable of guiding

Figure 8–3.   Booth's disk-pin memory in final form. (Photograph courtesy of Dr. A. D. Booth.)

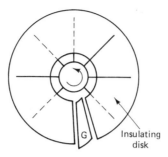

Figure 8–4. A diagram showing Booth's rotating wire mechanical memory system.

the fine wires through the slot in the sheet, from the upper to the lower surface, or vice versa if the guide vane was rotated the other way. An electrical contact placed on the upper surface of the sheet would be able to detect those wires currently riding over it. By being able to detect the position of the wires as being either above or below the disk, the mechanism could function as a binary storage device. A mechanical memory of a similar design was actually used on one of Booth's early computers (the ARC) for a number of years when the ARC's magnetic drum was removed to become the main storage unit for a subsequent machine (the SEC).

8.2.4 Delay-Line Systems

The first device to gain widespread acceptance as a reliable memory system was the acoustic delay line. This was used in machines such as EDSAC, ED-VAC, UNIVAC I, the Pilot ACE, SEAC, LEO I, and many others. The basic concept behind the device was to attempt to delay a series of pulses, representing a binary number, for a few milliseconds which, although a very short time, was a relatively long period as compared to the electronic cycle time of the machine. After they had been delayed for a short time, the pulses would be fed back into the delay line system to again store them for a further short period. Repeated short delays would add up to long-term storage.

The mercury delay line was actually developed by William Shockley of Bell Labs and was improved upon by J. Presper Eckert, one of the people who designed and built ENIAC, while he was working on radar-related research at the start of the Second World War. The mechanism, shown in Figure 8–5, would take a series of electrical pulses and convert them into sound waves by the use of a piezoelectric quartz crystal. The sound waves would then make their way, relatively slowly, down the mercury-filled tube. At the far end of the tube, the sound waves would be detected by another quartz crystal and the pulses, amplified and reshaped, would then be fed back into the front of the delay line again.

Mercury was generally chosen as the medium in an acoustic delay line because the speed of sound in mercury (1.5 mm per microsecond) was such that tubes of one to two meters in length would provide for a delay of between

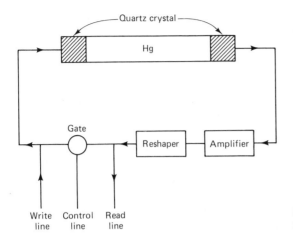

Figure 8–5. A mercury delay line memory system.

0.5 and 1 millisecond, and because the acoustical impedance of mercury was comparable to that of the quartz transducer. The importance of a good impedance match was not only that a strong signal would be transmitted through the mercury but that the entire signal arriving at the other end would be absorbed by the transducer and not reflected back down the tube to interfere with other signals. The impedance was not perfectly matched, so there was a small problem in dealing with a signal which would echo back down the tube. This echo problem was overcome in several different ways. If a very long delay line was used, the echo signal would have to traverse the length of the tube twice before the echo would be detected at the receiving end and, in that time, it would have decayed to the point where it was usually below the level of noise in the system, thus causing no problem. On the other hand, if short delay lines were used, techniques had to be employed to make the quartz crystals nonreflective. This usually took the form of suspending the quartz in the mercury in front of the actual end of the tube and constructing the end plug from some highly sound-absorbent material.

Because it was only possible to "read" a delay-line memory when the pulses were detected at the far end of the tube, delays of any more than a millisecond were counterproductive. A delay line would, depending on the rate at which pulses were fed into it, normally store something like 1000 binary bits of information at any given instant. If a longer delay, or greater storage capacity were required, it was possible to bend or fold the mercury tubes into a compact box without disrupting the sound transmission properties.

There were two basic problems to be overcome in the construction of mercury delay lines:

• getting good acoustic contact between the mercury and the quartz piezoelectric crystals

- getting over the problem that the velocity of sound in mercury is very temperature dependent

The first of these problems was solved by filling the tubes with alcohol (which had the ability to "wet" both the quartz and the mercury) and then displacing it with mercury. This procedure left a very thin film of alcohol between the quartz and the mercury which tended to enhance, rather than degrade, the acoustic contact between the two substances. The temperature problem was potentially the most serious because the speed of sound in mercury will vary about one part in 3000 for each change of temperature by one degree centigrade. This means that, if you store 3000 bits of information in a mercury delay line, but cannot keep the temperature constant to at least one half degree, you may be able to read the bits arriving at the end of the tube, but you will not know which bit you are detecting. The usual solution was to enclose the mercury lines in a very carefully controlled oven which could then be kept at a constant temperature several degrees above that of the room in which they had to operate.

This design required that any computer relying on mercury delay line technology for its memory system had to undergo a considerable period of warmup and temperature stabilization before it was usable. Many attempts were made to overcome this temperature dependence by constructing delay lines from other substances. A number of different liquids were tried and even a delay line made from solid quartz was experimented with, but each of these solutions had its own problems and the majority of the working devices remained based on mercury. Allen Turing did some theoretical studies as to what materials might make suitable delay lines, and he was heard to remark many different times that the ideal substance would be a mixture of alcohol and water. He seriously proposed that London Dry Gin might turn out to have the perfect set of properties for the best delay line medium.

The mercury tubes formed only a small part of the overall storage mechanism in a delay line system. A great deal of electronics was necessary to detect and reshape the pulses before they were fed back into the tubes. If we take the EDVAC memory as a typical example, it required 11 vacuum tubes to control the signals for each 1000-bit mercury delay line. This circuitry had to be more than just a simple amplifier because the internal reflections and attenuation suffered by the signal during its passage down the delay line would distort the pulse entirely out of shape. Another problem to be contended with was that mercury was not a good carrier of low-frequency sound, thus the pulses were generally used to modulate a high-frequency carrier wave which was the signal actually transmitted down the tube. Care had to be taken in the choice of the combination of tube length and the frequency used in order to avoid generating standing waves in the tubes.

If the frequency was high enough, the sound would form a very narrow beam in the mercury, and it was possible to fit several delay lines into one large mercury bath with little or no shielding between them. Having a large mercury bath containing several delay lines was an advantage because it would be more temperature stable than a smaller collection of individual tubes, but the majority of working systems still opted for the individual tube delay line because of its greater ease of access if it should ever be necessary to service an individual line. The one mercury bath system was used in an experimental machine constructed by Eckert and Mauchly which became known as BINAC. It used a very high carrier frequency (12 megacycles), which resulted in very tight beams being projected from the quartz transducer. They were able to incorporate 18 separate delay lines in one mercury tank with only minimal shielding between the lines.

Another technical problem with this system was that the electronic system required to perform the modulation, demodulation, amplification, and reshaping of the pulses was constructed mainly of vacuum tubes, and the heat given off by them would adversely affect the temperature stability of the delay lines. This was usually overcome by placing the electronic components at a distance from the delay lines, but this also led to the greater possibility of the connection wires between them picking up stray electrical noise and disrupting the contents of the memory. Specially shielded coaxial cables were usually employed to guard against stray pulses being picked up due to interference from the nearby electronic equipment. It was usually the case that the associated electronics were both physically larger and more expensive than the actual mercury delay lines themselves.

Many variations of the basic delay line system were tried. The inventive A. D. Booth even attempted to construct a delay line memory from air by mounting a loudspeaker on one wall of a room and a microphone on the other wall. It was, in principle, a reasonable idea for an inexpensive delay line, but in practice it did not work because the multiple reflections of sound waves from the floor, ceiling, and other walls destroyed the pulse shape to such an extent that it could not be easily detected. Another of Booth's attempts was to use a child's toy, usually called a "Slinky," consisting of a long coiled spring. He hung the Slinky from a support and attached a relay tongue to one end; by energizing the relay the tongue would move and cause a pulse to be transmitted down the spring which could be detected at the far end. The system worked and he was able to store several bits of information. However, standing waves soon developed in the spring and he abandoned it to spend his time on more rewarding projects.

A 1951 modification, by Booth and the Ferranti Co., of the acoustic delay line was the magnetostrictive delay line. This consisted of a single thin wire or tube (marked W in Figure 8–6), generally made of very fine nickel wire, together with two coils placed around either end of the wire. A pulse through the left-hand coil would induce a magnetic field which would cause a longitudinal compression wave to travel down the wire. When this wave passed under the right-hand coil, it would induce a small current into the coil which

Figure 8-6. The magnetostrictive delay line memory system.

could be detected. It was often necessary to put a small permanent magnet above the "receiving" coil to increase the output voltage. In order to eliminate the reflection of the wave from the ends of the wire, it was necessary to clamp the ends in some soft sound-absorbing medium. Everything from rubber clamps, tubes of grease, and wads of paper to children's modeling clay were used in different systems.

The speed of sound is very much higher in solid nickel than it is in mercury, so wires of about 5 m in length were generally needed to achieve delays of about 1 millisecond. Nickel had the great advantage that it was a good carrier of low frequency sound so it was not necessary to modulate a high-frequency carrier wave as was needed when mercury was the acoustic medium. Similarly, temperature control was not so critical in the nickel delay line, and it could usually be mounted directly in a rack in the same way as the other computer components. Magnetostrictive delay lines of up to 40 feet long were constructed and worked reliably. The longer delay lines did not have to be stretched

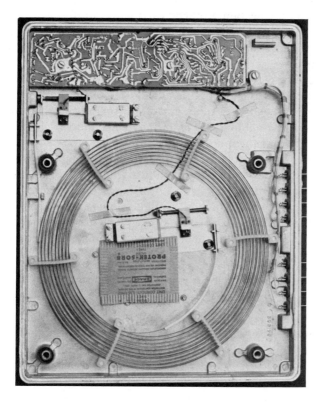

Figure 8-7. A solid wire delay line taken from an IBM terminal controller, circa 1975.

out tight in order to work and were often simply wrapped around some soft core, such as a sponge, so that they would fit into a physically small volume.

A further development of the magnetostrictive delay line occurred when a large number of coils were put at intervals of about 0.25 in. along the nickel wire. Information could be recorded on the wire by passing a heavy current through these coils and magnetizing the small section of nickel wire running through the coil. Either a north-south or a south-north magnet could be produced depending on the direction of the current flow. When a "reading" pulse was sent down the wire, generated by the leftmost coil, the movement of the small magnetized section within each coil could be detected by the voltage it induced in the coil around it. Thus one magnetostrictive delay line could be used to permanently store a limited number of bits.

Even when other devices, such as the magnetic core, replaced the delay line as a reasonable candidate for the main memory, the device was still being used as short-term memory in different parts of a computer. The usual place that a delay line could be found was as a temporary memory element in a controller for a number of video terminals. The information flowing to and from the terminals would be stored in the delay line until either the computer or the terminal was ready to deal with it. This application lasted until the mid-1970s when the function was taken over by large-scale integrated circuits.

8.2.5 Electrostatic Storage Mechanisms

The problem with the delay line was that the information, although stored, was not always immediately available, and it was necessary to wait until it reached the end of the delay mechanism before it could be used. This was overcome by the development of the first truly high-speed random access memory by F. C. Williams and his assistant T. Kilburn at Manchester University in England. At the end of the Second World War, Williams was working at the British Telecommunications Research Establishment, and, since there was no longer a pressing need for better and better forms of radar, he turned his attention to digital storage devices. It should be noted in passing that Williams did not have to turn his attention far, because storage devices were an integral part of certain radar systems—in fact, the mercury delay line was originally developed by Eckert as a radar-related project. It is entirely possible that Williams actually got some of his early ideas from the Moore School, because the topic of using CRTs (cathode ray tubes) as a memory device was mentioned by Eckert in one of the Moore School lectures during the summer of 1946. Although Williams was not at the lectures, he was certainly in touch with some of the people who attended the class. Eckert's ideas on the use of a CRT for a memory (which he called an "iconoscope") were only very rudimentary at this stage and, regardless of where the initial idea came from, Williams certainly deserves the credit for making it into a working reality.

Toward the end of 1946 Williams applied for a patent on his cathode ray tube storage device and moved to take up a position at Manchester University. Kilburn joined him there and, by the end of 1947, they produced a working model which could store 1000 bits of information. Progress was rapid and, by the middle of 1948, they were able to demonstrate a working memory that could store several thousand bits and retain its information for a period of hours.

The operation of the Williams' tube memory is based on the fact that, when a beam of electrons strikes the phosphor surface of a cathode ray tube, it not only produces a spot of light, but it also leaves a charged spot on the surface of the phosphor which will persist for about 0.2 seconds before it leaks away. If this charged spot can be detected and regenerated at the rate of at least five times per second, the problem of creating long-term storage is solved in the same way as it was with an acoustic delay line.

When the electron beam is used to write a series of dots and dashes on the face of the tube, the electron charge surrounding the dot will be different from the charge which surrounds a dash. After writing the binary dots and dashes, the electron beam can again be passed over the face of the tube and the electron current leaking through the front glass can be detected by a wire mesh over the face of the tube. This leaking current will be modified by the charged areas on the phosphor in such a way that it is possible to detect the difference when the beam is passing over a dot or a dash. The "reading" beam will tend to modify the information stored in the tube because of the disruptive nature of the electron beam on the pattern of charges. This fact led to the thought that two tubes would be needed, one to which information would be written and the other from which it would be read. By continually reversing the roles of the two tubes, a permanent storage device could be created.

The reading of the memory was accomplished by the electron beam scanning in a series of horizontal sweeps across the face of the tube. Williams and Kilburn were able to show that the pattern of electrons around either a dot or a dash was sufficiently widely distributed around the actual dot or dash so that the difference between them could be detected while the reading beam was still approaching that area of the phosphor. This enabled the construction of a memory system in which a low power reading beam would be scanned across the face of the tube and, when the system detected that a dot or a dash was about to be encountered, the beam power could be increased to rewrite the dot or dash back into the same spot from which it had just been detected. Thus only one tube was needed to manage a refreshed cathode ray tube store. The typical arrangement of such a system is shown in Figure 8–8.

The main reason why the Williams' tube memory was used for a lot of the early prototype computers, and even for some of the later production machines such as the IBM 701, was because it relied on known technology and could be constructed from standard components. Care had to be taken when selecting the CRTs to be used because even imperfections too small to be visible on the surface of the phosphor were enough to cause storage losses of one or

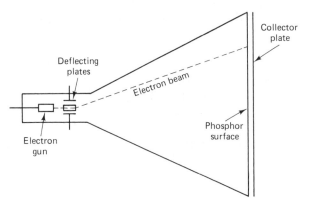

Figure 8–8. The Williams' tube electrostatic memory system.

more bits. Even the best quality tubes were not always good enough to withstand the exacting requirements of the computer memory usage but, by suitably adjusting the bias voltage on the beam-directing plates, the pattern of dots and dashes could be moved over the surface of the tube until a position was found which would give good results. Instead of dot-dash encoding, some of the later Williams' tube memories used a system of having the electron beam either tightly focused or slightly dispersed. This resulted in a memory system which was not quite so critical of small flaws in the surface of the phosphor and, as a result, the price of constructing a memory decreased slightly.

The first CRT memories were serial systems with the full binary word being stored on part of a single-sweep line of the tube. The refresh cycle of these tubes would generally be done so that it was interleaved with the reading of information. Alternate 240-microsecond time periods were devoted to re-

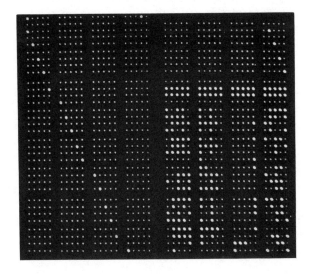

Figure 8–9. The front face of a Williams' tube in use.

fresh and reading sweeps of the tube. The parallel machines, such as the one developed by von Neumann at the Institute of Advanced Study in Princeton, required that the whole word be accessed in one instant rather than picking the bits off one at a time in a horizontal sweep across the tube. This, in turn, meant that each bit of a word had to be stored on a different CRT. The IAS machine, which had a 40-bit word, needed 40 different CRTs for the memory. For such parallel machines, the electron beam, rather than systematically sweeping from side to side of the tube, had to focus at different spot locations in random order. Because there was no longer a systematic processing of the storage tube's surface, the problem arose of just when, and how often, the refresh cycle should occur on such a tube. It was not reasonable to refresh the whole tube after reading only one bit; on the other hand, the system could not continue to read information in the same locality for very long before significant trouble, known as the "read-around" problem, occurred.

The read-around problem arose from the fact that, as the reading beam was focused on one area of the tube, the electrons would tend to spread out over adjacent areas. This was quite acceptable unless the beam was kept focused on one particular area for too long, because the electrons would then spread out far enough to disrupt adjacent bits of information. Unfortunately the effect was cumulative and many reads around one location would tend to build up the electron cloud to the point where it could destroy information in the immediate neighborhood. Eventually each installation found its own compromise to this situation and the refresh cycle would be initiated as often as the local engineers deemed it necessary. The full screen was usually refreshed after every 30 or 40 reading accesses, although some installations found that they lost information unless the refresh cycle was initiated after only 10 to 15 reading accesses. The differences in how often the refresh cycle needed to be done usually stemmed from the quality of CRTs in use. A simple change to different CRTs would often correct the difficulties causing the read-around problem. When the refresh cycle had to be performed too often it made the memory system spend so much of its time in this mode that it lost its effectiveness as a device for a high-speed parallel memory.

Another form of the electrostatic storage tube was developed at the RCA Laboratories in the United States by a team led by Jan Rajchman. Rajchman noted that the reliability of the Williams' tube depended on its ability to focus a stream of electrons at exactly the same place on the tube's surface each and every time it needed to read or write a single bit. This focusing mechanism was an analog process involving the voltages applied to the beam deflection plates in the CRT. This mixture of analog operations in a digital device was both prone to inaccuracies and was, esthetically, not a very nice mixture of the two techniques. Rajchman's team produced a purely digital electrostatic storage tube, called the "Selectron," which used a number of nickel-plated steel rings embedded in a mica wafer as the actual storage elements.

The small steel rings were kept at one of two different voltages in order to store the binary zeros and ones. A beam of electrons could either pass through the ring or be deflected from it, depending on the voltage level of the ring. The information stored by the ring would be detected by the presence or absence of the electron stream on the far side of the ring.

The selection of which ring was to be interrogated was the unique digital design feature of the Selectron. A series of horizontal and vertical bars crisscrossed the surface of the mica wafer forming little square windows, in the middle of which were placed the little steel rings. A voltage could be applied to various groups of these horizontal and vertical bars to electrically "open" or "close" any selected window to the beam of reading electrons. The situation is illustrated graphically in Figure 8–10. The mica wafer was bombarded by a low-power stream of electrons, and these would be allowed through a given window to fall upon the steel ring which, in turn, would either stop them or allow them to pass through to the detection device on the other side. The writing mechanism also employed the same window selection grid to permit a higher power beam of electrons to raise or lower the potential of the steel rings.

Although the Selectron idea was sound, the manufacturing difficulties were such that the tube was used only to a minor extent. Plans for using the Selectron memory for the IAS machine were eventually abandoned and the Williams' tube memory used instead. Initial plans called for each Selectron to be able to store 4096 bits, but eventually, after considerable effort, about 2,000 Selectron tubes were produced, each of which was limited to storing 256 bits. They found their main use as the central memory element for the Rand Johnniac computer (named after John von Neumann, an honor he was known not to have appreciated).

A different electrostatic scheme, using neon lamps, was developed by Louis Couffignal in France, as a modification of the idea that had been tried during the war by Zuse and Schreyer. This was based on the fact that neon lamps require a higher voltage to start them conducting (glowing) than to keep them in that state. If it takes, for example, 2 volts to start a lamp conducting but only 1 volt to keep it in that state, then when a potential of 1.5 volts is

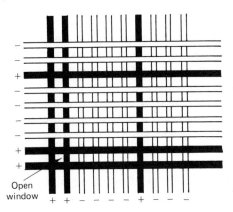

Open
window

Figure 8–10. A diagram of the Selectron tube memory window system.

applied to a nonconducting lamp nothing will happen. If a further pulse is applied momentarily to raise the potential over 2 volts, the lamp will strike and remain conducting until another, negative, pulse is applied to turn it off by dropping the voltage below 1 volt. The system is obviously capable of being used as a binary store by simply detecting the presence or absence of a current flow. Couffignal ran into problems when he tried to construct a neon memory of sufficient size to be useful, because it turned out that neon tubes tend to age at different rates and the voltage levels necessary to start conduction and keep it going would fluctuate widely as they aged. Couffignal eventually gave up the idea and experimented with other devices.

8.2.6 Rotating Magnetic Memories

The production of magnetic voice recording equipment naturally suggested that this medium might offer possibilities for the construction of a computer memory. The usual practice of using magnetic tape or magnetic wire recording materials had to be modified because of the slow access times which resulted from the use of a long tape. The concept of depositing a nickel or ferrite coating on a rotating drum occurred to many people at the same time, and many different experiments were conducted to determine the best material to use. The results were so satisfactory that the rotating magnetic drum, in combination with the Williams' tube and the mercury delay line, became the main form of memory on most of the early machines. The problem with relying on a drum as the sole memory device for a computer was that the average access time was quite long as compared to the electronic speeds of the computer's control unit. Most installations eventually went to the two-level memory concept, in which high-speed memory, served by something like a Williams' tube, was backed up by a large capacity magnetic drum store of some type. The expression, common among the first generation British computer people, "to bring (information) 'down' from the drum" is a direct result of the fact that the back-up drum was installed in a room above that used for the main Williams' tube memories on an early machine at Manchester University; thus the information was literally brought down from the floor above.

The operating mechanisms of magnetic drums and disks are too well known to be a suitable subject for discussion here, except for a few remarks about the early experiments. Immediately after the Second World War the shortage of magnetic materials, especially in Britain, was so great that recourse was made to any scheme that could be shown to work. As was stated earlier, a few of the early experimenters admit to having visited German research laboratories, in their capacities as consultants to the Allied governments, simply to gain access to some magnetic materials for their own projects. The usual form of the read/record head was a small electromagnet made out of thin steel laminations or, in more modern times, thin ferrite laminations. Because of the combination of the need for small size (about 0.1 in. wide) and the shortage of suitable materials and forming techniques, several experiments were done to produce a read/record head consisting of a single wire around which was bent a very thin strip of magnetic iron. The general configuration is shown in Figure 8–11. This simple head was used in a number of the early drums and worked remarkably well.

Dr. A. D. Booth, mentioned earlier in connection with mechanical memories, was one of the leading proponents of the magnetic drum. The computers he built were, in general, an order of magnitude slower than those under development by others and, as such, were suitable candidates for relying on a drum as the memory device. Booth recognized that one of the main difficulties in getting a strong signal out of a drum's read head was the necessity to keep the head at least a small distance away from the surface of the drum. The head could not be put in direct contact with the surface because the resulting wear would remove all the magnetic material. In order to get a strong signal, he attempted to construct a "floppy" disk memory consisting of a thin paper disk coated with magnetic material which could rotate with one pole of the read/record head above the disk and the other below it. He reasoned that all the magnetic flux would then pass directly through the disk and provide a very strong signal for both writing new information and reading it back again. He was able to obtain some oxide-coated paper disks from the American firm which manufactured "Mail-a-Voice" recording machines and incorporated these into a simple experimental disk store. The theory was that, when the disks were spinning rapidly, they would be held flat by centrifugal forces, and the high-speed layer of air near the disk surface would act to keep the poles of the recording head from actually touching the disk—much the same idea as that used in today's disk pack design. Unfortunately he underestimated the uniformity of the paper disks and the fluttering that would develop when they were rotated at 3,000 rpm. After his machine had rapidly destroyed all the disks at his disposal, he was forced to return to the construction of magnetic drum memories and the development of proper disk drives was put back a number of years.

In 1947 Booth and his father machined a brass cylinder 2 in. in diameter and 8 in. long which they then plated with nickel. By January 1, 1948, they had constructed a working magnetic drum from it. By May of that same year the

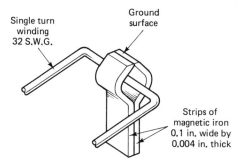

Single turn winding 32 S.W.G.

Ground surface

Strips of magnetic iron 0.1 in. wide by 0.004 in. thick

Figure 8–11. A drawing of a single-wire read/record head for a magnetic drum.

drum was installed and working in the experimental ARC (Automatic Relay Computer) which Booth was constructing for the British Rubber Producers' Research Association Laboratories. Booth and his father continued to experiment with modifications to the ARC's drum memory, and by 1952 they were producing large drum memories for others to use. Some of these drums were exported to the United States and, on the whole, they performed reliably, some lasting for as long as ten years without difficulty.

At the same time that Booth was conducting his experiments, many others were attempting to construct magnetic memories of one form or another. Although they all had the same types of successes and failures, one is worth mentioning because of its unique design. The Institute of Advanced Study in Princeton had started on the construction of their computer with the idea that the Selectron would be used for the main (4096-word, 40-bit) memory and punched paper tape would act as the main data input medium. It was not long before they had to abandon the Selectron in favor of a modification of the Williams' tube and, at the same time, they began to realize that punched paper tape would be too slow for the type of machine they hoped would result. They, therefore, decided to attempt the development of a high-speed input/output sys-

Figure 8–12. An early magnetic drum memory. This one was 5 in. in diameter, and had 32 read/write heads, and a total capacity of 1024 words of 32 bits each. Its speed was 6,000 RPM. (Illustration courtesy of Dr. A. D. Booth.)

tem based on magnetic wire recording techniques. An old bicycle was torn apart to provide two large wheel rims, around which was wrapped a long strand of magnetic recording wire. The wire ran from one rim, over the read/record head, and was taken up by the other rim. The whole system was driven by a small motor and a simple set of differential gears. Although the system worked, and would have likely been used as primarily an auxiliary memory rather than an input/output device, the wire quickly cut into the read/record head and the whole system had to be abandoned.

The use of magnetic wire as a form of secondary memory was attempted by several different groups, but they all abandoned it as impractical because of the technical problems of dealing with very thin (0.004 in. diameter) steel wire. The wire would tend to kink and, if a break occurred, it was impossible to repair in any satisfactory way. The National Bureau of Standards machine, SEAC, managed to use some commercially available wire cartridges that were part of standard dictating equipment to provide their staff with a device on which to record programs, data, or intermediate results. This seemed to work to most people's satisfaction, but the scheme was never adopted on a large scale.

Figure 8–13. The IAS experimental magnetic wire memory unit constructed from an old bicycle. (Photograph courtesy of the Institute for Advanced Study, Princeton.)

8.2.7 Static Magnetic Memories

The magnetic core memory was the first real system to offer a basis for a large-scale reliable memory at reasonable cost. It was developed in the late 1940s and, although used in 1952 for a test machine at MIT and later installed in their computer known as "Whirlwind," it did not really become a major item until later in the 1950s.

Several people participated in its development. J. Forrester, a professor at MIT, Dudley Buch, Jan Rajchman of RCA, An Wang, the founder of Wang Laboratories, and Frederick Viehe, an inspector of streets and sidewalks for the Los Angeles Department of Public Works, all played a part in its development from a vague concept to a working reality. The roles of most of these men are reasonably clear, with the exception of the mysterious Frederick Viehe. Viehe kept a small laboratory in his home and was often to be found working there on some new project. In 1947 Viehe filed a patent application which included a description of the use of a magnetic core to store information. Viehe did very little with this invention but, in 1956, IBM purchased the rights to his patent for a considerable amount of money (enough that he was able to quit his job with the Los Angeles Department of Public Works). Viehe seems to have had little success in exploiting any of his other electronic creations. In 1960 he died of exposure while attempting to test another of his inventions in the Mojave desert.

The RCA team had been working on magnetic cores as replacements for some of the logic components in their machines. In the days before the transistor, the core seemed like it might be an answer to replacing the vacuum tube in certain logic applications. An Wang's early experiments were done while working with Howard Aiken at Harvard. His 1949 patent indicates that the Harvard team was interested in them as potential pulse transfer control devices. The MIT group, who had some previous experience with coincident current memory systems (such as the scheme using neon tubes described earlier) put together the concept of using two wires running at right angles through the core to control which core received a high enough magnetic field to cause it to change state. The RCA group actually filed a memory patent first, but they later withdrew it in favor of IBM, who had purchased MIT's patent rights, in exchange for several licensing advantages.

The commercial availability of magnetic core memory was the great watershed point in the development of computers. From that time on they became very much more reliable and useful tools. Some indication of the dramatic changes caused by the introduction of core memory can be seen from its first effect on the MIT Whirlwind machine. Whirlwind had used an electrostatic memory much like the Williams tube in design. The difference was that the charge pattern was kept on a mica wafer within the tube rather than on the phosphor surface. When this system was scrapped in favor of a primitive core memory, the Whirlwind doubled its operating speed and quadrupled the input data rate. The maintenance time on the memory fell from four hours per day to two hours per week, the mean time between memory failure rose from two hours to two weeks, and a whole group of technicians were freed up to work on another project. It must be admitted that the Whirlwind was a bit exceptional in the dramatic performance improvements, but it does indicate the type of changes which resulted from the adoption of static magnetic memory devices.

8.3 THE BRITISH SCENE

8.3.1 Introduction

The British, partly because of their experience with the electronic Colossus machine, were very quick to actually construct working electronic computers. Once the basic ideas of a stored program computer had been described in von Neumann's paper *First Draft on a Report on the EDVAC*, and the ideas further discussed during the famous Moore School lectures during the summer of 1946, three projects were immediately started in Britain, one each at Cambridge and Manchester universities and another at the government-sponsored National Physical Laboratory. A further project was to start up a few months later at Birkbeck College in London. The first three projects all involved quite large and sophisticated computers, although not nearly as ambitious as those being designed in the United States, while the Birkbeck College project, under the direction of A. D. Booth, was a small-scale effort only partially funded by industry and institutional support.

While the researchers on the American side of the Atlantic were having a difficult time with the design of their large and sophisticated computer projects, the smaller and more technologically feasible British projects were finished and their users were beginning to discover the problems of debugging programs. This resulted in an early British lead in the design of software systems and, in at least one or two areas, allowed British firms to produce certain hardware advancements which were not incorporated in the American commercial computers for several years.

There is no doubt that it was one of the British projects which had the honor of being the world's first functional stored-program electronic computer; however, exactly which machine deserves this honor is a matter of debate. If you allow that a machine which shows some function, no matter how small, is considered operational then the prize goes to the Manchester University project. On the other hand, if your definition of a working computer includes the fact that it must be able to run nontrivial programs on a regular basis, then it goes to the EDSAC at Cambridge. This is not the place to debate the arguments for one side or the other, so the facts will simply be presented and you can decide for yourself which definition of a working electronic stored-program computer you prefer.

Several early British computer projects are specifically not considered in the following discussion. The Harwell electronic computer will not be discussed because it falls into the class of small relay-based machines, even though it did have a 90-word electronic memory. The Imperial College Computing Engine was a relay-based device which took its instructions from a punched paper tape, in much the same way as the early Zuse or Aiken machines, and thus is of no great interest in explaining subsequent developments. The Royal Aircraft Establishment Sequence Controlled Calculator (RASCAL) was interesting in that it was an electronic machine with a magnetic drum memory designed to operate on floating-point decimal numbers, but it was never a factor in the later development of either computing machines or methods. There were several other early computer projects, of various sizes, started in Britain, but these too will be ignored for reasons similar to those just mentioned.

8.3.2 The Manchester Machine

At the end of the Second World War, a number of people with expertise in the fields of electronics and computing all managed to obtain jobs at Manchester University. The section on computer memory devices has already described how Freddy Williams and Tom Kilburn left the Telecommunications Research Establishment and took their ideas for an electrostatic memory device to the Department of Electrical Engineering at Manchester University. M. H. A. Newman, who had earlier been in charge of the secret devices, such as Colossus, in the Government Code and Cipher School at Bletchley Park, had joined the Department of Mathematics at Manchester, and, after an abortive attempt to construct a computer at the National Physical Laboratory, Alan Turing was also to join him there. Another former Colossus man, I. J. Good, also joined the Manchester team so that, fortuitously, the Manchester computer project did have the advantage of a senior staff who had had strong associations with the secret war-time code-breaking work.

It should be pointed out that the project was not actually conducted by Manchester University, but rather by the Royal Society Computer Laboratory which was housed at Manchester University. Newman, who was a member of the Royal Society, had managed to convince them to give him a grant to set up a "Computer Laboratory" in order to investigate the possibilities of actually constructing an electronic digital computer. The grant was awarded in July of 1946, and Newman promptly set about collecting an appropriate staff. Williams and Kilburn arrived later that same year and Turing joined them in September of 1948. Although "Royal Society Computer Laboratory" sounds impressive, the reality was certainly not:

It was one room in a Victorian building whose architectural features are best described as "late lavatorial." The walls were of brown glazed brick and the door was labelled "Magnetism Room."[4]

The first project undertaken by this group was to construct a small prototype computer to test out Williams' electrostatic memory ideas. It was to be a serial machine, performing its operations one bit at a time. This tiny test-bed machine first operated on June 21, 1948, and thus ranks as the first fully electronic machine ever to execute a stored program. The fact that it could execute a stored program does not imply that it was a fully working computer because the machine was extremely limited in its scope. It had a memory of 32 words, each of 32 bits, stored on a single Williams' tube cathode ray tube, while two additional CRTs were used to store (1) an accumulator and (2) the memory location and actual bit pattern of the instruction under execution. The instruction set was limited to say the least. It consisted of an instruction to take a value from memory, negate it, and load it into the accumulator, another to subtract a value from the accumulator, one to write the accumulator value back into memory, a conditional branch depending on the value in the accumulator, and a stop instruction. The input was performed by a bank of switches which could be set to change any single bit in the memory, and output depended on a person's writing down the bit pattern shown on the surface of the memory CRT. As Williams describes it:

> When first built, a program was laboriously inserted and the start switch pressed. Immediately the spots on the display tube entered a mad dance.
>
> In early trials it was a dance of death leading to no useful result, and what was even worse, without yielding any clue as to what was wrong. But one day it stopped and there, shining brightly in the expected place, was the expected answer. It was a moment to remember. This was July 1948 and nothing was ever the same again. We knew that only time and effort were needed to make a machine of meaningful size. We doubled our effort immediately by taking on a second technician.[5] [Williams is incorrect, the actual date was June 21, 1948.]

This very simple machine was used to execute a few small problems just to check that it was, in fact, working. A division routine, using the long division paper and pencil method, was created and used to divide $(2^{30}-1)$ by 31, the answer being found in about 1.5 seconds. This same routine was used to show that 314,159,265 and 217,828,183 (which are the numbers π and e, each multiplied by 100,000,000) were relatively prime to one another. The longest running program was one which would determine the largest factor of $(2^{30}-1)$ by

[4]F. C. Williams, "Early Computers at Manchester University," *The Radio and Electronic Engineer*, 45 (No. 7), 328.

[5]Ibid., p. 330.

trying every number from $(2^{18}-1)$ downward, the division being done by repeated subtraction. This showed that the machine would run without error for at least 52 minutes during which time some 3.5 million instructions were executed. No real problems were ever solved on this machine because its memory size was so limited that it could not deal with them. The program for the last mentioned problem consisted of 17 machine instructions which only left enough memory available for the few intermediate results that were needed to keep track of the calculation.

Once this prototype computer had been shown to work, plans were devised for its expansion. It was realized that to have a machine capable of solving real problems, the memory size would have to be drastically increased. In order to have a memory of 4,000 words, over 100 CRTs would have been needed if the information density were to stay the same as in the prototype machine. Rather than putting effort into schemes for increasing the density of storage, the team decided that a two-level memory, incorporating a magnetic drum acting as the main storage element which would feed its contents to the CRT for fast access, was the way they should proceed. By April of 1949 the prototype had been upgraded to a machine with a memory consisting of two CRTs capable of storing 128 words of 40 bits and a drum capable of storing 1,024 words. The arithmetic facilities had also been improved by the addition of a multiplication unit.

The drum, which used the single wire read/write head developed by A. D. Booth, was located in the room above the "Magnetism Room," which housed the main electronics, because it tended to generate electrical noise which would disrupt the information stored in the CRTs. It was designed so that the information flowing to or from the drum was always in synchronization with the electron beam sweeping the surface of the CRT. By keeping the two devices in step with one another, it was possible to transfer information from one to the other with no delays being caused by waiting for the drum to rotate to the proper spot or waiting for the CRT electron beam to begin another sweep of the tube face. This synchronization meant that some form of control circuit had to be devised to guarantee that the drum, spinning at 2,300 rpm, was never more than plus or minus 1/100 of a degree away from where it should have been. Remarkable as it sounds, that proved quite an easy task, although there were some interesting times as they were trying to get it to work. As Williams relates, when talking about their early attempts at testing the two levels of memory:

> Transfers between the stores were achieved by setting switches, then running to the bottom of the stairs and shouting "We are ready to receive track 17 on tube 1." The process was repeated for tube 2 and the machine set working. When it wished to disgorge information, it stopped and the reverse process was initiated.[6]

[6]Ibid., pp. 328–29.

Figure 8–14. The Manchester Machine as of June 1949. The operating controls and a monitor CRT are seen in the middle rack. The memory and arithmetic units are behind the photographer. (Photograph courtesy of Manchester University.)

It was only a short time, of course, before this rather primitive method of drum access was replaced by a more automatic process.

The most interesting aspect of this version of the prototype machine was the inclusion of a third auxiliary CRT device, called the B unit because the two other auxiliary CRTs had been named A (for accumulator) and C (for control). This B unit only stored two numbers, referred to as B0 and B1, which were the first index registers to be incorporated into a working machine. Each instruction contained a special b bit which, depending on its being set to either 0 or 1, would cause the contents of B0 or B1 to be added to the instruction before a memory fetch or store was actually done. By making sure that B0 always contained the value zero, the use of B1 as a general-purpose index register was enabled whenever the b bit of an instruction was set. The value of these "b lines," as they were called, was soon realized and some form of index register was incorporated in almost every computer planned or constructed from that time on.

By October 1949 various other improvements had been made to the machine. The automatic control system between the two levels of memory was functioning properly, and could be invoked under program control to transfer any track on the drum to or from either of the CRT electrostatic memory units. The input and output hardware was improved by incorporating circuits, designed by Alan Turing, which would transmit 5-bit character codes into or out of the last five bits of the accumulator. The actual teleprinter equipment used for this machine was obtained by Turing through contacts he had at the Foreign Office Department of Communications at Bletchley Park. It included a German keyboard paper tape punch which had been "liberated" during the war and had the nasty habit of producing a 0 when the operator wanted a 1. This improved prototype machine was at last a useful computer that could be used to calculate Riemann functions and to do ray tracing through a lens system.

Turing's programming assistant, Cicely Popplewell, gives a graphic description of the problems one had trying to operate the prototype machine:

> Operating the machine required considerable physical stamina. Starting in the machine room one alerted the engineer and then used the hand switches to bring down and enter the input program. A bright band on the monitor tube indicated that the waiting loop had been entered. When this had been achieved, one ran upstairs and put the tape in the reader and then returned to the machine room. If the machine was still obeying the input loop one called to the engineer to switch

Figure 8–15.   T. Kilburn (left) and F. Williams (right) at the operating controls of the Mark I. (Photograph courtesy of Manchester University.)

on the writing current, and cleared the accumulator (allowing the control to emerge from the loop). With luck, the tape was read. As soon as the pattern on the monitor showed that input was ended the engineer switched off the write current to the drum. Programs which wrote to the drum during the execution phase were considered very daring. As every vehicle that drove past was a potential source of spurious digits, it usually took many attempts to get a tape in— each attempt needing another trip up to the tape room.[7]

In November of 1948, when the prototype computer was seen to be a useful design, a local Manchester electronics manufacturer, Ferranti Limited, was asked to produce a properly engineered version of the machine. By late 1949, when modifications to the prototype machine were shown to be feasible, specifications were set down and Ferranti began the actual construction work, which was completed in February 1951. This started a very close association between Ferranti and Manchester University which was to result in many advances in the design of computer hardware, the most outstanding of which was the design and construction of the virtual memory ATLAS computers in the late 50s and early 60s.

The initial Ferranti machine, known variously as MADAM, Manchester Electronic Computer Mark II, Ferranti Mark I, MUDC, or MUEDC, was usually just called the Mark I. This has given rise to some confusion because the prototype machine was also usually referred to as Mark I. It consisted of 4,000 vacuum tubes, 12,000 resistors, and 2,500 capacitors. In September 1952, Ferranti sold a copy of the Mark I to the University of Toronto where it was used for general computation; one of its most famous tasks was to do some of the design calculations for the St. Lawrence Seaway. Ferranti later sold seven more copies of a slightly modified machine known as the Mark I*. The price varied depending on the exact facilities supplied, but it was usually possible to obtain a machine for under $500,000.

The Ferranti Mark I had more facilities than the last version of the prototype machine. The electrostatic memory had been doubled to 256 words, each of 40 bits, stored on eight CRTs, and the drum had been increased to a total capacity of 16,384 words. The multiplication circuits were changed which reduced the time taken for that instruction to 2.16 milliseconds (as compared to 1.2 milliseconds for an addition), and automatic facilities were added to allow either addition or subtraction of the final product from the accumulator. With a 40-bit word available, each instruction was allowed to span 20 bits, and this provided enough room to allow for three b bits, which meant that a total of eight "B lines" were available to use as index registers. In addition, the "B lines" were associated with their own addition and subtraction circuitry which enabled them to be used as short, 20-bit counters for loops. The looping instructions were modified so that some of them would branch only if a given

---

[7]As quoted in M. Campbell-Kelly, "Programming the Mark I: Early Programming Activity at the University of Manchester," *Annals of the History of Computing*, 2 (No. 2), 135.

Figure 8–16. The Ferranti Mark I, as delivered to Manchester University in February 1951. (Photograph courtesy of Manchester University.)

"B line" had the correct sign. This was an interesting feature because, rather than have eight different instructions to test the signs of the different "B lines," each time a "B line" was used its sign was stored in a special circuit and only one instruction was available to test the sign of the last used "B line." The input and output were done via five-hole punched paper tape; the speed of reading was 200 characters per second and punched output was accomplished at ten characters per second.

The Ferranti Mark I had a total of 64 possible instruction codes, all of which actually did something, but only 50 of them were properly defined. Programmers were discouraged from using the undefined ones. Some of the operations were designed because of specific requests; for example, Newman asked for an instruction that would determine the number of binary 1s in a word in order to solve problems in number theory, while Turing wanted an instruction which would obtain a random number from a noise source. The branch instructions were interesting in that, rather than containing an absolute branch address, they referred to a memory word whose contents was the destination of the branch. This meant that it was quite easy to write table-driven programs simply by having the table of destination address changed to reflect the user's requirements. The design of the "B line" system also resulted in some interesting programming situations because, unlike modern index registers which are only added to the address portion of the instruction, the "B line" was added to the whole instruction. This not only resulted in modification to the address specified in the instruction but, if the number stored in the "B line" was large enough, it could modify the b bits or even the instruction code itself. This led to some programmers' exercising their intellects in the production of very curious code.

Some measure of the speed of the Mark I can be obtained by noting the times taken to perform several standard functions. A number of subroutines were kept on the drum, and they could be brought down into the electrostatic memory and executed as needed. It took about 0.03 seconds to transfer a subroutine, after which functions such as square roots, logarithms, and trigonometric functions could be calculated in about 0.1 second.

After the Mark I had been operating for a year, two problems were found in its basic design. The drum (which was 6 in. in diameter, 8.5 in. long and rotated at 1,950 rpm) was found to be generating errors at the rate of a few digits per million transferred. The difficulty turned out to be the packing density of information and, when a new drum of 12 in. diameter was substituted, the system worked fine. The second, and more difficult, problem concerned the power supplies. The team had decided to use dc machines to provide the high voltage power supplies to the machine. Unfortunately these also tended to supply quite a bit of very high-frequency noise, caused by brush arcing, along with the dc voltage. This high-frequency noise tended to cause problems with the timing circuits for the electrostatic memory devices. The problem was a continuing one and required a periodic dismantling of the dc generators, which of course shut down the machine, to replace the commutators and brushes.

8.3.3 The Cambridge Machine—EDSAC

In October 1937, just before the Second World War, Cambridge University had a small research and service department called the "University Mathematical Laboratory." This was set up mainly to operate the University's differential analyzer, but the staff were also to engage in research projects directed toward other methods of computation. The staff was small—Maurice Wilkes was its only full-time member and he worked under Professor J. E. Lennard-Jones who acted as the UML's part-time director. The war interrupted the UML's activities before any real work was ever accomplished, and Wilkes left Cambridge to join other scientists in mathematical projects related to the war. When the war was over, Wilkes returned to Cambridge in September 1945 and was appointed to the directorship of the UML.

Wilkes had already heard about some of the computing work that was going on in the United States from D. R. Hartree, then a professor at Manchester University, who was soon to join the faculty at Cambridge, and he learned even more when L. J. Comrie visited him in May 1946 after returning from a trip to America. Comrie had a copy of the *First Draft on a Report on the EDVAC* which had been produced by von Neumann and, as there were no Xerox machines in those days, Wilkes spent almost the whole of the following night reading and making notes from it before Comrie had to leave the next day.

Because of his position as director of the UML, and likely because of his contacts with Hartree and Comrie, Wilkes was one of the invited participants in the series of lectures that were to be given at the Moore School of Engineering during the summer of 1946. He managed to get a trans-Atlantic passage which, although it arrived too late for him to attend the first few lectures, was probably one of the most important trips taken by anyone that year. The content of the Moore School lectures so impressed him that he began to think of constructing his own digital computer while he was still in Philadelphia.

He was very pragmatic in his design, always wanting to have a machine on which he could run real programs rather than simply speculating on what would happen if certain types of machine design or programming constructs were available. This led him to use the technology that was readily available to him, rather than engage in any research programs to develop new forms of memory or arithmetic circuits. In addition to having a very pragmatic attitude, Wilkes knew that the UML's budget would not enable him to indulge in any development efforts which might lead to dead ends or result in delays in producing the final product.

In late 1946 the Williams' tube memory was still just a gleam in Fred Williams' eye, so Wilkes opted for a design which would use the mercury acoustic delay lines. Once the major decision on the memory had been taken, the other aspects of the machine just naturally fell into place. The serial nature of the delay-line storage demanded that the machine process its bits in serial fashion, and this determined the ultimate design of the arithmetic and control sections of the computer. Although no working acoustic delay-line memory had yet been constructed, Wilkes was fortunate in meeting a Cambridge research student, T. Gold, who had returned to Cambridge after doing some work on mercury delay lines for the Admiralty Signals Establishment during the war. Gold, whose work had actually been intended as a method of echo cancellation for radar receivers, was able to supply Wilkes with all the necessary information about the design and problems to be expected from a mercury-based delay line. This was all that Wilkes needed and, before long, he had designed and constructed a memory consisting of 16 steel tubes each of which was capable of storing 32 words of 17 bits each (16 bits plus a sign bit).

Wilkes' machine was called EDSAC, which stood for "Electronic Delay Storage Automatic Calculator," and was named after the Moore School EDVAC design which had first given him the basic idea. He was quite inexperienced in managing a large construction project and freely admits that he started the project with only enough money to take it through the initial design stage and simply hoped that "something would turn up." He was very lucky that one of the executives of J. Lyons and Co. Ltd., a very large British firm which supplied baked goods to hundreds of small stores and cafes throughout the country, had heard of his work while on a study tour in the United States.

Figure 8–17. M. V. Wilkes looking at the mercury delay lines for EDSAC.

The Lyons firm had an accounting and supply problem which, they hoped, might be eased by some form of automatic computer. They gave the UML some money but, more importantly, they loaned one of their best technical people, E. H. Lennaerts, to the UML for over a year. Early in 1947 W. Renwick joined the team and made many suggestions which resulted in the design being quickly finished and the actual construction started shortly afterwards.

The final design was about five times as big as the machine Wilkes first envisaged when he was still in Philadelphia and, of course, the projected cost was a great deal more than the UML's budget could provide. Help was obtained from several different sources, primarily a British government research agency and the central University Grants Committee. Wilkes was always very reluctant to estimate the cost of the complete machine, but he did indicate, when asked a formal question during a 1951 conference, that the final cost must have been under $1,000,000 but that it was never actually worked out because it was simply considered as part of the ongoing University research program.

The EDSAC design team faced the same problems as many of the other early computer designers. They had to develop circuits which would deal with transient currents and not mistake them for proper wave forms. The problems with the design of the mercury acoustic delay lines and their sensitivity to electrical noise and temperature changes have already been mentioned in Section 8.2. Wilkes once calculated that, if each unit in the computer were to be designed to the same standards as went into the design of radar sets, the actual project would take his small team about 20 years to complete. Because of this time problem the team decided that they had to be conservative in the basic requirements, but that they must also cut corners in the design and construction phases of the project in order to see results quickly. This led them to use a basic clock cycle time of only 500,000 hz instead of the 1 Mhz, or even higher, cycle times which were being discussed by other potential computer designers. This, of course, resulted in a slower machine than many which were to come after it, but it allowed them to use components and design techniques which were well within the range of their technological resources.

EDSAC was first demonstrated in May of 1949, almost a full year behind the first trial run of a working stored-program machine at Manchester. However, unlike the Manchester machine, EDSAC was not a simple test-bed prototype, but a full-sized machine capable of solving realistic problems. It went into regular use as a service machine only about eight months after it first ran a program, and remained in continuous use until the summer of 1956. Of course programming the machine was not easy, but Wilkes soon started a project to develop a series of subroutines which would be useful to anyone wishing to do realistic work on EDSAC.

The big thing about a subroutine is that the operator must be able to call several of them in succession from some type of driver program. However, the first thoughts about producing "canned" sets of code to perform various jobs required that they simply be strung together on the input paper tape so that

Figure 8–18. The Cambridge University EDSAC computer.

control would naturally pass from one to the next when each bit of code finished executing. At this point, a particularly bright graduate student, David J. Wheeler, devised a scheme whereby a series of machine instructions would store the address of where execution was taking place, jump to a subroutine, execute the subroutine code, and then jump back to where it had left off executing the main program. The programming scheme he used for this became known as the "Wheeler Jump," but it was not long before it became incorporated in the hardware of other machines and was simply referred to by the more prosaic "subroutine jump" we know today.

EDSAC was a single-address machine, which meant that all instructions had to manipulate data by transferring it into and out of a single accumulator. Unlike the Manchester machine it contained no index registers, but the usefulness of this additional hardware was so apparent that one was added to it in 1955. Fortunately only 16 of the 17 bits available in the memory word were being used to encode the instructions, so an extra bit was available to indicate that the contents of the index register were to be added to the address under examination. There were only 18 instructions available in the initial machine. These included:

- add
- subtract
- multiply
- transfer instructions for moving information to and from the accumulator and the special multiply register
- two conditional branch instructions depending on the contents of the accumulator
- commands to read or print a single character
- left and right shifts of the accumulator
- an instruction to round off the contents of the accumulator
- a stop instruction which would ring the warning bell

One of the most interesting features of the machine was that there was no simple branch instruction. Any branching had to be done via one of the conditional branch instructions which meant that the user had to know the sign of the number currently in the accumulator before deciding which of the two conditional branch instructions to use. If the contents of the accumulator was unknown, it was necessary to set it to zero (or some other known value) before a branch instruction could be executed. An unconditional branch was incorporated into the machine when some extensive modifications were being done in the early 1950s. Most simple commands took about 1.5 milliseconds to execute but a multiplication took 4.5 milliseconds. Division was done by programming, and the division subroutine took about 200 milliseconds. All numbers inside the machine were assumed to be fractions in the range +1 to

−1, so that the programmer had to keep track of the amount of shifting that had to be done to properly scale the results at output time. Although the memory was considered as being divided into 17-bit words (16 bits for the number and one for the sign), it was actually designed to store a 35-bit word. The two 17-bit words were stored in the upper and lower halves of one full 35-bit word, the extra bit being lost due to electronic switching time when only a half word was accessed. Most of the EDSAC instructions could either operate on a short 17-bit word or the long 35-bit word.

The peripheral devices were simple five-hole paper tape readers and teleprinters. They caused more trouble than the electronics for, although they only operated at less than ten characters per second, they were mechanical devices which tended to quickly get out of adjustment. When the machine began to be used as a service bureau for the University, the paper tape reader was replaced with a photoelectric reader which could manage 50 characters per second. This improved the speed at which both programs and data could be fed into the machine and also increased the reliability considerably. The increased speed of input was a significant factor in improving the efficiency of the machine for, just as with today's beginning programmers, the execution phase of a program seldom got beyond the point of reading it into memory.

A very simple bootstrap loader had been designed by Wheeler and built into a read-only memory, a series of telephone exchange stepping switches. This small program was copied into the mercury delay-line memory by an automatic process whenever the start switch was pressed. After being copied into the main memory, this loader would be executed to read the problem program from the paper tape reader. The actual instructions consisted of three fields punched on the paper tape. The first was one of the 18-single letter operation codes (A for add, S for subtract, T for transfer the contents of the accumulator to memory, and so on). The next was the decimal address of the memory word being manipulated, and finally came either the letter L or the letter S (standing for "long" or "short") which indicated whether the operation was to be applied to a long (35-bit) or a short (17-bit) memory word.

By August 1949 a very much more advanced set of "initial orders" (as the bootstrap loader was called) were written by Wheeler and installed in the same read-only memory. These not only provided the same facilities (for example, translation from the decimal addresses punched on the paper tape to the binary addresses in instructions) as the original loader, but also managed to deal with the problem of relocating the various parts of a program (main program, subroutines, and data areas) at loading time so that it was unnecessary to have many different copies of a subroutine operating out of different areas of memory. Wheeler had to squeeze this loading program into a routine of no more than 41 instructions because that was the total storage space available in the stepping switches. He used every space-saving programming trick he could think of and eventually got this very complex routine down to only 40 instructions. The extra storage location in the read-only memory was used to store a special constant so that the library of subroutines could be made a little bit shorter. Wheeler has often been given credit as one of the world's most inventive programmers for his production of this set of "initial orders."

EDSAC holds a prime place in the history of the world's first computers, not only because it was the first full-scale operational electronic digital computer but because its ability to construct programs from relocatable subroutines, and to link them together at load time, provided a model for almost all others to follow. The model was well explained by one of the most influential textbooks of this early era, *The Preparation of Programs for an Electronic Digital Computer*, which was written by Wilkes, Wheeler and Gill (Stan Gill was another graduate student who contributed a lot to the early systems software) and published in 1951. The form of constructing programs and how they should be linked together to form a load module, as described in this book, reappears many times for different computers being constructed in different countries. It provided the basic ideas as to how one should go about creating a computing system rather than simply providing a bit of hardware to be used only by a few specialists.

One of the spin-offs of EDSAC was the first computer to be used for commercial data processing. As was mentioned earlier, J. Lyons & Co. had sent T. R. Thompson to the United States to study the effects of war-time developments on office management. Thompson's report to his superiors was so enthusiastic that they allowed him to begin a study project aimed at determining if an electronic computer could help in the company offices. Thompson's first step was to decide that it was not worth his time to reinvent the wheel, and he sent one of his technical people to work with Wilkes in the hope that they could both benefit from a shared project. In the end, Lyons produced a re-engineered version of the EDSAC for their own use. They called this machine LEO for Lyons Electronic Office. It was to be the first of many different machines (LEO I, LEO II, LEO III . . .) produced by this same group. The technical computer group was eventually reorganized by the parent company as LEO Computers Ltd.

The construction of LEO was started in the summer of 1949 and it was operational in the fall of 1951. It used 64 delay lines which gave it a total storage capacity of 2048 words of 17 bits each. Rather than constructing an "oven" in order to keep the mercury delay lines at a stable temperature, the LEO group built them into a constant temperature enclosure with one delay line acting as a master frequency control unit. Depending on the speed at which pulses were found to travel in the master unit, the frequency being used to transmit the pulses in the other units would be varied so as to keep a standard time regardless of the delay-line temperature. This eliminated the need to wait for long periods while the memory temperature stabilized after the machine was turned on.

LEO initially used the same type of five-hole paper tape as was being used in Cambridge, but later went to a mix of input and output equipment including cards, paper tape, and mechanical printers. There were special instructions in the machine which would cause switches to flip between different input and output units so that programs could read from more than one paper tape reader at a time. This enabled the programming of such commercially oriented jobs as merging together data punched on two different paper tapes. LEO was also used to experiment with an early form of an endless loop magnetic tape reader/recorder. It was designed by Standard Telephones and Cables Ltd. and consisted of a long loop of tape which could be passed over separate reading and recording heads before it was allowed to fall back into its holding box. The main use of this device was to record data being produced by standard teleprinter devices and then have it read into LEO at the high speeds obtainable by magnetic media.

Lyons used LEO I to derive the optimum mix for their brands of tea, to compute different kinds of tax tables, to process the payroll, and to assist in research on crystallography. The speed of the machine can be suggested by the fact that a complete calculation of an employee's wages and deductions would take about 1.5 seconds, as compared with a total of 8 minutes for the same job done by an experienced human clerk. LEO I remained in service with the J. Lyons Co. for 14 years until it was eventually replaced by more modern equipment in 1965.

8.3.4 The NPL Pilot Ace

After the war was over, Alan Turing left his position with the code-breaking people at Bletchley Park and, although he still held a Fellowship at King's College Cambridge, he joined the staff at the National Physical Laboratory (NPL). This was largely due to the fact that he and J. R. Womersley, who had just been appointed as the first superintendent of the newly created Mathematics Division of the NPL, had talked about the possibilities of constructing electronic computing machines. Womersley was quite receptive to the proposal that Turing should spend his time in the design of an electronic computer. Turing arrived at the NPL in the fall of 1945 and immediately set to work considering exactly what features an electronic computer should have. Progress was very rapid, and by the spring of 1946 he had set out the basic design for four different versions of his machine and was hard at work on the fifth. Like Babbage a hundred years earlier, he was able to take his experience in producing a design and immediately use it to produce a better version.

The preliminary versions of the Automatic Computing Engine (ACE) were all done by Turing simply because he was the only person at the NPL who happened to have this interest. Womersley had other groups to set up and, although they naturally discussed the project, he could not provide any material help until May of 1946 when J. H. Wilkinson arrived at the NPL and was assigned to Turing on a half-time basis. Jim Wilkinson was a mathematician who had spent the war years working to find numerical solutions to ballistic and explosive problems so, although well qualified, he had no experience and very little knowledge about the design of electronics or what would be needed in order to create an electronic computer. Later that same year Mike Woodger joined the group and the three of them were able to put substantial efforts into the design project for versions 5, 6, and 7 of the ACE.

The design steps involved setting out the basic components of a machine and the types of control structures and programming techniques it would need. The next step was to write programs for this design and then to decide on the features that might make for either easier coding or more rapid execution of the resulting code. These considerations were then taken into account when producing the next design version of the ACE.

Four other poeple were added to the ACE team in 1947, and between the seven of them they wrote programs for almost all the basic operations of numerical analysis, even though these programs were never destined to run on a real machine. These included full-code segments for simple problems such as square root routines and floating-point and multilength arithmetic up to full programs to solve systems of linear equations and other similar matrix operations. It must have been rather frustrating to put all this effort in, over a three-year period, before starting the actual construction of any hardware, but it yielded huge dividends when the resulting machine, although small by even the standards of that time, turned out to be very powerful. It was easily able to match the speeds of machines many times its size in memory capacity and brute force arithmetic speed. Part of the reason the resulting machine was to be so fast was that Turing designed the system with a microsecond clock. Not only was this faster than some of the other early computers, but it also introduced some technical problems, such as the fact that the wave fronts of successive bits in the delay line were only 0.06 in. apart, which had to be overcome by new techniques.

Several different designs were suggested beyond version 5 of the ACE but, for reasons which will become obvious later, it is worth considering that version in detail. It was to be an unusual machine from the standpoint of modern architecture, but one that had merit. Almost all the machines then under construction, or even being considered, tended to have a large memory and a small, single-word register which was used as an accumulator for all the arithmetic functions. Turing's design, on the other hand, called for a mercury delay-line memory system consisting of 200 individual delay lines, each capable of storing 32 binary words (each 32 bits long) with a delay of about one millisecond. Rather than having an accumulator, the machine was designed so that all instructions simply routed information from one "source" (generally a delay line) to a "destination" (again, usually a delay line). Several of the delay lines automatically manipulated incoming information, for example, by adding it to or subtracting it from data already stored in the line. These functional delay lines were very short, about 2 in. long, and only capable of holding one binary number each, although a few longer delay lines were provided which would hold double length results.

This architecture meant that the machine instructions did not contain any operation code, but that the operation being performed was implied by the source or destination then in use. For example, Figure 8–19, which is actually a simplified version of the Pilot ACE machine, had a data path (called a "highway") which effectively ran around the outside of the machine and connected together all the sources and destinations. The notation DLi refers to Delay Line i (the main storage) while TSi and DSi were the Temporary Store (single-word delay lines) and Double Store (two-word delay lines). If a data word was sent to destination 16, it was stored in TS16 with no further action taking place. If it was sent to destination 17, it would be added to the number already stored in TS16. If a number was taken from source 17 and sent to destination 26, it had the effect of negating the quantity held in TS26.

All this design work took place between 1945 and 1948. There was always the intention that, at some time, the NPL would undertake to construct the ACE, but the decision was taken to subcontract out the actual hardware rather than setting up an electronics lab within the NPL. This decision was, in hindsight, a bad one. It resulted in little or no actual progress being made in starting

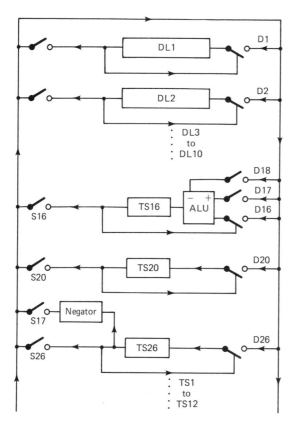

Figure 8–19. A simplified diagram form of the Pilot ACE system.

on the construction of any of the various versions of the ACE. In 1947 two things happened which actually got the initial construction work started. In January of that year Harry Huskey joined the ACE group while he was on a sabbatical leave, and, quite independent of that development, the decision was taken to establish an electronics group at the NPL. Although both of these events had a beneficial side, they were also to prove minor disasters.

Huskey had gained experience in digital electronics when he had worked on the ENIAC project with Eckert and Mauchly and, perhaps because of this experience, was quite anxious that the NPL actually start on some concrete construction project. He was also anxious that others see palpable results from the work done during his time at the NPL. At about this same time, Turing had become quite disillusioned with the progress being made on the ACE and made plans to leave later that year for his own sabbatical to King's College. Huskey, although always having very friendly relations with the rest of the ACE group, never got along very well with Turing. In fact, their relationship was so stormy that several members of the group thought they might eventually come to blows.

On the surface, it seemed that the establishment of an electronics division within the NPL would greatly facilitate the eventual construction of ACE through both expertise and manpower. In reality, however, the head of the electronics section was much more concerned with industrial electronic problems than in allocating his very scarce resources to a research project from the mathematics section. Thus actual progress was slowed to a snail's pace at best.

Eventually Huskey talked the ACE group, less Turing who was preparing to leave, into abandoning the grand design of ACE and attempting to construct a very small machine just to test out Turing's ideas of computer design. Because the version 5 machine was both the most carefully worked out design and one of the more easily implemented versions, they decided that this pilot project should construct a stripped down model of this version of ACE. It was officially designated the "test assembly."

Progress was slow, mainly because of a lack of real commitment from the electronics section and because it was only Huskey and D. W. Davies of the ACE team that had enough experience with digital electronics to be able to effectively design circuits. The project came to a standstill when Huskey returned to America, and the ACE team, having lost its natural leaders in Turing and Huskey, had real morale problems. Turing came back to the NPL in the spring of 1948 but was still upset over the lack of any real progress and left almost immediately to join Williams and Kilburn at the Manchester University computer project.

The real breakthrough came when the head of the NPL electronics section resigned and his replacement was open-minded enough to suggest to the ACE group that they take complete charge of the actual construction of the "test assembly." They quickly accepted the offer, abandoned the work on the "test assembly," and set about doing a redesign of version 5 to make the electronics as simple as possible. This machine quickly became known as the Pilot ACE.

Construction was started in early 1949 and, even though there had been a lot of earlier friction between the ACE group and the electronics section, they now worked together very well under the new arrangement. Progress was rapid, the first completed sections arriving from the workshops by the fall of 1949. Enough sections had been constructed by Christmas of that year that they could even consider the possibility of actually running one of their programs.

As usual with most computer projects, it is easy to complete the first 95 percent but very difficult to finish the last 5 percent of the project. The actual first run is best described by Jim Wilkinson:

> Towards the end of the day on May 10, 1950, we had working all the basic pulse circuits, the control unit, one long delay line, and a short delay line fitted with an additive and a subtractive input. The punched card input and output had not yet been added, and the only method of inserting instructions was via 32 switches on which we could set up one instruction at a time. Unfortunately, the amplifier on the delay line was barely adequate, and the probability of remembering a pulse pattern for as long as a minute was not very high. This was particularly true in the late hours of the afternoon since the mains voltage tended to drop because of national overload, and this affected the marginal circuits adversely.
>
> We concocted a very elementary program consisting of a few instructions only . . . but each time the memory would fail before we could complete the input. We decided to wait until the mains voltage recovered somewhat and then to try again. Finally we succeeded in inserting the whole program . . . and the lights came up slowly one by one. We switched off for the day knowing that the computer was working.[8]

Their little test program was simply designed to turn on the output lights one by one at a rate which was controlled by the number set on the panel switches at the time. This little test program was officially called "successive digits" but was known for years afterwards as "suck digs." It became the standard test program to be used when checking out the machine after any service or when first starting it up in the morning. Even when a properly engineered version of the Pilot ACE, the English Electric DEUCE computer, was constructed, the suck digs program was still in use at all the installations.

The director of the NPL was summoned to see the working machine and, although he indicated that the suck digs program was "scarcely epoch making," pressured the Pilot ACE team to hold a public demonstration for the press as soon as possible. After a few more improvements were made to the machine, a three-day press conference was called. The first day was for the popular press, the second for the technical press, and the third for various interested groups including the officials of the NPL and the main personnel from both the Man-

[8]J. H. Wilkinson, "Turing's Work at the National Physical Laboratory and the Construction of the Pilot ACE, DEUCE, and ACE," in *A History of Computing in the 20th Century*, ed. N. Metropolis et al. (New York: Academic Press, 1980), p. 109.

Figure 8–20. Some fine adjustments being made to the short mercury delay lines on the Pilot Ace. (Photograph courtesy of the National Physical Laboratory.)

chester and Cambridge computer projects. As usual with these types of demonstrations, the main memory on the Pilot ACE refused to work until just before the actual demonstration. Frantic efforts at repair were made and the system worked perfectly for the three-day period, and then promptly refused to work again for several weeks.

The Pilot ACE was, of course, smaller than any of the full ACE designs. When the machine was first put into productive use it consisted of a delay-line memory which held only 300 words of 32 bits each, the special TS delay lines for addition and subtraction, and another special unit for multiplication.

With such a small memory the ACE team had to devise many different techniques to cram both the machine instructions and data into efficient form. A large matrix could simply not be held in the delay lines, so projects like multiplying a matrix by a vector would be done by the following scheme:

1. The matrix elements would be punched on cards in a binary code, each number taking up 32 positions along one row of a card. This allowed for 12 numbers per card.

2. As the cards were being read in, the actual multiplication of the number just read and the corresponding vector would take place during the 15 milliseconds it took the card to move through the reader from one row to the next, the result either being punched out or stored in a delay line depending on the number of elements involved.

This same scheme was used on the English Electric DEUCE computer. A lot of thought and effort went into careful timing of the instructions so that a loop could be done in the very short time it took a card to pass from one row to the next in the reader. There was nothing so frustrating as finding that your loop took just two or three milliseconds too long for you to catch the next number as it came by the read brushes.

Part of the sophistication of the instruction set was its ability to deal with the problem of obtaining the next instruction in the program sequence. With a mercury delay-line system, if the instruction currently being executed took anything other than a trivial length of time, the next instruction in physical sequence would have already been moved past the reading end of the delay line and recycled back to the start of the tube. This meant that the machine had to delay all execution until that instruction again reached the output end of the tube, a process which would take about one millisecond. The Pilot ACE instruction set not only specified the source and destination of the operands, but also contained an address as to where the next instruction in logical sequence could be found. This meant that if you knew a particular instruction would take n microseconds to execute, you put the following instruction into a mercury delay line in such a position that it would be available exactly n microseconds after the first one. This resulted in very complex programs because the instructions, rather than being in physical sequence, were scattered all over the available memory space. With all of these speed-up features, the Pilot ACE was actually a very fast machine. Although containing only 800 vacuum tubes, it could do matrix arithmetic problems several times faster than the 3000 tube EDSAC machine at Cambridge.

Program branches were performed by moving either a 0 or a 1 to destination 25. The address of where to find the next instruction in sequence would then be modified to either accept it from the location specified or from the next physical location in the delay-line memory, depending on the contents of TS25.

Additional speed-up features were incorporated into the instruction set so that, for example, a simple form of vector or pipeline processing was possible. If it was necessary to add up a list of 200 numbers, then the numbers were put into a delay line and the instruction was given to move a number from that delay line into TS17 (which you will recall would add its input to the data already stored). An additional part of the instruction told the machine how

Figure 8–21.   Jim Wilkinson at the console of the Pilot ACE; his right arm is obscuring a CRT monitor. (Photograph courtesy of the National Physical Laboratory.)

long it should keep doing the instruction, so that if the instruction was "move from 2 to 17 for 200 cycles" it would add up all 200 numbers emerging from delay line 2 with only one instruction.

Like most early machines the Pilot ACE underwent modifications during its lifetime. Various small changes were made to the circuits, but the most important change was the addition of a magnetic drum as an additional memory device. This removed the necessity to used punched cards as intermediate storage devices and allowed the machine to deal with much larger matrix problems in a very much easier way.

The chairman of the giant industrial firm of English Electric happened to be a member of the NPL Executive Committee during the time that the plans for the Pilot ACE were being formulated. This led him to propose that English Electric produce a properly engineered version of the machine for their own use. The resulting machine, the DEUCE, was finished in 1954, and two more were constructed in 1955 for the NPL and the Royal Aircraft Establishment. Soon other commercial and academic institutions were placing orders. The

DEUCE, of which 32 were eventually manufactured, turned out to be one of the main computing machines used in Britain during the late 50s and early 60s.

The DEUCE computer was built for ease of service. The central portion of the machine was actually hollow, and a door at the back allowed access to the ranks of vacuum tubes that lined each side of the machine. The University of Glasgow in Scotland used a DEUCE as its major computer during the early 1960s. Their chief technician had the habit of coming in to work dressed in a kilt, clearly not suitable attire when attempting to service eletronic and mechanical equipment. He solved the problem by keeping his working clothes inside the DEUCE and using the inside of the computer as a private changing room every morning before starting work. Other members of the Glasgow staff would occasionally hang their swim suits or damp towels inside the machine to dry out after having taken a break at the university pool during lunch hour. Undoubtedly many other installations used the inside of DEUCE for similar activities. It was a common rumor that the space was also used by romantically inclined couples to gain a few minutes privacy on the night shift. A few minutes was all that was possible because it would often get quite warm inside DEUCE!

The NPL actually produced a full version of the ACE in 1959 but, by that time, the idea of a mercury delay-line machine had been replaced by the advent of core memory. The full ACE functioned very well but was no longer an important machine in terms of its architecture.

The control panel and part of the main electronics of the Pilot ACE now reside in the computer display of the Science Museum in London.

8.4 THE AMERICAN SCENE

8.4.1 The American Background

By the time the Second World War was over, the development of digital electronics in America was well advanced. The Moore School had produced the ENIAC and had laid out the development of the concept of the stored-program computer. It would seem that, with this background, it would be only a matter of months before the Moore School would start on the actual construction of the EDVAC stored-program machine. Things do not always turn out as planned, however. The Moore School was torn with internal strife, von Neumann had a large falling out with Eckert and Mauchly, and it became difficult to find funding for the post-war developments. Thus it was several years before any stored-program computer became a reality in America. The early lead in this field was lost to the British.

The first section of Chapter 8 has already mentioned that von Neumann's famous report, *First Draft of a Report on the EDVAC*, caused a lot of problems and hard feelings at the Moore School. These problems were to escalate because of other actions on the part of von Neumann and the university administrators. Eckert and Mauchly were the main driving force behind the development of the ENIAC and had formed the concept of a stored-program computer before von Neumann came on the scene. John von Neumann obviously contributed a lot to the thinking of the Moore School team, but his publishing of the EDVAC document was considered, by Eckert and Mauchly, as an attempt to gain credit for the ideas himself. This problem was aggravated by the fact that the Moore School personnel were constrained by the Official Secrets Act from publishing anything about either the ENIAC or the EDVAC while von Neumann, who was not a full member of the team, was under no such restriction. At the same time, the problem arose as to what to do about patents on the ENIAC and EDVAC design. Eckert and Mauchly were of the opinion, as were some of the rest of the staff, that the patent rights were to belong to the individuals who participated in the inventions. The University of Pennsylvania, on the other hand, was equally firm in their belief that any patents were to be in the name of the University rather than any individual.

One of the first post-war considerations was that a joint venture be formed between the Moore School and von Neumann, at the Institute of Advanced Study in Princeton, together with other academic and industrial interests, to produce a working stored-program digital computer. Initially this seemed like a good idea, but the falling out of the key members of such a group made it quickly clear that such a project was doomed to failure. The bad relations were made worse when von Neumann, in an attempt to get his own project started at the IAS, had a meeting with representatives from RCA and the United States Weather Bureau to discuss the possible design and use of a computer. On January 10, 1946, the *New York Times* published an article with the headline "Electronics to Aid Weather Forecasting" which reported on the meetings between von Neumann and the industry and government officials. The article made no mention of the work of the Moore School on the ENIAC and EDVAC, which is not very surprising because they were still officially under wraps, but it did serve to strain relations between the groups even further. The article implied that von Neumann and RCA were the leading group in electronic computing and that theirs was the only real project of any consequence going on in the world.

To make matters even worse, the end of the war caused the Moore School's administration to take a close look at the way the money from the ENIAC contracts (the EDVAC development contract was an addition to the basic ENIAC contract) was being spent and the accounting methods being used to keep track of the expenditures between ENIAC and EDVAC developments. Dean Pender, of the Moore School, appointed Irven Travis to take charge of all research and development projects in an effort to keep some sort of control over the situation. Travis had worked in the Naval Ordnance Department as an administrator of contracts and, before the war, had held a position at the Moore School. In a lot of ways the choice of Travis to be the person to bring some order into the Moore School's affairs was an ideal one, since he had an association with the school, some knowledge of digital electronics, and administrative experience with war-related contracts. Unfortunately Travis was eager to reform the system quickly and, when he demanded that all Moore School people sign their patent rights over to the university, it was the final straw that broke the team apart. Eckert and Mauchly felt that they had no choice but to resign from the Moore School, and several of the most senior engineering people followed their example. Thus, by March of 1946, what had looked like a very strong situation for the further development of computers had turned into one in which von Neumann was attempting to get backing for the construction of a machine at the IAS, the Moore School was left without any leadership in their development of the EDVAC project, and the senior members of the Eckert-Mauchly team were without jobs and looking around to see if they could find some government or academic institute that would fund the construction of their computer.

Although Eckert and Mauchly were no longer associated with the Moore School, they continued to press for patent rights on their ENIAC and EDVAC developments. This move was regarded as having some priority because they had hoped to use these patents to set themselves on a sound footing for their future business interests. It was also in the interests of the Moore School and the military that this problem be resolved because the Armed Forces had an agreement that they could use the patents and they were fearful of losing this opportunity. In the end the process dragged on until April 3, 1947, when a meeting took place between all the interested parties. During this meeting the lawyer for the military pointed out that one could only patent something within one year from the time it had first been described in a publication. It was their opinion that von Neumann's distribution of his *First Draft of a Report on the EDVAC* constituted a publication in the legal sense and, because over a year had elapsed, the concepts for EDVAC were no longer patentable. This, needless to say, simply increased the bitterness that was felt between the various members of the group.

The one good thing that did come out of all this mess was the course on digital techniques offered by the Moore School during the summer of 1946. The Moore School had always had a commitment to foster the transfer of technology from an academic setting into industry. Because of this, and because of the increased demand for information from outside interests, they organized a series of lectures with the title "Theory and Techniques for Design of Electronic Digital Computers" which ran from July 8 to August 31, 1946. Although Eckert and Mauchly had left the Moore School several months earlier, they were rehired to deliver some of the lectures. They were joined by George Stibitz, D. R. Hartree from England, von Neumann and Goldstine from the IAS, Howard Aiken from Harvard, and several others from industry and the ENIAC development team. Invitations were sent out to all groups known to be interested in computer development for them to send a representative to the lectures.

The course was rather loose in its organization. The mornings were to be used for formal lectures and the afternoon was set aside for laboratory exercises and discussion groups. Lecture topics were often rearranged to accommodate the interests of the audience and lectures were occasionally changed at very short notice because of other commitments or simply because somebody forgot to tell the lecturer that it was his turn that particular day. Despite the apparent lack of organization, the course was one of the fundamental turning points in the development of computers. It has already been pointed out that Wilkes returned to Cambridge from the Moore School lectures and immediately began the design of his EDSAC machine. Similar activities occurred with a number of the participants and it was a direct result of this course that several different computer projects were started.

By 1947 there were several different groups active in an attempt to construct a computer. The Moore School was still working, rather slowly, on the EDVAC, von Neumann had obtained funding from the United States Army and Navy and from RCA for his machine at the Institute for Advanced Study, Project Whirlwind was underway at MIT, and Eckert and Mauchly had managed to obtain initial contracts for the design of a machine for the National Bureau of Standards and the Census Bureau. Out of the Eckert and Mauchly contracts were to come, via various routes, the machines known as BINAC and UNIVAC.

One other line of major importance has not yet been mentioned. It evolved from the same types of secret code-breaking work as the British Colossus machines. During the war years, the United States Navy was engaged in the design and construction of machines to help in breaking enemy codes. This project led, after the war, to several of the ex-Navy personnel founding a small company, Engineering Research Associates, in an effort to keep together the main members of the war-time team. The ERA took on several contracts with the Navy to construct secret equipment, about which almost nothing is known. The ERA later tried to introduce a commercial line of computers and met with some initial success. The firm was later bought out by Remmington Rand and, together with the Eckert-Mauchly Computer Corporation, formed the basis of the Univac division of Sperry Rand.

8.4.2 *The Electronic Discrete Variable Arithmetic Computer (EDVAC)*

As has already been mentioned, the Moore School team had conceived the idea of the EDVAC while constructing the ENIAC. It was the first stored-program electronic digital computer to have been thought of, if not the first actually constructed and running. Most of the background to this machine was detailed in earlier sections, but it is worth recapping the situation as it existed in the summer of 1946.

Eckert, Mauchly, and von Neumann had broken off their association with the Moore School and, although the basic concept of the EDVAC had been formulated earlier, these leading members of the design group no longer had any input as far as the detailed design and construction of the units was concerned. The idea of a mercury delay-line memory had been shown to be feasible, some preliminary design of adding circuits had been done, and the general shape of the machine, as set out in von Neumann's *First Draft of a Report on the EDVAC,* was available as the guiding light for those members of the design team still at the Moore School.

The initial design for EDVAC, as reported by von Neumann, called for a machine which would use a mercury delay-line memory and, as a consequence, be serial in that it processed a word of bits one bit at a time. The von Neumann report makes it quite clear that the team had considered the possibility of constructing a parallel machine, in which each bit of a word would be processed in parallel to all others, but that the final decision was taken for a serial computer because of the fact that the electronics would be simpler than in a parallel machine. When discussing the possibilities of increasing the arithmetic speed of EDVAC by doing parallel processing in the arithmetic elements, von Neumann noted:

> Accelerating these arithmetical operations does therefore not seem necessary—at least not until we have become thoroughly and practically familiar with the use of very high speed devices of this kind, and also properly understood and started to exploit the entirely new possibilities for numerical treatment of complicated problems which they open up. . . . The device should be as simple as possible, that is, contain as few elements as possible. This can be achieved by never performing two operations simultaneously, if this would cause a significant increase in the number of elements required. The result will be that the device will work more reliably and the vacuum tubes can be driven to shorter reaction times than otherwise.[9]

Another consideration which governed the basic design of the machine was that Eckert felt quite sure that a mercury delay-line memory would not only be feasible but that it would only require some slight modification of the radar mercury delay line to come up with a working model. The problem of developing a parallel memory was, at that time, a very difficult one with no obvious solution.

In March of 1946, when Eckert and Mauchly resigned, Kite Sharpless took over as head of the EDVAC project. He was soon joined by a number of people, some of whom had earlier experience on the ENIAC, as they were released from their military duties. One of the new staff, Herman Lukoff, was given the job of creating a working mercury delay-line memory. He managed to solve the problem of temperature dependence of the delay-line capacity, not by having the memory in a controlled temperature oven, but by creating the electronics to vary the spacing between pulses so that a constant number of pulses were

---

[9]John von Neumann, "First Draft of a Report on the EDVAC," in B. Randell, ed., *The Origins of Digital Computers, Selected Papers* (New York: Springer Verlag, 1973), p. 364.

always stored in the delay line regardless of its temperature. By the spring of 1947 they had a memory system working well enough that they were able to demonstrate it during a meeting of the Institute of Radio Engineers held in New York in March of that year. During the demonstration things began to go seriously wrong, much to Lukoff's embarrassment because the engineers viewing the display were pressing him for explanations. The problem was finally tracked down to the Army Signal Corps who were demonstrating a new radar unit and had not bothered to switch off the beam. Every time the radar antenna rotated in their direction it sent extraneous pulses into the electronics which were then circulated through the mercury, corrupting the stored data. When the radar beam was turned off the memory worked fine.

By the summer of 1947 the memory system had been shown to work reliably but progress was again halted when Kite Sharpless and some of his friends left to form their own firm, Technitrol Engineering, for the manufacture and sale of electrical components. Another new head of the EDVAC project was appointed but he was not a computer expert and had to spend much of his time attempting to catch up on elementary basics. The morale of the place once again went down hill and the more experienced staff tended to leave. Herman Lukoff, for example, left to join Eckert and Mauchly in their new venture which,

Figure 8-22. The EDVAC at the Moore School of Engineering.

by then, had the formal name of Electronic Control Company. Irven Travis, the director of research at the Moore School, attempted to bring in several different consultants in an effort to get the project moving, but they all suffered from the same basic lack of knowledge of digital electronics as did the new project head. Eventually even Travis left to establish a computer research division within Burroughs. Richard Snyder was then named chief engineer and saw the EDVAC project through to its conclusion in 1952, very much later than many projects which had been inspired by its initial design.

In fairness to the EDVAC people, it must be pointed out that their project was much more ambitious than a lot of their early competition. Not only did they have to spend time in developing the standard computer components such as memory, arithmetic units, control circuitry, and so on, but they also attempted to devise some highly sophisticated peripheral input and output equipment. The first plans called for a magnetic wire to be used as an auxiliary input/output system. This was to be a nickel-coated bronze wire which could store about 20,000 words of data. The idea was that, instead of using slow card or paper tape peripherals, this very fast magnetic wire recorder would become the fundamental means of entering data and obtaining results. Off-line machines, having a typewriter keyboard, would record material on the wire, and off-line printers would read the results and produce readable copy. This scheme had a lot of merit in that the peripherals available at that time were impossibly slow compared to the internal speeds of the machine. The idea received a lot of attention but was eventually abandoned because of extreme technical difficulties. The EDVAC people had to resort to a photoelectric paper tape reader (1000 characters per second) as the main input device backed up by an IBM card reader (100 cards per minute).

Additional enhancements over a simple raw machine were made to ensure accuracy of the calculated results. Perhaps the most famous of these was the dual arithmetic unit. Each arithmetic operation was performed twice, by different circuits, and the results compared to make sure that no error had occurred. Several small registers were constructed to contain the instruction that had just been executed and the memory location from which it was fetched, together with the same information about the previous instruction. These registers were very useful in debugging a program that had run wild. Anyone who has ever had the experience of attempting to debug a program that contained a wild jump to some remote part of memory will readily understand how such a set of registers could prove useful. Additional debugging facilities were included to cause the machine to halt if any one of several specific memory addresses happened to be accessed by an instruction about to be executed.

The mercury delay-line memory system consisted of 126 delay lines capable of storing 1024 words, each of 44 bits. Each delay line was 58 cm long. The clock pulses were generated at the rate of one million per second, which meant that exactly 384 pulses could be stored in each delay line (eight words plus four blank clock pulses separating each word). The electronics were very efficient—only about ten vacuum tubes were needed for the reshaping, amplification, and switching of pulses from one unit to another. By the time the machine was finished, an auxiliary magnetic drum memory had been added to the system to give an additional 4,000 words of memory for data storage.

The instruction set was rather limited. One instruction would fit into each word, taking 4 bits for the operation code, and the rest was divided into four addresses of 10 bits each. This gave a total of 16 possible instructions, but only 12 were really used. The four addresses in each instruction were used to specify the first and second operands, the destination of the result, and the address of the next instruction in sequence. This latter address was used to implement an optimum coding scheme similar to the one done for the Pilot ACE at the British National Physical Laboratory.

When the machine was finished in 1952 it stood 7 ft high, took up 500 sq ft of floor area, contained just over 3,500 vacuum tubes of 19 different types, and about 27,000 other electronic components such as diodes, resistors, and so on. It could perform an addition in about 1 millisecond (the time varied depending on where the operands were in the delay-line memory), and multiplication or division took about 3 milliseconds each. It was delivered to the U.S. Army Ordnance Corps Ballistic Research Laboratory at Aberdeen Proving Grounds where it joined the original ENIAC in calculations related to ballistic trajectories and other military problems.

8.4.3 The Institute for Advanced Study Machine

When von Neumann and Goldstine finally left their associations with the Moore School to return to the Institute for Advanced Study at Princeton, they went with the idea of spearheading a drive to actually construct a digital computer. At first sight this seemed like a foolish move because the IAS was known as an ivory tower institute and did not have any of the infrastructure, such as laboratory space or workshops, that would obviously be needed to start such a project. Their first idea was that the IAS, the Moore School, RCA, and other academic, government, and industrial institutions should collaborate to produce one machine. This very quickly came to nothing because of the different attitudes of the people involved and the personal difficulties that had arisen between von Neumann and the senior members of the Moore School staff.

It was largely the great regard in which von Neumann was held which allowed him to obtain the funding for his project. He convinced the same military groups that funded the ENIAC and EDVAC projects to provide the major resources for his own machine and, together with some help from the Atomic Energy Commission and RCA, he set about making sure that the IAS would provide the basic workshops and research space. The fact that the Army would support his machine as well as the EDVAC project is not all that surprising because, in those days, it was not certain which machine design would eventually prove to be superior, or even work, and the military wanted to make sure that their eggs were in more than one basket.

Just when von Neumann was getting started, about March of 1946, Eckert and Mauchly were having their final patent problems with the Moore School. Seeing this as his chance to obtain one of the world's leading authorities on digital electronics, von Neumann put aside any personal feelings he happened to have and invited Eckert to join him as the project leader. The offer stayed open for several months but Eckert's ideas on the patent rights of inventors conflicted so much with the IAS's insistence on open research that von Neumann eventually had to withdraw the offer and gave the job to Julian Bigelow. Bigelow had been working with Norbert Wiener of MIT during the war, and it was probably Wiener's friendship with von Neumann which resulted in Bigelow's being offered the position.

When Bigelow came to Princeton in June of 1946 he found that von Neumann already had a small, but highly skilled, staff of five engineers who were ready to start work. The first job was to establish some of the basic facilities at the IAS and then to see if any of von Neumann's ideas were really workable given the constraints of the technology available and the shortages that had been imposed by post-war conditions. Contracts had to be set up between the group and the funding agencies and contact arrangements made with the other institutes which hoped to participate in the project. It was initially proposed that, as each portion of the IAS machine was designed, copies of the plans would be sent to the Los Alamos Laboratory, the University of Illinois, Oak Ridge National Laboratory, Argonne National Laboratory, and the Rand Corporation so that they could construct copies of the IAS machine for their own use. Copies of the IAS machine were made but each of these institutes, and others which were later to join the scheme, produced modified versions of the machine, no two of which were ever identical.

Although von Neumann was adamant, in the EDVAC report, that any first machine should be serial in nature, he reversed his decision when it came time to plan his own machine. The people from RCA convinced him that they could construct a device—the selectron mentioned in Section 8.2—which would serve as the basis for a parallel memory system. With this assurance, he decided that the potential for increased arithmetic speeds with a parallel computer would be worth the risk of relying on the development of the selectron. As was pointed out during the earlier discussion of the selectron, this gamble turned out to be very risky indeed. It was only the development of the Williams' tube memory system which enabled the IAS machine to eventually be constructed. Except for the special memory tube, the machine was to be constructed using only those components which were available off the shelf. This design decision, which was violated from time to time in order to experiment with different ideas, was taken in order that the project could proceed as quickly as possible. The engineering team were well aware that any special order devices would likely take at least two years to develop and then might not be very reliable when they were delivered.

The first design sketch called for a machine with about 4,000 words of central memory, each having 40 bits. The arithmetic circuits, and consequently the memory also, was to operate at a clock rate of one megacycle. Rather than having a central clock to keep all units synchronized, each unit was to function on its own time scale and emit a signal when it had finished its operation. This asynchronous nature of the machine, combined with the parallel arithmetic and memory access, meant that the design team had to solve a large number of problems which had never been considered before by any digital electronics group. It is to their very great credit that they managed to find workable solutions in a very short time.

The first really major step came with the realization that, unlike a serial machine having only one data path where information simply flows from one unit to the next, having 40 parallel data paths introduces major problems in timing the arrival of information to the different components. If one of the parallel data paths happened to have a slightly longer delay than another, then it would be possible to lose information if all 40 bits did not arrive at the component, say an adder, at precisely the same instant. It became obvious that what was needed was a very large number of flip-flops, then called trigger circuits, to hold the information as it arrived and allow it to be strobed out in truly parallel form. Thus one of the first major jobs was to build instruments that would enable the group to experiment with constructing very high-speed vacuum tube flip-flops. It should be kept in mind that this was no trivial exercise, since they had nothing in the way of test equipment to give them any measurements in the megacycle switching times they hoped to achieve. The best they could do was to use old radar equipment as their oscilloscope and to create their own pulse generators by sampling the output of old radar delay lines.

By the summer of 1947 the team had designed the basic components of the arithmetic unit and were quite certain of their ability to actually get the electronics to work. This confidence was quickly removed when sample circuits, to add up 10 bits in parallel, failed to perform properly under test conditions. The engineers spent several weeks attempting to tune the circuits, but no matter what they did the timing problems would simply not go away. Finally Bigelow called a meeting of the engineering staff to consider the whole problem right from the start. In a matter of a few hours they realized that their basic design systems were at fault. Unlike Eckert, when he designed the ENIAC circuits, they had not taken into account the potential worst-case situations when selecting components or considering the fundamental design. Their individual units tended to operate correctly but, when combined into assemblies of ten or more, the worst-case conditions were almost always cropping up. From this meeting the "new look" in circuit design was born. It demanded that in all cases the design allow for such things as the vacuum tube's conductance being a factor of two outside of specifications, resistors being considered as varying from their stated values by at least 10 percent, and so on. In addition all components were to be tested to make sure that they were accurate to no worse than half of these conditions before they would be accepted for inclusion in the machine. With these "new look" rules, the design of the individual components was redone and, when they were hooked together, they ran first time.

About that same time, the problem of an additional storage facility was being considered. It was beginning to be obvious that the selectron production was in trouble at RCA. Even if the selectron remained the basic memory device, the IAS people realized that they might have to limit the memory to less than the 4,000 words called for in the design. In order to produce a back-up memory, they took the same route as the EDVAC people in considering a nickel-coated bronze wire as the basis for a magnetic wire memory. The result was the famous "bicycle wheel" endless loop wire memory that has already been discussed in Section 8.2. The failure of this device led to some concern as to what they might possibly use for a back-up memory, but they decided to put the project on hold for a few months because they knew that several firms had started the experimental production of nylon and mylar based magnetic tapes. The destructive potential of this new material was a great deal less than that of bronze wire which, because it was moving at rates of 100 feet per second, wore notches in the read heads, so they decided to simply wait and see what technical developments might be produced to solve their problems.

By the spring of 1948 it was very obvious that the development of the selectron had run into real technical problems, and a crash program was undertaken to find some other parallel memory device. The only potential candidate was a magnetic drum with 40 read/write heads which would enable the machine to store one bit of each word on a different track. In order to get a high-speed memory it would be necessary to have several different sets of read/write heads positioned around the drum so that the machine did not have to wait for one complete rotation, in the worst case, for a given word of information to be located. Some calculations showed that the drum would have to rotate at 30,000 rpm if they used two sets of read/write heads, or 15,000 rpm if they used four, Either of these choices was unacceptable because, even at these very high rotation rates, the speed of accessing memory would have slowed down the machine so much that it would have thrown away any gain they may have had from the use of the parallel transmission of data. However, no other technology appeared capable of creating a parallel memory and they had gone too far with the design of the parallel machine to abandon it now. They took every possible precaution in the construction of a drum, even down to having it machined when it was already rotating on its own bearings in order that a later mounting would not throw off the alignment. At these rotation speeds the drum had to be quite small (5 in. diameter), and this meant that the resulting surface would only store about 2,000 words, half the number called for in the design. The problem of designing a read/write head capable of writing on the drum in microsecond time intervals was solved by using a single-wire head, similar to the Booth single-wire head already described in Section 8.2. The drum memory was actually ready to undergo testing when, in the spring of 1948, they heard about the work of Freddy Williams in Manchester.

Freddy Williams' construction of a CRT-based memory system was communicated to the group when Hartree came on a visit from Britain. Shortly afterwards, Williams sent them a copy of a paper he had written as a preliminary report on the idea. The problem of a memory device was getting so worrisome that one of the senior engineers, Jim Pomerene, began to do some initial experiments while Bigelow set off for Manchester to see what he could find out in person. After three weeks Bigelow phoned the IAS to report on his findings, only to discover that Pomerene had already managed to lash up a Williams' tube system which would store 16 bits for an indefinite length of time. The whole scheme looked so promising that Bigelow came home and the decision was immediately taken to abandon the selectron and attempt the construction of a parallel memory consisting of 40 CRTs, each one storing one bit of a computer word.

There were, of course, many problems in both the design and construction of such a large number of Williams' tube memory systems, not the least of which was to find 40 tubes with the same characteristics. The problem of blank spots on the phosphor, encountered by Williams in Manchester, was magnified many times over for the IAS group and only solved by setting up a test bed and processing several hundred war surplus tubes and, later, fresh tubes from a manufacturer's inventory before an acceptable set were found. Another fundamental problem was that the system was very sensitive to electromagnetic noise from adjacent electronics, the fluorescent lights in the room, and the spark plugs of passing automobiles. This was solved by constructing special metal shielding around each tube and its associated equipment. The memory system worked well, but was a little disappointing because it would only accommodate 1024 words. It was installed under the main electronics, and the front faces of 20 of the tubes can be seen in the photograph of the IAS machine.

The problems of "read around" and refreshing the screen described in Section 8.2 had to be approached in a different way from the mechanism used on a serial machine. In serial mode, the reading or writing of a word of information was done by taking a number of adjacent bits from one tube while in parallel machines only a single bit from each tube would be accessed at one time. Special circuits were constructed to refresh the information, each tube working in parallel with the others and, when the computer required access to a particular word, this refresh cycle would be interrupted, the access given, and the refresh cycle continued from where it left off. Unfortunately the refresh cycle timing was of the same order of magnitude as the basic addition time of the machine. This meant that if a long sequence of simple addition, subtraction, or data movement instructions was executed, it might take enough time to

Figure 8–23. John von Neumann and the Institute for Advanced Study Computer. The Williams' tubes can be seen protruding from the lower section of the computer. (Photograph courtesy of the Institute for Advanced Study, Princeton, N.J.)

forego the refresh cycle and thus data would be lost. Thus it was necessary to make sure that the programmer never created loops that contained only "short" instructions. If necessary, a dummy multiply or divide instruction would be introduced into a loop in order to give the memory time to refresh and thus clean up any problems that may have been building up because of the read-around effect.

The essential parts of the entire machine were available by January of 1951, and the IAS people began to see that it might be possible to consider running a program in the near future. The system was checked out and various shortcuts were introduced to make it into an operating machine in the shortest possible time. These included putting in dummy units in place of fully functional ones and creating a dc power supply by the simple expedient of using a large number of storage batteries. Even with all of these shortcuts it still took until the middle of that year before realistic programs could be run. The first major test was a long series of calculations connected with the design of the hydrogen bomb. This problem was programmed by the Los Alamos research center and required that the machine run 24 hours per day for 60 days. Duplicate runs were made to ensure that the answers were correct and several hardware errors were caught during this test run. Development, of course, continued, and the machine was officially dedicated in a public way on June 10, 1952. It continued to be enhanced, most notably with the installation of a magnetic drum and the replacement of its slow paper tape readers and punches with higher speed card equipment, until it reached the end of its useful life in 1960 when it was donated to the Smithsonian Institution in Washington, D.C.

Various copies of the IAS machine were eventually constructed: The Rand Corporation called theirs JOHNNIAC after John von Neumann, the Los Alamos machine was known as MANIAC, the Argonne National Laboratory constructed the AVIDAC, the ORACLE and GEORGE, and the University of Illinois built the ORDVAC for the Aberdeen Proving Ground and the ILLIAC I for themselves. Some of these machines were available for use at about the same time as the original IAS copy. The MANIAC and the ORDVAC were both ready for use in the spring of 1952 and the others were not far behind. Copies were not limited to being produced in the United States, the most famous of the several foreign copies undoubtedly being the SILLIAC constructed in Sidney, Australia.

When the machine was finished, it came as a bit of a surprise to most people working on serial computers just how few vacuum tubes the IAS machine contained. It was quite true that some sections of the machine were more complex than the corresponding parts of a serial computer, the memory being the most notable example, but the basic control circuits were capable of being set up in a very much simpler way. The fact that all the bits of an instruction were available at one time, rather than being presented from the end of a memory line one at a time, resulted in the central control being a simple set of gates rather than a complex device which had to take into account changes over a period of time. The IAS machine eventually contained only about 2,300 vacuum tubes as compared to the 3,500 used in the serial EDVAC. It was also quite small by the standards of the day, measuring only 6 ft long, 8 ft high, and 2 ft wide. Part of its compactness was due to the use of miniature tubes (6J6) containing two triodes each. Each tube was about a third the size of those used in ENIAC and EDVAC.

Instructions were each 20 bits long so it was possible to pack two of them in each memory word. This resulted in some slight speed-up of the machine because it was only necessary to access memory for instructions after every second major instruction execution cycle. The 20 bits were divided equally into two 10-bit sections, one for the instruction code and the other for a memory address. All operations were of the simple, one-address style of moving information between the memory and a single internal register for arithmetic. The space of 10 bits for the instruction code gave the scope for a huge instruction set, but in reality only about 15 instructions were available on the basic machine. A single-address instruction code was sufficient for the IAS machine because, unlike the EDVAC or Pilot ACE serial machines, the truly random-access memory meant that it had no need for optimum coding schemes. Considering the long word length of 40 bits, it was one of the most powerful computers of its day. Simple addition instructions required about 60 microseconds execution time while a multiplication took about five times as long.

The memory was complex and costly, but the performance of the machine set the design standard for the very fast parallel computers of the future.

8.4.4 The Eckert-Mauchly Machines, BINAC and UNIVAC

Eckert and Mauchly were able to see the deteriorating situation at the Moore School before it came to a head in the spring of 1946. They had made sure that people in various government agencies were aware of the achievements that had been made at the Moore School and aware of the men behind those achievements. In particular, they had contacted the Census Bureau and laid the groundwork for that agency's interest in obtaining some electronic computing help with their massive statistical work. When they left the Moore School and formed the Electronic Control Company, they again approached the Census Bureau and suggested that this new company would be willing to take on the job of actually constructing a machine.

The idea was well received by the Census Bureau, and a series of negotiations was begun to see just how a contract could be set up. Unfortunately for Eckert and Mauchly, the Census Bureau was constrained by law from entering into research and development contracts. The only thing they could legally do was to purchase a fully developed system. Eckert and Mauchly certainly did not have the resources even to start considering such a project on their own so they came up with a scheme that would involve a three-way arrangement between themselves, the Census Bureau, and the National Bureau of Standards. The idea was that the Census Bureau would obtain about $300,000 from the Army Ordnance Department, transfer this money to the National Bureau of Standards, and then the NBS would fund the development of a computer for use by all the concerned parties. What, on the face of it, looked like a simple arrangement was, in reality, to give nothing but trouble. The rules governing the NBS were simpler than those involving the Census Bureau, but they still required the NBS to go through several different steps before they could award a contract. Consultants had to be brought in to prepare reports (George Stibitz who designed the early Bell Laboratory machines was the main consultant), and different firms had to be contacted to provide evidence that organizations other than the Electric Control Company could offer bids on the contract. It was late in September of 1946 before a formal contract was signed between Eckert, Mauchly, and NBS and, even then, it was only for a $75,000 study into the specifications for a computer.

The study was to take only a few months. In reality it took the better part of a year before any proper results were available. Even when dealing with the NBS, rather than the Census Bureau, there were problems about getting the money to actually do the work. Once again the lawyers stepped in and pointed out that the NBS could contract out research, but that it could only pay when the research had actually been finished. Fortunately the NBS people were very understanding, broke the research study into a number of small parts, and paid out when each part was actually done.

The machine being contemplated was to be of the stored-program variety, with the initial study to be around the design of a serial mercury delay-line memory. It was initially called an EDVAC-type machine for the purposes of drafting the contract but, because of their friction with the Moore School, Eckert and Mauchly amended the agreement on May 24, 1947, to call it UNIVAC (UNIVersal Automatic Computer).

It had seemed obvious to Eckert and Mauchly that the design and construction of their machine would eventually cost about $400,000. When the Census Bureau could only manage to get $300,000, and then the NBS would only sign a "study" contract for $75,000, it looked like they might go bankrupt before they even got off the ground. The partners continued with the project only because they were sure that a market existed for these machines and that they could interest industrial firms in purchasing copies once one was functioning in the Census Bureau. The financial problems became so acute that they had to abandon their idea of a partnership and incorporate the firm in order to attract outside investors. They called the new firm the Eckert-Mauchly Computer Corporation. It came into being in December of 1948 with Mauchly as president because of his expertise in dealing with businessmen and government officials and Eckert as vice president and chief technical officer of the company.

In 1948 the NBS actually agreed to go ahead with the development work for UNIVAC and signed a contract. By that time the Eckert-Mauchly people were in a very awkward position. Because of the very limited income they had from the NBS contract over the last 18 months, they had searched around to find some other firm or agency that would be willing to keep the company alive until the UNIVAC development contracts would be awarded. Their search brought them into contact with the Northrop Aircraft Company, which agreed to fund the development of a Binary Automatic Computer (BINAC). In October 1947 Northrop signed a contract for the construction of a computer to be finished by May 15, 1948, and provided $80,000 development money with an additional $20,000 upon delivery of the machine. Had it been finished on time it would have been in contention with the British computers at Manchester and

Cambridge as the first working electronic stored-program computer. In reality it ran its first program in the late summer of 1949 and, as a consequence, became the first operational computer in America but not in the world.

Northrop had envisaged the BINAC as an experimental machine which might become the forerunner of a much smaller airborne guidance system for the Snark missile they had under development. In the end it saw very little use by Northrop; some employees even claim that, although it functioned in the Eckert-Mauchly workshop, it never ran when finally delivered. This has been disputed by a number of Northrop employees who indicate that it did run several small problems after it had been delivered to their California location, but that it was never in good enough shape to be used as a production machine. It would appear that a large part of the problem stemmed from the fact that Northrop took delivery in the Eckert-Mauchly workshop in Philadelphia and did not appreciate the fact that shipping a very sophisticated, highly experimental machine required more than simply building crates and calling in the moving men.

The BIN in BINAC stood for "binary" and this was significant in at least two respects. First, the design called for a serial machine which would be capable of performing high-speed arithmetic on binary numbers with no provision to store characters or decimal digits. Secondly, BINAC was really two machines in one; every part of the machine was constructed as a pair of systems to check each operation. Any instruction would be executed once by each unit, the result compared between the units and, if identical, the next instruction in sequence would be initiated. If any discrepancy was found between the two halves of the machine, it halted.

Mercury delay lines provided the memory, each half having a capacity of 512 words of 31 bits each. The design of the delay line was interesting in that only one large mercury tank was used; the individual delay lines were kept separate by means of a very high-frequency carrier signal which was capable of being constrained into a narrow beam of energy.

Besides the innovative approach of using two parallel machines to check each other and the one large tank design of the mercury delay lines, the BINAC was the first to employ magnetic tape as a secondary memory and auxiliary input device. The magnetic tape industry had just begun to develop plastic-based recording tapes for audio use, and these were incorporated into a unit they called a "converter" for use on BINAC. The experiment was important to the Eckert-Mauchly firm because the design of UNIVAC called for magnetic tape storage of data. The small plastic-based audio tapes proved to be unsatisfactory so Eckert-Mauchly redesigned the system to work with nickel-coated bronze tapes for the UNIVAC.

When Northrop took delivery of the BINAC in September of 1949 and paid Eckert-Mauchly the remainder of the $100,000 contract price, an accounting showed that the total costs of the machine had been $278,000. This, of course, left the Eckert-Mauchly firm in an almost bankrupt state, but it did

Figure 8–24. The BINAC computer in the Eckert-Mauchly factory. The two large upright cabinets contained the two central processing units, while the delay-line memory is in the rounded structure at the far left. (Photograph courtesy of the Sperry Corporation.)

indicate that they were capable of producing an electronic digital computer. The fact that they were able to show prospective clients some large sections of completed hardware resulted in their obtaining several orders for the still speculative UNIVAC. Three of the machines were destined for use by government agencies, two for use by the A. C. Nielsen Company in its accounting departments, and the final machine was for the Prudential Insurance Company which was having difficulties both in accounting and in the computing of new sets of actuarial tables.

Although the Eckert-Mauchly Company had received some small advances on these UNIVAC orders as well as some other investment money from the American Totalisator Company, its financial position remained very insecure. In an attempt to persuade firms to order copies of the UNIVAC, the company had lowered the prices of the machines to the point where they were unable to finance the ever growing demands for larger staff and workshops. The situation came to a head in late 1949 when it became obvious to even the most optimistic members of the firm that they were facing total bankruptcy. Finally in February of 1950 the Eckert-Mauchly Computer Corporation was sold to Remington-Rand who, while they retained the services of both Eckert and Mauchly, put one of their senior executives in overall charge of the operation. Mauchly later ran into problems of security clearance and had to be transferred to Remington-Rand's sales division. He later left to set up his own consultancy firm, but Eckert remained and eventually became a vice president of Sperry-Rand.

When Remington-Rand had determined that the contracts for UNIVAC were seriously underpriced, the firm attempted to have them renegotiated. The eventual result was the cancellation of both the Prudential and the A.C. Nielsen agreements while, because of legal difficulties, the three contracts with the government remained as they were originally written. The first UNIVAC was delivered to the Census Bureau on March 31, 1951, and the remaining two were shipped within the next 18 months. The UNIVAC thus became the second electronic computer to be produced under contract for a commercial customer, only being beaten by Ferranti's delivery of the Mark I to Manchester University

Figure 8–25. John Mauchly (left) and Pres Eckert (right) circa 1975. (Photograph courtesy of the Sperry Corporation.)

about a month earlier. A further 43 UNIVACs were produced for sale to both government and industry; these established Remington-Rand as the world's first large-scale computer company.

In keeping with the earlier Eckert-Mauchly machines (other than the EN-IAC), the UNIVAC was a serial machine based upon a mercury delay-line memory. The memory could store 1000 words of 12 alphanumeric characters (11 decimal digits plus sign) each with an average access time of 222 microseconds (maximum of 400 microseconds). Each of the 45 possible instructions could be stored in a half word, consisting of the operation code and a single address. There were four separate accumulators which could take part in arithmetic operations. The whole system was controlled by a 2.25 MHz clock which resulted in operation times of approximately 0.5 milliseconds for an addition, 2 milliseconds for multiplication, and 4 milliseconds for division—the actual time being dependent on the access time for the operands. Each arithmetic operation was checked by having the result computed by two independent arithmetic units, a design concept held over from the BINAC. Additional checks were done on data transfers by means of a parity bit on each character.

The final machine required over 5,000 vacuum tubes, arranged in a rectangular frame about 10 ft wide, 14 ft long and 9 ft high. A small door led into the interior of the chassis and allowed access for checking and replacement of the tubes. The initial models were all air cooled while later versions had a water cooling system. The UNIVAC remained in production, with a total of 46 installations, until 1957 when Remington-Rand replaced it with the more sophisticated UNIVAC II. In the meantime Remington-Rand had produced several other lines of computer equipment which developed from their later acquisition of Engineering Research Associates.

As mentioned earlier, the UNIVAC was designed for use with magnetic tape as the standard bulk data storage medium. Because of their earlier problems with plastic-based tapes, Eckert-Mauchly decided to use ½ in. wide nickel-coated bronze tapes. These were capable of recording data at 128 characters per inch and had an input/output speed of 12,800 characters per second. The tapes, although generally more reliable than the plastic-coated audiotapes used with BINAC, were subject to errors where the nickel coating had not properly adhered to the bronze. This problem was overcome by simply punching a hole directly into the bronze tape immediately before the error zone and, when a photocell detected the hole about to pass over the read/write head, the tape drive simply skipped the tape forward a few inches.

A complete set of peripherals for the UNIVAC consisted of UNITYPERS (electric typewriters) which were used as the main console control device, up to 10 UNISERVOS (magnetic tape units), and UNIPRINTERS which could copy information from the magnetic tapes to printers. A number of installations also opted for additional peripheral equipment to copy both the 80-column IBM and 90-column Remington-Rand punched cards to and from magnetic tapes, con-

Figure 8–26. The UNIVAC I computer being used to predict the 1952 presidential election. Here Walter Cronkite is being shown the machine by Pres Eckert. (Photograph courtesy of the Sperry Corporation.)

vert punched paper tape to and from magnetic tape formats, create magnetic tapes from electric typewriter input, and reproduce information from one magnetic tape to another.

One of the most dramatic events in the early days of computer usage took place on the evening of the 1952 presidential election. Several months earlier the CBS network had arranged to have a UNIVAC machine attempt to predict the outcome of the election based on a sample of the early returns. Various statistics were gathered and the programs written in preparation for the event. The actual runs were to be done on the fifth UNIVAC which was still on the construction room floor, but CBS set up a dummy control panel in their New York studios (with the control lights wired up to Christmas tree light flashers) just to give a convincing backdrop for the television audience. At 8:30 that evening, after only a very few results were available, the UNIVAC predicted a landslide victory for Eisenhower over Stevenson. Quick conferences between the computer people, election officials, and CBS resulted in the decision that something must be wrong and the risk of publishing this result was not worth taking. Several fudge factor constants were inserted into the routines but, again, UNIVAC predicted an overwhelming victory for Eisenhower. Again the system was checked and a further adjustment of some constants resulted in a more modest prediction of an Eisenhower win by only the small margin of 8 to 7. This prediction was eventually broadcast at 9:15 p.m. In fact, Eisenhower won by almost exactly the landslide first predicted by UNIVAC, and many television and computer people went to bed that night feeling very sorry they had not taken advantage of the publicity they could have had for the developing computer industry.

Eckert, Mauchly, and the engineers in their various companies went on to make further substantial contributions to the art of electronic computing. Although the entrepreneurial efforts of these two were always financial failures, the Eckert-Mauchly partnership was instrumental in the establishment of a viable computer industry in the United States, and their basic design ideas were to shape the developing Remington-Rand product line for many years to come. Seldom has a pair of individuals, while not making a success of their own business ventures, had such a tremendous impact on developments in their field.

8.4.5 The SEAC and SWAC Machines

The SEAC. In 1938 the United States government sponsored a depression relief program which included setting up a group of unemployed people to do the arithmetic tasks involved in creating new sets of mathematical tables. This project came under the direction of the National Bureau of Standards (NBS) in Washington, D.C. By 1945 the types of work being done by this group had changed so much that the NBS established a special division, the National Applied Mathematics Laboratories, to put the projects on a more secure administrative foundation. Part of the reason for founding this agency was the desire of the U.S. Navy to establish one national body which would provide leadership in the development of new computational technology as well as supply a service for performing large statistical and applied mathematical calculations. The Applied Mathematics Laboratories were to be divided into four almost independent groups; a Computation Laboratory, a Machine Development Laboratory, a Statistical Engineering Laboratory, and an Institute for Numerical Analysis. The first three were to be located in Washington while the Institute for Numerical Analysis was to be situated near the University of California in Los Angeles.

The earlier discussion of the Eckert-Mauchly computers has already indicated that the NBS was interested in obtaining a copy of the Eckert-Mauchly UNIVAC for use in the Applied Mathematics Laboratories. The impetus for NBS's interest in the UNIVAC had come from the Office of the Air Comptroller of the U.S. Air Force who had been developing a project known as SCOOP (Scientific Computing of Optimal Programs) to provide for the use of operations research techniques in military administration. One of the leading figures in operations research at that time was Dr. George Dantzig who grew very impatient at the length of time being taken by both Eckert-Mauchly and the IAS to bring their machines into operation. In late 1948 he managed to convince the Air Force that they should provide some extra financing to the Applied Mathematics Laboratories for them to produce a very small computer which would fill the need for computing power until either the IAS machine or the UNIVAC was operational.

The machine, initially known as the National Bureau of Standards Interim Computer but later called SEAC for Standards Eastern Automatic Computer, was to be of very modest proportions in order that it could be finished quickly. It was to use a mercury delay-line memory, to be purchased from the same people who were developing the EDVAC memory system, and was to have only simple numeric input and output capabilities. The input/output was initially so simple that it consisted of a single teletype with attached paper tape reader and punch, the communication being done in hexadecimal notation.

Every conceivable shortcut was taken in order for the design to be kept to a minimum. The instruction set was to be limited to a few variations on only seven basic instructions: fixed point addition, subtraction, multiplication, division, comparison, and input/output. The clock rate was to be kept down to one MHz in order to avoid any complications with very high-frequency circuits, and the memory was to only store eight words, of 45 bits each, in each of the 64 acoustic delay lines to yield a total capacity of 512 words. Because of the general suspicion that vacuum tubes were unreliable, even at the low clock rate to be used, the basic design called for them to be used only as amplification devices while all the logic gates and pulse reshaping circuits were to employ the newly developed germanium diodes. Even such critical circuits as short delay gates were avoided by the simple expedient of having very long wires wrapped into coils so that the required delay would be inherent in the time it took the pulse to travel through the wire. All these techniques resulted in a machine which, while containing only 750 vacuum tubes, required over 10,000 diodes. The major maintenance problem with the machine was not the usual one with tube failure, but with badly soldered joints on the diodes. A typical preventive maintenance technique was to shake the whole machine by jumping up and down on the wooden floors and seeing if this resulted in any failure of the diagnostic routines.

The original design of the SEAC was such that each instruction contained five fields: the operation, the address of the two operands, an address for where the result was to be stored, and the address of the next instruction to be executed. This last address was to permit the same type of optimum coding as was available on the Pilot ACE at the National Physical Laboratory in Britain. This scheme immediately led to two major problems: (1) the address fields were limited to 10 bits and consequently the maximum memory size could only be 1024 words, and (2) each 10-bit address required two and a half hexadecimal char-

Figure 8–27. Standards Eastern Automatic Computer (SEAC). Note the reel-less magnetic tape unit on the right. (Photograph courtesy of the National Bureau of Standards.)

acters to represent it on the input tape. The latter was the most serious problem because it meant that it was extremely difficult for programmers to accurately prepare their tapes. During the early stages of construction it was decided to add a series of ten toggle switches which could convert the machine from its standard four-address mode to a three-address mode which would allow for future memory expansion and easier programming. In its later years it tended to run for half the time as a four-address machine and for the other half as a three-address machine with larger memory capacity.

The NBS managed a demonstration of the machine in April of 1950, and one month later it was in full production solving an optical ray tracing problem. This made it the first fully operational machine in the United States, although the BINAC had actually run some test programs about nine months earlier. It remained in active service, with constant modifications and extensions, until shut off for the last time in 1964 after 70,254 hours of operation.

Several of the later modifications are interesting in that they enhanced the machine but tended to retain the elementary nature of the original design philosophy. The most notable of these were two different attempts to provide magnetic tape recording for the SEAC.

The first used small commercial dictating machine cartridges of magnetic wire to record programs and data. Information was initially punched on paper tape and then fed into a special machine which would record the data on the magnetic wire cartridge. The cartridge could then be read by SEAC at a rate of about 600 characters per second. Great care had to be taken when using this equipment because it took the magnetic wire almost two seconds to get up to speed and the user had to make sure that there was enough blank wire between records to allow for this time delay.

The second attempt at magnetic tape was equally ingenious. It involved the more standard form of magnetic tape but avoided the problems inherent in the design of mechanisms to control the take-up and supply reels. Two very simple glass-sided containers were mounted on either side of the read/write head and the tape simply spilled off the drive rollers into these baskets. The glass sides were mounted close together so that the tape would simply form loops on top of earlier loops and thus avoid any potential tangling problems. A problem did arise with the tape picking up a static charge as it rubbed over earlier loops, but this was solved by using special tape with a metallic backing and low-level radioactive isotopes to discharge the static as it built up. Up to 200 feet of tape could be accommodated in each container. The technique did not die out with the SEAC; RCA used a similar scheme as a buffer between the read head and the take-up reels, and at least one computer manufactured in the Soviet Union used the same type of containers for its very wide 2 in. magnetic tape.

The SWAC.   At the same time as the decision was taken to build SEAC, the NBS took the decision to set up their Institute for Numerical Analysis in Los Angeles. Harry Huskey who, a year earlier, had spent a year working on the Pilot ACE project at the National Physical Laboratory in Britain joined the Institute for Numerical Analysis in December 1948 and started the INA computer construction project in January of 1949. Huskey's British experience, combined with the fact that the NBS did not want to put all its hopes in only one type of computer design, resulted in Huskey's opting for a parallel type of machine based on the Williams' tube memory scheme developed at Manchester University. This would involve working with technology that had not yet proved itself, so the NBS insisted that the design be compatible with a magnetic drum as the main memory if the Williams' tubes proved unsatisfactory.

Like the SEAC, the SWAC (Standards Western Automatic Computer) was to serve as an interim machine until commercial models became available. Consequently, time was considered important and the design of the machine was still in progress when the basic construction of the chassis was begun. Fortunately Huskey's experience at the NPL and on the ENIAC proved its worth, and the design stages were kept far enough ahead of the construction crews so that nothing had to be torn down and reconstructed. Part of their ability to overlap the design and construction stages came from the fact that they were a small group (six engineers, four technicians, and Huskey) and thus the communication between the various subprojects was always easy.

Very early on, the SWAC crew decided that all the circuits would be constructed in small plug-in units containing only about ten tubes each, so that any problems could easily be isolated to very small sections of circuits and quickly replaced. Rather than construct special cathode ray tubes for the memory they decided to rely on commercially available units, and this resulted in some problems constructing an adequate memory. It had originally been proposed to have a parallel memory of 1024 words of 37 bits each, but they finally had to settle for only 256 words of main memory. The main difficulty was with microscopic flaws on the surface of the tubes. These were eventually traced down to tiny specks of carbonized lint embedded in the phosphor which had apparently come from the fact that the tubes were manufactured in a reconverted mattress factory. Another serious problem was the fact that the techniques developed for the serial Manchester memory to minimize the read-around problem were unsuitable for use in a parallel memory scheme.

Each instruction on the SWAC contained four addresses and thus took up a full word of memory. This tended to limit the complexity of programs because of the very small memory size, but this was alleviated by the addition of an 8,000 word magnetic drum which could transfer information to and from the main memory in 32-word blocks.

Programming was quite simple as there were only eight basic instructions available: add, subtract, multiply (both single and double length), comparison, data extraction, input, and output. The arithmetic system was quite interesting in that special care had been taken to design circuits which would very quickly propagate a carry through all 37 bits of a word. This required the use of very high currents which would create a severe drain on the power supplies when doing multiplication of a word which contained all ones. In fact the difference between the current required for multiplying all ones instead of all zeros could be as much as 15 amps. This was used to good effect in preparing diagnostic routines which would incorporate sequences of instructions to cause power shifts of as much as 20 amps every tenth of a second. It was felt that if the machine were able to pass these diagnostic tests, it would not fail when running similar production programs. SWAC was, in general, remarkably reliable for a first-generation machine. Some of the early programs required run times as large as a few hundred hours and were regularly run without undue difficulty.

When it was finally finished, in July of 1950, it was the fastest machine in the world. The parallel design and high-speed Williams' tube memory resulted in its being capable of adding together two numbers and storing away the result in only 64 microseconds while multiplication took only 384 microseconds. It retained its leadership in speed until the more sophisticated IAS machine was finished a year later. The SWAC continued to be used by the Institute for Numerical Analysis for both theoretical and practical calculations until the NBS decided to disband the Institute in 1954. It was then taken to the University of California at Los Angeles where it continued a productive life until late in 1967. Like the other early machines, it changed over the years with the addition of new facilities and modification of older ones. The most notable addition was a modified IBM punched card system capable of reading and punching the first 74 columns (two binary words) from each of 11 rows in the card.

Figure 8–28. Standards Western Automatic Computer (SWAC). The CRT storage system is contained in the large cabinet directly behind the console. (Photograph courtesy of the National Bureau of Standards.)

8.4.6 Project Whirlwind

The last early project to be described in the chapter, the Whirlwind computer developed at MIT, should be classed as one of the two or three most important projects undertaken prior to the mid-1950s. Although presented last in this litany of project descriptions, Project Whirlwind parallels the development of the computer itself in useful offshoots.

The start of the project came in 1943 when the head of the U.S. Navy Special Devices Division of the Bureau of Aeronautics, Louis de Florez, asked for some help from the MIT engineers to produce an airplane stability and control analyzer. De Florez had been involved in the development of several different flight training simulators during the war. He realized that if he could get a device which could be changed to simulate different types of aircraft it would speed up the training and give the Navy the opportunity to "test fly" experimental aircraft. What he had in mind was some form of fancy analog computer, much like the differential analyzers built at MIT by Vannevar Bush, which could be controlled to simulate different aircraft. The analog computer would then, in turn, control the simulator's response to the pilot's maneuvers.

When de Florez presented his ideas to the Servomechanisms Laboratory of MIT, a very bright young graduate student, Jay Forrester, was asked to look into the project. By October of 1944 Forrester had produced a rough plan for a one-year pilot study that would cost about $200,000. Even though the Navy was willing to spend almost any amount during the war years, they thought that it might be more prudent to fund a preliminary study project to the tune of only $75,000. Forrester soon found that the mechanisms needed for the simulator's cockpit were rather straightforward and posed no real problem; however, the control mechanisms for the simulator were another story entirely. Any of the analog techniques available were too slow to calculate the responses to a pilot's actions and control the flight simulator in real time. By May of 1945 the Navy, in desperate need to revamp its flight training, agreed to provide over $800,000 in order that Forrester's group could at least try to produce a workable device.

Things began to get worse and worse until Forrester happened to be talking to another graduate student, Perry Crawford, in September of 1945 and Crawford began describing how an electronic digital control system might be able to solve some of the speed problems inherent in the analog system. Forrester began to investigate this digital alternative and went to see the only electronic digital device at the time, the ENIAC, in November of that year. By late 1945 all work on the analog system had been abandoned and the design begun for a purely digital control system. This need for real-time speed was one of the major factors influencing the whole Whirlwind project and was to be both the major motivation and the largest stumbling block in the design of their equipment.

The first efforts were directed toward the design of a computer along the lines of the EDVAC being discussed at the Moore School. This was a serial machine but, because of the slow nature of the mercury delay-line memory, Forrester's group attempted to design a system based on similar ideas to the Williams' tube CRT memory. The main memory was to be read-only in nature, using punched cards placed in front of the CRT as the basic storage medium with a smaller read/write memory of more conventional design. Work on the design progressed until about the middle of 1946 when sample programs were devised in an attempt to see if the timing constraints of the simulator could be met. These were "executed" by a human who noted the times taken by each group of instructions for the proposed machine. Although the times were potentially within range of those required, the safety factor was small and the decision was taken to scrap this design and attempt to create a parallel machine in order to take advantage of the increased speed of operation of such a device. At about this time the Project Whirlwind staff were attending some of the talks being given at the Moore School lectures and these may have had some influence on the choice of machine design.

By now the war was over and the U.S. Navy was not so anxious to spend great sums of money for peace-time research, so a new contract was negotiated in which MIT agreed to construct a small pilot computer by the end of June 1947 (about a year away) and start on a full-sized machine only when the pilot project had shown some promise of actually being capable of controlling an airplane simulation. The chief engineer, Robert R. Everett, began to rough out block diagrams for the new machine. His ability to turn a theoretical idea into a realistic design was to be the source of a lot of the solutions to computer engineering problems in the next few years. Twenty years later Everett left MIT to become president of the Mitre Corporation when the group was set up to carry on the work of Project Whirlwind.

The design called for a parallel machine with a word length of 16 bits and a single-address instruction format. The memory was to be a special variant of the Williams' tube in which a mica wafer was mounted inside the tube to act as the electron gun target, rather than simply focus the beam on the standard phosphor surface. The 16-bit word length was chosen simply because team members thought they might like to have about 2000 words of memory, which would take 11 bits of address space in each instruction, and if they allowed for up to 32 operation codes it would take another 5 bits.

Being funded on a relatively lavish scale by the Navy, the MIT group had the luxury of being able to construct their own memory tubes and purchase specially designed vacuum tubes for much of the circuitry. These circuit tubes were, of course, very expensive but they did help to reduce both circuit design and maintenance problems. As can be seen from Figures 8–29 through 8–31, the construction details were not only very carefully designed but also executed on a lavish scale.

One of the many interesting construction details was that the machine was designed to run at different clock speeds. It could be debugged by gen-

Figure 8–29. The Whirlwind under construction, September 2, 1948. (Photograph courtesy of the MITRE Corporation Archives.)

erating clock pulses one at a time or it could run in production mode at the full clock frequency. This led to severe problems with the operation of flip-flop gates which tended to "forget" which state they were in if they were not pulsed at frequent intervals. Even under normal operating clock speeds it was conceivable that a particular flip-flop would not get used for long enough for trouble to set in. The solution finally adopted was to have the machine stop what it was doing every 20 microseconds, have a special pulse issued which would cause all the flip-flops to turn over, pulse them again to return them to their original state, then continue with the normal machine operation. This rather unorthodox design worked rather well, much to the surprise of many; however, it was eventually abandoned in favor of dc coupled gates which eliminated the flip-flop resetting entirely.

The changing needs from war-time aircraft simulation to peace-time research gradually began to be recognized by the Navy and in turn by the Whirlwind administration. In 1948 the decision was taken to abandon the concept of a control system for aircraft simulation and concentrate simply on the production of a working digital computer. The Navy was reducing its research budget and, by 1949, the Whirlwind project was consuming one tenth of the entire research budget of the Office of Naval Research. At this point the Navy took a hard look and decided that it had better things to do with its funds. Thus the financial side of the project came into a deep crisis for which there was no obvious solution. This was unfortunate because, by the beginning of 1950, the computer was actually operational, although a lot of work still remained in order for it to be classed as a fully developed system. For example, the memory only had a capacity of 256 words at this time and its speed was such that the design goal of 50,000 operations per second was reduced to 20,000 operations per second.

The early 1950s were a time of great concern for American military planners because of the possibility of attack by low flying long-range bombers. The air defense capabilities were such that it was impossible to coordinate the information from many different radar stations in order to detect and follow low flying aircraft. The Air Force was in desperate need of a system to manage its detection/interception problems, and Project Whirlwind was in equally desperate need of a financial backer. The real-time nature of the Whirlwind seemed well suited to the type of radar control problems that were being faced. The U.S. Government Air Defense System Engineering Committee got together with the Whirlwind engineers, and a simple demonstration soon convinced the Air Force that they should take over the funding for the Whirlwind.

For the new air traffic control project, the Whirlwind was fitted with a cathode ray tube which would display data obtained from a radar installation near Cape Cod. The CRT was connected, via two digital-to-analog converters, to two of Whirlwind's registers, and this allowed a program to generate a bright spot on the display simply by putting the coordinates into these two registers. Information could be written on the tube by sections of program which would

Figure 8–30. The Whirlwind control room, 1951. Jay W. Forrester (left) and Robert R. Everett (right) are standing. (Photograph courtesy of the MITRE Corporation Archives.)

display numerals as a sequence of dots. A light pen was also developed to enable an operator to select certain display features for further processing. Information came from the radar installation via telephone lines, but there was no easy way for Whirlwind to interrupt what it was doing and access this information as it arrived. The solution to this problem involved recording the radar data on a magnetic drum, so that when the computer had finished a processing step, it would read a track from the drum to get the latest radar update. This magnetic drum buffer was such a success that it was kept as part of the system when the Air Force developed its SAGE air defense system based on the Whirlwind. Several other additions were required in order to make the Whirlwind usable in its new role; chief among these was a second magnetic drum to hold the 20,000 machine code instructions required for the air control system, and the development of a magnetic core memory by J. Forrester.

The creation of a working magnetic core memory was, as has already been pointed out in the earlier section on computer memory systems, a fundamental turning point in the development of computer architectures. With the replacement of the electrostatic memory by Forrester's magnetic cores in 1952, the reliability of the machine reached such a high standard that it was possible to consider using it for actual air traffic control, and the basic speed of the machine had increased to reach its original design of 50,000 operations per second. Many demonstrations were put on for senior Air Force officers during which Strategic Air Command bombers would attempt to penetrate the Cape Cod system and Whirlwind would be used to give guidance information to intercepting fighter planes.

When the military decided that they should go all out to develop a

Figure 8–31. Jay. W. Forrester, Patrick Youtz, and Stephen Dodd check the operation of the electrostatic storage tubes on the Whirlwind. The tube on the right has had its magnetic shield removed. (Photograph courtesy of the MITRE Corporation Archives.)

continent-wide radar detection system, they moved a lot of the Whirlwind staff to the Mitre Corporation which had been specifically set up to construct the SAGE (Semiautomatic Ground Environment) Air Defense System. Rather than carry on with the construction of the military versions of Whirlwind, they were contracted out to International Business Machines. These machines were officially known by the Air Force designation of AN/FSQ7. This contract with IBM was one of the great influences upon that company and helped give the basic expertise that launched it as one of the world's leading computer suppliers in the mid-1950s.

It was the AN/FSQ7, rather than the initial Whirlwind, that really showed just how viable were the technical advances made during the early MIT days. It showed that it really was possible to design and construct a real-time, digital, magnetic core computer that would function under strict demands of both speed and reliability.

The AN/FSQ7 was the first full-production machine with a magnetic core memory, and the experience that IBM obtained in its construction was to play a big part in its subsequent commercial line of computers. It was also the first machine that kept a standby computer in reserve in case of machine failure. The standby AN/FSQ7 was kept powered up at all times, while the first machine recorded the current radar status information on a shared drum in order to ensure ultra-reliable service. This system resulted in an average of only 24 hours per year when at least one machine was not fully operational.

The first AN/FSQ7 began operation in 1958, and a total of 24 were eventually installed, often in underground bunkers. Each weighed 250 tons, contained 50,000 vacuum tubes, and had a 3,000 kilowatt power supply for its operation. Although the AN/FSQ7 was eventually outclassed by better technology, it provided the central air defense radar system computing for North America until the early 1980s.

FURTHER READING

BIGLOW, J. (1980). "Computer Development at IAS Princeton," in *A History of Computing in the Twentieth Century*, ed. N. Metropolis et al. New York: Academic Press, pp. 291–310.

BOOTH, A. D., and K. H. V. BOOTH (1953). *Automatic Digital Calculators*. London: Butterworths.

BOWDEN, B. V. (1953). *Faster than Thought*. London: Pitman and Sons Ltd.

BURKS, A. W. (1980). "From ENIAC to the Stored Program Computer: Two Revolutions in Computers," *A History of Computing in the Twentieth Century*, ed. N. Metropolis et al. New York: Academic Press, pp. 311–44.

BURKS, A. W., and A. R. BURKS (1981). "The ENIAC: First General Purpose Electronic Computer," *Annals of the History of Computing*, 39 (No. 4), 310–99.

CAMPBELL-KELLY, M. (1980a). "Programming the EDSAC: Early Programming Activity at the University of Cambridge," *Annals of the History of Computing*, 2 (No. 1), 7–36.

———. (1980b). "Programming the Mark I: Early Programming Activity at the University of Manchester," *Annals of the History of Computing*, 2 (No. 2), 130–68.

———. (1981). "Programming the Pilot ACE: Early Programming Activity at the National Physical Laboratory," *Annals of the History of Computing*, 3 (No. 2), 133–62.

ECKERT, J. P. (1944). "Report on the Magnetic Calculating Machine," excerpts reprinted in Stern *From ENIAC to UNIVAC*, N. Stern (Bedford, Mass.: Digital Press, 1981), pp. 28–75.

EVERETT, R. R. (1976). "*Whirlwind*," a lecture given at the Los Alamos Computer History Conference, June 10–15, 1976. (Reprinted in Metropolis et al.)

———. (1980). "Whirlwind," in *A History of Computing in the Twentieth Century*, ed. N. Metropolis et al. New York: Academic Press, pp. 365–84.

——· (1983). The SAGE system, *Annals of the History of Computing*, 5, (No. 4), entire issue.

GARDNER, W. D. (1976). "An Wang's Early Work in Core Memories," *Datamation*, March, pp. 161–64.

GIBBS, G. R. (1965), "The LEO I," *Datamation*, May, pp. 40–41.

GOLDSTINE, H. H. (1972). *The Computer from Pascal to von Neuman*. Princeton: Princeton University Press.

GOTLIEB, C. C., and J. N. P. HUME (1958). *High Speed Data Processing*. New York: McGraw-Hill.

HOLLINGDALE, S. H. (1959). *High Speed Computing—Methods and Applications*. Aylesbury: The English Universities Press Ltd.

HUSKEY, H. (1976), "The SWAC: The National Bureau of Standards Western Automatic Computer," a lecture given at the Los Alamos Computer History Conference, June 10–15, 1976. (Reprinted in Metropolis et al.)

——· (1980a). "The SWAC: National Bureau of Standards Western Automatic Computer," in *A History of Computing in the Twentieth Century*, ed. N. Metropolis et al. New York: Academic Press, pp. 419–32.

——· (1980b). "The National Bureau of Standards Western Automatic Computer (SWAC)," *Annals of the History of Computing*, 2 (No. 2), 111–21.

KILBURN, T. (1949), "The University of Manchester High Speed Digital Computing Machine," *Nature*, 164, 684.

LAVINGTON, S. H. (1976). "Computer Development at Manchester University," a lecture given at the Los Alamos Computer History Conference, June 10–15, 1976. (Reprinted in Metropolis et al.)

LUKOFF, H. (1979). *From Dits to Bits . . . A Personal History of the Electronic Computer*. Forest Grove, OR.: Robotics Press

METROPOLIS, N., and J. WORLTON (1980). "A Trilogy on Errors in the History of Computing," *Annals of the History of Computing*, 2 (No. 1), 49–59.

METROPOLIS, N., et al. (1980). *A History of Computing in the Twentieth Century*. New York: Academic Press.

PATTERSON, G. W. (1947). *Theory and Techniques for Design of Electronic Digital Computers*. The University of Pennsylvania, Moore School of Electrical Engineering, Report Number 47–21. (To be reprinted in 1985 by MIT Press, together with the versions of lectures that were not printed in 1947 because of security classifications.)

PINKERTON, J. M. M. (1954). "Operating and Engineering Experience Gained with LEO," in *Automatic Digital Computation*, Proceedings of a symposium held at the National Physical Laboratory, March 25–28, 1953, pp. 21–34. London: H. M. Stationery Office.

POLLARD, B. W. (1951). "The Design, Construction, and Performance of a Large Scale General Purpose Digital Computer," *Review of Electronic Digital Computers*, American Institute of Electrical Engineers, Proceedings of the Joint AIEE-IRE Conference held in Philadelphia, Dec. 10–12, 1951.

RAJCHMAN, J. (1951). "The Selective Electrostatic Storage Tube," *RCA Review*, March, pp. 53–87.

RANDELL, B. (1973). *The Origins of Digital Computers, Selected Papers.* New York: Springer Verlag.

REDMOND, K. C. and T. M. SMITH (1980). *Project Whirlwind: The History of a Pioneer Computer.* Bedford, Mass.: Digital Press.

SLUTZ, R. J. (1980). "Memories of the Bureau of Standards' SEAC," in *A History of Computing in the Twentieth Century,* ed. N. Metropolis et al., New York: Academic Press, pp. 471–78.

STERN, N. (1980). "The BINAC: A Case Study in the History of Technology," *Annals of the History of Computing,* 1, 9–20.

——— (1980). "John von Neumann's Influence on Electronic Digital Computing, 1944–1946," *Annals of the History of Computing,* 2 (No. 4), 349–62.

——— (1981). *From ENIAC to UNIVAC, An Appraisal of the Eckert-Mauchly Computers.* Bedford, Mass.: Digital Press.

TOMASH, E., and A. A. COHEN (1979). "The Birth of the ERA: Engineering Research Associates, Inc., 1946–1955," *Annals of the History of Computing,* 1 (No. 2), 83–97.

TURING, A. (1972). *A M. Turing's Original Proposal for the Development of an Electronic Computer.* Division of Computer Science, National Physical Laboratory.

VON NEUMANN, J. (1945). "First Draft of a Report on the EDVAC," Moore School report. Reprinted in From ENIAC to UNIVAC, ed. N. Stern (Bedford, Mass.: Digital Press, 1981), pp. 177–246.

WILKES, M. V. (1949). "The E.D.S.A.C.," *Report on a Conference on High Speed Automatic Calculating Machines, 22–25 June 1949.* Cambridge: University Mathematical Laboratory.

WILKES, M. V., WHELLER, D. J., and S. GILL (1951). *The Preparation of Programs for an Electronic Digital Computer.* Cambridge, Mass.: Addison-Wesley (Reprinted by Tomash Publishers, 1983.)

WILKES, M. V. (1951). "The EDSAC Computer," *Joint AIEE—IRE Computer Conference,* Dec. 10–12, 1951, Philadelphia.

——— (1952). "The EDSAC Computer," *Review of Electronic Digital Computers,* Proceedings of the Joint AIEE-IRE Computer Conference, Philadelphia, Dec. 10–12, 1951, pp. 79–83.

——— (1954). "The EDSAC," in *Automatic Digital Computation,* Proceedings of a symposium held at the National Physical Laboratory, March 25–28, 1953, pp. 17–20. London: H. M. Stationery Office.

——— (1956). *Automatic Digital Computers.* London: Methuen & Co.

——— (1975). "Early Computer Developments at Cambridge, " *The Radio and Electronic Engineer,* 45 (No. 7), 332–35.

WILKINSON, J. H. (1975). "The Pilot ACE at the National Physical Laboratory," *The Radio and Electronic Engineer,* 45 (No. 7), 336–40.

——— (1980). "Turing's Work at the National Physical Laboratory and the Construction of the Pilot ACE, DEUCE, and ACE," in *A History of Computing in the 20th Century,* ed. N. Metropolis et al. New York: Academic Press, pp. 101–14.

WILLIAMS, F. C. (1949). "Cathode Ray Tube Storage," in *Report on a Conference on High Speed Automatic Computing Machines,* July 22–25, 1949, ed. M. V. Wilkes (Cambridge, England: The University Mathematical Laboratory).

——· (1954). "MADAM, Automatic Digital Computation," Proceedings of a symposium held at the National Physical Laboratory, March 25–28, 1953. London: H. M. Stationery Office.

——· (1975). "Early Computers at Manchester University," *The Radio and Electronic Engineer*, 45 (No. 7), 327–31.

WILLIAMS, F. C., and T. KILBURN (1951). "The University of Manchester Computing Machine," *Review of Electronic Digital Computers*, American Institute of Electrical Engineers, (Proceedings of the Joint AIEE-IRE Conference held in Philadelphia, Dec. 10–12, 1951.)

——· (1952). "The University of Manchester Computing Machine," *Joint AIEE—IRE Computer Conference*, Dec. 10–12, 1951, Philadelphia.

WILLIAMS, F. C., and J. C. WEST (1951). "The Position Synchronisation of a Rotating Drum," *Journal, Institution of Electrical Engineers*, 98, part II (No. 61).

WOODGER, M. (1969). "In the Beginning. . . ," *Computer Weekly*, April 17, pp. 8–9.

9

Later Developments

9.1 INTRODUCTION

After the inital development of the electronic digital computer in various academic and research establishments, the main job of both innovation and production fell to the commercial sector. This was the case not only because of the free market economy but also because the vast amounts of capital and manpower that were needed were not readily available in the academic institutions. This was particularly the case in Britain where every effort was being made to recover from war-time setbacks, and the government simply did not have the resources to support advanced university research.

It is quite impractical to follow all the different organizations that opted for entry into the commercial development of computers. Even a list of their names would, besides being very tedious, take up about two pages, and to attempt a survey of their products would require a book at least as large as this one. As a consequence, this last chapter will examine only one line of equipment, that produced by IBM, with only occasional side trips to look at particularly noteworthy machines produced by other firms. This is not intended to imply that IBM were the leaders in the field—indeed they often were behind other, smaller firms in some of their product developments, but their story is typical of the kind of work that was going on in the larger organizations. The one other reason for following the IBM developments is, of course, because they have had such a huge impact on the computer industry.

IBM's involvement in computer development has spread into every sector of the industry, and it would be hard to find any computer product which has not been influenced by the IBM design philosophy or engineering standards. Their product line, even before 1960, consisted of several different scientific and business computers while, by the mid-1960s, they were actively selling about 20 different machines designed to fill the needs of various computer users. It is not only tedious to consider each of these machine lines in detail, but also a useless exercise because a lot of them were not of any great importance in the evolution of the computer. As a consequence, this chapter will examine the contributions of IBM by concentrating on their entry into the computer business with the NORC, 700 series and 7000 series machines. This leaves out a lot of the interesting material dealing with some of their other best-selling lines of commercial equipment—for example, the very useful workhorse computer known as the 650—and totally ignores the development of the small scientific computers such as the 1620 and 1130 machines.

After we look at the basic development of these lines of equipment, we devote a section to the abortive attempt at producing a few notable supercomputers. Here it is worthwhile to deviate from the strict IBM line to note the parallel development of the IBM STRETCH and UNIVAC LARC computers. Included also in this section is a discussion of the English ATLAS computer which, with its virtual memory and design for ease of implementation of the operating system, was to be quite influential in subsequent computer architecture.

The final section will deal with the advent of the IBM System/360 series of computers. This particular sequence of machines was to have such a corner on the market that many other firms brought out /360 look-alikes in order to cash in on their popularity. These look-alikes originated not only among competing domestic firms but could also be found in several foreign countries, the British ICL 2900 series and the Russian Riad computers being notable examples.

Obviously many other topics and trend-setting machines could have been considered here, but hopefully the ones we chose will give the reader some intimation of the progress of computer development between 1950 and 1965 while not overpowering with detail. Such fundamental advances as the development of the very large Control Data Corporation 6000 series, Digital Equipment Corporation's line of minicomputers, or the Canadian design of the

FP6000 which became the basis of the very successful British ICL 1900 series computers would also have made for fascinating reading. However, information on these machines is readily available in large libraries.

It is well known in the computer science field that programmers tend to think of the first machine they ever used as being one of the most interesting. Readers interested in the details of a particular device, say a CDC 6400, need only ask around until they find someone who was initially trained on the machine, and the chances are close to 100 percent that this person is willing to spend several hours extolling the glories of the 6400 and how all other machines are somehow inferior.

9.2 THE EARLY MACHINES OF IBM

9.2.1 The NORC

The NORC (Naval Ordnance Research Calculator) was not part of IBM's commercial line of machines but it did have an effect on the design of the first commercial machine, the IBM 701. Between 1946 and 1950 a research project was undertaken at IBM's Watson Scientific Computing Laboratory in Columbia University to see just how much progress could be made in electronic circuit design for digital computers. One of IBM's senior design engineers, Byron Havens, had been doing research into circuits capable of operating at speeds of less than a microsecond with the eventual goal of producing "the most powerful and effective calculator which the state of the art would permit."[1] Very few potential customers existed for such a device but the U.S. Navy's Bureau of Ordnance was having difficulty in solving large computational problems, mainly ballistic calculations, and they soon came to an arrangement with IBM to construct NORC. IBM had always cultivated the image of a company that was willing to offer its services in the national interest, and they continued with that policy by offering to produce the NORC on a nonprofit basis.

NORC was to be based on a memory consisting of 264 Williams' tubes which would store 3,600 words of 16 decimal digits each. The decimal digits were, of course, coded on the Williams' tubes in binary notation. Each word actually contained a 17th digit which was used as a check digit to catch errors when information was transmitted from one unit of the machine to another. In addition to each word of memory having a check digit, each column of information on the Williams' tubes also contained a check digit, and the pair of them could be used to locate and correct any single bit error in the memory. Reliability was a prime consideration and the result was a machine which was

---

[1] J. F. Brennan, *The IBM Watson Laboratory at Columbia University: A History* (Armonk, N.Y.: IBM, 1971), p. 26.

available 92 percent of the time, a record which was the envy of many installations for years to come.

NORC was capable of executing 15,000 operations per second. This speed was achieved through the combined effects of Haven's microsecond delay circuits and a very fast arithmetic unit that performed an addition in 15 microseconds and a multiplication in 31 microseconds. The multiply unit used the same type of design that we have already seen on the early mechanical machines, that of automatically producing all nine multiples of the multiplicand and then selectively adding these together, as required by the digits of the multiplier, to produce the final result. Because the NORC operated electronically rather than electromechanically, it was able to optimize this process so that all nine multiples were produced in parallel. A pipeline of 12 adders took the digits of these multiples and produced a single digit of the result each microsecond. All arithmetic operations were checked by independent circuits that performed a "casting out nines" process on the operands and the result to ensure reliable operation.

Various other pioneering efforts were done on the NORC design that were to yield dividends for future IBM machines. Chief among these was a memory control system, devised by the assistant manager of the project, W. J. Deerhake, which would largely eliminate the read-around problem usually encountered with the Williams' tube memory. This solution freed programmers from checking when their programs made repeated references to adjacent storage locations and thus simplified the actual operation of the system. A second major effort was to produce a quantum advance in the design of magnetic tape units. NORC was equipped with eight specially designed tape drives that were each capable of reading or writing 70,000 digits per second, five times faster than any other existing equipment. These tape drives, which recorded each digit as four binary bits across the tape, were designed at the IBM Poughkeepsie facility at about the same time as the tape drives for their commercial 700 series machines.

NORC was designed as a sequence of individual units to be constructed independently in various IBM installations by various subcontractors from the New York area. By the time it was fully finished it contained over 9,000 vacuum tubes, 25,000 diodes, and several hundred thousand other electronic elements. The parts were finally assembled in the Watson Laboratory of Columbia University in late 1953, and the whole machine, finished late in 1954, was presented to the Navy on December 2 of that year. Six months later it was moved to the Naval Proving Ground at Dahlgren, Virginia, where it was the main computing facility for three years. Although the Navy supplemented their facilities with the addition of more modern machines in 1958, the NORC continued in active use until 1968.

During the presentation ceremony, the NORC was demonstrated to the Naval officials by having it calculate the first 3,000 digits of π. John von Neu-

Figure 9–1. The NORC. (Photograph courtesy of IBM archives.)

mann, who by that time had been involved in computer construction for several years, was the guest speaker. He finished his speech by noting:

> In planning new computing machines, in fact, in planning anything new, in trying to enlarge the number of parameters with which one can work, it is customary and very proper to consider what the demand is, what the price is, whether it will be more profitable to do it in a bold way or in a cautious way, and so on. This type of consideration is certainly necessary. Things would very quickly go to pieces if these rules were not observed in 99 cases out of 100. It is very important, however, that there should be one case in a hundred where it is done differently. . . . That is, to do something that the U.S. Navy did in this case, and what IBM did in this case: to write specifications simply calling for the most advanced machine which is possible in the present state of the art. I hope that this will be done again soon and that it will never be forgotten.[2]

[2]Ibid., p. 29.

IBM was to wait for only a few years before attempting to follow von Neumann's advice and again try to produce a cost-no-object, state of the art computer known as STRETCH.

9.2.2 The 700–7000 Series Machines

When NORC was still in the design stage, IBM decided that they had sufficient resources to undertake up to three other electronic projects. At first the idea was to meet various needs by constructing individual machines aimed at different sectors of the defense industry. However, a quick tour of potential customers showed that a large number of them had almost identical problems, so the strategy became one of concentrating the resources in order to design a single machine which could be produced in quantity and used by a number of different firms. As most of the potential customers for this device were government defense agencies, and the original mandate of the team had been to look into special machines that could be useful in the Korean War effort, the project was called the Defense Calculator. It was estimated that about $3,000,000 would be needed to design and construct a prototype engineering model. With this figure in mind, a rough estimate of the rental of such a machine was developed, and the industrial and government agencies again canvassed to determine the potential market. Much to everyone's amazement they quickly received 30 letters of intent, and IBM started a crash program to produce what eventually became known as the 701 computer.

The decision to produce the 701 was made in 1951, although a lot of the ground work had been done earlier. For example, the engineering side of IBM had actually built a computer, called the Test Assembly, that consisted of an IBM 604 arithmetic unit with a Williams' tube memory and small drum. The Test Assembly was operational by September of 1950, and this gave the engineers confidence that things such as a Williams' tube memory were not beyond their capabilities. Another early research project was a study of the use of magnetic tape to replace the standard IBM punched card. The early summer of 1950 saw the completion of a design for an experimental Tape Processing Machine which incorporated not only experimental magnetic tape units but also a simple electronic computer to drive them. The early work on the NORC had provided IBM with the elementary high-speed pulse circuits designed by Havens, and these were incorporated into the arithmetic and control unit designs. All of this preparatory work gave IBM a substantial advantage over its competition in the design of a new computer. It meant that the first 701 was ready less than two years after the project was formally approved.

By the spring of 1952 the design and production of the first 701 units were well enough advanced that it was obvious the initial estimated rental of $8,000 per month was seriously low. New calculations showed that the rental would have to be about $15,000 per month. Because of the cost adjustment, only five of the original 30 orders were reconfirmed (most of the others were reconfirmed later), but this was enough to start the actual production. The first of the production machines was shipped from the Poughkeepsie factory to IBM World Headquarters in New York during the last week of 1952. It was set up in the space formerly occupied by the SSEC.

The 701 was a parallel binary machine whose basic design followed that of the von Neumann computer at the Institute for Advanced Study. Rather than use the elementary peripheral equipment of the IAS machine, IBM opted for card readers and punches as the basic input/output devices with modified accounting machine printers (150 lines per minute), a magnetic drum backing store, and magnetic tapes for bulk data storage. The hardware was deliberately kept as simple as possible with no provision for floating-point operations, indexing, or the automatic conversion from decimal to binary or binary to decimal. The engineers realized that these omissions would probably result in later modifications and, therefore, left at least 25 percent of the space in each of the major units empty to accommodate engineering changes.

As with many of the early machines, the memory for the 701 proved to be the most troublesome unit in both the manufacture and operation of the computer. It consisted of multiple Williams' tube electrostatic memory units having a total capacity of 4096 words of 36 bits each, although the machine could be obtained with only 2048 words if the customer wished. Several schemes were incorporated in an effort to reduce the read-around problem, the most interesting being to have adjacent addresses stored in physically different portions of the tubes. Since most programs contain sequences of instructions that are in logically adjacent addresses and access data from nearby groups of memory words, this scheme aimed at ensuring that sequential memory accesses were scattered over the surface of the tubes. When the first memory unit was under test, it would perform very well for several minutes at a time, then suddenly corrupt all its information. The problem was eventually traced to the use of wire-wound resistors in the circuits controlling the electron beam deflection. The very fast switching times would induce large voltage transients in the resistor coils, and these would occasionally short across the wire insulation. When higher quality resistors were used, the memory worked well, although it had the usual problems associated with any cathode ray tube system.

The Williams' tubes were mounted so that their faces were visible through glass doors on the front of the unit. This easy visual access to the contents of the memory was the cause of acute embarrassment during the formal unveiling of the machine in the spring of 1953. The usual group of dignitaries and press people had been invited for the occasion. The 701 was demonstrated, speeches were made, and the IBM engineers responsible for ensuring a faultless performance of the machine were just beginning to relax when a press photographer decided to take a close-up of the front of the memory tubes. When his flashbulb went off, the entire memory system reset itself to random bit patterns. After this episode all the 701 memory units were fitted with darkened glass panels to prevent such accidents in the future.

If we don't count the first engineering prototype, there were a total of nineteen 701s installed. The first went to the IBM World Headquarters in New York late in 1952, and the last was delivered to the U.S. Weather Bureau early in 1955. The majority of these units were used by the military or defense-related corporations: Three went to atomic energy laboratories, eight to aircraft companies, three to large corporations, two to government agencies, and two to the U.S. Navy. Hundreds of people, from aircraft engineers to Navy supply clerks, who had never seen a computer before were suddenly confronted with the need to find out how these devices operated. Bits of software, originally written in binary machine code, were exchanged among installations, and techniques developed at one site were soon finding their way to other users. The first elementary attempts at producing assemblers soon developed into larger projects involving more and more sophisticated translating schemes, and a whole new software industry came into being. Users of the 701 later formed the backbone of the organization known as SHARE, which was responsible for both the dissemination of software and applying pressure on IBM to produce more useful general software products.

By May of 1954 seventeen model 701s had been delivered to customers,

Figure 9–2.   The IBM 701 installed at IBM World Headquarters, New York, 1952. (Photograph courtesy of IBM archives.)

and IBM had plans to produce a successor machine, the 704. The eighteenth 701 was a late order and was initially refused because the production line had already been shut down, but IBM was pressured to construct it out of leftover spare parts. The concurrent development of the SAGE computers had shown that magnetic core memories were not only more reliable than the Williams' tube, but could be produced for about the same cost as the electrostatic systems. This led to the introduction of a modified 701, initially called the 701A but later changed to the 704, which was to be based on magnetic core memory and have full floating-point arithmetic and three index registers. A number of 701 customers opted simply to replace their electrostatic memory with the new magnetic core unit, but firms wanting to order a new machine were forced into purchasing the 704.

The switch to the more easily programmed 704 (the 704 had 75 different instructions available as compared to 33 on the 701) paved the ground for one of the most important developments of the early computing industry. John Backus had been employed in various capacities at IBM since the days of the SSEC and thus was in a good position to see the developing needs of programmers. He was also familiar with some of the early assemblers that had been available on both IBM's 701 and the other early computers produced by UNIVAC and with the loaders available on machines such as the Cambridge EDSAC. He asked for some time and resources to spend on a project to develop a translator for taking mathematical formulae and converting them into machine code to be run on the 704. Fortunately Cuthbert Hurd, a senior IBM administrator and manager of the 700 series projects, agreed and Backus went on to develop FORTRAN. The story of software projects such as this is unfortunately not within the scope of this work, but interested readers will be able to find many references to these developments in the literature cited in the last few sections of this book.

As the first 701 was being delivered to IBM World Headquarters in early 1953, needs were beginning to be expressed for a commercial data-processing machine to match the 701's scientific calculating speeds. In part, IBM's response to these needs can be viewed as a way of offering competition to UNIVAC, which was gaining a foothold in the larger data-processing institutions. Although the 701 was a good machine for scientific work, it was not easy to program it for the manipulation of character-based, variable-length records. In September 1953 IBM announced the development of the 702, a serial, character-oriented machine with a variable word length.

Engineering on the 702 proceeded slowly, so that the first machine was only delivered to a customer in 1955, several years after UNIVAC had been readily available. A total of only fourteen 702s were produced, but the machine did help to establish certain features that were to remain a part of the computer scene for many years. Foremost among these was the development of a new tape drive which set a very high standard for commercial plastic-based magnetic tapes. It could store twice as much information as the tape drives associated with the 701 and transfer it to and from the computer at twice the data rate. This one development was responsible for the entire industry's finally abandoning the metal-backed tapes used on the UNIVAC and switching to IBM-style tape units.

As with the 701, the 702 went through a process of technology upgrading to incorporate the latest forms of memory and a more sophisticated instruction set. The result was known as the 705 and this version of the machine sold very well. Initially, 95 of the machines were installed, beginning in 1956, but two further upgrades of the 40,000-character memory (to 60,000 characters in 1957 and 80,000 characters in 1959) resulted in the installation of a further 63 and 32 machines, respectively.

The constant advance of technology, particularly with respect to the production of higher speed memories and the ability to control transfers to and from peripheral devices concurrently with the execution of programs, led to one further development in the 700 series. In January of 1957 IBM announced a further modification of the 701–704 machines to be known as the 709. This was a very high-speed parallel scientific computer that quickly started replacing the earlier machines when the first deliveries began in 1958. It was essentially "upward compatible" with the earlier 700 series scientific machines but incorporated a great many technological changes that made it both faster and more reliable. Reliability is, of course, only relative, and the fact that vacuum tubes were still being used in the circuits meant that more than one of these machines were known to have caught fire at an awkward moment, usually when processing a critical job for which the results were needed the next morning at the latest.

Figure 9–3.   The IBM 705, circa 1954. (Photograph courtesy of IBM archives.)

The advent of the transistor dramatically changed the way in which computers were assembled but did not at first affect much in their organization. The transistor was invented in 1948 and thus had been around from very early in the computer era, but there were many problems to be solved before transistors could be employed on a large-scale in computer construction. Philco Corporation was the first to employ high-speed transistors in their 1958 production of a machine known as the Transac S-2000, and UNIVAC was not far behind with the development of a transistor machine for military uses. In response to a request for a high-speed transistor computer for use on the Ballistic Missile Early Warning System, IBM initially produced a version of the 709 known as the 709TX. This was quickly developed for their commercial market as the IBM 7090. It ran about five times as fast as the 709 with, of course, much fewer problems for the user in the way of power supplies and air-conditioning requirements.

Once the switch to transistor circuitry was underway, most of IBM's earlier machines were redesigned to take advantage of the newer technology. In order to meet the demand for a scientific machine cheaper than the 7090, the 7040 and 7044 machines were brought on the market, and the customer's data-processing needs were met by redesigning the 705 to produce the 7080. Each of these machines went through its own particular evolution in the next few years; the 7090, for example, was again upgraded to a machine known as the 7094.

As faster and faster transistor-based machines were being produced, the slowness of peripheral devices such as card readers and line printers was felt as an impediment to the overall processing speed of the system. This led in 1960 to the development of separate, stand-alone computers such as the 1401, whose job was simply to load data onto magnetic tape and copy results from tape to the line printer. As more and more jobs were assigned to these smaller

Figure 9–4. The IBM 7090. (Photograph courtesy of IBM archives.)

machines, a whole separate line of machines came into being, from the simple 1401 to the massive 1410 and 7010 computers.

Any computer company that was able to survive into the 1960s either tended to develop along the same lines as IBM or concentrated its efforts on special applications such as process control, complex scientific calculators, or smaller business-oriented machines. Thus by the early 1960s the major firms all had several different incompatible lines of equipment, often with several versions of each machine in the line, while the smaller corporations contented themselves with one or two machines designed for special-purpose applications. All of this was to change with IBM's announcement of System/360 in 1964, but first we should go back a bit and look at some abortive attempts to produce super-computers.

9.3 EARLY SUPER-COMPUTERS

9.3.1 The Stretch

In 1955, when IBM had finished the NORC and was just switching from their 701–702 line to the 704 and 705, they initiated a research project to determine the possibilities of constructing a computer at least a hundred times as powerful as anything yet made. The impetus behind the project came from the Los Alamos Scientific Laboratory of the U.S. Atomic Energy Commission, whose need for computation power could not be met by anything currently available. Rather than start on a one-of-a-kind machine, as they had done with the NORC, IBM decided to enter the project with commercial objectives in mind and formally called the machine the IBM 7030, with the intention that it fit into their 7000 series line of processers. Informally it was always known as "Stretch."

Stretch was the first major IBM product to be designed with transistor electronics. IBM had been one of the leaders in the development of disk storage technology with their introduction of the RAMAC 305 random-access disk system in 1957, and the Stretch designers took advantage of this in their creation of special random-access disk drives. Additional fundamental advances were made in the areas of high-speed magnetic core memory and sophisticated pipeline processing of instructions. All of these techniques were to appear in later IBM production computers.

The switch to high-speed transistor circuits increased the basic processor speed by a factor of 10 over the 704, and the 2-microsecond core memory was about six times faster than that on the 704 or SAGE systems. This was still not enough to result in a two-orders-of-magnitude speed increase over earlier systems so the designers decided to take advantage of the fact that memory tends to be idle during parts of the instruction decoding process and also during parts of the actual arithmetic operations. This spare time was utilized by devising a special instruction look-ahead scheme which would start the decoding and execution of one instruction and then go on to access and partially decode the following five instructions in memory. It is always the case that the instruction being executed could either modify or entirely eliminate the need for some of the next five instructions, thus the control scheme had to be extremely complex to allow for the possibility of abandoning one of the six instructions during the time that it was being executed.

This philosophy of overlapping the operations of the machine extended to all the basic components. The memory was split into multiple banks, each with its own access circuits, and logically adjacent memory locations were actually stored in different banks. This meant that, although the cycle time for each memory bank was 2 microseconds, it was possible to fetch instructions or data every 0.5 microsecond on average. Further enhancement of the system resulted from having a special memory control processor to coordinate the transfer of information between the peripherals and the memory banks without interrupting the main machine and also to "prefetch" any information it thought might be required. This resulted in new information being accessible once every 0.2 microseconds.

The arithmetic unit was as complex as the others, with both serial and parallel arithmetic circuitry. The parallel unit would process the majority of the floating-point arithmetic, while the serial unit would take care of the exponents of the numbers. There were two basic forms of instructions on the Stretch—those that dealt with fixed-length operations and those that dealt with variable-length operations. The fixed-length operations were ones that manipulated a 64-bit word as a unit, and the variable-length instructions would specify the starting and ending bits of a "byte" to be used as an operand or result. These bytes could extend across a word boundary if necessary. The serial nature of the byte operations required the construction of additional special-purpose serial arithmetic units. Because the different units operated independently, the whole machine had to have 3,000 different internal registers and over 450 separate arithmetic circuits.

The result was a very powerful machine with the most complex electronic circuitry that had ever been attempted. As can be seen from the following table, the goal of two-orders-of-magnitude increase in speed was achieved for some arithmetic operations as compared to the 704 but not managed at all for the variable-length operations as compared to the 705.

| Operation | Time in microseconds | | |
	IBM 704	IBM 705	Stretch
Floating add	84	—	1
Floating multiply	204	—	1.8
Floating divide	216	—	7
Five-digit add	—	119	3.5
Five-digit multiply	—	799	40
Five-digit divide	—	4828	65

The first Stretch was delivered to the Los Alamos Laboratories in 1961; subsequently seven others were shipped to high technology centers in England, France, and the United States. Almost all of these were used in atomic energy agencies or defense-related industries. One of the Stretch machines was modified to include a special device for manipulating alphabetic characters, and the result, known as the Harvest machine, was used by the U.S. National Security Agency in their code-breaking work. Most of these machines continued to give useful service until the early 1970s when they were replaced by more modern equipment.

Besides the advances in technology and organization that have already been described, Stretch was responsible for several other innovations that became standard on computers produced in later years. The disk drives developed for the project were the first to incorporate multiple read/write arms in a single movable system, and their capacity (2,000,000 words) and high-speed data transfer rates were far in advance of any competing product. Almost all computers manufactured after Stretch abandoned the use of a drum for high-speed backing store and switched to the removable disk pack format. In connection with disk development, techniques of encoding the information were produced so that any single error was automatically corrected before the information was transferred to the main machine.

Stretch was also responsible for a quantum leap in the actual design and

Figure 9–5. An overall view of the Stretch (IBM 7030), circa 1960. (Photograph courtesy of IBM archives.)

construction of computer electronics. The IBM 704 was used to simulate the different aspects of the instruction look-ahead system, and the final design was based on the results of that simulation. In addition, the 704 was used to design the back panel wiring diagrams and produce the instruction tapes for the automatic wiring machines. Because of the huge size of the system, methods were developed to automatically assemble and test the individual printed circuit boards. This not only speeded up the construction but also added to the reliability of the final product.

The first Stretch would have been delivered to Los Alamos in late 1960, rather than 1961, except for the intervention of the U.S. Air Force. We have already described how IBM produced their first transistorized version of the 709, the 709TX, in answer to the need for powerful machines to run the Ballistic Missile Early Warning System. In order to accommodate the production of the

Figure 9–6.   A close-up of the Stretch technical control panel. (Photograph courtesy of IBM archives.)

709TX, the Stretch project was put on hold for a few months while the advanced production facilities were devoted to the creation of what eventually became the 7090.

Because Stretch failed to meet its goal of two-orders-of-magnitude increase in speed, it never really became a financially viable product for IBM. It was the intention that Stretch become the largest member of a new line of equipment which united the scientific processing capability of the 704 and 709 with the data-processing capability of the 705, but that scheme had to wait a few years until the advent of the System/360.

9.3.2 The LARC

During the late 1950s UNIVAC was the only large firm in a position to compete effectively with IBM in the production of both large and small computers. When IBM started the Stretch project, UNIVAC also looked into the possibility of producing a machine in the super-computer class. Just as with IBM, the pressure to develop such a system came from one of their atomic energy customers, the Lawrence Radiation Laboratory in Livermore, California. Thus the LARC (Livermore Atomic Research Computer) was destined for the same types of uses as the Stretch.

Most of the large computers had either been designed for scientific computing, with fixed word length and floating-point arithmetic, or for data-processing applications with memory subdivided into character-sized bytes. The Stretch was the first big machine to combine both fixed- and variable-length word sizes in one machine, and the LARC was perhaps the last big project to be designed around a decimal-only memory storage scheme. The memory was divided into independent banks, as in Stretch, with each bank capable of storing 2,500 words of 12 decimal digits (11 digits plus sign) each. The basic LARC system contained eight banks for a total of 20,000 words of storage, but it was possible to add extra banks to bring the total up to 97,500 words if necessary. With the eight basic overlapped units it was possible to provide access to a memory word every 0.5 microseconds on average.

The basic system was composed of two essentially independent computers, one for controlling the input and output operations and the other dedicated to performing the arithmetic. Provision was made for an additional arithmetic processor to be added to the system if further performance enhancements were required. The arithmetic units could execute a floating-point addition instruction in 4 microseconds, while floating-point multiplication took only 8 microseconds. The machine was thus somewhat slower than its Stretch equivalent but was still better than an order of magnitude faster than most other computers available at the time. It was certainly far superior to the 1103A (UNIVAC's fastest machine when LARC was proposed in 1956) which was itself slightly faster than the IBM 704, but perhaps not quite as reliable.

Rather than rely on the new technology disk drives, UNIVAC utilized their

Figure 9-7. The LARC computer at the Lawrence Livermore Radiation Laboratory. (Photograph courtesy of the Lawrence Livermore Radiation Laboratory.)

own expertise in high-speed drums for the LARC. It was possible to install up to 24 drums, each capable of storing 250,000 words, but only two drums were really necessary. By storing adjacent drum tracks on alternate drums it was possible to keep up a continuous transfer of information to and from the main memory of about 2,500 words in 80 milliseconds.

The LARC was a technical success in that it really was a much faster machine than anything in the UNIVAC line but, like the Stretch, the manufacturing costs were so high, and the potential customer demand so low, that UNIVAC decided it could not support it as a regular part of its offerings. Only two LARCs were ever installed, the first at the Lawrence Radiation Labs in 1960 and the second at the U.S. Navy Research and Development Center in Washington, D.C., a short time later. Both machines continued in active use until 1969.

It is only natural to compare Stretch and LARC because they were both projects far in advance of the current state of the industry and both were destined for atomic energy research establishments. However, this is not quite fair. LARC was a project which, in 1956, had its design built around components (such as the surface barrier transistor and 4-microsecond magnetic core memory) which were either readily available or well known to laboratory engineers. Stretch, on the other hand, was conceived as a machine which would rely on components still very much in the experimental stage of their evolution—for example, the drift transistor and 2-microsecond core memory. This difference of approach resulted in two very different machines, but both were tremendous technological achievements that led to many innovations in both companies' commercial computing machines.

9.3.3 The Atlas

For the last of our super-computer stories we must return to England and take up the story of computing machine design at the University of Manchester. After Fred Williams and Tom Kilburn had produced their initial machine, Ferranti Ltd. joined with them to produce several commercial computers, chief among them the "Greek" series of machines known by the names Mercury, Pegasus, Orion, and so on. This combination of university research under Tom Kilburn with the production facilities of Ferranti was particularly fruitful, producing many different machines for both scientific, commercial, and military users in Britain.

In 1956 a team under Tom Kilburn began to investigate the possibility of constructing a very powerful machine, known as Atlas, of about the same class as Stretch or LARC. The Atlas followed its American cousins in that it was not a commercial success, but a number of innovations in its architecture were to be very influential in later developments. Among the most interesting features on Atlas were the provision of a virtual memory scheme and the idea of an "extracode" instruction—essentially a system interrupt to a section of code, usually kept in a special section of read-only memory that was part of the kernel of the operating system. These, along with a few other minor innovations of Atlas, were to become fundamental for the design of large computing systems in the mid-1960s.

Kilburn realized that to have a very high-speed machine he had to have access to very large amounts of memory. The prototype of the Atlas could address a memory space of 1,000,000 words of 48 bits each. Attempting to provide a full magnetic core implementation of this size was beyond the budget of any computer development project in the late 1950s. Previous machines had partially solved the memory size problem by providing a high-speed drum, but this required the programmer to read and write information to and from the drum as it was needed. The Atlas departed from this philosophy by having a real core memory of only 16,000 words and a drum of a further 96,000 words which would automatically swap information with the core memory as required.

The main memory was subdivided into 512 word "pages," and associated with each page was a page address register which contained the address of the block of information that was currently occupying that physical location in memory. Every time the computer wanted to access a word, the address of the required word was automatically compared to all the page address registers to see if that word was currently in the main memory. If the word was found, access was granted. If the word was not currently in main memory, a special interrupt would suspend the program execution, and an automatic transfer would take place to retrieve the required page from the high-speed drum.

Even though the examination of the page registers was performed in hardware, it did slow down the processing of instructions. In response to this problem, a special arrangement was made so that accessing the next instruction would not cause the page registers to be checked. Another system coped with the occasional errors generated by attempting to access an instruction across a page boundary. A special learning program kept track of which pages were swapped in and out of the core memory and attempted to choose which page to swap, depending on the past performance of the application program.

Because a program could be suspended during a drum transfer caused by a page interrupt, the Atlas had to be designed from the beginning as a time-shared computer capable of having several different jobs in its memory at any given instant, automatically switching from one to another as the information demanded by a particular process became available. All of the checks that had to be made to keep one job from accidentally corrupting another resulted in a control unit of great complexity but, even with all this overhead, the Atlas was remarkably efficient. If the job mix was chosen carefully, it could achieve over 80 percent utilization of the central processing unit. Some later machines, particularly the first versions of the IBM /360/67, only managed to utilize about 8 percent of their CPUs!

Kilburn's team realized that they would need a very complex operating system for their machine so they incorporated a number of design features to allow for both the easier creation of the operating system and for higher efficiency during running time. The most important design feature was an "extracode" which could be called from a production program via a software interrupt. There was a read-only memory of 8,000 words which was composed of a wire mesh into which ferrite rods were inserted. The design, usually referred to as a "hairbrush" memory, contained the central kernel of the operating system. These routines were normally available for use by production programs and included arithmetic routines, such as sine and log functions, as well as the usual types of jobs necessary for controlling peripherals, overseeing storage allocation, accounting, and other operating system functions. These extracode routines could access a special high-speed (1.8 microsecond cycle time) scratch-pad memory for their own use. This, combined with the fact that the "hair brush" memory cycle time was only 0.4 microseconds, resulted in ultra fast execution of the basic underlying software of the machine. The concept of the extracode was immediately taken up by many designers and appeared in many subsequent machines. The IBM System/360 operating system supervisor calls (SVCs) stems directly from the Atlas extracode concept.

Just as in Stretch and LARC, the speed of Atlas was obtained by extensive overlapping of the instruction times in the independent units of the computer. The machine not only had a very fast arithmetic unit, but also had an entirely separate set of arithmetic circuits for performing the address calculations involving the index registers, which Manchester persisted in calling "B lines"—the notation developed on the original Manchester computer of 1948. Each single address instruction contained the possibility of the address being modified by two "B lines"—a base register and an index register—so this part of the instruction decoding process had to be extremely fast in order to keep the machine operating at maximum speed.

Atlas fell between the Stretch and the LARC as far as the individual instruction execution speed was concerned. A floating-point addition would take between 1.4 and 2 microseconds depending on the number of "B line" modifications that were done to the address. Multiplication was 4.7 microseconds, and floating-point division required 13.6 microseconds. In any computer system the number of floating-point operations done is usually less than the number of "housekeeping" instructions needed for indexing arrays and so forth. When this is taken into consideration, the very fast index registers and integer arithmetic ciruits gave the machine an overall speed of about one instruction execution every 2 microseconds.

There were 128 index registers, of which 90 were available to the applications programmer, 30 reserved for use by the extracode routines, seven for use by the hardware for control purposes, and the last, register B0, always contained the constant zero. One hundred twenty of these registers were constructed from special high-speed core memory components with a switching time of only 0.7 microseconds, while the last eight were electronic flip-flop registers with essentially zero access time.

As mentioned earlier, Atlas was not a commercial success. Only three Atlas machines were ever installed, one at the University of Manchester in 1962, a second at the University of London in 1963, and the third at Atlas Computer Laboratory at Chilton in 1964. The Chilton installation was used as a service bureau by a number of British universities and research establishments. It was the largest of the Atlas machines, with 48,000 words of main core memory and 30 magnetic tape decks for bulk storage of information. All three machines were heavily used for about nine years.

A slightly smaller version of the Atlas, known as the Titan or Atlas 2, was produced with larger main memory and no paging drums. Three of these machines were installed, one at Cambridge University, one at the Computer Aided Design Centre in Cambridge, and the last at the Atomic Weapons Research Establishment at Aldermaston.

Atlas proved that it was possible to have a multiprogramming machine with a paged memory and sophisticated operating system. It was a technical achievement of great importance and one which set the standard for very large computer systems for a number of years. It is unfortunate that one of the planned abilities of Atlas, the use of individual time-sharing terminals, was scrapped in the early design phase because of budget limitations. Had this been incorporated into the machine, we would likely have seen the mass-produced time-shared computer system being commercially available a few years earlier than it actually was.

9.4 THE IBM/360 SERIES OF MACHINES

By 1959 IBM, like many of the other larger computer corporations, particularly those that had grown by absorbing smaller firms and their product lines, was beginning to face real difficulties with the fact that they had a very wide range of computers installed in a diverse customer base. Each customer was essentially bound to the machine that they were using with little or no room for growth. It was true that the 709 user could migrate to the 7090, and later to the 7094, when more computer power was needed, but this migration was often difficult because of the slightly different hardware specification of the machines, different peripherals available on each, and the different software products that made a transparent switch anything but a simple matter of exchanging one box of electronics for another.

Another problem that was starting to cause concern was the fact that the vast majority of computers available on the open market were designed for efficient operation in only one of the two major applications areas, either commercial data processing or scientific computation. Typical users were finding that their scientific staff was recognizing a need for data manipulation and file control facilities found on commercial machines, while their sales and production staffs were starting to use the developing operations research methods that presumed massive amounts of scientific calculations. It was very often impossible even to transfer data between several machines used in one firm, let alone develop programs on one which would run on another. Any attempt to reconcile the differences in design between commercial and scientific models had usually resulted in machines which would do neither job well. The occasional design which seemed to have some merit would usually fall through the cracks when the designing firm was absorbed into the ever-growing major corporations or, if it was the child of a major group, not enough effort was ever put into the creation and marketing to show a positive impact on the overall progress of computer design.

At this time IBM had three internal divisions: the General Products Division, the Data Systems Division, and the World Trade Laboratories. Each of these was responsible for the design of new equipment and the general enhancement of the older lines of computers. IBM's senior management had given the job of creating a new line of machines, designed to supply the needs of the 1960s, to the Data Systems Division. They had already started on their project, to be known as the 8000 series of computers, when they found that, because of internal rivalry, they were getting very little cooperation from the other divisions. In January of 1961 the decision was taken to scrap the 8000 series of machines and expand the original 7000 series in order that IBM might have a temporary line of modern designs which could be sold while an all-new family of computers was being investigated.

There was a lot of discussion within IBM's engineering management as to what the new series of machines should look like and, in November of 1961, IBM formed a senior working group, known as the SPREAD committee, which was to report on IBM's machine design goals for the next decade and to create both an engineering and a marketing plan to unify the efforts of the various IBM divisions. Just three days before the end of 1961 the SPREAD Report was released: Nothing would ever be the same again in the commercial world of computer corporations!

The report suggested that IBM devote itself to the production of a family of compatible computers ranging from the smallest commercial machines, like the 1401, to models even more powerful than the Stretch machines for its scientific customers. Each processor was to be capable of executing all valid programs as long as it conformed to the memory capacity and peripheral devices available. A new operating system was to be developed which would enable these processors not only to perform the same types of jobs as the earlier product lines, but also to incorporate such new ideas as on-line random-access processing, the integration of communication facilities between computers at remote sites, the operation of multiple processor configurations, and multiprogramming to achieve efficient on-line operation of terminals.

In order to achieve these objectives, a number of basic design decisions were taken. Decimal digits and alphabetic characters were to be stored in 8-bit bytes, each of which should be addressable within the memory. Operations on variable-length fields would be permitted for fields as short as one byte or as long as the memory capacity of the machine. The memory capacity was to be increased several orders of magnitude from earlier machines by allowing base and index registers to modify the addresses contained in an instruction. Floating-point operations would be standard on the larger models and available as an option on the smaller ones. A full range of interrupts was envisaged to enable the operating system to control any program and data transfer and thus to allow unattended operation of the machine. A goal of international marketability meant that the alphabetic character set must incorporate non-English characters and the arithmetic facilities must be flexible enough to deal with nondecimal monetary units such as Sterling. A new super-language had to be developed in order to incorporate both the scientific and commercial processing requirements. The initial members of the new family should be five separate processors capable of spanning the range from adding two 5-digit numbers in 1 microsecond all the way down to one capable of doing the same job in 200 microseconds.

In order to design a family of machines which met all these initial design criteria, it was necessary to make tradeoffs between the basic goals of engineering sophistication and the resulting cost of the machines. Very early on, IBM recognized the impracticality of individual designs for each member of the family and determined to rely on a system of microcode in read-only memory to implement the instruction set for the majority of machines. In order to ensure some form of standardization and to pave the way for ease of repair in the resulting machines, the committee decided to use microcoded implementation throughout, except where it could be shown that a hardwired control would be at least two thirds of the cost of a microcoded one. In effect, IBM intended to have a number of different machines, all of which, however, would simulate, through microcode control, the operation of the one standard system /360 design.

Because integrated circuit design was still in the experimental stage, IBM's management decided to rely on miniature circuits in which very small individual transistors would be placed, along with the other components, on a ceramic substrate. They called this new form of circuit packages Solid Logic Technology, and it became the intermediate bridge between discrete component circuits and the newer monolithic integrated circuits that were to arrive on the scene only a matter of months later. This type of circuitry allowed for a considerable degree of automation in the production of basic machine components.

System automation became so complete that certain machines were manufactured with all the options plus a simple set of toggle switches that permitted the customer to disable any of them not actually ordered. Many customers in university settings immediately took advantage of this situation to reconfigure the system to their own design. The author remembers one very embarrassing incident when the floating-point unit on a /360 ceased to function and a trouble call was placed to IBM. A few minutes later the IBM representative phoned back confused and informed the operations personnel that he must have misunderstood the original call because IBM's records showed that our machine did not have the floating-point unit installed!

On April 7, 1964, IBM invaded the market with an announcement of over 150 new products, services, and devices. These were all centered around the new System /360 family of computers and ranged from the new Solid Logic Technology, through the 029 keypunch with expanded character sets and new magnetic tape and disk drives, to the central machines of the new computer line. Of these, the six initial models were the 30, 40, 50, 60, 62, and 70, with the higher numbers indicating a machine with more memory and facilities.

It very quickly became apparent that these models would not fill all the gaps in customer requirements, which led to replacement of some of the original models with ones for specific applications. At the bottom end of the scale an incompatible model 20 was produced for those users needing minimal facilities, essentially to replace the older punched card tabulating equipment. A special scientific version, known as model 44, was produced which did not have the full /360 instruction set but which was a very cost-effective machine for high-speed real-time applications. At the more complex end of the line, the models 60, 62, and 70 were withdrawn and replaced by models 65 and 75.

In an attempt to lure some of their customer base away from the older 1400 series of equipment, IBM announced that some models of the /360 could have their microcode changed so as to emulate the workings of a 1401, rather than the standard /360 model. This did influence some customers to obtain the newer equipment, but at times it resulted in the machines' being used in very strange ways. Some firms were reluctant to give up their old punched card based accounting schemes but required more power than was available from the very old electromechanical accounting machines. They usually moved to a very small computer like a 1401 and used a system that resembled their original accounting machines. When the /360 came along, a number of them opted for the 1401 emulation scheme, and this resulted in a number of machines being used to emulate a 1401 which, in turn, was emulating even older punched card equipment. This awkward arrangement was still to be seen in several installations as late as the latter part of the 1970s.

Several serious shortcomings in the System /360, particularly a weakness in virtual memory address translation, resulted in IBM's losing several large orders from Bell Labs and MIT shortly after the April 7th announcement. This, combined with the fact that Control Data Corporation was also producing a very large and powerful 6000 series of computers, prompted IBM to announce another member of the /360 family, the model 67. The model 67 was not entirely compatible with the /360 line but it did introduce an Atlas-like paging system with the hardware address translation and other facilities that were necessary for efficient operation of a machine via time-shared terminals.

Figure 9–8.   The smallest member of the IBM/360 (Model 20) contrasted with the turn-of-the-century Hollerith Tabulating Machine. (Photograph courtesy of IBM archives.)

In response to the competition from CDC, three new high-speed versions—models 91, 92, and 95—were announced. Model 91 employed the same overlapped, look-ahead, pipeline architecture as Stretch and had a very fast core memory of 750 nanoseconds. Models 92 and 95 were essentially the same machine with up to 1,000,000 bytes of core memory being replaced by the new 120-nanosecond thin film memory. This resulted in a machine which could execute instructions at the rate of about one every 60 nanoseconds. Like Stretch, the 90 series models of the /360 family were never a commercial success. IBM withdrew them in 1967 and announced that they would produce only the 20 that were currently on order. This caused CDC to conclude that IBM's announcement was simply a marketing ploy to prevent customers from switching to their large 6000 and 7000 series machines. The result was a lawsuit that was to tie up both firms in legal difficulties for several years.

Almost immediately after the IBM announcement of the System /360, the other large computer companies followed with their own "families" of compatible machines. In 1965 RCA launched its Spectra 70 series of machines which were roughly comparable in power to the /360 models 30, 40, and 50. Even the smaller firms, such as National Cash Register, eventually joined the competition with their 1968 announcement of a "Century" series of machines. The most interesting of the various competing families was the RCA Spectra 70 series because it was almost exactly compatible with the /360 hardware. As other groups joined the bandwagon, many different lines of equipment were produced to execute programs written for the /360 architecture. The Spectra 70 series was produced in Britain by ICT and marketed as the System 4; it appeared in similar forms in different countries before RCA decided to abandon the computer manufacturing business. Perhaps the two most famous rivals of the IBM /360 were the series of Riad machines produced as a joint effort by several Eastern European nations and the series of machines constructed by Gene Amdahl, after leaving the IBM /360 project, for direct domestic competition with IBM.

It has been estimated that the initial research and development cost of introducing the /360 series of machines amounted to at least $500,000,000, and of course each successive model of the series increased the total outlay. Taking into account all the costs of developing the different /360 models, plus the costs for the subsequent /370 series machines (which incorporated the dynamic address translation scheme of the model 65), outsiders have estimated that IBM has taken a *five billion dollar* gamble. It has paid off handsomely!

FURTHER READING

BELL, C. G., AND A. NEWELL (1971). *Computer Structures: Readings and Examples*. New York: McGraw-Hill.

BUCHHOLZ, W. (1962). *Planning a Computer System (Project Stretch)*. New York: Mc-Graw-Hill.

EVANS, B. O. (1983). "Introduction to the SPREAD Report," *Annals of the History of Computing*, 5 (No. 1), 4–5.

GALLER, B., ET AL. (1983). "Discussion of the SPREAD Report," *Annals of the History of Computing*, 5 (No. 1), 27–44.

HAANSTRA, J. W. (1961). "Final Report of SPREAD Task Group," reprinted in *Annals of the History of Computing*, 5 (No. 1), 6–26.

HURD, C. C. (1980). "Computer Development at IBM," in *A History of Computing in the Twentieth Century*, N. Metropolis, ed. New York: Academic Press, pp. 389–418.

——. (1981). "Early Computers at IBM," *Annals of the History of Computing*, 2 (No. 3), 163–82.

——. (1983). "Special Issue: IBM 701," *Annals of the History of Computing*, 5 (No. 3), entire issue.

KILBURN, T. D., ET AL. (1962). "One Level Storage System," *IRE Transactions*, 2 (No. 2), 223–35.

LAVINGTON, S. H. (1975). *A History of Manchester Computers*. Manchester, England: NCC Publications.

VON NEUMANN, J. (1981), "The NORC and Problems of High Speed Computing," *Annals of the History of Computing*, 3 (No. 3), 274–79. (A reprint of von Neumann's 1954 talk.)

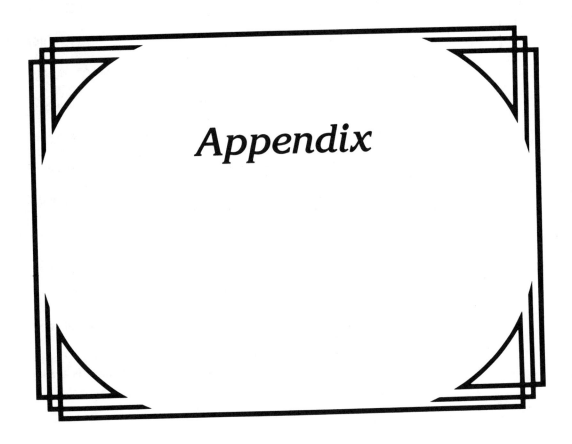

Appendix

Below are listed the approximate dates of major events cited in this book. The reader is encouraged to consult the actual text or the reference materials cited at the end of each chapter for exact dates.

ca. 6000 B.C.	Ishango bone type of tally stick in use
1800 B.C.	Well developed additive number system in use in Egypt
1300 B.C.	Direct evidence exists as to the Chinese using a positional number system
ca. 600 B.C.	Major developments start to take place in Chinese arithmetic
213 B.C.	Chi Hwang-ti orders all books in China to be burned and scholars to be put to death
ca. 800	Chinese start to use a zero, probably introduced from India

ca. 850	Al-Khowarizmi publishes his *Arithmetic*
ca. 1000	Gerbert describes an abacus using "apices"
1120	Adelard of Bath publishes *Dixit Algorismi*, his translation of Al-Khowarizmi's *Arithmetic*
ca. 1200	First minted jetons appear in Italy
1202	Fibonacci publishes his *Liber Abaci*
1220	Alexander De Villa Dei publishes *Carmen de Algorismo*
1250	Sacrobosco publishes his *Algorismus Vulgaris*
ca. 1300	Modern wire-and-bead abacus replaces older Chinese calculating rods
1392	Geoffrey Chaucer publishes the first English-language description on the uses of an astrolabe
ca. 1500	Inca quipu reaches its highest form of development
	Use of quadrant gaining popularity in Europe
1542	Robert Record publishes his English-language book on arithmetic
ca. 1600	Modern wire-and-bead abacus first recorded in use in Japan
1614	John Napier publishes his *Cannon of Logarithms*
1617	John Napier publishes *Rabdologia* describing "Napier's bones" and "Multiplicationis Promptuarium"
ca. 1620	Use of sector gaining popularity in Europe
1620	Robert Napier publishes John Napier's work *Constructio*
1622	William Oughtred invents the circular form of the slide rule
1623	Wilhelm Schickard invents first true mechanical calculating machine
1623	*The Works of that Famous Mathematician Mr. Edmund Gunter* published
1624	Henry Briggs publishes first set of modern logarithms
1628	Adrian Vlacq publishes the first complete set of modern logarithms
1642	Pascal invents his adding machine
ca. 1650	Sliding stick form of the slide rule developed
1666	Gaspard Schott publishes *Organum Mathematicum*
1672	Samuel Morland publishes *The Description and Use of Two Arithmetic Instruments*
1673	Rene Grillet describes the general form of his adding machine

1674	Leibnitz' calculating machine constructed
1786	J. H. Muller publishes an idea for an automatic difference engine
ca. 1822	Thomas de Colmar invents his calculating machine
1822	Charles Babbage starts on a model of the Difference Engine
1826	Use of tally sticks abolished in England Charles Babbage publishes his tables of logarithms
1834	Charles Babbage conceives of the Analytical Engine
1842	British government abandons support for the construction of Babbage's Difference Engine
1850	Amedee Mannheim creates the "Mannheim Slide Rule"
1853	The Scheutz team produce the world's first automatic difference engine
ca. 1880	True variable-toothed gear invented
1886	Dorr E. Felt completes his first production comptometer
ca. 1890	Mechanical disk-sphere-cylinder integrators developed to a usable state
1891	Genaille-Lucas rulers described
1908	Percy Ludgate proposes a new design for an analytical engine
1928	Punched card equipment attached as output devices to standard mechanical calculators in Germany
1928	Punched card machines in use by L. J. Comrie to calculate the motions of the moon
1929	IBM founds the Columbia University Statistical Bureau and donates some punched card equipment
1930	V. Bush's differential analyzer constructed at MIT
1931	L. J. Comrie converts a National Accounting Machine into a difference engine
1932	Large-scale electronic counters first used to count events in a physics experiment by C. E. Wynn-Williams at Cambridge
1934	Konrad Zuse realizes that an automatic calculator would only need a control, a memory, and an arithmetic unit
1934	Moore School differential analyzer operational
1935	IBM manufactures the 601 multiplying punch
1936	Konrad Zuse applies for a patent on his mechanical memory

1937	John Atanasoff conceives of the ABC machine
	George Stibitz experiments with relays for performing calculations at Bell Labs
	Howard Aiken and IBM join forces to produce the Harvard Mark I
1938	Konrad Zuse completes his Z1 machine
1939, Apr.	Construction started on the Complex Number Calculator at Bell Labs
1939	Construction started on the Harvard Mark I
1939	Konrad Zuse completes his Z2 machine
1940, Jan. 8	Bell Labs Complex Number Calculator operational
1940, Sept. 11	Complex Number Calculator demonstrated via a remote terminal at the American Mathematical Association Meeting
1941, Dec. 5	Konrad Zuse completes his Z3 machine—the world's first fully operational calculating machine with automatic control of its operations
1942, Aug.	John Mauchly writes "The Use of High Speed Vacuum Tube Devices for Calculating"
1942	The ABC machine almost operational when work is abandoned because of the war
1943, Jan.	Harvard Mark I operational in IBM Endicott Labs
1943, Mar.	First contacts between U.S. Army and the Moore School for the production of the ENIAC
1943, Apr.	"Heath Robinson" machine working at Bletchley Park on code-breaking problems
1943, May 31	Construction of the ENIAC started at the Moore School
1943, Sept.	Bell Labs Relay Interpolator operational
1943, Dec.	Colossus machine working at Bletchley Park on code-breaking problems
1943	Project Whirlwind started as an analog flight simulator project at MIT
1944, Jan.	Early thoughts about stored-program computers arise at the Moore School
1944, May	Mark I moved from IBM Endicott Labs to Harvard University
1944, June	Bell Labs Model III operational
1944, July	Two accumulators of the ENIAC operational
1944, Sept.	John von Neumann visits ENIAC project for the first time

1944, Oct.	U.S. Army extends the ENIAC contract to cover research on the EDVAC stored-program computer
1944	IBM produces the Pluggable Sequence Relay Calculator for the U.S. Army
1945, Mar.	Bell Labs Model IV operational
1945, spring	ENIAC working well
1945, June	John von Neumann publishes *First Draft on a Report on the EDVAC,* which first described the basic details of a stored-program computer
1945, fall	Alan Turing arrives at the National Physical Laboratory
1945, late	Project Whirlwind switched from analog to digital electronics
1946, spring	Turing's designs for the ACE are well underway
1946, Mar.	Eckert and Mauchly leave the Moore School to found their own firm, Electronic Control Company
1946, Mar.	John von Neumann attempting to set up computer project at the Institute for Advanced Study
1946, May	Jim Wilkinson joins Turing at the National Physical Laboratory
1946, May	M. V. Wilkes sees a copy of the *First Draft on a Report on the EDVAC*
1946, June	J. Bigelow joins von Neumann and Goldstine at the IAS project
1946, July	Computer Laboratory founded at Manchester University via grant from the Royal Society
1946, July	Bell Labs Model V operational
1946, July	Moore School lectures—a turning point in the spread of information about the electronic digital computer
1946, Aug.	M. V. Wilkes considers construction of a computer at Cambridge (EDSAC)
1946, Sept.	F. C. Williams and T. Kilburn join computer project at Manchester University
1946, late	F. C. Williams applies for a patent on his electrostatic memory tube
1947, Jan.	Harry Huskey arrives at the National Physical Laboratory
1947, Mar.	Delay-line memory for the EDVAC working at the Moore School
1947, summer	Electronics for the IAS machine redesigned to the "new look" versions
1947, July	Harvard Mark II operational

1947, Oct.	Contract for BINAC placed with the Electronic Control Company by Northrup Aviation
1947, late	F. C. Williams has working model of his memory system
1947	Construction started on EDSAC at Cambridge
	ENIAC converted into elementary stored-program computer via the use of function tables
1948, Jan.	IBM unveils the SSEC at their World Headquarters in New York
1948, Jan.	A. D. Booth has working magnetic drum memory
1948, spring	Selectron abandoned as the IAS machine memory device in favor of the Williams' tube
1948, June 21	Manchester University prototype computer in limited operation
1948, Sept.	Alan Turing joins computer project at Manchester University
1948, Dec.	Electronic Control Company refounded as the Eckert-Mauchly Computer Corporation
1948, late	SEAC started at the National Bureau of Standards
1948	Contract drawn up between Eckert-Mauchly Computers and the U.S. Census Bureau for the production of UNIVAC
	IBM produces the 604 multiplying punch based on vacuum tube technology
	Transistor invented
1949, Jan.	SWAC started at the National Bureau of Standards Institute for Numerical Analysis
1949, early	Construction started on Pilot ACE at the National Physical Laboratory
1949, May	Cambridge EDSAC fully operational
1949, Aug.	Construction started on LEO I, a copy of the EDSAC
1949, Aug.	Relocating loader added to "initial orders" of EDSAC
1949, Sept.	Harvard Mark III operational
1949, Sept.	BINAC delivered to Northrup Aviation by Eckert-Mauchly Computer Corporation
1949, Oct.	Manchester University computer fully operational
1950, early	Project Whirlwind in limited operation
1950, Feb.	Eckert-Mauchly Computer Corporation sold to Remington-Rand
1950, Apr.	SEAC operational at the National Bureau of Standards
1950, May 10	Pilot ACE working at the National Physical Laboratory

1950, July	SWAC operational
1950, Nov.	Bell Labs Model VI operational
1950	Konrad Zuse installs the refurbished Z4 at the ETH in Zurich
1951, Feb.	First Ferranti Mark I version of the Manchester University machine delivered to Manchester University
1951, Mar. 31	First UNIVAC delivered to U.S. Census Bureau
1951, summer	IAS machine in limited operation
1951, fall	LEO I fully operational
1951	IBM decides to produce the 701 computer
1951	*The Preparation of Programs for an Electronic Digital Computer* published by Wilkes, Wheeler, and Gill
1952, spring	MANIAC and ORDVAC copies of the IAS machine operational
1952, June 10	IAS machine fully operational
1952, Sept.	A Ferranti Mark I installed at the University of Toronto
1952, Dec.	First IBM 701 delivered to IBM World Headquarters
1952	EDVAC finally finished at the Moore School
	Harvard Mark IV operational
	Core memory installed on the Whirlwind I
	Core memory module added to the ENIAC
1953, Sept.	IBM announces the development of the 702 for commercial calculation
1954, May	IBM plans to develop the 704 as a successor to the 701
1954, Dec. 2	NORC delivered and operational
1954	DEUCE machine constructed by English Electric based on the Pilot ACE
1955	IBM considers building the Stretch computer
	First IBM 702 delivered
	Index registers added to Cambridge EDSAC
1955, Oct.	ENIAC shut off
1956	First IBM 705 delivered
	UNIVAC considers construction of LARC
	ATLAS computer project started at Manchester University in conjunction with Ferranti Ltd.
1957, Jan.	IBM announces the 709
1957	IBM introduces the RAMAC 305 disk storage system
1958	First IBM 709 delivered

	Philco delivers a transistorized computer, TRANSAC S–2000
	First AN/FSQ7 operational for SAGE system
1959	ACE machine constructed at the National Physical Laboratory
	Harvard Mark I shut down for the last time
1960	IBM starts delivery of its 1400 series machines
	First UNIVAC LARC delivered to Lawrence Radiation Labs
1961	First Stretch computer delivered to Los Alamos
1961, Nov.	IBM forms the SPREAD committee which decided to produce the System /360 series
1962	First ATLAS installed at Manchester University
1964, Apr.	IBM announces the System /360
1964	Control Data delivers the first 6600
1965	RCA Spectra 70 series announced
1968	NCR Century series announced

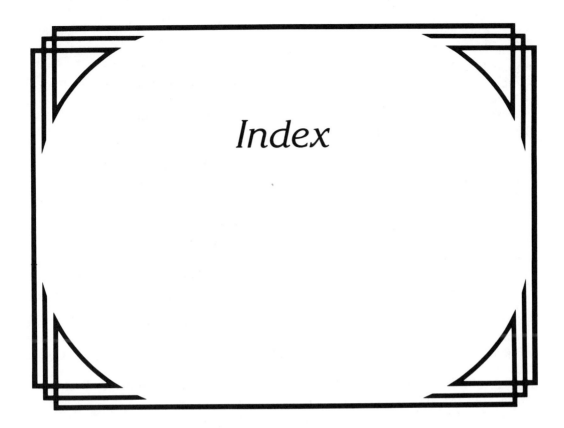

Index